Alternate Translation

of the

OLD TESTAMENT

(Selected Scriptures)

For My Parents
Louis and Evelyn Goldstein
My daughter Maria, and
My Granddaughters, Sarina & Juliette

Published @ Long Island, NY December, 2025

ISBN: 13: 978-0692799963
ISBN: 10: 0692799966

Alternate Translation of the Old Testament
Sheila R. Vitale

Living Epistles Ministries
Sheila R. Vitale
P O Box 562
Port Jefferson Station, NY 11776-0562 USA
(631) 331-1493

TABLE OF AUTHORITIES

1. **Brown Driver & Briggs' Hebrew Lexicon**, Woodside Bible Fellowship, Ontario, Canada, Licensed From The Institute for Creation Research.

2. **Englishman's Greek-Hebrew Concordance**.

3. **Gesenius' Hebrew and Chaldee Lexicon to the Old Testament** Scriptures, Baker Book House, Grand Rapids, Michigan.

4. **The Interlinear Bible** (Jay P. Green, Sr.), Hendrickson Publisher's, Peabody, Massachusetts 01961-3473.

5. **The Interlinear Bible (transliterated), Biblesoft and International Bible Translators, Inc**.

6. **Nave's Topical Bible**.

7. **Nelson's Bible Dictionary**, Thomas Nelson, Inc., Publishers, Nashville, Tennessee.

8. **Strong's Exhaustive Concordance** (James Strong) Thomas Nelson, Inc., Publishers, Nashville, Tennessee.

9. **Strong's Hebrew And Chaldee Dictionary** (James Strong), Thomas Nelson, Inc., Publishers, Nashville, Tennessee.

10. **Strong's Greek Dictionary** (James Strong), Thomas Nelson, Inc., Publishers, Nashville, Tennessee.

11. **The New Thayer's Greek-English Lexicon Of The New Testament**, Hendrickson Publisher's, Peabody, Massachusetts 01961-3473.

12. **Unger's Bible Dictionary** (Merrill F. Unger), The Moody Bible Institute of Chicago, Chicago, Illinois 60610.

13. **1979 Authorized Version** (AV), The On-Line Bible

14. **Stephanus Greek Text**, The On-Line Bible

15. **Green's Literal Translation**, The On-Line Bible

Numbers In Brackets [###] Indicate The Message Where The Alternate Translation Was Researched And Worked Up. **[Version Date: 09/10/2024]**

Living Epistles Ministries
Sheila R. Vitale
Pastor, Teacher, Founder
PO Box 562
Port Jefferson Station, NY 11776 USA

Alternate Translation® of the OLD TESTAMENT©

Selected Scriptures
Translated, Edited and compiled by
Sheila R. Vitale

Alternate Translation®
of the
OLD TESTAMENT©

THE ALTERNATE TRANSLATION BIBLE

1. Is An Esoteric Understanding Of The Scripture.

2. Is Not Intended To Replace Traditional Translations.

More Facts about **the Alternate Translation Bible** may be found at the end of this Volume.

Living Epistles Ministries
Sheila R. Vitale
Pastor, Teacher & Founder

Ministry Staff
Anthony Milton, Teacher (South Carolina)
Brooke Paige, Teacher (New York)
Dele Adegbite, Teacher (London-Nigeria)
Margaret Mobolaji-Lawal, Leader (Lagos, Nigeria)
Sandra Aldrich (MN) (July 7, 1975 – April 18, 2021)

Administrative Staff
Susan Panebianco, Office Manager

Editorial Staff
Rose Herczeg, Editor

Technical Staff
Lape Mobolaji-Lawal, Database Administrator

Ministry Illustrators
Cecilia H. Bryant (Oct. 18, 1921 – Oct. 23, 2013)
Fidelis Onwubueke

Music Staff
Don Gervais, Singer, Lyricist and Guitarist
(June 30, 1956 – October 21, 2024)
June Eble, Singer, Lyricist and Clarinetist
(July 20, 1931 – Jan. 24, 2024)
Rita L. Rora, Singer, Lyricist and Guitarist

Table of Contents

The Alternate Translation Bible© (ATB)

The Old Testament

Alternate Translation of the Old Testament©
Alternate Translation, Exodus, Chapter 32
(Crime of the Calf)©
Alternate Translation, Daniel, Chapter 8©
Alternate Translation, Daniel, Chapter 11©

The New Testament

Alternate Translation of the New Testament©
Alternate Translation, 2 Thessalonians, Chapter 2
(Sophia)©
Alternate Translation, 1st John, Chapter 5©
Alternate Translation, The Book of Colossians
(To The Church At Colosse) ©
Alternate Translation, The Book of Corinthians, Chapter 11
(Corinthian Confusion) ©
Alternate Translation, The Book of Jude
(The Common Salvation)©
Alternate Translation of The Book of the Revelation of
Jesus Christ to St. John©
Traducción Alternada del Libro de Revelación de Jesucristo©

THE ALTERNATE TRANSLATION BIBLE

1. Is An Esoteric Understanding Of The Scripture.
2. Is Not Intended To Replace Traditional Translations.

More Facts about **The Alternate Translation Bible** may be found at the end of this Volume.

Alternate Translation

of the

OLD TESTAMENT

(Selected Scriptures)

PREFACE

Why Another Translation?

The King James Translators were not spiritual men. They were scholars who, themselves, perceived the Deity of the Scripture as an unforgiving, punishing God. But there is another Message, a spiritual understanding of the Scripture called *the Doctrine of Christ*, which reveals a loving God, whose sole intention towards mankind is to deliver us from destruction and death.

There are many definitions for each word in the English dictionary, and many translations for each Hebrew and Greek word in the original text of the Scripture.

The King James Translators dealt with the problem of one Hebrew source word appearing several times in a single Chapter, by using a different English word each time that the Hebrew word appears. The English word choices of the translator, then, are directly related to 1) his knowledge of the Word of God, 2) the degree to which he is influenced by the Spirit of Revelation, and 3) the accepted understanding of the Word of God at the time.

The Spirit of Revelation influences the translator to choose legitimate *Alternate Translations* from the Hebrew and Greek lexicons listed in the front of the *Alternate Translation Bible*, to express the spiritual intent of the Scripture. The Alternate English Translations for some of the Hebrew and Greek words in the Scripture are just as legitimate as the choices made by the King James Translators, but they render a radically different, and much more positive Translation than the Authorized Version.

Multiple English translations for the same Hebrew or Greek word in the King James text are perfectly legitimate examples of Translator's License, and simply prove our point:

The King James Translators, themselves, used multiple definitions of the same Hebrew and Greek Word.

The *Alternate Translation Bible* is a Spiritual Translation of the Scripture which is as legitimate to the Spiritual Mind as the King James translation is to the Carnal Mind. The *Alternate Translation Bible* sounds radically different than the King James and other translations, because it must be Spiritually Discerned (1 Cor. 2:14).

A knowledge of the True Intent of the author of the Scripture and a desire to understand the message that he intended to convey, should be the top priority for all genuine seekers of *Truth*.

God is the Living Word that feeds Mankind through imperfect vessels. Beware of idolatry for the King James, or any other Translation, because *all translations* are the work of imperfect mortal men. Seek God and He will direct your paths (Pro 3:6).

May the Spirit of Truth expose all of our wrong thinking, and may the Truth intended by the author of the Word cleave to our heart and mind, because the Spirit of Truth awakens our potential for Eternal Life (1 Cor 15:4).

Romans 8:1-14

1. There is therefore now no condemnation to them which are in Christ Jesus, who walk not after the flesh, but after the Spirit.

2. For the law of the Spirit of life in Christ Jesus hath made me free from the law of sin and death.

3. For what the law could not do, in that it was weak through the flesh, God sending his own Son in the likeness of sinful flesh, and for sin, condemned sin in the flesh:

4. That the righteousness of the law might be fulfilled in us, who walk not after the flesh, but after the Spirit.

5. FOR THEY THAT ARE AFTER THE FLESH DO MIND THE THINGS OF THE FLESH; BUT THEY THAT ARE AFTER THE SPIRIT THE THINGS OF THE SPIRIT.

6. FOR TO BE CARNALLY MINDED IS DEATH; BUT TO BE SPIRITUALLY MINDED IS LIFE AND PEACE.

7. BECAUSE THE CARNAL MIND IS ENMITY AGAINST GOD: FOR IT IS NOT SUBJECT TO THE LAW OF GOD, NEITHER INDEED CAN BE.

8. SO THEN THEY THAT ARE IN THE FLESH CANNOT PLEASE GOD.

9. BUT YE ARE NOT IN THE FLESH, BUT IN THE SPIRIT, IF SO BE THAT THE SPIRIT OF GOD DWELL IN YOU. NOW IF ANY MAN HAVE NOT THE SPIRIT OF CHRIST, HE IS NONE OF HIS.

10. AND IF CHRIST BE IN YOU, THE BODY IS DEAD BECAUSE OF SIN; BUT THE SPIRIT IS LIFE BECAUSE OF RIGHTEOUSNESS.

11. BUT IF THE SPIRIT OF HIM THAT RAISED UP JESUS FROM THE DEAD DWELL IN YOU, HE THAT RAISED UP CHRIST FROM THE DEAD SHALL ALSO QUICKEN YOUR MORTAL BODIES BY HIS SPIRIT THAT DWELLETH IN YOU.

12. THEREFORE, BRETHREN, WE ARE DEBTORS, NOT TO THE FLESH, TO LIVE AFTER THE FLESH.

13. FOR IF YE LIVE AFTER THE FLESH, YE SHALL DIE: BUT IF YE THROUGH THE SPIRIT DO MORTIFY THE DEEDS OF THE BODY, YE SHALL LIVE.

Multiple Versions

There are many instances of multiple versions of a Scripture verse, or a series of verses. The translator has included these redundancies so that the reader can experience the progression of her understanding of the Scripture over the years. The number within the brackets that precedes each translation is the number of the Message that produced the translation. The names of the Messages are listed in the *LEM Media Catalogue*, which can be viewed on the *LEM Website*:

http://www.lemdatabase.org/lem/CatalogueFiles/LEM-MediaCatalogue.pdf

Some numbers within brackets have a "C" after them, which indicates that the translation is the product of a *Christ-Centered Kabbalah* Message. The names of *CCK* Messages are listed in the *CCK Media Catalogue*, which can be viewed on the *CCK Website*:

http://www.lemdatabase.org/lem/CatalogueFiles/CCK-MediaCatalogue.pdf

Also, if there are any illustrations associated with the work-up(s) of the translation(s), links to those illustrations have been inserted next to the *linked Message Names* on the *LEM or the CCK Website.* (See, *Alternate Translations Are Progressive.*)

http://livingepistles.org/#parentVerticalTab1

http://christ-centeredkabbalah.org/#tl3

In addition, fully-annotated versions of *Alternate Translations* (references and bookmarks) are included wherever an *Alternate Translation* has been made into a book. The name of the book is noted between the brackets, instead of the Message Number, wherever the translation has been made into a book.

Preparing To Translate

Three Hebrew-English dictionaries, three Interlinear Texts, and multiple Bible Dictionaries (see, Table of Authorities at the beginning of this book) are used to search out the meaning of each Hebrew and Greek word of the *Alternate Translation Bible*. English dictionaries, encyclopedias and search engines are also employed to acquire as much information as possible about obviously and not so obviously related topics revealed through the *Alternate Translations*. Each word and verse is seriously prayed over to discover God's spiritual message behind the written words.

References and footnotes are attached to some translations. Others have only references, and many are not annotated. Footnotes for new translations have not been included since 2016, but references are always included if the *Alternate Translation* is annotated. Some fully annotated *Alternate Translations* (footnotes and references) have been made into books. Transcripts of other *Alternate Translations* which are fully annotated are available for sale from the publisher.

The research material for each *Alternate Translation* is faithfully preserved in the Archival Notes for the Living Epistles Ministries or Christ-Centered Kabbalah Message where it was rendered.

It is not unusual for the verse structure of the *Alternate Translations* to be rearranged so that they can be read as one continuous message. Accordingly, some paragraph numbers are out of order (*3* before *2*, for example) and some paragraphs are divided into *a* and *b* and interspersed (*2a, 3a, 2b, 3b,* for example).

Alternate Translations Are Progressive

Alternate Translations are rendered for each verse in its entirety. After that, all of the translated verses are read together as one whole revelation to confirm their synchronicity, reveal additional, deep nuances of the whole revelation, and to expose any inconsistencies or errors.

Alternate Translations are progressive in that the *Alternate Translation* for each verse is affected by the *Alternate Translations* for previous and subsequent verses. A newly translated verse, for example, will be influenced by previous *Alternate Translations*, and sometimes the *Alternate Translation* for the new verse causes changes in previously translated verses.

The Word of God Is Alive

The *Alternate Translation* of one whole chapter of Scripture is a living organism that evolves and grows in scope. The Spirit of Revelation refines the *Alternate Translations* as the translator reads and re-reads them. Eventually, all of the thoughts, understanding and influences of the Carnal Mind are removed, and the optimal understanding for that particular time is reached.

Written words are vessels that clothe the spiritual word, just like the body is a vessel that carries the soul in this world. It might even be said that the spiritual understanding of a written word is the soul of that written word.

Unveiling the spiritual meaning of a word shatters its hard exterior, so that the spiritual contents flow out and blend with the spiritual contents of the other vessels. Then, the *Spirit of Revelation* takes hold of the Word of God in this *liquid form,* goes beyond the letter of the Word, and reveals the esoteric message of the Word of God to a particular people, at an appointed time.

Sheila R. Vitale

THE BOOK OF

AMOS

Chapter 3

[240]

3.01 Hear the Word that [I], Jehovah, have spoken against you, O Israel, against the whole family that I brought up from the land of Egypt, saying,

3.02a You are the only families of the earth that I have known intimately,

3.03 [And since] two cannot have a peaceful and fruitful relationship unless they think like thoughts,

3.02b I will deal with your iniquities from above, [in order] to set all of you upright,

3.05a Because Abel does not have the spiritual strength to restrain Cain,[R-1] [who] offers [herself] up

[R-1] Job 41:10

3.04a To Satan, [the unconscious part of] the mind[R-1] [whose] fierce sound,[R-2] is [only] noise [to Jehovah], separates [Abel] the mortal man, from [Righteous] Adam,[R-3] and [Leviathan] captures him,[R-4] [but Jehovah] shall cast down [Satan],

[R-1] Zeph 2:13 (AT)
Is 14:11 (AT)
Dan 12:10 (AT)
Rev 13:15
[R-2] Zeph 1:14 (AT)
[R-3] Zeph 2:5, 6 (AT)
[R-4] Matt 12:29 (AT)

3.05b [And Righteous Adam shall be] strong enough to overcome [Leviathan, [R-2] because] he possesses the breath of Jehovah's [life, and] capture [him],

[R-2] Rom 8:20-21 (AT)

3.04b And Abel,[R-5] the mortal, man, Adam's dead [root system], shall flow spontaneously and freely.

[R-5] Ps 72:16 (AT)

[Unknown]

3.12 [Adam rose from the dead in] Elijah[1] and snatched Abel away from Cain,[2] and this is how the Israelites in Samaria shall be delivered from their idolatrous[R] and adulterous relationship with Satan, and [this is how] the Gentiles shall be delivered from their common law marriage to [Leviathan].[3]

[R] Mic 1:7

3.14 And in the day that I bring judgment upon Israel because of their sins, I shall judge the men of Judah also,[R-1] and their spiritual strength shall be cut off,[R-2] and they shall become mortal men,[4]

[R-1] Rev 20:11-14
[R-2] Zeph 3:04b (AT)

3.15 And the many-membered physical expression of the Wild Animal that Satan lives in[R-1] shall become empty[R-2] and

---

[1] Righteous Adam was resurrected in the man, Elijah.

[2] The Spirit of Elijah joins with Abel, Adam's root system within a mortal man, to raise Adam from the dead (Zeph 3:08a [AT] (Footnote continued – See, Appendix)

[3] The incarnating spirit marries the bestial background [threads] of the creation by weaving himself through them. (Footnote continued – See, Appendix)

[4] Judgment on spiritual men ***always*** manifests as loss of the spiritual benefits they acquired from their relationship with Jehovah (Dan. 4:25).

cease to exist,[5] when I crucify Leviathan, **R-3** and Abel, [6] the mortal msn [that is] Adam['s dead root system], is awakened, and matures into everlasting life,[7] says Jehovah.**R-4**

R-1 Ps 104:26 (AT)
Deut 32:32
R-2 Rev 14:14-15 (AT)
R-3 Gal 2:20
R-4 Jn 8:35
Rev 14:16 (AT)
Rev 21:2 (AT)

Chapter 5

[368.8]
5.01 [I am forgiving Israel's family for murdering Abel] because of their remorseful wailing, so listen to the truth [about what happened to you], and understand it [so that you can be delivered from hell]:

5.19a The waters underneath the firmament twisted together with the Earth and the Serpent[8] who revealed Adam's

---

5 ***The Devil*** is the personality that is in agreement with the carnal mind. The ***old man*** (Rom 6:6; Eph 4:22; Col 3:9) [the Serpent's household within mortal man], dies, and will cease to exist (Jn 3:30) when the ***new man*** (Eph 2:14, 4:24; Col 3:10) possesses the Woman [personality] and the house [physical body] (Mk 3:27).

6 The Spirit of Elijah is awakening Abel, Adam's dead root system, within mortal man, to raise Adam from the dead and restore his priesthood (Gen 4:4[AT]). Abel matures into the resurrected Adam, who covers the fallen, mortal mind of the individual (his old identity). (Footnote continued – See, Appendix)

7 We experience ***everlasting life*** in the visible, spiritual world, after we are emancipated from the physical body.

8 The Serpent is the Tree of the Knowledge of Good & Evil.

potential to sin[R-1] came into existence, and the Serpent[9] knew the Woman, and she bare the mortal female, Cain [R-2] instead of Elohim's immortal Son.[R-3 10]

[R-2] Rom 5:14
[R-2] Gen 4:1 (AT)
[R-3] Dan 9:25-27 (AT)
Zeph 1:2 (AT)
Zech 6:1 (AT)

5.03c Nevertheless, [despite Adam's fall from immortality into mortality], Abel appeared [in the mortal world] with the righteous authority of Jehovah's priest[R-1]

[R-1] Gen 4:2 (AT)
Matt 23:35

5.19b But Cain obeyed the Serpent's suggestion [to rebel against] Abel, and the Serpent, [who is] the bestial background threads of the Living Beast,[R-1] wove itself together with the Woman,[11] [R-2] and Adam['s righteous nature] disappeared behind

---

[9] The Interlinear Text of Gen 2:21 says that Jehovah put ***Adam*** (Strong's #121) into a deep sleep, which means that ***Adam*** descended, and was joined to the level of consciousness called ***Adamah*** (Strong's #127), the spiritual ***ground***. (Footnote continued – See, Appendix)

[10] Adam is the Tree that Jehovah planted in mankind, the spiritual earth, to give it Life. Today, since Adam died, only Abel, Adam's root system, and Cain, the dual stump of that Tree (Job 14:9), can be found in mortal humanity. Righteous Adam was resurrected in Jesus of Nazareth, who was glorified, and is presently in the process of regenerating mortal mankind with His glorified life.

[11] Spiritual sexuality has nothing to do with the sex of the physical body. Spiritual sexuality is the unification of spirit and soul. Spirit is male, and soul is female.

the [unrighteous nature of the Serpent], and the Living Beast became a Wild Animal,[12]

R-1 Gen 2:20 (AT)
R-2 Gen 4:10 (AT)
1 Ki 19:5 (AT)
Job 7:5b (AT)

5.03b And this is how the Serpent came to be swelling up into a full stature of evil within [Jehovah's] Living Beast that became a Wild Animal,

5.03c But Righteous Adam shall gather Israel, Jehovah's family,[13] to himself again,

5.03a Says my Lord, Jehovah,

5.04 But [while you are waiting for this to happen], Jehovah promises you life through union with His Spirit;

5.06a Therefore, all you teachers of Jehovah's Word, find out what Jehovah requires of you [and do it], before Jehovah sends Righteous Adam to attack [Leviathan], your [fallen, mortal mind],[14] and destroy [him],

---

[12] The background threads of the creation can be likened to the cloth background of a tapestry. The [primordial] Serpent wove the image of Leviathan, the sea serpent, her own spiritual sexual male organ, over Adam, the mosaic that Jehovah wove into the background threads of the creation, and the Living Beast became a spiritually female, Wild Animal. (Footnote continued – See, Appendix)

[13] Righteous Resurrected Adam shall be regenerated within the peoples of natural and spiritual Israel. All of the human beings that Righteous Adam is appearing in are members of ***Jehovah's family***.

[14] Jehovah's righteous Sowing and Reaping Judgment causes the individual to experience much grief, destroys the Carnal Mind, and can result in physical death. Repentance, a change of opinion concerning attitudes, thoughts and behavior that are unacceptable to Jehovah, introduces the element of mercy into Jehovah's righteous, but destructive judgment, and reconfigures it into a life-changing lesson that works, ultimately, for the good of the individual being corrected.

5.05a Because Satan is overflowing [Jehovah's restraints],[R]

[R] Gen 11:6-9
Gen 11:6-7 (AT)
Rev 17:8 (AT)
Rev 20:3, 7-9

5.06b And no one in [Israel's] family can stop her,

5.05b Because they are all worshiping Satan, the spirit [that is the unconscious part of] their own mortal mind, by seeking [her counsel],[15] [R]

And Abel is going underground [again], and the [primordial] Serpent is marrying [the Woman again, and Israel is going into] captivity [again],

[R] Matt.3:7

5.08a But wherever Abel is [still] invested with priestly authority,

5.07a Those Israelites shall overthrow the fiery serpent [within themselves],

5.09a And loose the ox, who is together with them,

5.08b And put her in [the right moral] order,[R]

[R] Rev 12:1

5.08c When [Elijah] summons Satan, [fallen] Adam's hidden, widowed spirit, out of the sea [of the unconscious part of the mind, and [Elijah] pours Jehovah's nature forth upon the personalities of the earth[en bodies],

5.07b And lays [a] righteous [foundation] in the Earth,[R-2] but [the Israelites who will not repent] will experience wormwood judgment,

[R-2] Amos 9:6
Dan 7:14, 27 (AT)

---

[15] Satan's counsel is the wisdom of the carnal mind.

5.09b So that you may enter in, and be added to, Elijah's defensed City,

5.10 But you detest Elohim's Sons teaching about spiritual completeness [through Elijah], and are horrified when they correct you in public,

5.11b So, [Satan], the lower waters of creation, is twisting together with the earth[en personalities] again,

5.11a And Leviathan is seizing Adam,

5.02a And Cain [within you] is regaining her strength, and murdering Abel again,

5.11c And Leviathan is crucifying Adam, and [the Serpent] is weaving together with [the Woman again],

5.02b And Abel[16] [is under] the ground [again], so that [Leviathan] can rise up

5.11e And trample upon Adam, and cast him down, and marry his widowed spirit [again].

5.12 [So, you see], I, Jehovah, have experienced the strong rebellion and the countless sins of the Serpent, [who] vexed Adam, [who] married [a foreign] wife and oppressed the justified [men of Israel], and abused those who are bound, and turned them away from me, the one they need, toward the mortal side of the visible world, [rather than] vindicating [them];

5.15a So despise the fiery serpent, and join your human spirit to Elijah

5.13 By keeping silent when someone with Kingdom Age insight is speaking righteous [judgment] to [Cain], your evil side,

5.14a And shun evil by demanding [a high standard of] morality for yourself, because you want [Adam] to rise from the dead [in you],

---

[16] ***Abel*** is the righteous personality of the individual Israelite.

5.15b So that [Adam, Jehovah's] justice, can be permanently placed in the doorway to hell [R] where [Satan is waiting to trick you], and, perhaps, Jehovah will have mercy on Abel, [that] which remains of Adam[17] after he took that foreign wife,[18]

[R] Gen 4:7

5.14b And Jehovah shall set you upright, and you shall be amongst Elijah's soldiers, ***IF YOU ANSWER THE CALL.***

5.16a So, says Jehovah, this is why Elijah, the general of my armies,

5.17 Is crucifying [R] the fallen, mortal minds of all of Israel's family, and they are wailing,

[R] Gal 2:20

5.16b And all the sinners that Abel's priestly authority has been restored in, are crying out loud [also], and everyone outside of Israel is saying, "Alas, alas, Israel's visible expression of grief and loud wailing,[R-1] are publicly exposing their realization that they [are Cain], the servant [and not the Son]." [R-2]

[R-1] Rev 18:9
[R-2] Jn 8:35

5.18a Woe unto you who desire the Kingdom Age for your own selfish purposes.[R-1] How can this Age be for you? [R-2]

5.20a Since this is the [spiritual] day that Jehovah

---

[17] All that remains of Adam after his fall from immortality into mortality, is his human spirit [Jehovah's breath of life]. Adam's widowed spirit in mortal man, is called ***the human spirit***.

[18] Elohim, Adam's living mind, married the ox that it formed out of the ground, and the creature became a Living Beast. (Footnote continued – See, Appendix)

5.18b Covers Leviathan, with [Adam's] Light,[R-3]

[R-1] Matt 3:7
[R-2] Mal 3:2
[R-3] Eccl 12:2 (AT)
Dan 12:3 (AT)

5.20b And [Elijah's] brilliant spirit shall possess Satan, and Leviathan,[19] the sun [of this world that] darkened [Adam], Jehovah's timeline, shall set,

5.22b [But at this present time], your sin [offering] is unacceptable to me,

5.25a Because you bring your animal sacrifices with insincere promises;

5.22a Indeed, [when] Leviathan, the sea serpent, rises up [within you], you sacrifice Adam, and [Satan] receives your voluntary offering in return for a friendly alliance with her,

5.25b And you are surviving by the Serpent's instincts during this age, and are subject to her law,

5.21a So I will not breathe my Spirit into your dead services [anymore, and] your religious parades [that make my people walk in circles] will stop.

5.23 I know that Leviathan, [not Adam], is the fruit of your ground, so take your angry, emotional protests [of innocence] away from me

5.24 And let Elijah, bring [Satan], the spiritual urine, to a rolling boil,[R] [and let] a continual stream of moral virtue [flow in its place],

[R] Rev 3:16

5.26 And because you raised up [Baalzebub], the image of the prince [of the] angels, and made statues of him, Leviathan, the sea serpent's reign as king [over my] house[hold];

---

[19] Elijah shall weave his Spirit through the widowed spirit of Satan, the background threads (Footnote continued – See, Appendix)

5.27 Therefore, because of all this, Jehovah is promising to expose Satan in Elohim's soldiers, so that [her speech] can be silenced in Israel.

Chapter 6

[1245.1.C]

6.01 Woe to you [Israelites of God] who feel secure in [spiritual] Jerusalem, [20] and trust in the power of [spiritual] Samaria, [that idolatrous nation] called ["the United States of America"], the chief of the nations that the [souls of] the house of Israel came into,

6.02 [Because spiritual] Syrians, Iraqis and Turks, are crossing over into their territory [to have] spiritual sexual intercourse [with their mind, **while] the Palestinians are being crushed like grapes in a winepress,**[R-1] [because the spiritual] authority [that rules through] the territory [of the spiritual Syrians, Iraqis and Turks] is greater than [the spiritual authority of the Holy Spirit that is limited by the sins of the Israelites of God, [R-2]

[R-1] Is 63:3
[R-2] Gal 6:16

6.03 Because the doctrine that the Israelites of God[R-1] teach], that the evil day[R-2] [when Messiah shall judge their sins], is far away, has brought the throne of [Lucifer],[R-3] the Violent

[20] Jerusalem is the spiritual city formed from all of the spiritual intellectual souls of the Israel of God.

One, near [enough to the Israelites of God] to have spiritual sexual intercourse [with their mind, and]

R-1 Gal 6:16
R-2 Pro 16:4
Mal 3:2
R-3 Is 14:12

6.04 The third [21] [of Lucifer's ten] spheres of power, has extended [itself, through Leviathan, the pride of the Israelites of God], to have spiritual sexual intercourse [with their mind, and Satan] is consuming the lambkins [22] [that are gestating] in the midst of the personalities of the flock [R] of [the household of] the Israelites [of God],

R Zech 10:3

6.05a The skin bags [23] [that]

6.06a The wine of the Holy Spirit] pours out from like] a drink offering [R-1] [to Jehovah, and who Messiah] smears with the best oil, [R-2]

R-1 Lev 23:13
R-2 Lev 8:12

6.05b Interpenetrates and prophesies [R] through,

R 1 Cor 13:2

---

[21] The third sphere of power brings understanding, so the third sphere of Lucifer, would suggest misunderstanding, or false doctrine.

[22] The spiritual offspring of the Lamb of God within the Spiritual Israelites.

[23] Human bodies.

6.06b ([Which prophecy has the same spiritual effect as] the sound [that] was made [by] David's musical instrument),[24] [R]

[R] 1 Sam 16:23

But, [despite all this favor, the Israelites of God] do not empathize with those [**Palestinians**] who are suffering for the sake of [R] righteousness

[R] Ps 146:7
Matt 23:44-45

6.08 From Jacob's prideful hate speech, [and that is the reason why] Jehovah, the God of battle, desires to complete [R] Adonai [25] [within the mortal personalities of the Israel of God, rather than] shut up the Holy Spirit [that flows out from spiritual Jerusalem], the city [of God], to satisfy [the personalities that are Jehovah's] palaces;

[R] Col 2:10

6.07 [Indeed, Jehovah, the God of battle], shall reveal [Messiah], their leader, at the appointed time,[R-1] [and Messiah] shall stand the captive [Israelites of God] upright,[R-2] and turn [them] away [R-3] from [believing and serving] those [spiritual Syrians, Iraqis and Turks], who feast [R-4] extravagantly [on their souls, and

[R-1] Heb 2:3
Gal 4:2
[R-2] Lk 4:18
[R-3] Is 42:1
[R-4] Ps 14:4, 53:4

---

[24] David's instrument calmed the murderous rage within King Saul.

[25] ***Adonai*** is the Name of God that is within the spiritual Israelite.

6.10 Messiah], the uncle [26] [of the Israelites of God that came into the United States of America], shall speak to [the personalities of] the house[hold of the Israelites of God, and, say:

"[Is] the one who lives forever still with you?"

[And wherever Adonai], the highest part [of the Israelites of God responds, Messiah] shall lift [R-1] [that] personality up [above its fallen nature, and] bring [it] out from the burning house,[R-2]

[But, the personalities of the Israelites of God that do] not recognize [Messiah], the Name of Jehovah speaking [through the personality of a mortal man, or] hear [Adonai, the highest part of the Israelites of God], speaking in the silence [27] [R-3] of the unconscious part of the mind [saying "it is me speaking through that person, listen to him,"

[R-1] Mk 16:18
[R-2] Is 1:11
Mal 4:2-3
Rev 18:1
[R-3] 1 Ki 19:12

6.9a Shall die,[R-2] even if the tenth [sphere of Messiah's power is] united with what is left [R-1] [of their personalities];

[R-1] 1 Thes 4:15
[R-2] Is 40:6-8
1 Pet 1:24

6.11a Look [at what]

6.09b Shall come to pass [for those personalities of] the household [of the Israel of God]!

6.11b Jehovah shall give the order and [Messiah] shall strike the great [Spirit-filled] house [of the Israel of God] with

---

[26] The man who rescues the Israelites of God will be a blood relative.

[27] ***The speaking silence*** is the state of consciousness where a man can hear the voice of God.

deception,[R-1] and [strike] the less esteemed house [28] [of the Israel of God], with separation; [R-2]

[R-1] 2 Thes 2:11
[R-2] Num 15:30-31

6.12 Now, [tell me]:

Should Adonai guard the animal souls that she engraved[R-2] with the nature of Righteous Adam, [which] changed them into [Jehovah's war] horse, [R-1]

[R-1] Zech 10:3
[R-2] Ez 9:4

6.12 [When] they teach that righteous judgment is a bitter poison? [R]

[R] Jn 9:34

6.13 [And should she guard the souls of] the Israelites of God [that] lack the spiritual food[29] that generates the power [of God but, nevertheless], say [that] there is no power [that can] take the power [R] of [the Holy Spirit] away [from] their vessels?

[R] Acts 1:8

6.14 Look [at what] I am saying [all you people of God, who are] the house[hold of the Israel of God that came into the United States of America, and understand that it is] I, Jehovah, the God who wages war against [his own people,[R] who] has raised up the nation [of spiritual] Syria [to come] against [the mind of the Israelites of God, and] they shall afflict you with the spiritual power of the natural man.

[R] Dan 7:21

---

[28] People of God that are not Spirit-filled.

[29] ***The spiritual understanding of the Word of God*** is spiritual food. It is more powerful than ***the understanding that can be gleaned from the letter of the Word***.

Chapter 9

[161]

9.01 I recognized that Adam, was fully raised from the dead in me, and He was commanding that Leviathan should be attacked, **R-1** and that my human spirit should separate from her,**R-2** and he was saying, ***let Leviathan be slaughtered. Indeed, the man who tries to save himself shall not escape the slaughter of his fallen, mortal mind.***[30]

R-1 Is 40:1-3 (AT)
Jer 6:4
Joel 3:9
R-2 Zech 11:12 (AT)

9.02 If they dig themselves into hell, the Spirit of Elijah shall snatch them to safety by marrying them there [while they are still in hell],**R-1** and if they climb up into heaven,[31] **R-2** [Elijah and Adam] shall force them into submission while they are in heaven,

R-1 Dan 7:21 (AT)
Rom 5:8
R-2 Gen 11:4
Dan 7:23, 25 (AT)

9.03 And if their hearts are hard because Adam is completely hidden behind Leviathan,**R-1** Adonai shall send Satan

---

[30] Leviathan's union with Cain shall be broken apart, and Abel shall be liberated (Heb 4:12).

[31] ***Heaven*** is ***understanding***. Elijah and Adam will judge the sins of spiritual Israelites who understand why it is necessary, as well as those who do not understand.

[in the unconscious mind] to judge them and expose their sins,[R-2] and, then, [after they repent, Elijah] shall marry them.

[R-1] Joel 3:3 (AT)
Amos 5:19 (AT)
[R-2] Dan 7:25 (AT)
1 Tim 1:20

9.04 But if they are overtaken by their enemies, Adonai shall command [Elijah], and he shall not do good to their enemies, but evil, and they shall be slain,

9.05 And I, Jehovah, the God of battle, shall command it, and Leviathan, mortal man's carnal mind, shall be injured[R-1] and cast down, and Adam shall rise from the dead,[R-2] and the whole earth shall sink down, and be dissolved, [R-3] and become the bed of Jehovah's river of life,

[R-1] Rev 9:10
[R-2] Zeph 3:8a (AT)
[R-3] Dan 7:25 (AT)
2 Pet 3:10 (AT)

9.06 Because it is Elijah who enables men to enter into heaven [R-1] by giving Jehovah's nature to the whole Wild Animal,[R-2] and when Elijah becomes their foundation in the Earth,[R-3] [Adam], Jehovah's image, expands into a visible, spiritual [R-4] world. [32]

[R-1] Matt 5:20
Jn 3:13
[R-2] Gen 2:7
[R-3] Amos 5:7b
Dan 7:14, 27 (AT)
[R-4] Dan 8:8-12 (AT)

9.07 Are not you, [Israel, who] belongs to me, like the children of the Ethiopians, says Jehovah? Are not Israel, the mate that I brought up out of the land of Egypt, [like] the Philistines

---

[32] See Book, ***Mind, Hell & Death***, Chapter V, by Sheila R. Vitale (Christ-Centered Kabbalah, Long Island, NY, July 2017).

[and] the Syrians [that worship] the wreathed serpent, the wall [that separates them from me]?

9.08 Be careful! [Says] Jehovah: I see what you are doing [through] the eyes [of] Adonai [within my prophets, and

I shall destroy the earth[en] personalities of the kingdom [of God, because of their sins,], except that I will not completely destroy [the earthen personalities of the kingdom of God, who are of the spiritual] house[hold] of Jacob, says Jehovah,

9.09 Look, Adonai shall [give] directions [to] the house of Israel [that] Elohim separated [from] all the nations [of Canaan, and their] earth[en soul], the sieve that separatees [them from Elohim], shall fall down, and not separate [from Elohim again],

9.10 But my people who say [that] they do not have to confront [their] sins, [and that] the curses [of Jehovah's righteous Sowing & Reaping] Judgment shall not overtake [them], shall die,

9.11 And in that day, Jehovah] shall repair [Adonai], the broken wall, and [Jehovah], the eternal timeline, shall overthrow [the Serpent, and the angels] shall be rejoined [to Elohim Jehovah, and Adam, who was] cast down, shall stand up and fence in [his] beloved house[hold],

9.12 And everyone who is manifesting [Adam, the mind that expresses] my nature, says Jehovah, the one who is doing this great work, [shall inherit] the ox that I formed from the red earth, that [the Serpent] is devouring; **[R]**

[R] Num 19:2-10
Heb 9:13

9.13 The days are coming, says Jehovah, that the Spirit of Elijah shall draw near to [Abel], Adam's root system,**[R-1]** and

[Elijah's reproductive seed] shall fall in drops,[33] and [Adam] shall crush Leviathan,**R-2** and pull the ox out of the pit,[34] and separate the human spirit from Satan,**R-3** and engrave the ox with Jehovah's image,**R-4** and [this is how] hell shall be covered over.

R-1 Dan 7:21 (AT)
R-2 Rev 14:19 (AT)
R-3 Dan 7:7 (AT)
Heb 4:12
R-4 Rev 2:17 (AT)

9.14 And I will turn away the captivity of my people, Israel, and the Spirit of Elijah shall be planted in them,**R-1** and they shall rebuild [Jehovah's] altar that was torn down,[35] and they shall dwell in Adam's renewed mind,**R-2** and drink of Elijah's Spirit, and [Adam] shall sacrifice Leviathan to Jehovah,**R-3** and [Adam, their immortal] mind, shall engage in spiritual intercourse [of the mind] with [Elijah].**R-4**

R-1 Amos 9:9 (AT)
Dan 7:14, 26 (AT)
R-2 Zeph 3:2 (AT)
R-3 Rom 8:11
R-4 Rev 21:2, 9 (AT)

---

[33] The phrase ***fall in drops***, (1 Pet 1:2) suggests the impartation of the life of God to the members of fallen Adam. Elijah's fertile seed shall graft to Abel, Adam's root system, in the members of mortal humanity, and, Adam, the Son of God, shall rise from the dead within them. (See, Lk 22:44)

[34] The Serpent killed Adam, and his ox fell into a spiritual, watery pit, which can be likened to a black hole. (See, Message #234, ***Physics & Multiple Incarnations In Righteous Adam***, and Message #341, ***The Physics Of Creation***.)

[35] Jehovah's altar was torn down three times: When Adam died, when Abel died, and when Noah died.

9.15 And I will give them authority[R-1] over Leviathan, and they will not lose the [righteous] mind of [Adam] that I've given them, any more, says Jehovah.[R-2]

[R-1] Gen 1:26

[R-2] Dan 7:14 (AT)
Ez 18:4

BOOK OF

1 CHRONICLES

Chapter 4

[1121.4.C]

4.22-23 Jehovah shall arise with fiery judgment to turn back the deceiver [that] changed the Word [of God, the spiritual] bread that forms the clay bodies of Judah and Israel into enclosures [that] the King marries and makes his] ministers, [but, thereafter], grow old and are removed.

BOOK OF

2 CHRONICLES

Chapter 1

[unknown]
1.09 Now [that] the people you have made me king over have overcome the fiery serpent, their mortal subconscious mind, let Elohim's sons who were spoken into existence along with our Father, Adam, be made immortal princes.

Chapter 34

[unknown]
34.04 And they separated [their human spirit from Satan, the polluted] waters [of the creation, who] crippled [the Seraph], their intellect[ual understanding of the Word of God], overthrew [Adam, their] spiritual cover, [who became the Serpent that married [the Woman and] increased into Leviathan, the sea serpent, [and] turned [Abel] into small dust, [36] in the same way that the fiery serpent, the intellect[ual understanding of the Word of God of the fallen priests], burnt the resurrected Adam upon their altars as a sacrifice to Balim, and pronounced Judah and

---

[36] The primordial Serpent swallowed up Elohim's clean waters, (Job 40:23) and Abel dried out and became dust.

mortal Jerusalem morally clean,[37] so that they could experience the animal existence.**[R]**

R Zeph 3:4a (AT)

---

[37] They were pronounced morally clean by he works of the Law.

THE BOOK OF

DANIEL

Chapter 2

[1240.1.C]

2.16 And Daniel went inward and desired of the Shechinah], the king [within himself], that he would be given the dream that occurred in "the time" that was lost to the king [of Babylon, so] that [the Shechinah], the king [within himself], could show the king [of Babylon] the interpretation,

[31.7]

2.31 You saw, O King and, behold, a very large, idolatrous form of the one who has exceedingly great power to exist, appeared before you, but she is only a proud shadow of what she will be in the future,[R-1] and can only creep along the earth[R-2] in this stage of her development, because of her premature birth. [R-3]

[R-1] Rom 5:14 (AT)
[R-2] Gen 3:14
[R-3] Job 3:16

2.32-33 The part of her that experiences pleasure, is made from that weak, pale, fearful material, the rubbish [of the surface part] of the Earth,[R] and her reproductive seed, the part of her that understands and reasons, is Adam's widowed spirit[ual intellect].

[R] Is 14:11 (AT)

Each of her two parts is overflowing into the visible, physical world and standing on the Earth: Her spirit[ual intellect] is appearing as Mind, and the waters of the creation mixed with the rubbish of the Earth, are appearing as animals who are capable of containing spiritual life.[R]

[R] Is 14:11 (AT)

2.34 You looked until [Elijah], the foundation stone of the Living Beast was supernaturally established[R-1] and nailed Himself to the human spirit, overlaid [the confused intellect of] the fiery serpent, tread [Satan] underfoot,[38] [R-2] and became one with Adam's widowed spirit[ual intellect, which was joined to] Leviathan, the sea serpent, who pierced through into the visible, physical world[R-3] and is now appearing in the Earth as the children of Belial;[R-4] And [Elijah] judged the Woman,[R-5] and Adam's fallen, mortal mind broke up.[R-6]

[R-1] Dan 7:14, 22 (AT)
[R-2] Dan 8:6-7 (AT)
Rev 20:3
[R-3] Dan 8:8-9 (AT)
Job 40:24 (AT)
[R-4] Zeph 2:5-6 (AT)
[R-5] Eccl 12:3 (AT)
Song 8:7 (AT)
Dan 8:13 (AT)
[R-6] Dan 7:25 (AT)
Rev 20:12-13

2.35 Then the fiery serpent, Satan and the whole Wild Animal [that were joined to the spiritual garbage of the earth], were combined into one membranous outer covering for Elijah[R-1] and, in the harvest season,[R-2] when Adam is separated from the fiery serpent [their confused spiritual intellect] with [the judgment[R-3] of] repeated blows and whippings, he will overtake

---

[38] ***Piercing through*** [into the heart], ***overlaying*** [the confused intellect of the fiery serpent] and ***treading under*** [Satan], are the three steps which lead up to the spiritual experience known as ***full stature*** (Eph 4:13), the first of three experiences which result in the individual's liberation from hell and death.

the many members of the Wild Animal, and bring [the age[R-4] of] their spiritually dead existence to an end;

[R-1] Dan 8:6-7 (AT)
[R-2] Rev 14:15-20
[R-3] Dan 7:25 (AT)
Rev 20:12-13
[R-4] Matt 13:39

And Elijah crushed the [the fallen Adam], who is the shadow[R-1] of Himself, and the resurrected Adam became one with Elijah,[R-2] and they became the sharp rock[R-3] that completes[R-4] the Wild Animal that is lacking [righteousness],[R-5] and the Wild Animal that the Leviathan made was swallowed up by the resurrected Adam, and Elijah.

[R-1] Rev 14:18-20
[R-2] 1 Cor 15:45-47
[R-3] Deut 32:4
[R-4] Col 2:10
[R-5] Col 2:10
2 Pet 1:1

[1240.2.C]
2.36 And this [is] the dream and interpretation [that] I will declare to the personality of the king:

2.37a The God of Heaven has given you the rationale, [moral] authority, and [military] power [to rule over] the Kingdom [of Judah, which makes] you a King of kings,

2.38 And he has given [these spiritually] male children, where the Angels of Heaven dwell [together with their] best[ial souls], into your hands, and made you a ruler over them all.

You are this Head of Gold,

2,27b Oh King,

2.39 And after your [GOLDEN MONARCHIAL rule over the spiritually male children of Judah], they shall be under [the authority of] the BRASS [Kingdom of Angels that are born with] all the earth[en personalities of the spiritually male children of Judah, and the angels of the Brasen Kingdom shall enforce

Jehovah's Righteous Sowing & Reaping Judgment upon the bestial nature of the spiritually male children of Judah, until the King of] another, third, [SILVER] Kingdom [of Heaven], shall arise, [and He shall SAVE the spiritually male children of Judah from the sins of the angels that judge their bestial nature],

2.40 And the fourth Kingdom of [God, the regenerated Name], Jehovah Elohim, shall be strong [enough] to weaken the bad angels [that] broke up the whole [Name, Jehovah Elohim, and] beat all of the earth[en] personalities [of the spiritually male children of Judah] into powder, [stripping them of their spirituality and rendering them as brute beasts; Indeed, Elohim shall end the immoral marriages between] all the bad angels that broke up the whole [Name, Jehovah Elohim, and] all [the bestial personalities of the spiritually male children of Judah that] they beat into powder, [which changed them from sons of God into brute beasts],

2.41 And, as you saw, [the Fourth] Kingdom [of God, represented by] the toes of the feet, is part potter's clay, and part angel, but, the angels [of the Kingdom of God shall be permanently] fixed [in the immortal Name, Jehovah], so you shall see only clods of the clay [that they are] mixed [with],

2.42 And, as the toes of the feet were part angel, and part clay, [so, too], shall the larger, [angelic] part of the Kingdom [of God] be powerful, and [the other, clay] part, fragile,

2.43 And just as you saw the angels mixed with the clay clods, [the angels] shall mingle with the human descendants [of the Third Kingdom of Salvation], but [these angels of the Third Kingdom] shall not be bound to [the heirs of Salvation, just] as the angels were not mixed with the clay [in your dream],

2.44 And in the days of these kings, the God of Heaven shall establish a kingdom [that] shall not be perpetually destroyed, [or] left to other people, [but] it shall break in pieces, and bring to an end, all these [other] kingdoms, [and] it shall stand for ever,

2.45 And you saw the power of God cut the seed of God's Angels away from the clay of [humanity, and] save [the lives of the people] without the judgment [of God] breaking [their] mind in pieces, to make known what shall come to pass after this [time so that] you, the king, can trust that this dream [came from heaven, and] rely on [the interpretation coming to pass],

And now that you understand the interpretation of the dream, [if you think that it is] reliable and you trust [it, pay me the prophet's reward of 30 pieces of] silver, [and Jehovah's righteous Sowing & Reaping] judgment shall [release the foundation] stone, [which is held captive by] the mind that is not [of God, and] the mountain [that attaches Righteous Adam to the God world], will circumcise [your heart].

[31.7]
2.48 Then the king made Daniel a great man and gave him many gifts.

Chapter 4

[982.3.C]
4.32 And [the watchers] shall drive away your male side, and [make] you to dwell with the beasts of the field, and the moth, [Jehovah's Righteous Sowing and Reaping Judgment], shall consume [the Second Adam, the Lord from heaven, within] you, continually,, until you recognize that [Jehovah] is higher than men, [and] appoints whoever he pleases to rule over the kingdom,

4.32 And [the watchers] shall drive the traveler out from [the Temple of] Man, and you shall live with the beasts of the field, and the moth, [Jehovah's Righteous Sowing and Reaping Judgment], shall consume [the Second Adam, the Lord from heaven, within] you, for seven spiritual time periods, until you recognize that the Supernal Mother has preeminence [over] the Kingdom of Men, and permits [whoever] she wishes, to live in [the Temple of Man], and

4.33 At the same time that the Word [of the Lord] was revealed to Nebuchadnezzar, [whose] spirit stretched out like a bird as strong as an eagle, [and whose] body was drenched with the Spirit [of the Supernal Mother who is in] heaven, [the watchers] from above, drove the traveler, [Nebuchadnezzar's male] side, out [of the Temple] of Man, and the moth, [Jehovah's Righteous Sowing & Reaping] Judgment, consumed [the Second Adam who had been formed within Nebuchadnezzar],

Chapter 5

[Message # Unknown]
5.11 There is a man in the kingdom . . . whom the king, thy father . . . made master of the magicians, astrologers, Chaldeans and soothsayers.

5.25 ***MENE*** - Jehovah has divided you from Elijah, as a recompense for living out of, and doing the fiery serpent's wicked works, when Abel's righteousness was available to you.

TEKEL - Your spiritual development is measured against Adam and you are found to be lacking the quality of His life.

PERES - Your personality is an unclean Wild Animal [mortal and dead]**[R-1]** and is, therefore, given over [by Jehovah] to Satan.**[R-2]**

R-1 Rev 13:18
R-2 2 Cor 4:4
1 Tim 1:20

Chapter 7

[71]

7.02 Daniel responded to his night vision by telling about it: And there they were, the spirits that were in right standing with Jehovah when they were one with Him, before they unfolded and germinated forth as the [spiritual] plant life of this visible, physical world,[R-1] and they were breaking forth from Adam's widowed spirit, and descending upon the very large Living Beast, like a child issuing from the womb.[R-2]

R-1 Zech 6:1,6 (AT)
R-2 Gen 2:11 (AT)

7.03 And they were huge, with a domineering nature, and they represented the full reproductive potential of the Living Beast which was appearing in the visible, spiritual world; and the first three were completely different from the fourth one.

7.04 The Living Beast that came before all of the others was Adam,[R-1] Elohim's Son, a highly exalted, fierce spiritual warrior, who dwelt in the high place of Jehovah's Spirit,[R-2] and I continued to look at the vision, until I saw the [soul] waters of the creation murder Adam and incarnate by Adam's widowed spirit,[R-3] and [Satan and Leviathan], a mortal foundation, was laid into Elohim's Living Beast, and he became a mortal [Wild Animal],[R-4]

R-1 1 Cor 15:45
R-2 Ez 28:13-15
R-3 Gen 4:1-2 (AT)
R-4 Dan 8:8-9 (AT)
Zeph 2:5-6 (AT)

7.05a And there she was, a different Animal, one inferior in authority and subordinate to the first, and this [Leviathan, the sea serpent] was a wild, raging war-monger, who increased [by bringing] Cain [into existence], who incarnated as a mortal woman without Jehovah's image,[R]

[R] Is 27:1

7.06 Then, after all that I had already seen, I looked again, and there it was, a different one, [which was] wild, ravenous and stained with sin, and this Wild Animal had everything she needed to incarnate and function in the visible, physical world, because ruling authority over mortal man, and over all of the Earth[R] is being granted to Satan.

[R] Rom 7:14

7.05b And she had three parts to her, Satan [unconscious mind], Leviathan [sub-conscious mind], and Cain [conscious mind], and she was mortal; and Satan and Leviathan and Cain said to themselves, "Let us incarnate, and be the accuser of all mankind,"[R] and

[R] Rev 12:10

7.07 After seeing everything in the sleeping trance that I just told you about, there it was! A fourth Living Beast that was spiritually complete;[R-1] [39] The spirit of [the male Righteous Adam] crucified [R-2] Elijah and [the First] Adam rose from the dead [R-3] and was appearing [R-4] in the many members of the Wild Animal which had multiplied to the fullest extent possible, and

[R-1] Col 2:10
[R-2] Gal 2:20
[R-2] 1 Cor 15:4
[R-3] Matt 27:53

They are terrifyingly strong,[R-2] with superior, dominant power,[R-3] and they have the great spiritual strength necessary to bring Leviathan into submission to their male spiritual authority, and burn her in the lake of fire, and boil Satan,

---

[39] The Righteous Adam is called *the Lord from heaven* because he is joined to Elohim. He is the root of Melchizedek (Gen 14:18), the personality that represents the Kingdom of Heaven, the priest of the Most High God that completed Elijah.

the unconscious mind of mortal man, as a sin offering, to separate the human spirit from her;**R-4** and Elijah is so different from the Living Beasts that came before him, that he appears perverted to them, but he has the power and authority to fulfill the law,**R-5** and

R-2 Ez 1:22 (AT)
R-3 Eph 1:21
R-4 Heb 4:12
R-5 Matt 5:17

7.08 Then I turned my attention to the power of the law**R-1** which was ruling in the Wild Animal,**R-2** and there it was, a different, despised source of spiritual power rising up from underneath her, and he made the law [of sin and death] **R-3** utterly useless by castrating Leviathan and destroying Satan.**R-4** And there it was! A form like unto the appearance of a mortal man who was incarnating upon Elijah's spiritual power base, and He had a mind that was proclaiming Jehovah's mighty works in the visible, physical world,**R-5** and

R-1 Rom 7:23
R-2 Rev 6:5 (AT)
R-3 Eph 2:15
R-4 1 Jn 3:8
R-5 Tit 2:11; 3:4

7.09 I continued to look at the vision until the Wild Animal that Adam is to rule over came into submission to him, and Jehovah's Spirit shined through [the First] Adam [who was formed from] the earth,**R-1** [and the Righteous Adam who is from] heaven**R-1** [came into existence], and the male Righteous Adam, the first one resurrected out from this existence known as death,**R2** possessed the Wild Animal, and dwelt with her as a wife; and

The spirit of the Wild Animal [that had illegally] increased into many human spirits in a visible, physical world, was cleansed from all sin when she married him, because the male Righteous Adam [from heaven] was covering [the First] Adam [in the earth], and the many-membered Body of the male Righteous Adam became Jehovah's lampstand,

R-1 1Cor 15:47
R-2 Rev 1:5

7.10 [Because] the male Righteous Adam was firmly fixed within the hearts of the Wild Animal's many members, and of the male Righteous Adam, the instrument by which Jehovah would sentence the Wild Animal,**R** rose from the dead, and ploughed Cain[40] until the Wild Animal came into the correct moral order,**R** and the male Righteous Adam engraved [the Wild Animal that became] an ox[41] with Elohim's nature, and Jehovah was revealed through the ox when the male Second Adam appeared, and [Elohim], the spirit of [the male Adam] vibrated forth and covered [Satan and Leviathan, the mind of] the ox, like a garment, and Jehovah was revealed in the visible, spiritual world through the male Righteous Adam, [who became] the spiritual [intellectual] mind of the ox,[42] and

R Rev 12:1

7.11 Then I continued to look at the vision within my own mind, and to hear the powerful things that Adam was speaking about, and as I continued to look, Satan was cut off, and her spiritual authority over the Wild Animal was dispersed and lapped up by the fire of God,**R** and

R Rev 21:10,14

7.12 This is how Adam was raised from the dead in the many-membered, sin-stained, mortal Wild Animal; Neverthe-

---

[40] *To plough* means to cut deep, as far as the unconscious part of the mind, to reveal sin (Lk 9:62).

[41] The Wild Animal became an ox, which is a castrated bull (Ez 1:10, and the ox became a cherub (Ez 10:14). This parable means that the First Adam who was made from the earth, experienced a moral fall and became a wild animal (Dan 4:33), but Elijah castrated him in Jacob (Gen 32:25,32) and Israel became Jehovah's servant (Ps 136:22, Is 44:21, 49:3). (See, also, Note [42].)

[42] The First Adam who became an ox, became a cherub when the male Righteous Adam became his mind (Ez 1:10, 10:14). (See, also, Note [41].)

less, their fleshly existence was prolonged until the season appointed for [their bodies] to waste away,[R] and

[R] Rev 14:15 (AT)

7.13 I continued to look into the visible, spiritual world because my [carnal] mind was prostrated under Adam, and there it was! The male Righteous Adam was crucifying the human spirit and Adam was rising from the dead [in his sons], and [the male Righteous Adam] was appearing in, and becoming one with, the many-membered Wild Animal that had been cleansed from sin; and as [Adam's sons] drew near to Jehovah and appeared in front of Him, they were set free from the visible, physical world of time and space, and became Jehovah's immortal Body in the visible, spiritual world, and

7.14 Elohim, the Spirit that produces life from within himself,[R] was set up in the Wild Animal, and became the foundation which provides mastery [over one's fallen, mortal mind], and [the male] Adam was given an immortal body so that all the peoples who know Jehovah, as well as those who don't know Him, and all nationalities and groups of people with different ethnic backgrounds, but who speak the same language, should find the strength to pierce through Leviathan, break away from Satan, and rise from the dead, [so that Adam] who is become incorruptible,[R] shall never lose control over the Living Beast [again], and he shall rule [his female side] for the life of the ages.

[R] 1 Cor 15:52

7.15 [Then], I, Daniel, was made holy in my human spirit[43] which is in the midst of my mortal mind, and spiritual communications from Jehovah were thrust into my mind, and

7.16 I approached the fourth Beast, which is Elohim's completed Living Beast, and ardently asked to know what the vision really meant, so [the spiritual man] assured me that the vision was from Jehovah and explained it to me, [saying],

---

[43] Elohim joined itself to Daniel's human spirit.

7.17 "These wonderful Living Beasts are spiritually mature human beings who are standing because they ascended up to Elohim's throne and became spiritual men whose mind and personality increased into their full spiritual potential, and they are ruling over their female side by Jehovah's authority;

7.18 "Indeed, the men who are joined to Elijah and Adam in their spirit have taken authority over their own fallen mind and become sinless, because Elohim and Adam, the Kingdom [of Heaven,[R] have become their mind, and they shall be joined to Elijah for the indefinite time period that shall be the greatest age of all the ages," and

R Matt 4:17

7.19 Then I asked to understand about the fourth Living Beast, and to be assured that I was being taught Jehovah's truth about the Beast that is so different from the others that he appears perverted to them. He is like one who used to have spiritual power, whose spirit fell down into an existence in the visible, physical world,[R-1] but now he has risen from the dead[R-2] with enough spiritual strength to bring this Wild Animal into submission to His male spiritual authority, and he is gloriously terrifying, and

R-1 Dan 5:21
Dan 7:4 (AT)
R-2 1 Cor 15:45

He is burning [judging][R-1] Leviathan [subconscious] as a sin offering, and boiling Satan[R-2] [unconscious mind] until the human spirit, which is increasing into [Elohim], the bridegroom who is marrying Adam, separates from the Wild Animal, and

R-1 Ez 1:27 (AT)
R-2 Jer 46:22 (AT)

7.20 I would like to know about the Law of Sin and Death[R-1] which is ruling in each and every one of this Wild Animal's members, and about the other Law[R-1] which is appearing from underneath her, which caused the criminal Cain to prostrate herself and serve Adam, the one who appears much more like lord and master of Elohim's Living Beast than any of the three other Living Beasts, which were designed to be joined to Him, and serve him,[R-2] and

[R-2] Rom 8:2
[R-2] Dan 7:7

7.21 I looked at the vision, and the same Spirit [of life] that fulfilled Jehovah's spiritual law in Elijah, drew the mortal, corrupt, sin-filled mind of Adam's [many-membered] Body near to Him,

7.22 So that Elijah[R] who overcame the visible, physical world of time and space, could reproduce His resurrected life in them,[44] and

[R] 1 Cor 15:45

The season arrived in which the mortal mind of the Wild Animal to which Elijah had loaned his righteousness, without requiring repentance of specific sin,[R] would be woven together with Himself, and made truly holy and

[R] Rom 11:29

Adam judged every individual member of the Wild Animal, and waged war against their sin-filled mind, and the many members of mortal humanity were cleansed from their sins when Elijah was laid as a spiritual foundation[R] in their heart, and

[R] 1 Cor 3:11

7.23 Then Daniel prophesied saying, "Thus saith Jehovah, "Adam is the mind that shall develop the highest spiritual potential of the Wild Animal through her submission to, and union with Elijah; Adam shall be different than Leviathan, and he shall humble the many members of the Wild Animal, and bring them into submission to himself, and under his Lordship, and he shall swallow [Satan] up, and separate them from every wicked personality trait which is not of Jehovah's nature, and

---

[44] Elijah transmigrated into Jesus of Nazareth and rescued his personal soul by joining it to Elohim, the third degree of power of the God World of Emanation.

7.24 "Elijah shall incarnate in this visible, physical world,[R-1] and [the man in whom he incarnates] shall become great,[R-2] and after him, a company of men shall appear and become great,[R-3] because Elijah shall loan them his righteousness without requiring repentance of specific sins,[R-4] and Elijah's Mind shall be different than the mind of the men who are great because of Elijah's ***loaned*** spiritual authority, and Adam shall fulfill the Law[R-5] of Sin and Death[R-6] in the minds of the Wild Animal's many members, and empower them to cease from sin, and

R-1 Matt 11:4
R-2 Lk 1:15,32
R-3 Jn 14:12
R-4 Rom 11:29
R-5 Matt 5:17
R-6 Rom 8:2

7.25 In anticipation of the next spiritual season of Jehovah's plan for maturing the whole Wild Animal, Elijah shall preach about himself rising from the dead,[R-1] the judgment of Elohim's Sons,[R-2] and Elijah's spiritual life replacing their religious systems; [R-3] and

R-1 Matt 27:63
R-2 Heb 9:27
R-3 Dan 9:27

Elohim's Sons shall be subjected to Elijah's authority, and he shall judge their sin-filled minds for three and one-half generations, and their fallen, mortal mind, shall decay,[R] and Elijah shall swallow [Satan] up, and

R Ez 1:24 (AT)

7.26 Elijah shall marry the first group[R-1] of mortal men to have their mind renewed[R-2] in Elohim's image, and they shall plant His life in the Wild Animal's[R-3] remaining members, but [Satan] shall continue to rule over them until Elijah is irrefutably installed as their king, [R-4] and Elijah shall rise from the dead in the Wild Animal's remaining members, and Elijah shall lay waste and bring to naught, Satan's spiritual military strength, [R-5] and

[R-1] Ez 48:14
Rom 11:16
[R-2] Eph 4:23
[R-3] Rev 9:2-3
[R-5] Heb 4:12

7.27 Adam shall swallow [Satan] up, and bring them under the authority of the new, combined Heavens,[45] and Elijah shall be the foundation[R-1] that is laid into the remaining members of the Wild Animal and, because Elijah is their mind, every member of the Wild Animal shall be made to understand [R-2] what Jehovah requires of him; and Elijah shall be raised from the dead[R-3] in each of them, and they shall break out of fallen [Adam's], mortal mind and pierce through into Elijah's Kingdom, and they shall live for the life of the ages.[R-4]

[R-1] 1 Cor 3:11
[R-2] Eph 1:8
[R-3] Rev 20:6
[R-4] 1 Thes 4:17

7.28 This is everything that Gabriel showed me, and [then] he separated himself from me; and after seeing all the thoughts that he gave me which were thrust mightily into my fallen, mortal mind, the thoughts of my fallen, mortal mind returned to me, and I exerted every effort to remember what He had shown me.

---

[45] *The combined Heavens* consists of the Kingdom of God and the Kingdom of Heaven.

Chapter 8

[143.10]

8.01 A vision appeared to me, Daniel, about the time that the Wild Animal was to become spiritual, and it was similar to the vision that I had seen earlier and,

8.02 As I realized that a divine revelation was being presented to me and tried to understand it, I was immersed in Elijah's Spirit, and as Elijah joined Himself to my human spirit which was still woven together with Cain, my mortal conscious mind, Adam was raised from the dead in me, and I was able to look at this divine revelation with Elohim's Mind, and

8.03a [When] I opened my spiritual eyes, I was seeing and understanding with Elohim's Mind, and there it was! [Adam], the Living Beast that Elohim made, and he had two spiritual laws in his mind, one ***passive*** and the other ***dominant***,[R-1] and [Adam], the Living Beast, was standing in full spiritual strength in the [spiritual] high place of the Earth, and he was both male [***positive/dominant***] and female [***negative/passive***],[R-2] and

R-1 Rom 8:2
R-2 Gen 1:27

8.04a I saw Elohim, the unconscious part of the mind of the [whole] Living Beast, and Righteous Adam, [the personality of the Kingdom of] Heaven, the subconscious part of the mind [of the whole Living Beast,] spreading himself into the Earth, and Adam was protecting the Living Beast from materializing in the Earth in a perverted form,

8.03b But, Adam's female [***negative/passive*** side] twisted together with the Snake,[46] [the earthen side of the Living Beast],

---

[46] Adam's wife twisted together with the Snake, who is a spiritual eunuch because her seed can only produce a conscious existence that

and] the mind [of a Wild Animal] came into existence [that] was stronger than Adam, Elohim's male ***[positive/dominant***] mind, and

8.04b Adam [***positive***] knew that [his ***negative*** female side that had twisted together with] the Snake, was strong enough to kill him and begin an independent existence,[47] and

8.05a As I turned to Gabriel to receive understanding, I saw the Woman [who came into existence when Adam's] female [side twisted together with the Snake, and] she had the vision of the spiritual land of Nod in her mind, and she rebelled against Adam, and brought her spiritual law out from under Adam's authority,[48] and the Snake appeared in the Earth and began to dominate

8.06-7a Adam, the Lord and Master of the [whole] Living Beast, which was both ***positive*** [***male/dominant***] and ***negative*** [***female/passive***],

8.05b But [the Snake] did not penetrate [Adam's ox] right away, and [the Woman and the Snake] fell upon Adam, the Living Beast, the one that I had seen standing in Eden in the Earth by the full spiritual authority of [the Kingdom of] Heaven, but [Adam] could not escape from the witchcraft power[49] of the Snake that stripped him of the strength he needed to sustain the

---

is disconnected from Jehovah. Adam carries Jehovah's virile seed, the only source of true life (Gen 4:25 [AT]).

47 This spiritual truth is revealed in Zech 5:11, for which there is no printed Alternate Translation. (See, Message #8, ***The Latter End***, for further explanation and study.)

48 The Woman's spiritual authority is passive when she is in submission to Adam, but aggressive, or dominant, when she twists together with the Snake.

49 Adam could not escape, because the enemy was his own wife, who was a part of him.

image of Eden in the Earth,[R-1] and [the Snake] took [Adam]'s ox for a wife,[R-2] and

[R-1] Gen 2:8, 6:2
[R-2] Gen 2:22 (AT)

8.06-7b I saw the Snake penetrate Adam's ox[50] and his spiritual seed flow into her, and [this is how] the Snake overthrew Adam,[R-1] and Adam's [female] spirit[ual side], which is now joined to a Wild Animal, became a harlot[R-2] because of the Snake's witchcraft,[R-3] and

[R-1] Gen 4:8
[R-2] Job 41:5,13 (AT)
Pro 26:11 (AT)
Eccl 12:3 (AT)
Ez 32:2 (AT)
Joel 3:3 (AT)
Zeph 3:4a (AT)
Rev 17:1 (AT)
[R-3] 1 Sam 15:23

8.08-9a The Snake [R-1] entered into Eden, the vision of the visible world that Adam was sustaining through his [female] spirit[ual side], and used violent spiritual military strength[R-2] to break the bones[51] of Adam, the Living Beast, and offer him up as a sacrifice to [his female side, who] had increased into Satan, the high priestess of the Wild Animal and Cain, the conscious part of its mortal mind, and that is how the Snake purchased Adam,

---

[50] Adam died to his spiritual manhood and Jehovah's breath incarnated as Satan, the unconscious part of the mind of the Wild Animal, Adam's ox incarnated as Cain, a mortal Woman (Gen 2:25 [AT]), the Snake increased into Leviathan, and the whole Wild Animal was engraved with the Snake's nature (Lk 3:7). (Footnote continued – See, Appendix)

[51] The bones that form the skeleton of the material body are the structure upon which the flesh hangs, and the bones of the skeleton hang on the spiritual flesh of Adam's personal souls (personalities), (Footnote continued – See, Appendix)

Elohim's wife, who died when [his female side committed adultery with] the Snake, and

[R-1] Matt 4:1 (AT)
[R-2] Heb 4:12

8.10 The Snake went beyond Nod, the visible, spiritual world, and caused Eden, the visible physical world, to appear [in front of it], and

8.08-9b [The Snake] incarnated in the visible, physical world[R] as Leviathan, [the subconscious part of the mind of mortal man, and that is how]

[R] Dan 7:5 (AT)

8.11 The many members of Adam, [the Living Beast], were given over to the custody of the Snake in Eden, [which is] beyond [Nod], the visible, spiritual world, because of [the Woman's] rebellion, and

[The Woman] broke forth upon the many members [of Adam], the Living Beast, and intertwined herself with them, and [Adam's] potential to incarnate [as the righteous mind] of the whole Living Beast] was permanently altered [from righteous] to good and evil, when [the Woman] incarnated as Satan and Cain[R] instead of Elohim's immortal Son, and

[R] Gen 3:1

8.12 This is how the Woman ***re***formed the many members of [Adam], Elohim's Living Beast, into her own image, and built a nation of earthy, sensual and devilish, physical humans, who would engage in continuous labor[R-1] in order to survive,[R-2] and they entered into the visible, physical earth [beyond] Nod, and this is how [Adam], the Living Beast, was overthrown;

[R-1] Ez 39:14
[R-2] Is 14:5 (AT)
Zeph 2:5-6 (AT)

8.13 Then I heard Jehovah speaking about his plan to raise Adam from the dead by judging the Woman,[R-1] and Adam[52] said to Jehovah, "How long will it be until your Warrior Spirit[53] is added to the saints so that they can put a yoke on Leviathan, [their proud subconscious mind] who tread [Righteous Adam] under foot[R-2] and brought him to ruin, and be delivered from Satan, their rebellious unconscious mind?" And

[R-1] Eccl 12:3 (AT)
Song 8:7 (AT)
Dan 2:34 (AT)
[R-2] Rom 8:20 (AT)

8.14 Jehovah said to Adam, "It shall take as long as is necessary for you to overcome Leviathan's present, illegal use of [your] spiritual substance, and then your righteousness[54] shall be restored," [55] and

[165]
8.15 When I understood that Jehovah was communicating with me through a vision, I asked for understanding, and there

---

[52] Adam was temporarily resurrected in Daniel's mind.

[53] Elijah is the spiritual Warrior that raises Adam from the dead.

Adam exists on multiple levels. One of his models fell, but a righteous model of Adam continued to exist. That righteous Adam is called *The Second Adam, the Lord from Heaven* (1 Cor 15:47) in the New Testament. (Footnote continued – See, Appendix)

[54] Adam's widowed spirit, which is appearing in mortal man as Satan, the unconscious part of the mind of the whole Living Beast, shall be restored to sinlessness [immortality] when Adam is raised from the dead (Matt 5:18; 1Cor 15:3-4) and subjects Cain (Dan 7:7 [AT]; Rom 8:21 [AT]).

[55] At the beginning of this discourse, Daniel's fallen, mortal mind was separate from Adam, but Gabriel paralyzed Leviathan, the source of Daniel's pride, so the Scripture says, ***and He*** [Adam, Daniel's only functioning mind], ***said to me***.

it was! A mature spiritual [Warrior] materialized in front of me and,

8.16 Between the time that I asked to understand the vision and the time that the Spiritual Warrior appeared, I heard a voice crying out, saying, "Gabriel," * enlighten this mortal mind with spiritual sight;" And

* See, Footnote 53, ¶ 3

8.17-18 I was in the deep sleep that the Wild Animal exists in, when Gabriel rushed upon me unexpectedly and lay on top of my fallen, mortal mind, [56] and I began to ascend into [the Kingdom of] Heaven* because of Gabriel's righteousness and, as Gabriel started to speak to me, the foundation of Jehovah's city, the holy Jerusalem,[R-1] began to appear in my mind and, because Elohim's promises [R-2] are about to bring this present age to an end,[R-3] Gabriel showed me, a descendant of Adam, how to distinguish between Righteous Adam and Leviathan, [my two minds], and

R-1 Rev 20:10 (AT)
R-2 Gen 9:11
R-3 Matt 13:39

* "The Kingdom of Heaven" is the unified Elohim and Jehovah functioning as the link between God and fallen Adam.

8.19 Gabriel said, "Look, I will help you to understand that the end of Jehovah's corrective judgment upon mankind is the reconciliation of the whole Wild Animal unto himself:[R]

R Zeph 1:17-18 (AT)

8.20-21 "There are two spiritual laws in the Living Beast that you saw: Adam, the ***positive/dominant*** Law, and the Woman, the ***negative/passive*** Law; Adam's ***positive/dominant*** authority was stronger than the Woman's ***negative/passive***

---

[56] ***Gabriel*** covered over Daniel's fallen, mortal mind, paralyzed Leviathan, and caught Daniel up into the Kingdom of Heaven, which the mind of righteous Adam. (See, also, Note 53).

authority until the Woman twisted together with [the Snake] and [became] the ***negative/dominant*** Law [of the whole Living Beast]; and

"The Woman's ***negative/dominant*** Law was stronger than Adam's ***positive/dominant*** Law, so the Snake was able to penetrate [Adam]**[R-1]** and break his bones,**[R-2]** and

"The Snake married Adam's ox, [57] and

"[The Woman] incarnated as Satan, who became the Wild Animal's high priestess and Cain [who] murdered Abel; And

"[The Snake who] stole [Adam's female] spirit[ual side] increased into Leviathan, the subconscious part of the mind of the [whole] Wild Animal, and

"These are the stages of the fall of the Living Beast, and

R-1 Gen 2:24 (AT)
R-2 Gen 2:22 (AT)

8.22 "This is how [Adam, Elohim's creation], the Living Beast, materialized in the visible, physical world in a perverted form**[R-1]** because of the Woman's**[R-2]** rebellion, but Adam's widowed spirit shall, nevertheless, separate from the Snake, not by [Adam's] ***positive/dominant*** authority, but by the [double portion of] the ***positive positive/dominant*** reproductive strength of Righteous Adam and Elohim,**[58]** and

R-1 Dan 7:7 (AT)
Dan 8:4 (AT)
R-2 Dan 7:5 (AT)
Rev 13:4

---

[57] Adam is the name of the whole Living Beast. The ox is the most external part, the human vessel that all the other parts dwell in.

[58] Adam is the ***positive/dominant*** spiritual law called "the Tree of Life." "The Snake" is the ***negative/dominant*** spiritual law called "the Tree of the Knowledge of Good and Evil." (Footnote continued – See, Appendix)

8.23 "At the end of the age [when the Snake's rulership comes to an end,[R-1] Elohim shall fortify a King[59] that has the mind of the Righteous Adam and understand mysteries,[R-3] and he shall appear[R-2] [in the visible, material world], and

[R-1] 2 Pet 2:4 (AT)
[R-2] Zech 3:8
[R-3] Dan 5:14, Rev 5:2

8.24a "Righteous Adam shall be strong enough to bind up[R-1] and destroy the fallen, mortal mind of the first members of the Wild Animal to mature[R-2] so that Jehovah's priests[60] can appear,[R-3] and they shall pass through [the resistance of Cain, the mortal conscious mind that opposes Righteous Abel], and flow over Leviathan like a river,, who paralyzes [mortal men with fear], and offer him up as a sin offering to Jehovah, and this is how the Second Adam, who became a King when [Elohim] Fortified him, shall give his single mind[R-4] to [Jehovah's priests], the first members of the Wild Animal to mature, and

[R-1] Matt 16:19
[R-2]Matt 12:29 (AT)
Rev 14:1-4 (AT)
[R-3] Rev 9:14-15 (AT)
[R-4] Col 3:22

8.25 "The Spirit of Elijah shall beget a Son through understanding, and the Spirit of Elijah and the Righteous Adam shall pass through [Cain who opposes righteous Abel], and they shall flow over [Leviathan] in the first fruits of the Woman, and

---

[59] This is a prophecy of Messiah. He is a king because his base is the Kingdom of Heaven. He is the King of Heaven.

[60] Jehovah's end-time priests are the sons of Zadok (Ez 40:46), who are descendants of Phinehas, son of Eleazar, son of Aaron, the High Priest. Jehovah gave the Covenant of Peace to Phinehas and his seed (Num 25:12), and that seed became flesh in Jesus of Nazareth through his mother, Mary. In the age to come Jehovah's priests will come from the tribe of Judah, the tribal designation of Joseph, Jesus' father.

8.25b "[Jehovah's male child] shall break forth from [the womb of the Woman,[R-1] and stand upon the foundation of [Michael],[R-2] the Chief Prince[R-3] of the many princes who are Elohim's Sons,[R-4] and this is how Elijah shall bring peace[R-5] to the Wild Animal, by binding[R-6] their fallen, mortal mind to himself;

[R-1] Rev 19:16
[R-2] 1 Cor 3:11
[R-3] Dan 10:13
[R-4] Jn 1:12
[R-5] Rev 14:14 (AT)
[R-6] Ps 118:27

8.26 "Elohim gave you that priestly vision about the mortal men who made an alliance with him,[R] but [Satan, Leviathan and Cain], your fallen mind, kept you from receiving it for many days," and

[R] Rom 8:14

8.27 Then I, Daniel, was separated from Adam, the one who rose from the dead [in me] after [Elijah] wounded my fallen, mortal mind so that I could receive the prophecy[R] that I was commanded to write down, but Leviathan, [the subconscious part of my mortal mind] confused my understanding of the vision and Gabriel's explanation of it, so that I could not remember any of it.

[R] Dan 8:2

Chapter 9

[177]
9.21-23 At the time I, Daniel, was speaking to Elohim and interceding on behalf of Israel, Gabriel, the man I had seen in the previous vision, said to me,

Elohim responded to you as soon as you began to pray for mercy. Therefore, because you're a delight to Jehovah, Elijah is spreading forth, entering into your fallen, mortal mind, and intertwining himself [with your human spirit] to give you understanding, as well as mercy.

And then Elijah wounded my fallen, mortal mind, [and] separated my human spirit from Satan,[R] and offered [my human spirit] up as a sacrifice to Jehovah, saying, ***now use Adam's Mind, which is given to you so that you can distinguish between Jehovah's truth and the fiery serpent's error.***

[R] Heb 4:12

And I received [the following] insight from Gabriel, and was comforted:

[830.1]

9.24 Seventy weeks are decreed upon your people, [until] the Righteous One comes from the eternal world in[to this world],

To anoint [the unconscious mind of the people who are] the sanctuaries of the holy city [of new Jerusalem, with the seed] of the Holy [One],

To seal off [Leviathan], the sin [nature of mortal mankind],

To cover over [Satan, the source of mankind's] morally evil [nature], and

To seal off the vision of the [false] prophet, [all of which will] put an end to [the Woman's] rebellion;

9.25 Know, therefore, and understand that from the going forth of the commandment to restore [Israel] and build Jerusalem, unto Messiah, the Prince, shall be seven weeks and 62 weeks, and [after that] the foundation and the street of the temple shall be built again, [and the second and third constructions shall take place] in times of great distress;

[1241.2.C]

9.26 And after 62 weeks, [Adam] shall be circumcised, [and] the Prince [of the Covenant] shall come to finish [the work of] the flood [and] end the war [that the Angels are waging against Jehovah], but Messiah shall not come into existence until [Adam], the sanctuary in [the midst of] the city of the people that belong [to Jehovah, that] was destroyed [when the Lizard] stunned [Adam and] maimed [his earthen personalities, making them unfit to marry Jehovah, is rebuilt],

9.27 [And Messiah, the Prince], shall confirm the covenant with many [people that he is] in the midst of, and] complete [them, and the Prince of the Covenant] shall unite [with the people [that Messiah] completes, [and] the people shall ascend, and [Jehovah] shall cease from consuming [the animal souls that the people] sacrifice [so that] the Shekinah [should ascend above their fallen soul, and the Lizard], the detestable thing that stunned [Adam and] maimed [his earthen personalities making them unfit to marry Jehovah], shall be completely destroyed [when] judgment is poured out upon [the Male Goat and the Lizard and his angels] are melted [in the Lake of Fire].

Chapter 11

[843]

WORLD OF POTENTIAL

A VISITATION

Daniel Seized

11.01 In the first year of Darius, the Mede, Adonay stood up [in me, Daniel], and seized [my human spirit, the core of my mind], the fortified place that belongs to [God], and

11.02 Now I [am able] to tell you the truth. Look!

The Fourth King

Three more kings shall stand up [after Darius, this present] Persian [king], and [Messiah] the fourth [king]**R-1** shall be greater than [Sophia] the whole Female Power, [who possesses] the ten [Rings of Power of the Snake**R-2** which was created on the Fifth Day,**R-3** because] [Messiah] shall have the ten [Rings of the Power of the (God) World of Emanation, and] the tenth [Ring of the (God) World of Emanation] shall awaken [the bones**R-4** of] the whole [Adam, the Son of God, which are sleeping] in the [spiritual] mud**R-5** of [the physical bodies that cover] the Kingdom [of the Dark World of Creation, and]

R-1 Dan 3:25
R-2 Gen 3:1
R-3 Gen 1:21-23
R-4 Ez 37:3-5
R-5 Gen 2:7

11.03 [Messiah, the fourth] king [that] stands up [shall be] a great ruler, and he shall reign**R** over the many [souls of humanity], and he shall do whatever he wants [to do], and

R Gen 3:16

THE COVENANT

Michael

11.04a At the end [of time],

11.05a [Michael], the Prince from [the God World of Creative Power], above, shall stand up, [and shall affect the material world] with actualized spiritual power, and

First Fruits

Michael, [the Prince of the Covenant], shall seize [the human spirits], the part of

11.04b These [sons of God that] belongs to him, [and

Messiah Crucified

[Leviathan, the King of the North], shall fasten [Messiah, the man that Michael, the Prince of the Covenant, is appearing in, to a tree,[R-1] but] [Messiah] shall rise [from the dead,[R-2] and] the elements] of the Dark Worlds shall burst apart, and

[R-1] Deut 21:23
Gal 3:13
[R-2] Is 26:19, 25:8
Job 19:25-26
Dan 12:12

The First Souls

11.05b A large number [of souls]

11.04c Shall separate[R-1] from the dominion [of Leviathan, the King of the North, and Michael, the Prince of the Covenant], shall give his female seed [to the people of the Covenant, and] they shall receive power,[R-2] and

[R-1] Ez 37:13
Matt 27:52
[R-2] Is 40:29
Acts 1:8

A Descendant of David

11.07 [Righteous Adam, the King of the South, the resurrected soul of Messiah], a descendent [of David],[R]

[R] Gen 49:10

11.06a Shall stand up out of [Abel,[R-1]

1) The personality of the female seed of Michael, the Prince of the Covenant, and][R-2]

2) The root system [of Righteous Adam, the King of the South, that Michael, the Prince of the Covenant], gave to [the people of the Covenant][R-3] and

R-1 Is 14:29
R-2 Dan 12:1
R-3 Heb 4:12

Michael's Female Seed

11.06b [Michael, the Prince of] the Covenant, shall attach his female seed to the people that are bound by [Leviathan], the King of the North, and

11.04c [A spiritual male child[R] shall sprout out of those seeds, and Righteous Adam], the King of the South, [shall arise within the people of the Covenant, and

R Is 7:14

11.05c [Righteous Adam], the King of the South, shall seize the female [Carnal Mind of Leviathan, the King of the North, that] governs

11.04d The people of [Michael], the Prince of the Covenant, [and the people of Michael, the Prince of the Covenant], shall join themselves to [the resurrected Righteous Adam, the King of the South, within the people of the Covenant, and Michael, the Prince of the Covenant], shall tear away [the emotional souls of the people of the Covenant], from [the four spiritual divisions of] the Kingdom [of the Dark Worlds, which] cannot be compared to the four spiritual divisions of [the Kingdom of] Heaven, and

Adam Born Again

[That is how the soul of Messiah] shall come [into his sons] at the end of time, to reconcile[R-1] [the Israel of God[R-2] to Jehovah], but

R-1 Rom 5:10
2 Cor 5:20
R-2 Gal 6:16

PEOPLE OF THE COVENANT

Sin

EVIL SONS

[Righteous Adam, the King of the South], shall not be able to deliver [the people of Michael, the Prince of the Covenant, from Leviathan, the King of the North]; neither [shall Righteous Adam, the King of the South within the people], be able to restrain the power of the Lizard, [the Prince of the Dark Worlds],**[R-1]** [because of the sins of the people],**[R-2]** and

R-1 Ez 28:1
Eph 2:2
R-2 Dan 9:26

The Kingdom

WAR AGAINST THE SAINTS

[Michael, the Prince of the Covenant], shall come with an army**[R-1]** [of the soul parts of the whole Adam, the Son of God], and they shall enter into the fortified [Carnal] Mind of [Leviathan], the King of the North [within the people of the Covenant, and the army of the soul parts of the whole Adam, the Son of God], shall make [war]**[R-2]** against [Leviathan, The King of the North, Within the people of the Covenant who are bound to Leviathan, the Carnal Mind of the King of the North], and [Michael, the Prince of the Covenant], shall seize [the souls of the people of the Covenant that belong to him, and

R-1 Ez 37:10
Joel 2:25
R-2 Dan 7:12

11.09 That is how Righteous Adam], the King of the South, shall come into his Kingdom, and [how the Whole Adam, the Son of God, shall return to [the material bodies of the people of the Covenant,[R-3] who are] his own land, but

[R-3] Dan 12:13

Cain's Spiritual Child

11.08 The Princes [of Israel], who are called *lesser*] *gods*, [because] they have the female seed [of Michael, the Prince of the Covenant], the gold[en foundation[R-1] of the spiritual building that produces full] salvation, shall assemble [together with the spiritual child that sprouts from Cain] within the vessels [that Michael, the Prince of the Covenant], prepared [for himself, and

[R-1] Is 28:16
Zech 4:9
1 Cor 3:11

Michael's Judgment

The people of the Covenant who are bound to Leviathan, the King of the North], shall go into exile[R-2] in [spiritual] Egypt for [all of] the years [that Leviathan], the King of the North, [continues] to stand up [in the people of the Covenant, because they will not leave behind] the delightful [emotional experiences they receive from the Holy Spirit], and

[R-2] Gen 15:13

Jehovah's Judgment

Holy Anger

11.10 [When Righteous Adam, the King of the South, reveals the idolatry that[R-1] the people of the Covenant [have for the gifts of the Holy Spirit, [the people of the Covenant] shall gather together with Leviathan, the King of the North], in the fortified place of [the Carnal Mind of Leviathan, the King of the North, with] the force of a large a crowd [to reject the Truth that the gifts of the Holy Spirit[R-2] are *supposed* to pass away, and

Jehovah's] wrath,[R-3] [his Righteous Sowing & Reaping Judgment, shall fall upon the people of the Covenant, and

[R-1] Dan 7:10
[R-2] 1 Cor 13:8-12
[R-3] Ex 16:20
Num 25:3
Lev 26:17

The Dark Unity

The Lizard, the Prince of the Dark Worlds], shall enter [into the people of the Covenant who reject the Truth about the gifts of the Holy Spirit, that they were always destined to pass away], to have spiritual sexual intercourse [with the Carnal Mind of Leviathan, the King of the North, within the people of the Covenant who reject the Truth about the gifts of the Holy Spirit, that they are supposed to pass away], and

Rebels Conquered

[The Lizard, the Prince of the Dark Worlds], shall conquer[R-4] [the people of the Covenant who reject the Truth about the gifts of the Holy Spirit, that they were always destined to pass away, and]

[R-4] Jer 22:8-9

Return To The Point of Departure

[The people of the Covenant] shall return to the place where [new converts] begin [their journey towards immortality,[R-5] and

[R-5] Dan 4:33

An Evil Child

[An evil spiritual child][R-6] shall be born within the people of the Covenant who reject the Truth that the gifts of the Holy Spirit are supposed to pass away], and

[R-6] Num 5:24, 27
2 Thes 2:3

MICHAEL'S MERCY

Satan's Waters Distilled

11.11a [Michael, the Prince of the Covenant], shall [enter into each individual soul, and] distill [Satan, the impure, spiritual underground blood supply of the fallen Sons of God, and Righteous Adam], the King of the South, shall come forth [within the people of the Covenant, who accept the Truth about the gifts of the Holy Spirit, that they are supposed to pass away],**[R-1]** and

R-1 Job 40:4, 42:3

War Against Leviathan

[The people of the Covenant who accept the Truth about the gifts of the Holy Spirit, that they are supposed to pass away], shall fight against [Leviathan, the Carnal Mind of]**[R-2]** the King of the North [within themselves, and]

R-2 Ex 23:27
Ps 18:40, 48

Michael's Male Seed

[Michael, the Prince of the Covenant], shall give [the people of the Covenant who fight against Leviathan, the Carnal Mind of the King of the North within themselves, the male seed**[R-3]** of his right] hand, [and the Sons of God

R-3 Rev 12:5

A LARGE CROWD

A GOLDEN FOUNDATION

Shall give the male and female seeds of Michael, the Prince of the Covenant], to a large crowd**[R-4]** [of the people of humanity, and

R-4 Rev 7:9

11.12a Those people of] the crowd [of humanity that receive the male and female seeds of Michael, the Prince of the Covenant, shall become spiritually] active,[R-5] and

[R-5] Zech 10:8

11.11b A crowd [of the people of humanity] shall stand up [upon the golden foundation[R] of

[R] 1 Cor 3:12

11.13a Righteous Adam, the King of the South], and the people [of the crowd of humanity who] stand up [in the Kingdoms of the Earth], shall turn back[R] [Leviathan], the King of the North, [and, after that],

[R] Ps 56:9

Teachers Of Truth

11.14 The people [who teach][R-1] the revelation [of God's Word] shall stand up[R-2] [in the Kingdoms of the Earth], but

[R-1] Dan 12:3
[R-2] Dan 12:2

Death By Pride

11.12b The hearts of [the people of] the crowd [of humanity who turned back the Carnal Mind of Leviathan, the King of the North], shall be lifted up [concerning their own self-importance,[R-1] and], they shall cast down the Wisdom[R-2] [of God, which is given to] strengthen [them], and

[R-1] Ez 28:5
[R-2] Dan 12:3, 10

A LARGER CROWD

Growing Pains

A Stumbling Stone

11.13b After that, a large crowd of many people, bigger than the former [crowd], shall come, but they shall stumble [over the humanity of the teachers of God's Wisdom], and

Tyrants Cometh

Tyrants[R-1] shall rise up [among] that large number [of people who reject God's Wisdom, and] the [spiritual] cities [of the Lizard, the Prince of the Dark Worlds], shall come with a great army to fortify [Leviathan, the King of the North, against Righteous Adam, the King of the South, within the people of the larger Crowd, and the people of the larger Crowd] shall stand up against [Righteous Adam], the King of the South, [and against the male] seed[R-2] [of Michael, the Prince of the Covenant, within in the Teachers of God's Wisdom], and

R-1 Gen 6:4 (AT)
R-2 Is 54:3
Gal 3:16

JUDGMENT

A Great Fall

[Many of the people of the larger crowd] shall fall[R-1] [from the spiritual height[R-2] that they attained to through the Wisdom[R-3] of the Word of God], and

R-1 Ez 31:10
R-2 Eph 4:13
R-3 Ez 28:3-5

Satan's Soldiers

11.15a The Lizard, [the Prince of the Dark Worlds], shall enter [into the larger crowd], to incarnate a spiritually female, military [unit of Satan's soldiers who] shall enforce [Jehovah's Righteous Sowing & Reaping Judgment[R-1] upon the people of the larger crowd who rejected the Wisdom of God, [which wisdom would have protected them from Jehovah's Sowing & Reaping Judgment, and Leviathan, the Carnal Mind of] the King of the North, [Jehovah's judgment[R-2] upon the people of the larger crowd, who [Michael, the Prince of the Covenant], made to be spiritual houses [for Righteous Adam, the King of the South, but became] the cities [of the Lizard, the Prince of the Dark Worlds, who] fortified [the Carnal Mind of Leviathan, the

King of North, within the people] against [Righteous Adam, the King of the South, when

R-1 1 Sam 2:10
Rom 1:28
R-2 Deut 28:41

Refusal To Recognize Sin

The people of the larger crowd] stumbled[R-3] over [the humanity of the Teachers of Wisdom, and refused to recognize their own sin nature,[R-4] and this is the reason why Leviathan, the King of the North], shall occupy [the people of the larger crowd], and neither

(1) The force [of the Holy Spirit within] the people of [Righteous Adam, the King of] the South, nor

(2) [Righteous Adam's] manifested[R-5] [sons, God's] elect,[R-6] shall be able to withstand

R-3 Is 8:14
R-4 Ez 18:20
R-5 Rom 8:19
R-6 2 Sam 23:6

An Unholy Conception

11.16a [The Lizard, the Prince of the Dark Worlds, when] the Lizard, the Prince of the Dark Worlds, comes [to the people of the larger crowd, to form the Carnal Mind of Leviathan, the King of the North, within them, and

11.15b To have spiritual sexual intercourse with the Carnal] Mind [of Leviathan, the King of the North, that the Lizard, the Prince of the Dark Worlds, formed within the people of the larger crowd], to complete [them in the image of Sophia, the Female Power, by impregnating them with the evil spiritual child[R-1] that Sophia, the Female Power], delights in,[R-2] and none of the personalities standing in the earth of [Jehovah's] gazelle shall be able to stand against[R-3] [the Lizard, the Prince of the Dark

Worlds, when he comes to impregnate them with his evil spiritual child, because they refused to acknowledge their sin nature, but]

R-1 Jer 6:19
Is 14:29
R-2 Pro 8:30
Is 14:29
R-3 Dan 8:6

RESCUE

A Savior Cometh

11.17 [Michael, the Prince of the Covenant], shall put the personalities of the upright[R-1] ones [who agree] with him, [in the right moral order,[R-2] and make them] whole, and [the Upright Ones who agree with Michael, the Prince of the Covenant], shall enter into the Kingdom of [Leviathan, the King of the North, and] [Michael, the Prince of the Covenant], shall do [whatever he pleases to] the daughters of [Sophia],[R-3] the Female Power, [who have the nature of the Lizard, the Prince of the Dark Worlds, and]

R-1 1 Sam 2:8
R-2 Judg 7:3
R-3 Num 25:1-3

A Holy Conception

The corrupt [daughters of Sophia, the Female Power, shall conceive the spiritual child[R] of Michael, the Prince of the Covenant, and

R Is 7:14

Measured For Righteousness

Michael, the Prince of the Covenant], shall give [those daughters of Sophia who have the nature of the Lizard, the Prince of the Dark Worlds], over to Satan to be tested, to prove [that they have been engraved[R-1] with the righteous] character [of Michael, the Prince of the Covenant, because the personalities who] do not measure up [to the righteous character of Michael, the Prince of the Covenant], do not belong to [Messiah,[R-2] and] they shall not come into existence[R-3] [in the World to Come; then, after that

[R-1] Ez 9:4
[R-2] Jn 6:37
[R-3] Obad 21

The One They Belong To

Failure To Recognize Messiah

11.19 Michael, the Prince of the Covenant], shall return [to the Crowd],

1) To fortify [Righteous Adam, the King of the South, within] the personalities [that are attached to the material bodies which are] his land, and

2) [To cause the people joined to Leviathan, the King of the North], to stumble[R-1] [over the humanity of the Teachers of Wisdom by not recognizing Righteous Adam, the King of the South, in the Teachers of Wisdom, or behind their own personalities, and

3) To cause the Lizard, the Prince of the Dark Worlds], to fall [down],[R-2] and cease to exist,[R-3] and

[R-1] Is 8:14
[R-2] Is 14:10
[R-3] Is 43:17, 65:25

The Upright Ones

11.18 [Michael], the Prince [of the Covenant], shall appoint [Righteous Adam, the King of the South], to occupy[R] the dry [side of the heart of] the many personalities [of the Upright Ones who are with him, so that] he can rest from [warring against Leviathan, the King of the North, the spiritual] sexual organ of [Sophia], the Female [Power], until she returns [humanity to Righteous Adam, the King of the South, the one that] they belong to, and

[R] Lk 19:13

WORLD OF ACTION

ANTICHRIST

11.20 [The Lizard], shall cross over from [the tenth Ring of Power of the Dark World of Creative Power, which is] the Kingdom [of the Lizard, into a mortal man, and the Lizard] shall stand upon [the sixth Ring of Power of Leviathan, the evil male child that shall be born within that mortal man, and the whole Reptile shall come into existence, and the man that the Whole Reptile shall be revealed through, shall be called, *Antichrist,* and

Antichrist] shall tyrannize [the people of Michael, the Prince of the Covenant], until [Michael, the Prince of the Covenant], crosses over into [a mortal man, and] stands upon**R-1** [the sixth Ring of Power of Righteous Adam, the spiritual male child that sprouts from the golden, female] foundation**R-2** [that Michael, the Prince of the Covenant, plants,**R-3** and crowns Righteous Adam, King of the World of Creation, which makes the sixth Ring of Power of Righteous Adam, called], *Beauty*, [shine, and

The whole Adam, who is the Son of God, shall come into existence and force the Lizard to withdraw**R-4** from Leviathan, the King of the North, and] in about [1,260] days, the [unholy] unity [between the Lizard, the Prince of the Dark World of Creative Power, and Leviathan, the evil male child who became King of the Dark World of Creation when the Lizard stood upon his sixth Ring of Power],

R-1 Zech 14:4
R-2 Pro 10:25
Is 28:16
R-3 Is 61:3
R-4 Judg 3:22

The Unholy Unity Severed

Shall burst [apart], not [because of] the warfare [between Leviathan, the King of the North, and Righteous Adam, the King of the South], nor [because of] the anger [of Jehovah, whose Righteous Sowing & Reaping Judgment, defeats

Leviathan, the King of the North, with pestilence, wild beasts or famine,[R] but because the whole Adam, who is the Son of God, overthrew the whole Reptile, and

[R] 2 Sam 24:13

THE TIME OF THE END

[The Lizard, the Prince of the Dark Worlds], shall fortify [Leviathan, the Carnal Mind of the King of the North within the people of the Larger Crowd],

1) To rule over the many [people of] the country,

2) To defend [the spiritual houses that Leviathan, the Carnal Mind of the King of the North, occupies, and]

3) To divide [the people of the nation] for profit, and

A Push From The North

Jehovah, [the God of Israel], shall look on, intently, as the influence of [the *other Antichrist*] increases, and

40a At the time of the end, [Leviathan], the King of the North, shall push[R] against [Righteous Adam], the King of the South, with the horns [of his spiritual power], to sweep [Righteous Adam, the King of the South], away, but

[R] Dan 8:8-9

A Moabite Woman

11.41a The first fruits[R-1] [of the regenerated Righteous Adam, the King of the South within the people, shall spring from the root[R-2] of a woman of] the children of Moab,[R-3] [and] [a soul] shall escape from [Leviathan,[R-4] the Carnal] Mind [of the King of the North, who is indebted to [the Lizard, the Prince of the Dark Worlds], for his existence in this World [of Action], and

R-1 1 Cor 15:20
Rev 1:5
R-2 Is 37:31
R-3 Ruth 1:4
Matt 1:5
R-4 Rom 8:7

Michael's Cavalry

[That soul that escapes from Leviathan, the King of the North], shall become the spiritual garment that covers [Michael, the Prince of the Covenant], the upper millstone, and [Michael, the Prince of the Covenant], shall also enter into [Jehovah's] gazelle, and

11.40b The [spiritual] cavalry[R-1] [of Michael, the Prince of the Covenant,], the upper millstone, shall pass over [into the Land of the Sleeping Death,[R-2] and]

R-1 Rev 19:14
R-2 Gen 4:16

The Nations

[Michael, the Prince of the Covenant], shall enter into the [human] ships[R] which are the household of [Leviathan, the King of the North], to cleanse them; but

R Ps 104:26

11.41b Many Edomites and Ammonites[R] shall stumble over [the mortal bodies that] the sons of God [appear in, and

R Deut 23:3

A Warmonger

A Foreign Enemy

11.42 Leviathan, the Carnal Mind of] the King of the North [of the *other Antichrist*], shall stretch forth towards the countries [of Iraq, Syria and Afghanistan], and the land of Egypt shall not escape [from his hand], and

11.43 [The *other Antichrist*], shall [also] extend his [ungodly] influence to Libya and Ethiopia, and

A DOMESTIC ENEMY

He shall take authority over

1) [The people that Abel], the gold[en foundation by which men are] saved, [resides in, and

2) The Constitution of the United States of America, the Law of the Land that the people] treasure, [and all the precious [principles upon which The United States of America, which is Spiritual] Egypt, [today, was founded]; but

Terrified of Exposure

11.44 [The *other Antichrist*] shall be terrified when he hears that [the secret that] he had been hiding [about his true intentions towards The United States of America, and towards the people of God] is out in the open, and

A Great Rage

[The *other Antichrist*] shall go forth in a great rage to exterminate [the people that Michael, the Prince of the Covenant, and Righteous Adam, the King of the South, who Jehovah sent] to destroy [him, are appearing in, but],

Michael

MESSIAH'S PRIESTS

11.45 [Michael, the Prince of the Covenant], shall establish his [spiritual] DNA**[R-1]** in the bodies [of the priests**[R-2]** who stand] between**[R-3]** the sea [of Galilee, which represents life], and the [Dead] sea, [which represents death,**[R-4]** and] [the priests of the Covenant] shall come to [the middle column of Righteous Adam, the King of the South], and

[R-1] Dan 7:12, 18 (AT)
[R-2] Gen 14:18
Heb 7:2-3
[R-3] Ez 22:30
[R-4] Josh 3:15-17

The Holy Unification

[The subjection of the priests of the Covenant to the *other Antichrist*], shall end when [the sixth Ring of Power, called], *Beauty*, [of

1) The *Midot* of Michael, the Prince of the Covenant, descends into the tenth Ring of Power, of the Princedom of Michael, the Prince of the Covenant, and

2) The tenth Ring of Power, of the Princedom of Michael, the Prince of the Covenant, descends into the regenerated Righteous Adam, the King of the South within the priests, and

3) Brings the holy sixth Ring of Power called], *Beauty*, [of Righteous Adam, the King of the South, into existence within the priests, which union crowns Righteous Adam, the King of the South within the priests, the *King of the World,*[R] because of The unified:

1) *Princedom* of Michael, the Prince of the Covenant, and

2) *The Kingdom* of Righteous Adam, King of the South], and

[R] Dan 2:37

THE OTHER ANTICHRIST

11.21a After that], a contemptuous person who shall not honor the authority of the Kingdom [of Heaven], shall stand up upon [the same spiritual] foundation [that the previous *Antichrist* stood up upon, and

The Promise of Safety

The *other* man called, *Antichrist*], shall come [to power by

11.24 Promising [the people of the Crowd], the security [that comes with] the abundance of health and wealth, [just like the previous *Antichrist* did], and

REDISTRIBUTION OF WEALTH

[When this *other* man called, *Antichrist*], enters nation[al office], he shall do what our father, [Abraham, our] father [Isaac, or our] Father, [Jacob], never did: [the *other Antichrist*] shall prey upon these [sons of God, and] take their property and possessions, by [illegal, en]force[d taxation], and [re]distribute [their property and possessions

SPIRITUAL CITIES

To the people who are spiritual] cities [for Sophia, the Female Power, who were made to be houses for Righteous Adam, the King of the South, but are ruled by Leviathan, the Carnal Mind of the King of the North, who] fortifies [them against Righteous Adam, the King of the South, which Carnal Mind, Sophia, the Female Power], intends to weave[R] [herself together with], as far [into the future] as [the end of] time, and

[R] Ex 25:20 (AT)

THE UPRIGHT ONES NOT DECEIVED

11.27a [The *other* man called, *Antichrist*], shall speak lies, [but] he shall not succeed [in deceiving the Upright Ones who agree with Michael, the Prince of the Covenant, because] they must continue [R-1] until the end [of this whole matter],[R-2] At the time appointed [by God], but

[R-1] Is 65:20
[R-2] Eccl 12:13

THE OTHERS SEDUCED

11.21b [The *other Antichrist* shall overpower the people of the crowd that honors] the Kingdom [of Heaven] with lies and deceit about [their health insurance], and

11.23 After [the *other Antichrist*] seduces[R] [the people of the Crowd to elect him for a second term], he shall ascend [above the Law of the Land], and become mighty with a small amount of people, and

[R] Gen 3:1-24

ILLEGAL USE OF THE LAW

11.25 [Leviathan, the King of the North, who occupies] the right side of the heart of the people [who are seduced by the *other Antichrist*, and can no longer distinguish between good and evil],[R-1] shall agitate[R-2] the people [of the crowd who are seduced by the *other Antichrist*], to [take legal] action against [the people that Righteous Adam], the King of the South, [occupies, and the people that Leviathan, the King of the North, dwells in

[R-1] Heb 5:14
[R-2] Is 22:18

The King of The South

A GREAT ARMY

Shall provoke [Righteous Adam], the King of the South, to gather his great army to battle against the mighty power of the Lizard, the Prince of the Dark Worlds, who seeks to interpenetrate himself [R-1] [with Leviathan, the Carnal Mind of the

King of the North, within the people that Righteous Adam, the King of the South, occupies], but his plan [shall fail**[R-2]** because

R-1 Ex 25:20 (AT)
R-2 Deut 28:15-68

CLEANSED FROM SIN

11.22 Michael], the Prince of the Covenant, shall burst forth [upon the people of the Crowd, and Michael, the Prince of the Covenant], shall pierce**[R]** [the people of the Crowd who are seduced into Provoking Righteous Adam, the King of the South], and Michael, the Prince of the Covenant], shall cleanse the people of the Crowd by a power [so strong that it can only be likened to the spiritual power that brought] the Flood [upon mankind]; indeed, [after that spiritual cleansing], the personality of

R Ps 22:16
Rev 1:7

LEVIATHAN CONQUERED

11.26 [Righteous Adam], the King of the South, shall burst forth from within [the people of the Crowd, and] they shall conquer [Leviathan, the King of the North], and [Leviathan, the King of the North], shall fall down,**[R]** and

R Is 14:12

SPIRITUAL FOOD

[The people of the Crowd shall eat [the spiritual] food [of the whole Adam, the unified] force [of

1) Michael, the Prince of the Covenant, above, and

2) Righteous Adam, the King of the South, below, and the people of the Crowd, shall understand that]

The King of The North

A Spiritual Place

11.27a The political and military violence and intrigue of these two Kings against [each other is happening] in a [spiritual] place [that is similar] to the heart [of the people of Michael, the Prince of the Covenant, and that

The Holy Covenant

11.28 Leviathan, the King of the North, as well as Adam, the King of the South, is occupying] their heart [and that is the reason why] they were against the holy Covenant [between Jehovah and the people of the Crowd], and [in agreement with the *other Antichrist* that he should do [whatever it pleased him to do], [but, Michael, the Prince of the Covenant], shall return [the souls of the people], the wealth of the great land [that Jehovah promised Abraham], to their [spiritual] starting point, and

Return of The Land

He shall return the land [of the material bodies of the people to Adam, their original owner], and

A Different Visitation

A People Who Knew Him

11.29 At the appointed time, [Michael, the Prince of the Covenant], shall return [to the people of the crowd], and he shall go to the dry [side of the heart of the people that Righteous Adam, the King of the South, occupies], but [this entrance into the crowd] shall be different than his two previous appearances;

An Unwelcome Change

11.30 [This time Michael, the Prince of the Covenant], shall go [to those people of the crowd who already know Jehovah, but shall be opposed to [the additions] that [Jehovah]

shall make to the Holy Covenant, [which shall include salvation for]

1) The brokenhearted,**R-1**

2) [Alcoholics, prostitutes and tax collectors], a segment of earthen humanity [that they consider to be undesirable,**R-2** and

3) The first grade of soul, which is attached to the marrow of the bones of] the physical body, and [the people of the crowd that know Jehovah], shall be enraged at [the change to the Covenant], but

R-1 Deut 27
Matt 25:43
R-2 Matt 21:31

Return To Jehovah

[After] they receive intelligence from [the God World of Emanation], above, they shall give up [observing the Law of Ordinances,**R-3** which was required by] the Holy Covenant [in the previous age], and they shall return [to Jehovah,**R-4** and]

R-3 Lev 18:3
Col 2:14
R-4 Song 6:13

Michael's Warfare

11.31 The Rings of Power [of Michael, the Prince of the Covenant], shall penetrate into [that] part [of the Kingdoms of the Earth that oppose Righteous Adam, the King of the South, and Righteous Adam, the King of the South], shall stand up in [the right side of their heart], the place [that is] consecrated**R** [to Michael, the Prince of the Covenant, and

R Ex 25:22

TELEPATHIC COMMUNICATION

Righteous Adam] shall turn off [Satan's broadcast,[R-1] which] defends [the continuation of] the daily [sacrifice],[R-2] and

[R-1] Amos 5:27 (AT)
1 Ki 19:14 (AT)
[R-2] Dan 8:11-12 (AT)

IDOLATRY FOR THE LAW

They shall deliver up [the Law that] they idolize,[R] [even though it is] overwhelming [to keep, and has caused] devastation [to come into their lives], but

[R] Is 9:1-17

11.32 Those [who give up the Law of Ordinances[R-1], and] Violate [the Law of the New] Covenant, as well, shall be morally soiled and separate[R-2] [from the Congregation of Israel], and

[R-1] Col 2:14
[R-2] Num 19:20

FAITH AND FEAR

11.33 Many of the people who acquire the spiritual intelligence to distinguish [between the Spirit of God and an evil spirit,[R-1] shall still] faint[R-2] [from

1) The fear of Righteous Adam's circumcising] knife,

2) [The thought of their spiritual power being] stolen,

3) [The sight of] the spiritual weapons [of their enemies, and

4) The fear of their enemies] capturing them, for [an undetermined number of] days, [and

[R-1] 2 Cor 11:14
[R-2] 2 Cor 4:16

11.34 At the time that the people who give up the Law of Ordinances begin] to faint,

THE SOUL OF MESSIAH

Another Kind of Incarnation

1) [The soul of Messiah shall clothe himself with a human personality, and

2) The soul of Messiah shall marry[R-1] that human personality[R-1] and that

3) Human personality] shall separate [from its fallen nature,[R-2] and

4) Produce] an humble seed[R-3] that shall help many to unite with [Michael, the Prince of the Covenant], but

[R-1] Is 62:4
[R-2] Lev 15:31
[R-3] Is 7:14

PHARAOH

11.35 Some [people of the Larger Crowd of humanity who acquire] spiritual intelligence shall [still] stumble [when it comes] to making the brick [for the male part of the foundation that Michael, the Prince of the Covenant], fuses [together with], to purify[R-1] [them] until the time appointed to end

1) [The adultery[R-2] between the Woman and the Snake, and

2) The transgression of spiritual incest between Sophia, the Female Power, and Cain,[R-2] the offspring of the Woman and the Snake], and

[R-1] Dan 12:10
[R-2] Is 57:3

A King

11.36 [That *other Antichrist* shall behave like] a king, [rather than a duly elected servant of the people, and]

A Corrupt Government

He shall raise himself above [the other branches of Government], and [he shall do whatever he wants [to do; and] [that *other Antichrist*] shall promote [policies that promise to do] things [for the people] that can only be accomplished by God, [and] he shall succeed [in destroying the nation that he swore to protect], until he brings to pass [the desired result of God's] curse, [which is] to maim [Jehovah's gazelle], and

One World Religion

11.37 He shall not recognize any difference between the God of [Abraham, Isaac and Jacob], the fathers [of Israel, and the gods of the Pagan Pantheon],[R-1] nor

R-1 Ps 86:8

Sexual Immorality

Shall he recognize any difference between the [sexual] delight [a man experiences with] a woman, [and the sexual delight that a man experiences with another man,[R-2] and] concerning [spiritual sex of the mind],[R-3] [The *other Antichrist*] shall not see any difference between

1) [Michael, the Prince of the Covenant, twisting together with the Mind of Righteous Adam, the King of the South within the people, to bring] the whole [Adam, the Son of] God,[R-4] into existence, and

2) [The Lizard, the Prince of the Dark Worlds, twisting together with Leviathan, the Carnal Mind of the

King of the North, to bring] the whole [Reptile into existence within the people of the Larger Crowd of humanity], and

R-2 Lev 20:13
R-3 1 Jn 3:15
R-4 Dan 3:25

ANOTHER GOD

11.38a [The Whole Reptile] shall influence the mind of [the people of Adam, the King of the South, and the *other Antichrist* shall incarnate]

11.39a The cities [of the Lizard, the Prince of the Dark Worlds, who serve Allah], the foreign god [of the *other Antichrist*,

11.38b Upon] the foundation of a god [that our] fathers did not know [or ever] gave power to, [and

11.38c The Lizard, the Prince of the Dark Worlds, shall overshadow the people of Righteous Adam, the King of the South, and],

THE KINGDOM OF GOD

No one, [neither god nor man, shall be able] to help the person called the *other Antichrist*[R-1] [Escape from the judgment that he truly deserves, at the hands of the Sons of God who serve the King of Kings[R-2] and the Prince of Princes].[R-3]

R-1 Dan 7:11 (AT)
R-2 1 Tim 6:15
Rev 17:14
Rev 19:16
R-3 Dan 8:25

Chapter 12

[142]

12.01 And in the end times, Michael, that great Prince[R-1] who is our righteousness, shall appear in His people, and Elohim's Sons shall enter into a period of conflict with their fallen, mortal mind,[R-2] the likes of which has not been seen since they came into existence. And the whole flock of your people shall be delivered at that time, and Elohim's Sons shall be witnesses to Adam's resurrection.[61]

[R-1] Dan 8:23-24 (AT)
[R-2] Rev 14:18

12.02 And the Wild Animal's many members, who are existing in the hell of their fallen, mortal mind, shall become aware of their spiritual side, some finding themselves dwelling in the Elijah's city [unconscious mind], and others dwelling in the fiery serpent's[R] hated city [subconscious mind].[62]

[R] Jn 5:29

12.03 And those who teach shall enlighten the whole flock, and turn them towards Elijah's righteousness,[R-1] and the Serpent shall be as bright[R-2] as Elijah, because of their union with Him,[R-3] and each of their spiritual bodies [mind + personality]

---

[61] Adam's resurrection from the dead (1 Cor 15:3-4) is evidenced by the miracle-working power which arises out of a sinless (Acts 4:33) and unending life (Heb 7:16).

[62] See, Message #278, Differentiated Spiritual Maturity.

shall be as a blazing star**[R-4]** which will be easily seen by the many members of the Wild Animal**[R-5]** during the Kingdom age.

R-1 1 Cor 1:30
R-2 Eccl 12:2 (AT)
Amos 5:18b (AT)
Is 6:2 ,6
R-3 1 Cor 6:17
R-4 Ps 104:4
R-5 Ez 1:13 (AT)

12.10 And Leviathan, the sea serpent, the collective subconscious mind of the guilty ones [many members of the Wild Animal], shall cause noisy upheavals**[R-1]** to keep Elohim's Sons from distinguishing between Cain, their fallen, mortal conscious mind, and Abel, their new, righteous mind, who is rising from the dead in their human spirits, and [the fiery serpent**[R-2]**] shall be refined in the lake of fire,**[R-3]** when the resurrected Adam is separated from the whole fallen, mortal mind.

R-1 Zeph 2:13 (AT)
Is 14:11 (AT)
Rev 13:15
R-2 Heb 4:12
R-3 Rev 20:10

12.11 And for the season that Jehovah's Living Beast is driven out of the Garden of Eden and bearing the Serpent's unclean image instead of Jehovah's**[R]** glorious image, her number is 1,290.[63]

R 1 Cor 15:49

---

[63] The number ***1,290*** signifies the spiritual, but ***mortal***, Woman who is inhabiting the lower heaven, of this visible, physical world (Rev 12:8). See, Message #140, ***Understanding Some Symbolic Numbers***.

12.12 Blessed is the one who pierces through[R-1] [Cain] his conscious [fallen] mind, and enters into the age of intimacy with Elijah:[R-2] His number is 1,335.[64]

[R-1] Rev 1:7 (AT)
[R-2] Jn 19:37
Heb 10:20

12.04 But the resolution of this matter for you, Daniel, is to forget about it until the end times, when Elijah pushes forth[R] into the whole flock, joins Himself to their human spirit, and raises Adam from the dead [the double portion].

[R] Mk 1:12 (AT)

12.05 Then I, Daniel, looked and saw a spiritual man [Adam],[R-1] who had dominion over his [subconscious] mind and his emotions [unconscious/female side].[R-2]

[R-1] Rev 19:13
[R-2] Rev 10:2

12.06 And I, Daniel, said to the righteous man who had dominion over the peoples, multitudes, nations and languages of the Wild Animal, How long will it take for these miracles to come to pass?

12.07 And I heard the righteous man who had the spiritual strength to visit both blessings and judgment[R-1] upon the peoples, multitudes, nations and languages of the Wild Animal, swear by His Father,[R-2] that all these miraculous events would take place when the supernatural ministry of Elohim's Sons appears in the earth,[R-3] [and Elohim's Sons] break the witchcraft power [that Satan exercises] over [and through] the saints,

[R-1] Rev 10:9
[R-2] Rev 10:1-3
[R-3] Rev 11:6

---

[64] The significance of the number ***1,335*** is: (Footnote continued – See, Appendix)

12.08 And I heard what the righteous man said, but I didn't understand him, so I asked another question, saying, O, my Lord, how shall all this that is about to happen affect my people?

12.09 And He said, continue on with your life, Daniel, because the wonderful events I have told you about, are blocked, and cannot take place until the end times.

12.13 But run the race,[R] and you shall arise in the last days,[65] and live in the flesh that Elijah allots to you.

[R] 1 Cor 9:24
Heb 12:1

---

[65] Adam, Elohim's mind (1 Cor 15:45), rises again in the last day, but not the personality. (Footnote continued – See, Appendix)

THE BOOK OF DEUTERONOMY

Chapter 14

[Message # Unknown]

14.01 Your consciousness is in the brow [of Jehovah's timeline, because you] are the children of Jehovah and Elohim, [but] you shall die [spiritually] and become [spiritual] widows, if the fiery serpent assembles herself [and marries Leviathan], the captain [of the Serpent's timeline].

Chapter 17

[945.4.C]

Slander Is Idolatry

17.01 Anyone who lets themselves be used to stain [the reputation of] a member of the community of Israel by looking for the opportunity to slander [them concerning] any immoral or unnatural matter, [is guilty of] the disgusting [sin of] idolatry, and Jehovah their God, will not receive their sacrifice;

Slander Causes Ungodly Thoughts & Emotions

17.02 [So], if any immoral thought or emotion, or unnatural [act that] transgresses the covenant [that] Jehovah your God gave [to Israel] be found concerning any man or woman, and

Slander Causes Lust For Pagan Gods

17.03 They have lusted for [Sophia], the moon [goddess], and gone and bowed down to [her, and to Tammuz, her] son, [or lusted for any of] the [other] gods and goddesses [that exist in] the spiritual world above [this material world], and labored for all [those] other gods, which I have not commanded [you to do], and

Investigation, The Godly Response To Slander

17.04 [If] it is obvious to you [that, after] inquiring with a good motive [and] understanding [the facts] intelligently [with your] righteous [mind], that the evidence that [you have uncovered] is true, [that] this disgusting thing was done in Israel,

The Slanderer Loves The 1st Adam

17.05 Then, [in that event], the man that desired the woman [who is] his [spiritual] mate [more than God], the mate that had the immoral and unnatural thoughts or desires, that man [who] lusted for the [spiritual] woman [who is] his mate [more than God], shall go [into the spiritual dimension of his soul] and stone [the spiritual woman who is] his mate with stones, [until the spiritual woman that is] his mate, dies; and

Two Spiritual Witnesses And Three

17.06 If [Moses (the Law) and Abraham's seed], the two female witnesses, say [that the man] should be killed [because of the immoral thoughts that the spiritual woman who is his mate put in his mind and emotions, or the unnatural acts that he has done], that man shôuld not die, [unless the Father and Righteous Adam in heaven, and young Adam, their Messenger in the earth], the three male witnesses, unanimously witness [that he has not killed the spiritual woman who put those immoral thoughts in his mind and emotions which led him to commit those unnatural acts],

Spiritual Judgment: Lake Of Fire

17.07 [Then, in that event], the unified mind of the [three] witnesses to [the immoral thoughts and unnatural acts] within all of the people [whose] mind is in the left [side of their heart], shall burn the center [column of] the immoral [woman who lusted for] unnatural acts with fire, and she shall die;

Judging An Unnatural Act

17.08 [So], when you have to make a judicial decision [that requires you] to discern the difference between the blood [that is shed when a murder is committed], and the blood [that is] shed [as a result of manslaughter], and [between] a motive [that benefited the guilty party] and a motive of [self-defense], and [whether there was permanent] damage or damage [that could be repaired], and

The Last Judge

17.09 You go to a priest, a descendant of Levi, and to the judge that exists in those days, [who has the authority to vindicate or punish the accused], and ask that he reveal the appropriate verdict to you, and

Obey Jehovah's Commandments

17.10 [Then], do what[ever the priest who is instructed by the judge] from above tells you [to do, and] you oppose [the First Adam], the part of you that is separated [from God], and choose to guard the whole [Adam, which is the instruction that] Jehovah delivered to you by the Spirit,

Resist The Devil

17.11 [Let your] heart [be influenced by] the spiritual speech [that comes from] above, [and let] your judicial decisions [be influenced by] the spiritual understanding of the law [that comes from] above; [and] do not to turn away from speaking [the truth about] an [immoral] issue [that exists within your mind or emotions, or an unnatural act that you have done, but] let your righteous side stand boldly opposite [the immoral thoughts and unnatural behavior of the First Adam, the spiritual woman that you are married to],

17.12 [Because] the arrogant man [who] has immoral thoughts and engages in the unnatural behavior [of the First Adam], lacks the intelligent [mind of God that] understands the ministry of the priest who stands in front of [the Shekinah], the God [who is] Jehovah's mate, [who] desires to vindicate [him, so] he shall die [when] he is cast into [the lake] that burns with fire,

17.13 [But], all the people [who] revere [God, shall have] the intelligent [mind of God that] understands [the ministry of the priest who stands in front of the Shekinah, and they shall resist the immoral thoughts and emotions of the First Adam, and not engage in his unnatural acts any] more,

17.14 [But when] you come into the land that Jehovah, your God, shall give you to possess and live in, [the spiritual woman who is your mate] shall say [to you], I will set a king over [you, from] all the nations that surround you,

17.15 But you shall set a king over yourself, [and] you shall set [a king over the spiritual woman in] the center [of your heart], [that] Jehovah your God shall choose [from among your] brethren; You shall not give a stranger that does not resemble you power [over you], by making him your king, and

17.16 [The king that Jehovah selects] shall not increase the people of [Judah, Jehovah's] mate, [into spiritual male war] horses, [because] increasing [Judah into spiritual male war] horses will turn them back to Egypt, [when] Jehovah said, [this people] belongs to [me, and] they shall continue in my lifestyle and not return [to the Egyptian lifestyle any] more;

17.17 Neither shall they increase the women that belong to them, nor greatly increase the money and commodities that belong to [them, so that] they do not return to Egypt in their heart, and

17.18 It shall come to pass [that the Messiah of Jehovah, your King], shall sit upon the throne [of] the kingdom [of God, and] he shall write a copy of this law [in the heart of the Israelites who are his] mate, [so] that [their personalities] reflect the personality of the Levite priests, and

17.19 It shall come to pass that Jehovah [your] God shall teach [Israel, his] mate, to morally revere [him, and Israel, his] mate, shall guard all the words of this law, and these decrees to do them, [and] it shall come to pass that they shall call out to [Jehovah, their God] all the days [of their] lives

17.20 With respect to prolonging their days in the kingdom of Israel, unless the animal side of his brethren rises up [against] the spiritual seed in the center of their heart, [and] they turn away from the right [path of following] the commandments to the dark side,

Chapter 19

[Message # Unknown]

19.14 The Serpent shall give back the dust [dead Abel] that Elohim twisted together with to form Adam, when Elijah possesses the land, which is His inheritance [not the Serpent's].

Chapter 21

[602.1.C]

21.10 When you go to war with [Cain within] your adversaries, and Jehovah and Elohim deliver them into your hands, and you take them captive,

21.11 Then [Cain], the [spiritual] woman within you, will appear to you as a beautiful woman,**R** and [try] to cling to you and take you, [Abel], for her [spiritual] wife,

R 2 Cor 11:14

21.12 [So, you should know that even though you have captured Cain], she has gone [into captivity] with her claws**R-1** extended [and will try] to separate herself from the [spiritual] house[hold that] you, her head,**R-2** joined her to,

R-1 1 Pet 5:8
R-2 Eph 5:23

21.13 And throw off your covering [to end her] exile;**R-1** So [Cain] will weep and moan for [Leviathan], her father, and [Satan], her mother, the moon of the [first] age [when it was very] hot, where they were behind [Jehovah], who set [Adam] upright,**R-2** and [Satan and Leviathan], her husband, will draw near to [Cain], and [Cain shall kill Abel within you again,**R-3** and] you shall belong to the widowed [spiritual] woman [again].

R-1 Col 1:18
R-2 Gen 2:15
R-3 Gen 4:8

21.14 And it shall come to pass that you shall chastise Satan,[the one who] sold [you for thirty pieces of] silver, and drive her to the bottom, and you shall look down on her.**R** and Cain shall surrender to you, [and] Cain within you shall no longer bend [Abel within you to her will, and] your animal nature shall be set free,

R Amos 8:6

[696.1]

21.23 The serpent that is entombed in the [spiritually] dead body [of a citizen of] the House[hold] of the Day, shall, indeed, not lodge permanently in the Tree [of Life in] the window above the window [where] the serpent is entombed,

21.22 [Wherefore], a judicial sentence of death [shall be rendered against] the [physical] body of a [spiritual] male [who] ascends above the [lower] window [of creation, while his nefesh grade of] soul is] nailed to the tree of death [that is] nailed to [a physical body in the lower window of creation].

Chapter 28

[392.1]

28.13 The Lord [Adam] shall be your head,[R] and the Serpent shall be a [tree] stump, if you listen to Jehovah and do what He says, but

[R] Deut 28:44 (AT)

28.44 [If you don't do what Jehovah says], Leviathan, the sea serpent, shall intertwine herself with the fiery serpent, and Leviathan, the sea serpent, intertwined with the fiery serpent, shall be your head[R] and you shall be their tail,

[R] Deut 28:13 (AT)

[859.3.C]

28.27 The Lord will smite you with the botch of Egypt, and with the scab, and with the itch, because of the pride, arrogance and presumption by which you resist the advice [of the teachers that God sends to you].

Chapter 32

[226.3]

32.23 The evil that comes from their fallen, mortal mind shall drive my Spirit away, and they shall pine away, and be consumed, and come to an end,

32.24 Their fallen, mortal minds shall fight against themselves [the resurrected Adam] with Satan's destructive poisonous storm, and strike them with hunger and sicknesses, which will exhaust and emaciate them,

32.25 And their children shall die violently, and they shall be filled with fear,

32.26 [But] I will break the fiery serpent, [Adam's] mortal**[R-1]** remains,[66] in pieces in those who are being judged,[67] and deliver the human spirit of the young spiritual men who are fighting the fiery serpent within themselves,[68] and the mature spiritual men who are fighting the fiery serpent and Leviathan, the sea serpent, [the collective subconscious mind of fallen, mortal man],[69] within their [individual subconscious mind, who are confessing their sins and repenting], and [I will also deliver

---

[66] Israel's agreement with his fallen, mortal mind brought all this evil upon himself. (Footnote continued – See, Appendix)

[67] See, first footnote to 1 Jn 2:13, ***Alternate Translation of the New Testament***, where these believers are called, ***little children.***

[68] Waging war against the fiery serpent in one's own mind results in a doctrinal understanding of how Adam was separated from Elohim and Jehovah at the beginning (1 Jn 2:13[AT]).

[69] Waging war against the fiery serpent in one's own mind, as well and in other men's minds* raises Adam (Footnote continued – See, Appendix)

the human spirit of] the spiritual men who are virgins[R-2] [that are being judged], because they follow Elijah everywhere.

R-1 Gen 4:1-2 (AT)
R-2 Rev 14:4

32.27-28 They have removed their personality from [the protection] my Spirit [gives them] against [the fallen, mortal mind], the enemy who knows that I, [Jehovah], protect Israel.

They are a nation void of counsel, and without understanding, saying, ***we are innocent; Jehovah hath not sent this enemy against us, and there is no reason to fear his wrath***.

32.29 Oh, if only Israel were wise, they would understand what I am talking about and recognize that Adam is in [the midst of] them,

32.30 And that Adam's Kingdom does not drive the fiery serpent underfoot, or rescue the many-membered, Wild Animal, until [they admit that their enemy is their own sin nature],

32.31 And that the resurrected Adam is not only ***their*** Saviour, but that he is also Saviour of the enemies that are fighting against them,

32.32 Because Leviathan, the sea serpent, has produced a people whose personalities are a dwelling place for Satan, [the unconscious part of the mind], and the fiery serpent, [the subconscious part of the mind],[R] and Satan and the fiery serpent can only produce more death,

R Ps 104:26 (AT)
Amos 3:15 (AT)

32.33 And the [pride of] the fiery serpent, [the subconscious part of] the mind of the evil, poisonous plant[R] hinders Adam's resurrection,

R Ps 58:04 (AT)
Ps 74:14 (AT)
Ps 140:1-3 (AT)
Ez 38:1-2 (AT)

32.34 Because Leviathan, the sea Serpent sealed up the provision [that] I stored for them in [Adam's] memory,

32.35 Therefore, revenge and payment for damages belong to me, says Jehovah; the day is at hand that I will judge[R] my Living Beast, which has become a mortal Wild Animal, and shake them free from Leviathan, the sea serpent, the one who owns them.

[R] Zeph 1:14 (AT)

32.36 [Yes], Jehovah shall destroy the fallen, mortal mind of Elohim's Sons, [restore Adam's life], and send them to minister to the nations,

32.37 And they shall say, ***where are your gods in whom you trusted and sought refuge?***

32.38 ***Which possessed your spirit and mind? Let them manifest as your mind and protect you now.***

32.39 So, you can see that I, even I, am the one who kills the Wild Animal's fallen, mortal mind and restores Adam's life; I shake her [fallen, mortal mind] and she is healed; Neither is there any one who can snatch her out of my hand,

32.40 Because I am raising Adam from the dead, and commanding that he should live for the life of the ages.

32.41 I shall avenge my enemies, and [the Woman] shall be safe and sound when I pierce through the fiery serpent and make [Adam's widowed spirit] whole, and [Adam] shall execute righteous judgment upon the Wild Animal's many members, and

32.42 I shall fill my Sons with Adam and Elijah, [Elohim's mind], and they shall join themselves to [Adam's slain, widowed spirit that the Serpent] captured, and this is how Adam and Elijah shall deliver them from their enemy, which is their own fallen, mortal mind.

32.43 Rejoice, all of the nations from which [Jehovah's] people are gathered, because [Elijah] shall break in pieces, the fiery serpent who stole the life of [Adam, Jehovah's] servant, and he shall boil Satan, and He shall atone for the Wild Animal, and for his people.

[268.2]

32.51 Moses, you struck the rock at Meribah[R-1] because Adam [who was resurrected in you][70] failed to separate from, and overlay the fiery serpent, the subconscious mind[R-2] you were born with,

[R-1] Ez 18:4

[R-2] Rom 8:6 (AT)

32.50 So you must die a natural death, [not as a punishment, but] because you are called to inherit the spiritual land [above the firmament], and not the physical land of Canaan,

32.49&52 But [don't be distressed, Moses, because] Adam will have another opportunity to wrestle with [the fiery serpent, fallen, mortal man's subconscious mind, when He incarnates again.

---

[70] ***Michael, the archangel*** (see, Jude 1:19) pierced Abel, Adam's root system within Moses, and raised Adam from the dead, but Moses, the personality, (Footnote continued – See, Appendix)

THE BOOK OF ECCLESIASTES

Chapter 7

[Message # Unknown]

7.14 Indeed, the evil one, recognizes that salvation is in the Fortified Adam, the good timeline, and sets her timeline against him. But the Serpent's use of Elohim['s breath] will end when fallen, mortal man recognizes the fiery serpent [within themselves].

Chapter 9

[228.1]

9.01 I searched out this whole matter and found that neither the Wild Animal's righteous members, nor the men who are alienated from Elohim in their mind, know that the whole creature is to be restored to the correct moral order, but the men that [Righteous] Adam is resurrected in become righteous and wise, because their relationship with [righteous Adam], enslaves their ungodly nature.**R**

R Is 33:19 (AT)

9.03 All of the evil men who are laboring on the earth, are experiencing the same mortal condition . . .

9.15 There was a poor, but wise, mortal man in the city, that humbled himself and repented, which delivered the whole city [out of its troubles], but those men who were strengthened because of that poor, mortal man, do not [even] remember him.

Chapter 10

[919.3.C]

10.01 [Men who] speak [the words of evil angels] are as morally offensive [to the people who can recognize the true] anointing, as dead flies [are repulsive to the natural man, but] the small amount of wisdom [that these false prophets have] impresses foolish [people, who give them] an honorable reputation.

[313.9]

10.08 The [believer] who searches out the spiritual part of this visible world [without Righteous Adam's permission],may fall into it and lose their salvation, because the Serpent ***re***forms [those such as these who enter into her world] into her own image.[71]

10.11 Surely, the serpent will not bite [you] unless [someone who] licks [the feet of] Ba'al profits from the incantation.

Chapter 11

[818.1]

1.01 Cast your [knowledge of], the Word [of God] upon [Primordial Adam], the personality of the waters above, and [the promised] Days of Abundance shall come into existence for you;

1.02 Give [understanding, loving kindness, judgment, justice, glory, victory and foundation], the seven parts of

[71] Satan is the spiritual part of this visible, physical world.

[Jehovah's] assemblage, to the female, the eighth [widowed, part within the people], because you do not know [what kind of] evil may happen [when] Elohim arrives on the earth;

1.03 Clouds [that] are full of rain, empty themselves upon the earth, and A tree that falls to the south or the north, will remain in the place that it falls, [and]

1.04 [Whoever] does not see the clouds, and does not [implement the provision of God] to guard himself, will reap what he sows;

1.05 Since you do not understand the actions of the God who made the whole Adam, you do not understand Elohim's way of life, [and] the bones of the spiritual [female] are filling up your [spiritual] womb,

1.06 So, sow your seed when the [sixth]Day breaks, and do not withhold [punishment from] your carnal mind, because you do not know whether [it] will turn out for your good and you will prosper, when the two, [the seven parts of Jehovah's assemblage and the female], unite,

Chapter 12

[1148.1]
12.01a In the days of your youth, in the days that

12.02 [Elohim] did not darken [R] the sun, or the light of the moon, or [the light of] the stars, or [cause] the clouds to return [again] after the rain [caused a Flood],

[R] Joel 2:10

12.01b You did not remember [R] your Creator, [which is] a sin, but [you shall remember him] in the years that [follow], when Elohim says, "I no longer have any pleasure in them."

[R] Deut 8:18
Titus 3:3-5

12.03a In that day,

12.04a The voice of the Shekinah shall rise up [above] the sound of all the daughters [R-1] of [Adam, who] grind [R-2] [spiritual food and feed it to the people through the lyrics of their] music, and

[R-1] Gen 6:1-2
[R-2] Lk 17:35

12.03b The concubines shall stop grinding [spiritual] food, [and] the few [souls that] guard [Jehovah's] house[hold while] they watch [R-1] [for him through] the lattice,[R-2] shall shake off the darkened [souls of] the strong mortal males who forcibly seized [R-3] them, and

[R-1] Matt 25:13
[R-2] So 2:9
[R-3] Gen 6:3
Jud 7:5-7

12.04b They shall sink down into the streets of the world below,[R] [and Jehovah] shall shut the swinging door,[R] and

[R] Gen 4:7

12.05 Everyone that is arrogant shall be afraid, [and] terror [shall pervade their] lifestyle, [but the daughters of Adam who are] pregnant [with the male offspring of the Sons of God] shall bloom like the almond tree, [even while plague of] the locusts frustrate Adam's passion to procreate, [and Elohim] returns to his eternal house, [and the concubines] go about the streets [of the world below] mourning [for their lovers],

12.06 Until Elohim, the fountain [of life from] above,

1) Breaks up [the process of] reincarnation in the hole [that Adam fell into], and

2) Stops the umbilical cord that brings salvation from receding, which breaks up the soul [that produces] the golden oil [of eternal life and] bursts apart the clay bodies, and

12.07 Turns [Abel] back [into] the dust of the earth [that Elohim brought] into existence,

[and] the spirit returns to God who gave it [to the man],

THE BOOK OF

EXODUS

Chapter 3

[624.8.C]

3.01 Now, it came to pass that Moses ruled over the animal nature of Jethro, his father-in-law, the high priest of Midian, and drove that animal nature under the authority of the desert [lifestyle[R-1] of Jehovah], and [Moses] came to the Mountains of God, [which] were dried up[R-2] [within himself],

R-1 Matt 3:1,3
R-2 Jer 23:10

3.02 And [Moses] saw the Angel of the Lord crucify [Abel,[R-1] the good side of the Seraph],[R-2] the fiery serpent [which] was near to him, [and] sever [Cain, the evil side of the Seraph, from Leviathan; and then Moses] saw [Adam rise up and] consume Leviathan,[R-3] [and after Adam consumed Leviathan, Moses] understood [why the Angel of the Lord] had crucified [Abel, the good side of the Seraph], the fiery [serpent in the midst of mortal man],[R-4]

R-1 Gal 2:20
R-2 Is 6:2
R-3 1 Ki 18:38
R-4 Mk 9:44, 46, 48

3.03 And Moses said [to himself], now that I have seen [and understand] this great vision[R-1] of Elohim crucifying [Abel] and [Adam] consuming Leviathan, I shall turn back[R-2] [to Jehovah],

R-1 Dan 8:16
R-2 Deut 30:1-3

3.04 And when Jehovah saw that Moses understood [the vision] and had turned back [from worshiping the Midianite gods], Elohim called to [Abel],the soul of Moses,**R-1** whom he had crucified, saying, Moses, and [Abel within Moses] said, here I am,**R-2**

R-1 Ps 42:11
R-2 1 Sam 3:6, 10

3.05 And Elohim said, Cain, the one who is presently occupying you, cannot approach this place where you are standing, [because it is] a holy Mountain, [the high place from where you can] overthrow Cain, and refuse to marry**R** [Leviathan, who rules] over [her],

R Rom 7:4

3.06 In addition, I [Am], the God of your father, says [that Cain, your animal] personality, is afraid [when] the God of Abraham, the God of Isaac and the God of Jacob, [is] near [enough] to look intently at [her],**R**

R Acts 10:4, 13:9-11

3.07 Because, Jehovah said, I have seen Cain browbeating**R-1** my people in Egypt, and I have seen [Abel], the obedient [part of their] personality, shrieking in anguish,**R-2** because he is experiencing [Cain's evil deeds],**R-2**

R-1 Ex 32:1
R-2 Gen 4:10

3.08 And I am come down to deliver [Abel], the good part of their earth[en personality], from [Pharaoh], the power of the Egyptians, by raising [Adam] up to the [good] land [of the heart] which is near to every direction, [and is also the place where Adam] stands up above the Canaanite Mountains of the Hittites, the Amorites, the Perizzites), the Hivites, and the Jebusites of the other side, [when] the Wisdom the Father, draws near to [him],

3.09 Because, I have seen the shrieks of [Abel], the root system of [Adam, the hope] of Israel,**R** coming towards me, and

I have seen the pressure that [Cain, who] assembles [together with Leviathan, the king of] Egypt, presses upon them,

R Jer 14:8
Acts 28:20

3.10 Now, therefore, walk [with me][R] and I shall send you to Pharaoh [so that I might] appear to my people and bring [Abel], the root system of [Adam, the hope] of Israel, out of Egypt,

R Amos 3:3

3.11 And Moses said to Elohim, [Should not] Jehovah and Adonay [be the ones who] go to Pharaoh to bring [Abel, the root system of Adam, the hope] of Israel, out of Egypt?

3.12 And Elohim said, You are up to the task because you belong to I AM, who has made [Abel within you] the slave/bond servant of [Jehovah], His high mountain, [and Jehovah] has engraved [Abel within you] with His nature,[R] and sent you to bring [His] people out of Egypt,

R Ez 9:3-4

3.13 And Moses said to Elohim, Do I understand you [correctly]? That I am to go to [Abel, the root system of Adam, the hope] of Israel, and say, The God of your fathers has sent me to tell you that you belong to Him? [But], they shall [surely say that the Holy Spirit, [who is] near to them [and] speaks [to them, is] the mark of Elohim's nature.[R]

R Num 12:1-2, 16:9-10

3.14 And Elohim said to Moses, [You are to go to Abel], the root system [of Adam, the hope] of [my people], Israel, and say, I AM has sent me [to tell you that] I AM [is] the self-existent One, [not the Holy Spirit],

3.15 And Elohim said to Moses, You shall also say this to [Abel], the root system [of Adam, the hope] of Israel, Jehovah, the God of your fathers, the God of Abraham, the God of Isaac, and the God of Jacob, has sent this [Adam] to remind you of His eternal Name [and the intimacy that you had with Him in the previous] age, [and to prepare you to be intimate with Him again in] the age to come,[R]

[R] Rom 5:6 (AT)
1 Pet 3:18 (AT)

3.16 [So], go and gather the elders of Israel together with [Adam within] yourself and say to them, Jehovah, the God of your fathers, appeared to me,[R-1] the God of Abraham, Isaac and Jacob, saying, I have deposited [my Holy Seed with this Adam called Moses, who] belongs to [me, to execute] the punishment that I would do to [Pharaoh, the high mountain who is appearing in] Egypt,[R-2]

[R-1] Ex 3:6
[R-2] Ex 6:1, 6

3.17 And, [as] I told you,[R] [when] you ascend into [my Holy] Mountain, wisdom will flow into [Abel], the root system [of Adam, the hope of Israel within you], to enable you [to overcome] the misery of [Leviathan, the king of] Egypt, [who is] joined to the Mountains of the Canaanites, the Hittites, and the Amorites and the Perizzites, and the Hivites and the Jebusites [of the other side],

[R] Vs 8

3.18 And [the elders of Israel shall listen to the voice of the widowed [Abel within themselves], and you, and the elders of Israel [who are] nailed to [Leviathan], the king of Egypt, shall go [to Pharaoh], and you shall say to him, Jehovah, the God of the Hebrews, has descended upon us at this time, to sacrifice [Leviathan], the fish[R] [that the Serpent] nailed us to after she kidnapped us, and to bring us into the desert lifestyle of the third day of Jehovah, our God,

[R] Mk 1:17
Jn 21:3

3.19 [And] I, [Elohim, the one who is] nailed to [Jehovah], assure you that Leviathan, the king of Egypt, shall release [Cain, the one who] belongs to him, and, [then, Abel] shall depart from the house[hold] of [Leviathan, Pharaoh's] violent mind,

3.20 [And Adam], the mind [that is] nailed to [Elohim], shall go forth and strike [Leviathan, his other] self, [and] the whole house[hold] of Leviathan, [the king of] Egypt, shall separate from the ox [that] I made, [and Adam's left] hand [of judgment] shall send [Leviathan, his other] self away, [and] I shall set Elohim], the unconscious [part of Adam's] mind, upright[R-1] in the center of the house,[R-2]

R-1 Matt 19:28
R-2 Is 30:20-21

3.21 And I shall give [my Son, Adam], who envisions [and calls into existence],[R-1] the world [to come,[R-2] to be] the husband [of] my people,[R-3] [and the world that Leviathan, the king of] Egypt, called into existence,[R-4] shall disappear,[R-5] but you shall not be left empty[R-6] [after Leviathan] departs,

R-1 Rom 4:17
R-2 Lk 18:30
Heb 6:5
R-3 Joel 2:16
Matt 9:15
R-4 Gen 14:3 (AT)
R-5 Is 34:4
Rev 6:14
R-6 Ex 11:2

3.22 Because you shall demand [that] the spirit of the woman, [even] the spirit of [Cain], the fellow citizen [that you are] nailed to, humble herself [before the elders of Adam's] house[hold who] fear [Jehovah,[R-1] and] turn aside from [following after Leviathan's] lifestyle;[R-2] and

Because [the elders of Israel, Adam's] weapons, shall judge [Cain],[R-3] the house[hold of Leviathan, who] lusts after [the things of this world,[R-4] and because Jehovah] has anointed [the elders of Israel Adam's] weapons, with the oil [of His Spirit,[R-5] and] put [Adam], His mantle,[R-6] above [Abel], the female [part of Adam's household], to defend Abel, [Adam's root system, against Leviathan who is] above [Cain], and snatch

[Cain] away from [Leviathan, the king of] Egypt, [so that] she may escape [from the lusts of this fallen world also].

R-1 Mal 4:2
R-2 Mk 1:15
Acts 17:30
R-3 1 Cor 6:3
R-4 Mk 4:19
1 Jn 2:16
R-5 Is 61:3
Acts 10:38
R-6 2 Ki 2:13-14

Chapter 4

[675.5]

4.02 And Jehovah said to [Moses], ***This*** Elohim is my rod of chastisement,

4.03 And [Jehovah] said [to Elohim], Cast down the [ascended fiery] serpent to the ground, and [Elohim] in the personality of Moses, cast down [the fiery serpent] to the ground, [and the fiery serpent] fled [from Elohim]

4.04 And Jehovah said to Moses, [Now, Young Adam], your [righteous] mind, can reach out and seize [the King of Egypt], the lower part [of Pharaoh within Moses], and [Young] Adam, [Moses' righteous] mind, reached out, and [Young] Adam, [Moses' righteous] mind, prevailed over the King of Egypt, because of [Elohim, Jehovah's] rod of chastisement,

4.06 And, IN ADDITION, Jehovah said to [Elohim}, Now bring [Young Adam, Moses' righteous] mind into his heart [so that the fiery serpent] will go into captivity, and [Elohim] brought [Young Adam, Moses' righteous] mind, into [Moses'] heart, and, behold, [Young Adam, Moses' righteous] mind, [was as] soap [to] the King of Egypt [in Moses' heart],

4.07 And [Jehovah] said [to Elohim], Bring [Young Adam, Moses' righteous] mind, into [Moses'] heart again, and [Elohim brought Adam, Moses' righteous] mind, into [Moses'] heart again, and, behold, [the fiery serpent] had gone into captivity, and [this is how Young Adam, Moses'] other inner man, was re-established [in Moses' heart],

4.09 And it shall come to pass, if they will not believe the second sign either, or listen to your voice, that you shall take [some] of the water of the [Nile] river, and pour it upon the dry land [of their heart], and the water that you take out of the [Nile] river shall become blood upon the dry land [of their heart].

[798.3]
4.14a And Moses became frustrated and angry, and Jehovah said, I know [that] you cannot speak [and that] Aaron, your brother, the Levite, [cannot] speak [either, but]

4.16a Elohim shall be a widowed mouth [to] you, [and your] widowed [mind] shall belong to Elohim, [and

4.15 Behold], Elohim shall speak my words to you, and put them in your mouth, and I will be with your mouth, and with [Aaron's] mouth, and I will teach you what you shall do; and

4.16b Elohim's mind in you] shall be [my] spokesperson to the people that belong to [me],

4.14b Look! [Elohim] is appearing, [in your] widowed heart, and when he encounters you, [you will experience calm] delight

[598.C]
4.21 Moses Returns to Egypt. Moses, go and return to Egypt, and [let the people] see all the miraculous signs that I have put in your mind to do, but Pharaoh will seize the hearts of the people and not let them go

4.26 Moses, the Unfaithful Husband. You are ending a relationship that was meant to be permanent, which makes you an unfaithful husband.

4.25 Moses' Spiritual Son. You are a husband that sheds the blood of his own [spiritual] son

Chapter 5

[675.10.C]

Telepathic Communication To The Elders

5.01 And Moses and Aaron went into the unconscious part of the mind [of the Elders] and told Pharaoh, this is what the Lord says to you: My people, Israel, are in a [spiritual] drunken stupor because of your seductive speech, [wherefore], you will release them to sacrifice [Leviathan to me], and

5.03 And [Moses and Aaron] said [to the people of Israel], the God of the Hebrews

Has encountered us, and

[Commanded] us to sacrifice the flesh of [Leviathan] to Jehovah, our God, [and]

To die to [Leviathan's] lifestyle, and

[To embrace] the doctrine [that teaches us how] to enter into the lifestyle of the third day [of creation],

So that we can avoid some dreaded disease or [foreign] military power falling upon us [because of our] craving for [the spiritual experiences and esoteric doctrine of the Egyptians], and

The Elders' Telepathic Response

5.02 Pharaoh [within the Elders] said, [Why] should we obey the voice of Jehovah and release Israel who are spiritually sexually connected to us, as well as to Jehovah? And

5.06a [Moses and Aaron] instructed Pharaoh [within the Elders] saying,

Conscious Communication To The Elders

5.05a Look, in the day [of Jubilee], many of the people of the land shall rest from the burdensome hard labor

5.06b [That] Satan, [Jehovah's] officer, exacts from [the people who violate Jehovah's Law, and in] the same day

5.05b [That Moses and Aaron] said [this] to Pharaoh [within the Elders],

Conscious Communication To The People

5.04 Elohim said to the King of Egypt [Pharaoh's spiritual child within the people, in the day of Jubilee], The people shall be loosed from the burdensome work of treading the path of [Leviathan's] lifestyle, and

5.07 [Righteous Adam], the [spiritual] food [which is the bread from heaven],

Shall exchange [the King of Egypt, Pharaoh's] increase [within] the people, for [Young Adam, Righteous Adam's increase, and

Young Adam] shall assemble [together with Elohim] through the judgment that forms [the spiritual] female building [that joins heaven and earth], like they were before [the fall], and

5.08 [At that time, the people] shall cry out, saying,

Let [our corruptible souls] be exchanged for [incorruptible souls, and

The people] shall die to [Leviathan's] lifestyle, [and]

Stop reverencing [the physical] bodies that Leviathan previously made for [Adam, to implement] the restrictions that [Jehovah] placed upon [them after they were cast out of the Garden, and

Their corruptible souls] shall be exchanged for [new, incorruptible souls] from above, and

[Young Adam] shall stand upright within the people], and

[Leviathan's scales] shall fall away [from their eyes],

5.09 And the men who labor in the rule of law, the work from above, who see through Satan's lying words, shall be vindicated; and

Pharaoh Within The Elders

Preach To Their Congregations

5.10 [The Elders who are Pharaoh's] officers, who] require [the people] to labor [for their spiritual food], went out and spoke to the people in this manner, saying, [If you believe Moses and Aaron], Pharaoh will not provide your spiritual food [any more],

5.12 Because [Righteous Adam, the left] hand [of God, will dash to pieces [Leviathan], the whole [spiritual man within the Elders of] the people of the land of Egypt, and gather [to himself, Abel], the part of the [spiritual] food that remains after [the fruit of the land] is harvested,

5.11 And [Elohim] shall seize [Young Adam, and the spiritual female building that joins heaven and earth like they were before [the fall shall appear, and [the people] shall die to [Leviathan's] lifestyle, and stop reverencing [their physical bodies, and Young Adam] shall be formed [within them], if [Abel] recognizes [Righteous Adam, Jehovah's spiritual] food, and

5.13 [Pharaoh within the Elders who] were oppressing [the people], egged [the people] on, saying, [Young Adam, the spiritual] speech of [Jehovah, will prevent the emergence of the Dragon], the completed work [that I have been bringing forth in you] since I began [to provide your] daily [spiritual] food, and

Pharaoh Within The Elders Opposes The Truth

In The Mind Of The Children Of Israel

5.14 [This is how Pharaoh within the Elders], the officers who oppressed the children of Israel that [Pharaoh] set them over, beat down the thoughts [of Young Adam, Jehovah's spiritual speech within the people, which was telling them that] Pharaoh [within their Elders] had failed to satisfy [Jehovah's] requirements for [providing] the [spiritual] food of the previous age, both in the past and [in this] present age; and

Pharaoh In The Elders Attack Preachers of Truth

5.20 [Pharaoh within the Elders] met Moses and Aaron who were standing erect [because Jehovah] had encountered them as they came forth from Pharaoh, and

5.21 [The Elders] said to [Aaron and Moses], Look at us, and let Jehovah judge [concerning what you have done], because you have made us to be a bad smell in Pharaoh's world, and you have put a sword in the hand of [the people] who serve [Pharaoh] in his world, to kill us, and

Moses Calls Upon Jehovah

5.22 Moses went back to Jehovah saying, Lord, why has Elohim done evil to the people that you sent me to?

5.23 Because, since I came to Pharaoh, [the Elders] speak [to the people] in your Name, [saying, Moses] has done evil to this people; neither has he delivered your people from the power of [the other side];

Moses Calls Upon Elohim

5.15a Then came [Moses], the officer [that Jehovah sent] to the children of Israel, and cried to Pharaoh [within the Elders who are] Elohim's widowed servants, saying, You have a moral obligation to [provide the spiritual food that]

5.16a Builds [Young Adam within the people], and

5.15b Complete [him, but] Pharaoh [within the Elders who are]

5.16b [Jehovah's] servants, are not providing the [spiritual] food [that] forms [Young Adam within the people]; and, look, [Pharaoh within the Elders], your servants, are stricken [because of] the sins of your people, and

5.17 [Elohim responded], saying, [The people] must forsake and abandon [the King of Egypt, Pharaoh's mind within themselves], and [Young Adam] will stand up [and join with Elohim] from above; and [Elohim] said, [The people that Young Adam is conceived in] must sacrifice [Leviathan] to Jehovah, and die to [Leviathan's] lifestyle, and

5.18 [When they do that], the amount of [spiritual] food [that the people need] to exchange [the King of Egypt within themselves for Young Adam], shall be given to [the people who] are presently laboring for Leviathan's [spiritual] food, but are moving towards [Righteous Adam], Jehovah's spiritual food], and

5.19 [Moses, Jehovah's officer], saw [that the fiery serpent, the internal] thoughts [of Satan, were continually evil, and that the man-made doctrine [of Hatmehyt], the fish [god, which] does not speak of the judgment [of the sin nature], produces [only] dried up spiritual bodies,

Chapter 6

[675.10.C]
6.01 Then Jehovah said to Moses, Now you shall see what I shall do to Pharaoh, whose persistent stubbornness is aborting [Young Adam in the people], and whose persistent stubbornness is [also] driving the [living] waters out of their land,

Chapter 7

[675.4.C]
7.06 And Aaron and Moses did as Jehovah commanded them to do, and [Adam's young son] stood upright [in Moses and Aaron],

7.07 And Moses, the son [of God], was 80 years old, and Aaron, the son [of God], was 83 years old, when [Adam's young son] stood upright [in Moses and Aaron], and [when] Aaron and Moses spoke to Pharaoh,

[OLM 11 24 99]
7.10 And Adam [within Moses] penetrated Pharaoh [within Aaron, and Adam] stood up [within Aaron], and [Adam within Aaron] cast down [the swine, the ascended fiery serpent within Aaron, and] Adam cast down the authority, correction and doctrine of Pharaoh's widowed personality, and [Adam within

Moses] set [the fiery serpent within Aaron] in Jehovah's moral order, and Elohim nailed the widowed personality of Aaron, his servant, to Moses], the [fiery] serpent [in] Jehovah's moral order, and righteous [Adam] appeared.

7.21 And [Leviathan], the fish that was in the river died, and Satan's morally offensive river became moral, and the Egyptians drank of the water of the river, and there was life [blood] throughout the land of Egypt.

Chapter 8

[440.2]

8.15 But, when Leviathan saw that Jehovah was relieving the Hebrew children [from their carnal mind, she stirred up Satan to] prevent [Abel], Jehovah's understanding, [from rising into] their heart,

8.16 And Jehovah said to Moses, Tell Aaron to stretch forth his branch of [the Fortified Adam], and strike into the dust of the earth, so that [Adam's] root system might be planted throughout all of the land of Egypt,

8.17 And Aaron stretched forth his righteous branch of the [Fortified Adam], and struck into the dust of the earth, and planted [Abel, the Fortified] Adam's root system, in the dust of the land, which is in all of the cattle[72] throughout the whole land of Egypt,

---

[72] Humanity, apart from the mind of God, is a herd of cattle. The planting of Abel, Adam's root system, in a [spiritual] Egyptian, elevates that man to Elohim's Son.

8.18 And the magicians used their enchantments to pluck up [Abel], the root system that [Aaron] planted in the cattle, but could not, and Adam's root system, endured.

8.19 So the magicians said to Leviathan, They are baptized into Elohim! Secure the heart! And Leviathan and the fiery serpent granted their request, because of Jehovah's promise.[R]

[R] Ps 105:8 (AT)

Chapter 9

[01/11/2025]
9.10 And they saw [Adam], the mate of the God of Israel, a highly polished, pure and precious foundation, the representation [of God's] handiwork [in] heaven, [and his] male organ [in the earthen personalities],

Chapter 10

[Message # Unknown]
10.10 And he said to them, Let it be so, since it appears that Jehovah is with you I will let you and the younger members of your household [who] can see the evil counterpart of their personality go.

Chapter 11

[12/20/2024]
11.06 And, so, Jehovah distinguished between the Israelites and the Egyptians among the mortal men of Israel [who served] the Dog, [that ancient Egyptian deity called, "Anubis,"

and all the prayers of all the prayer chains could not] prevent [the death of the Egyptians],

[1226.1.C]
11.07 And, so, Jehovah distinguished between the Israelites and the Egyptians among the mortal men of Israel [who served "Anubis," the ancient Egyptian] dog [god], and all the prayers of all the prayer chains could not] prevent [the death of the Egyptians],

Chapter 12

[1114.2.C]
12.51 And it came to pass in the same day that the Lord brought a crowd of people [who had] the seed of Israel out of the land of Egypt, that

Chapter 13

[1114.2.C]
13.01 Jehovah spoke to Moses, saying,

13.02 The Firstborn [Son of Man] shall sanctify all the virgins [who have] the seed of Israel, and they shall belong to me, and all the children of the Firstborn Son of man shall belong to me [also],

13:03 [Wherefore] Moses says to the people [in the wilderness], "Remember this day that Jehovah brought you out of Egypt, [when he gave you his] mind [so to that you would have] the strength to stop consuming this confusing [Egyptian] doctrine, and come out of the house [of worship that] bound you [to pagan gods],"

13.04 [Because], the day that you departed from [Egypt was the beginning of] a new season, [called] "The Third Day Of Creation," and

13.05 It shall come to pass when Jehovah brings you into the material world, that he shall provide the human wives [bodies],the spiritual child that imparts immortality, social prominence, spiritual and physical children, and the righteous perceptions of God, that he swore he would give to your fathers [in] this New Season, [and he will also provide you with] an abundance of physical food [for those] earth[en bodies], as well as spiritual wisdom for your souls, and

13.06 Your [spiritual soul] shall consume doctrine without confusion for seven days, and in the seventh day [you shall make] a feast to the Lord, and

13.07 Your [bestial soul] shall consume esoteric doctrine for seven days [also, during which] there shall be no confused doctrine, neither shall there be any confused perceptions within the boundaries [of your personalities], and

13.08 In the day that my Son is revealed in you, you shall say, "The Lord made me to cross over into [his mind, and] come out of the land of Egypt," and,

13.09 Your talking about the memory of what you saw with your [own] eyes shall be a sign that Jehovah's powerful mind brought you out of Egypt, and [that the Son of Man, his spiritual] Law, was born in [you after that];

13.10 Therefore, you shall keep this Law in this [New] Season, [so that the Son of Man is revealed in you] from day to day, and

13.11 It shall come to pass that, when you bring [your bestial side] into submission, [you shall enter] into the [immortal] bodies that the Lord promised your fathers that he would give to you, and

13.12 The manchild that comes forth [from your] best[ial side, shall impregnate all of Jehovah's virgins, [and] the manchild and all the [spiritual] males [that] come into existence, shall belong to Jehovah, and

13.13 The Firstborn [Son of] Mankind [shall be] the ransom for the male ass, the [bestial] part of the flock, and if the ransom for the whole [world] cannot accomplish the exchange, he shall force [the male ass] down under the manchild, the seed [of the woman], and

13.14 It shall come to pass that, in the future, when your son asks you, saying, "Why are you doing this?" You shall say to him, "Jehovah gave us his strong mind, which brought us out of the house [of worship where] we were bound to [the gods of] Egypt,

13.16 So that I should remember what I saw within [my own] mind when Jehovah's strength brought us out of the house [of worship where] we were bound to [the gods of] Egypt,

13.15 But when this happened Pharaoh was so dense that he would not let us go, so Jehovah slew all the Firstborn [physical males] in the land of Egypt, from the Firstborn of Mankind, [their] spiritual [side], to the Firstborn of [their] bestial [side], and this is the reason why I sacrifice every male [ass] that comes out of the womb of the Firstborn [bestial side of the physical males in the land of Egypt], by bringing him into submission] to Jehovah, but all the Firstborn of Mankind, I ransom.

Chapter 14

[1066.4.C]

14.01 And Jehovah spoke to Moses saying,

14.02a Speak to the children of Israel and

14.03a Tell [them]

14.02b To return to the starting point, [because Jehovah promised] the use of their material bodies to [Adam from above], the personality [of Jehovah, but] they have given the use of their material bodies to [Pharaoh], the personality of [Satan], the black hole of Egypt [in the unconscious part of their mind] and the enforcer of Jehovah's Righteous Sowing and Reaping Judgment,

14.03b [Who] has led the children of Israel astray, and driven them to surrender their material bodies to Pharaoh,

14.04 [Wherefore, Adam from above, my] mate, shall seize Pharaoh, [and lay it] heavily [upon Pharaoh's] heart to run after them, [so that] the whole Egyptian army should know that I, Jehovah, [Am the one who] stands [them] upright, and

14.05a [When] it was revealed to the King of Egypt that the people had fled [to Adam from above, who rules them from the right side of their] heart [center], and

14.06 [That Righteous Adam], the upper millstone [in the unconscious part of the mind of] the people he took to be himself [in the World of Action], had joined the battle,

14.05b Pharaoh and his servants turned against the people, saying, "[Adam from above], Elohim's mate, has made Israel stop serving [us]," and

14.07 He has taken 600 youths [in the World of Action], all [of them extensions of Adam, Jehovah's] upper millstone, [and given them] more [spiritual understanding] than the captains of Egypt, and

14.08 [Adam, the upper millstone], Jehovah's mate, seized Pharaoh, King of Egypt, [in the unconscious part of the mind of] the children of Israel, [because] he was pursuing the children of Israel [who had fled to Righteous Adam, who rules them from the right side of their] heart [center, and the children of Israel] went out [of Egypt by] the ascended mind [of Righteous Adam, the upper millstone],

14.09 [But], the Egyptians ran after their other selves in the unconscious part of their mind, and they overtook all [of their other] selves [who] had pitched their tents [with] the extensions of Adam, the upper millstone in the unconscious part of their mind, [who] were rejoicing [because they had escaped from] the power of the cavalry of [Cain], Pharaoh's spiritual child, and [Pharaoh], the personality of [Satan], the black hole of Egypt [in the unconscious part of their mind], and the enforcer of Jehovah's Righteous Sowing and Reaping Judgment, and

14.10 As Pharaoh approached the children of Israel, [Adam, Jehovah's] mate, who rules the children of Israel from the right side of their] heart [center], opened [their] eyes, [and] the children of Israel saw that the Egyptians, [their other selves], were dissolving [Adam's] union [with his Mother, the third personality of the God World in] the unconscious part of the mind, [and] they were very afraid, [and] the Hebrew children cried out in the Spirit to Jehovah [to save them], and

14.11 They [accused] Elohim [falsely in their mind], and said to Moses, "This Elohim took us out of Egypt to die in the desert because he wanted a people to express himself through, [and [there were no [unoccupied] sepulchers;

14.12 "Did we not tell you [while we were still] in Egypt, saying, "Leave us alone and let us serve the Egyptians, the mate of the [Leviathan, because] It is better to belong to the Egyptians, [the mate of [Leviathan and] serve them, than to die in the desert,"

14.13 [But] Moses said to the people, "Do not be afraid, [but, rather], be immovable, [and] you will see the salvation [of Adam from above], the mate of Jehovah Elohim, make you belong to Elohim [this] day, [and] you will see Elohim, the mate of [Jehovah], continue to do to the Egyptians, repeatedly, forever, [what] you see [them] doing [to the Egyptians] today, and

14.14 "You shall belong to Jehovah, and he shall feed you, and engrave [you with his nature], "and

14.15 Jehovah said to Moses, "Elohim is crying out in the Spirit to the children Israel, telling them to go forward,

14.16 "[But] they are confused [because they cannot distinguish between Elohim's Spirit and the destructive energy of the soul, so Adam from above], your mate [and their] spiritual speech, has risen up [to deliver them;" and Adam from above, Moses'] mate, stretched forth over the unconscious part of the mind of the children of Israel, and went into the unconscious part of their mind, [and] divided [Elohim's Spirit] from [the destructive energy of the soul], and

14.17 [The Hebrew children], Looked, [and they saw] Adonai, the mate [of Jehovah], going into the unconscious part of the mind of the Egyptians, and their heart was seized [with fear, which] made it difficult for [Cain, the female] drivers of all the chariots of Pharaoh's armies, [to pursue the Hebrew children], and

14.18 The Egyptians knew [that it was] Adonai Jehovah [who] made it difficult for [Cain, the female] drivers [of] Pharaoh's chariots [to run after the children of Israel], and

14.19 The angel of God that carried the personality [of Moses and] the [personal souls of the whole] Israelite camp, departed [from Moses' material body], and walked into the unconscious part of the mind [of the Hebrew children], and the thunder cloud that was standing in the personality of [Moses] departed [from his material body and stood up in the unconscious part of the mind [of the Hebrew children], and

14.20 He came between the camp of the Egyptians and the camp of Israel, and was a thundercloud to the destructive [energy of the soul], but a light to all [the earthen personalities of the Hebrew children], the mate of [Moses], so that the [destructive]

energy of the soul did not come near to [the earthen personalities of the Hebrew children], and

14.21 [Adam, Jehovah's] mate, stretched out [from] Moses' mind over the unconscious part of the mind [of the Hebrew children, and [Adam, the upper millstone], walked into the unconscious part of their mind, and] Jehovah's Spirit strengthened all the personalities [of the Hebrew children against the destructive opinion of] the soul, and [Adam, the upper millstone], Jehovah's mate, enabled the confused [earthen personalities] to divide [the opinion of] Elohim's reproductive force from the [destructive opinion of] the soul, and

14.22 The confused Hebrew children joined [the opinion of] Elohim's reproductive force to the right side [of their heart], and the destructive opinion of the soul to the left side [of their heart], and

14.23 [Adam, the upper millstone], the higher soul of all the material body-personal soul (personality) unities, [that] walked into the unconscious part of the mind [of the Hebrew children, which enabled them] to bisect [the opinion of Elohim's reproductive force and the destructive opinion of the soul in] the unconscious part of their mind, ran after [Leviathan], Pharaoh's upper millstone, and [after] the Egyptians, and

14.24 Adam below, the night watch [that] guards [the earthen personalities of the Hebrew children before] Melchizedek, the continuing existence of the next day appears, saw Jehovah moving towards the armies of the Egyptians, and the column of fire and the thundercloud, his mate, troubled the armies of the Egyptians, and

14.25 [The column of fire], the female power [that is] the mate [of the Thundercloud], turned away [Leviathan, the higher souls of the earthen personalities, which made it] very difficult [for the Egyptians] to go on, [and] they said, "We are becoming invisible, [because Adam, the upper millstone], Jehovah['s mate], is fighting [for the earthen] personalities [of the Hebrew children," and

14.26 Jehovah said to Moses, "Stretch out your mind over the unconscious part of the mind [of the Hebrew children, your] mate, [and walk into the unconscious part of their mind, and] over[flow] the Egyptians, and over[flow Leviathan, Pharaoh's] upper millstone, and over[flow Cain], the female drivers [of Pharaoh's chariots], and turn back the opinion [of the Hebrew children towards Elohim's reproductive force]," and

14.27 Moses stretched forth his mind over the unconscious part of the mind [of the Hebrew children, and Adam from above], Jehovah's mate, encountered [Leviathan, Pharaoh's upper millstone], and [Melchizedek], the morning [of the next day], roared at the Egyptians, and [the Egyptians] vanished when [Melchizedek], the continuing strength [of the Hebrew children] appeared, and [the Hebrew children] returned to the starting point [in] the unconscious part of their mind, and

14.28 The opinion of Elohim's reproductive force returned [the Hebrew children] to the starting point, and [Melchizedek, the morning of the next day], satisfied the egos of [the Hebrew children so that when Leviathan], the upper millstone, [Pharaoh's] mate, [and Cain, the female] driver of all the [chariots of] Pharaoh's armies, came to the unconscious part of the mind [of the Hebrew children], not one degree of the [destructive] energy of the soul in] the unconscious part of the mind [of the Hebrew children] rose to the surface [to feed from them],

14.29 Because the [earthen personalities] of the children of Israel [which had been] confused, [now] belonged to [Adam from above, and] they [were] joined to his right and his left side, and they walked [with him] in the midst of the unconscious part of the mind, [which was now dominated by the continual life of Melchizedek, the King to whom peace belongs, the morning of the next day of creation], and

14.31a Israel saw [Adam], the great mind that Elohim, Jehovah's mate, made [to help the Hebrew children overcome their] Egyptian [mind], and

14.30a Israel saw their Egyptian mate dead on the shore of the unconscious part of their mind. that day, and

14.31b The people revered Jehovah [and Adam, his] mate, and believed Jehovah and Moses his servant, and

14.30b That is how Jehovah saved Israel from their Egyptian mind.

Chapter 17

[1234.1.C]

17.06 Look! I will stand [Adam] up in the place above [the human] soul of the people [who are at the point of wanting] to kill your personality, [Moses, because] judgment [has made their] soul dry and desolate, and drinkable water shall come out of the soul [of Adam; And Jehovah] stood [Adam] upright [in the people, and Jehovah] was elevated in the eyes of the elders of Israel [when Adam] competed [them],

Chapter 20

[OLM 05 03 00]

20.01 And Elohim [within Moses] spoke all these words, saying,

20.02 I [Am] Jehovah, [the one] who delivers Elohim's sons from forced servitude [to the Dragon, the spiritual] waters [in the crown of Leviathan's timeline, which is] the [spiritual]

land of Egypt, [and from Satan, the spiritual] waters of [Leviathan, Satan's] house[hold],

20.03 [Wherefore], it shall come to pass that Cain, the alien personality that is above [Abel], shall belong to Elohim,

20.05a [And] Jehovah, [who] has an ardent zeal for you, [shall subdue]

20.04 Satan, the [pool of polluted] water [in the morally impure place that lies] under the separated personalities [of mortal mankind, and] the whole Leviathan, the household of Satan [in] the etheric [plane of consciousness, who] engraves [Adam, Elohim's] household in the upper window of creation [with Satan's nature], and forms [Elohim's sons into a] household [that produces good and evil mental] images,

20.05b [And Adam shall subdue Leviathan, who makes] Cain [within Elohim's sons] bow down to Satan, [the one who] enslaves you, [and Elohim's sons shall subdue Cain, the one who] punishes [Abel], the children [from] above, [and] the widowed [Abel], Cain's enemy, [shall subdue Cain by] depositing the internalized sins of their father, [Satan, in their path, whether they incarnate in] Leviathan's kingdom, [or in] Adam's Kingdom, and the sons of Elohim shall belong to I [Am],

20.06 [Who] appoints mercy to the widowed personalities of [Adam's] ox who are hedged about [by Adam, Jehovah's] Divine Law, and the widowed [personalities] who are [Elohim's] friends,

20.07 [But, while we wait for this great salvation], Satan [and] Leviathan [continue] to bring forth the nature of [their] own empty selves to accomplish [Satan's] purposes [in the personalities of mortal humanity, but I], Jehovah, am cleansing the sons of Elohim from sin, [so] they shall bring forth Jehovah's [nature and not] the nature [of Satan and Leviathan's own] empty selves,

20.08 [So, Jehovah, the one who has mercy], shall cleanse [the tarnished] morality [of Abel, your] male self, [and Abel] shall mature into Adam, [who shall deliver you from Satan and Leviathan],

20.10 [But] my son, King Adam, shall complete the sons of Elohim, [who] the Snake separated from Jehovah [and] fashioned into Cain, [Satan's] daughter, [so that] Abel, [would serve as Leviathan's] manservant, and Cain, the physical female animal, [would serve as Leviathan's] maidservant, [who blocks] the opening [to Adam's timeline, and] serves the collective [Leviathan], the household [of] Satan, the Alien Age [of] Intermission,

20.09 [And the personalities who] bear the mark of Satan, [the spiritual female], will be Leviathan's slave [for] the [entire] Age [of Intermission],

20.11 Because Jehovah made the heavens and the earth, and all [the species] that [are] in them, [and] set [Adam, Elohim's] household, the mother of [the personalities who] complete the ages, upright, [and, for this reason, King Adam who is] above, shall silence Satan, the Age of Intermission, [and King Adam shall make Leviathan] bow down to Jehovah, [and King Adam] shall cleanse [Abel], the morality [of your male self, and Jehovah] shall marry King Adam [within the personalities of mortal man],

20.12 [And for all of these reasons, King Adam], the [unified] mind that Jehovah gives to the sons [that] belong to Elohim, is a heavy burden upon Satan, the father, and Leviathan, the mother [of mortal man, because King Adam is the mind from] above that draws [Abel, Jehovah's royal seed] out [from under Cain's] ground,

20.13 [Wherefore], Cain [seeks to] murder [Abel], Leviathan [seeks to murder Adam],

20.14 [And] Satan commits adultery with Cain,

20.15 [Since] the Primordial Serpent deceived [Adam, who died to his immortality and became] Cain [and Abel],

20.16 [And this is the reason why] Cain [within the sons of Elohim] responds to Leviathan, the false witness [within the sons of Elohim], the household [of Jehovah], the one who has mercy,

20.17 [And] Satan and Leviathan desire [to marry Adam], the wife [of Jehovah], the one who has mercy [on Abel, Elohim's] male servant, [and on Cain, Elohim's] female servant, [who became the animal that is] nailed [to Leviathan, and on the human spirit that is] nailed to Satan, and [on] all the personalities that [are] separated [from Jehovah], the one who has mercy, [who] agree with Satan's thoughts.

[513.1]
20.24 The female personalities that are grateful [for my salvation] shall sacrifice [Cain within themselves] as a burnt offering, [and] Adam shall acquire [Abel], who belongs to me, and [the Spirit of Elijah] shall castrate Satan in [the female personalities that are grateful for my salvation], and I will enter into all of the female personalities that kneel down before [the one who comes in] my nature, and [Adam] shall engrave [the female personalities [that turn away from] Cain's lifestyle with my nature].

Chapter 21

[OLM 01 26 00]
21.23 I shall pay you back [for the evil you have done to my son, Adam, [by declaring your] evil personality [to be] good, says the Lord.

21.24 Yes, [I shall give you Righteous Adam] to cover your [naked] carnal mind,

21.25 [And Righteous Adam] shall penetrate the center of the neck center [of the counterfeit timeline, where] Leviathan [your spiritual sexual part], penetrates Cain, and [Righteous Adam] shall divide Cain from Satan,

[And you, the personality, shall depart from] Leviathan's physical, visible world [in the right side of the heart],

[And you shall enter into] Righteous Adam's visible, spiritual world, [in the left side of the heart, and from there you shall ascend into] the neck of Righteous Adam, [my glorious timeline].

Chapter 25

[393.8]
25.20 And the Cherubim[73] who are above the firmament, shall spread apart the opening in their skulls, and weave themselves together with [Adam, and ascend to his brow], at a right**R** angle.[74] And this is how the Cherubim shall liberate the personalities that are near to his crown.[75]

R Ez 1:19b (AT)

---

[73] The Cherubim are Elijah in the center of his brow, and Adam in the center of his neck.

[74] The Spirit of God interacts at a right angle with the human spirit in man's centers (Ez 1:19-20b).

[75] The personalities whose consciousness ascends from [the animal instincts at] the center of his root at the bottom of the spine, up to the center of his brow [6th].

Chapter 32

[690]

Fear Of Abandonment

32.01a Now, when Moses did not descend from the mountain [as quickly as] the people expected [him to, their hearts] fainted [from fear; and]

Emotional & Spiritual Weakness

32.01b They shamefully transferred their allegiance [from Moses] to Aaron, saying,

32.01c We do not know what happened to this man, Moses, [who] empowered us to ascend above the spiritual [waters] of Egypt,

32.01d [So, you, Aaron, must be the one who is supposed] to stand up [in spiritual power] and make our bodies the chariots that carry Elohim,

32.02a And Aaron said to [the people], Listen to me,

32.02b The mixed multitude, that idolatrous, male nature of the [Serpent's] Circular Universe, [has taken you to be his] wives, [and,

32.02c Unless the spiritual military] power of [Jehovah] rescues [Abel], the royal [female] seed of the Shekinah [within you],

32.02d You will be guilty of shedding the blood of [Abel all over again]; and

32.03a All the people listened to what Aaron [said about their being guilty of] shedding the blood of [Abel the Shekinah's] royal [female seed] again, and

32.05a The widowed personalities of [the people repented, and Righteous Adam,

A New Nature

32.04a Aaron's] splendid [spiritual] covering, interacted intimately with [Abel within the people, who] had said,

32.04b These [two men, Moses and Aaron, are] your gods, O Israel, which brought you up above the spiritual waters of the land of Egypt, and

32.06a [The people] drank [the Water of Life] from [the well of the Shekinah within Aaron], and

32.06b Ate [the manna that congeals into the female Adam], who produces the lamb, which represents the neck [of Righteous Adam], and

32.04c [Righteous Adam within Aaron], seized the [male calf] mind of [the mixed multitude within the people, and]

32.04d Engraved [Abel, the spiritual side of the male calf] mind, [with the nature of Jehovah], and

32.04e Shaped [Cain, the animal side of the male calf] mind [of the people which were engraved with the nature of Jehovah, into the female Adam], and

Spiritual Sacrifices

32.05b When Aaron saw that Righteous Adam, the [spiritual] altar [upon which the male calf mind of the mixed multitude] is [sacrificed, was re]built [within the people],

32.05c Aaron called for [the people] to bring forth [the male calf mind of the mixed multitude from within themselves, so that

32.05d The Shekinah's fiery stream within Aaron] could crush [the male calf mind which was formed as a result of Abel's adultery with the female power], and

32.05e Bring the next day [of creation into existence within them], and

32.06c The people offered up [their male calf mind, the fruit of Abel's adultery with the female power], as a peace offering [to Jehovah], and

32.03b That is how [Righteous Adam], the spiritual, [military] power [of Jehovah within] Aaron, rescued [Abel, the royal female seed of the Shekinah within the people, from] the idolatrous [calf nature of the mixed multitude of the Serpent's] Circular Universe, [and, after that],

32.05f The third day [of creation came into existence within the people], and

Aaron Mocked

32.06d [Jehovah] married the people [again, but]

32.06e [Cain, the animal side of the male calf mind of the mixed multitude], rose up to mock [Aaron]

32.08a Very soon [after Aaron rescued[R] the people, and Cain, the animal side of],

[R] Vs 4a

32.08b The male calf [mind of the mixed multitude],

32.08c Sacrificed [Abel, the royal female seed of the Shekinah, to Satan, the female power], and

32.08d [Satan], the female [power]

32.08e Interacted intimately with [Abel, who was under Cain's influence], and

32.08f [Abel] submitted to

32.08g [Cain, and to Satan, the female power], and that is how [Cain, the animal side of the mixed multitude,

32.08h Covered [over Abel, who is engraved with Jehovah's righteous nature, and]

32.08i Turned [the people] away from the lifestyle [that Moses] commanded them [to follow, and

32.08j The people spoke the blasphemous words [of the mixed multitude], saying,

32.08k [The male calf, mind of] these [Israelites, the fruit of the union of Abel and Satan, the female power], are your gods, O Israel, which empowered you to ascend above the spiritual [waters] of the material land of Egypt, and

Pharaoh's Neck

32.09a Jehovah said to Moses, I have looked into [the heart of] this people

32.07a Which ascended above the [spiritual] waters of [the material land of] Egypt, and

32.09b I see that

32.07b [Satan, the female power], has married [my nature that you, Moses, formed in] them, and

32.09c [Completed them, and that the people are expressing] the cruelty of [Pharaoh's] neck, and

Completed Personalities

32.07c Jehovah said to Moses, Go down to [the Circular world of the Universe of Separation], and

32.10a Burn the male [calf mind that] the Serpent [formed within the people], and

32.10b Complete [Cain, the personality of] the ox that is nailed to the [lower] window of [creation, and]

32.10c Complete [the physical bodies of] the ox, [the animal side of Israel], that great, widowed nation that is nailed to the [lower] window [of creation, so that

32.10d They may remain [in the earth]; and

Blind To Sin

32.11a Jehovah, the God [of Israel], said to Moses,

32.11b The personalities of my people [who] you are married to are spiritually sick [concerning their inability to recognize their sins], and

32.12e They have become] Egyptians [again], so

32.11c [Satan, the expression of my] anger [and the enforcer of my righteous Sowing & Reaping Judgment], is raging against the [idolatrous, male calf] mind [of the mixed multitude within] my people, who

32.11d Elohim, the great strength of my authority [in the earth, just] raised up above [the spiritual] waters of the material Land of Egypt, [and]

32.12a [Their false] gods are speaking to them [saying that you,

32.12b [Moses], had an evil motive for bringing them out of captivity, [and that

32.12c You intend] to slay them, [and]

32.12d Consume their [spiritual] energy, [which is] greater than the energy of their earthen bodies;

Jehovah's Promise

32.13a [But], I have remembered [my promise to] Abraham, Isaac and Israel, my servants, to whom I swore by my own self, saying,

32.13b [The female Adam, Abraham's] seed, shall increase into [many]

32.13c Permanently fixed points of [spiritual] light in the heaven [of the Universe of Asiyah], and

32.13d They shall be [the inner dimension of the immortal], earthen [bodies] that I told [Jacob] about, [who] I gave the [royal female] seed [of the Shekinah to], and

32.13e [Israel] shall possess eternal life; and

Reprieve

32.12b [That is the reason why] I am granting repentance [to my people, that] comes from an higher [authority than that of Satan], the rage of my anger, [so that]

32.12c The evil [that Satan, the enforcer of the Sowing & Reaping Judgment, is devising] against my widowed people, shall be turned back; and

32.14 Jehovah, breathed strongly against [Satan, the one who executes] the evil that [Jehovah] said he would do to his widowed people; and

A Spiritual Mind

32.15a Moses turned [toward the material world below], and

32.15b Went down [from the mountain of God] with two [additional spiritual grades], and

32.15c One [of the two is] the spiritual region [in Moses'] heart [which is] across from the [spiritual] waters [of the material land of Egypt], and

32.15d The [other] one of the two [is] the spiritual mind [that resides there, which is] engraved with the spiritual [authority of] the male [Adam],

32.15e The [true and faithful] witness [that]

Engraved By God

32.16a The work of God

32.15f Is written

32.16b In the framework [of a man's heart], and [that]

Sin Recognized

32.17a Joshua, [Moses' spiritual] mate, heard the loud shouts of the people [and] said to Moses,

32.17b [This] noise [is] the noise of the warlike military power [that opposes God, not the sound of people worshiping God, and]

The Second Witness

32.18a The Eternal One spoke [through Moses, who is spiritually] male [to Joshua], saying,

32.18b [It is true], I hear the voice [of Abel, who] Cain defeated,

32.18c Crying out [for the spiritual food that forms Adam's male [mind] within the people, even

32.18d While they] are obeying the voice of [Satan], the female power, and

Inclined To Do Evil

32.21 Moses said to Aaron, What sin did the people do that brought this great [judgment] upon them? and

32.22a Aaron said, Lord, [Moses], do not let your anger rise up [because the people] are saying,

32.23a We do not know what happened to this man, Moses, [who] empowered us to ascend above the spiritual [waters] of Egypt, [so,

32.23b You, Aaron, must be the one who is supposed] to stand up [in spiritual power] and make our bodies the chariots that carry Elohim, [because]

32.22b You know that the people are inclined to do evil, and

32.24a I [have already] told them that they must throw down the gold[en calf that they made, and that]

32.24b They will have to give up [the male calf mind] that [Satan, the female power], formed in them, [before they can] be circumcised in the Shekinah's fiery stream, [which

32.24c Frees Abel, the Shekinah's royal female seed within them], and reforms him [into the male Adam again]; and

Bound To Pharaoh

32.30a It came to pass, [that] the [next] day, after [Aaron spoke to Moses, that]

Widowhood

32.25b Moses saw that [Pharaoh], the enemy [of the Shekinah], had risen up [in spiritual power within the people]

32.25c [Who were Aaron's spiritual mate, and made Aaron] a widow, and a laughing stock, [and that]

32.25a The people were naked, [because] they were no longer bound [to Jehovah], and

A Great Sin

32.30b Moses said to the people, You have sinned a great sin, so

32.30c I will ascend before Jehovah [to see if], perhaps, [He will permit you] to atone for the sin of [the male calf, that the female power formed in you], and

Power For Themselves

32.31a Moses returned to Jehovah, and said, Alas, the people have sinned a great sin:

32.31b [These] Elohim have spun the [spiritual] gold [of the Shekinah into a source of spiritual power for] themselves; and

32.33a Jehovah said, [The people] have sinned against the Shekinah, and [according to my righteous Law],

32.33b They should be blotted out of my Book [of Life], and

Moses Intercedes

32.32a Moses [said], Please [give me] time [to teach the people how to not sin against you, so that]

32.32b You might forgive them [for making a golden calf], and

32.32c Blot out [the judgment for] the sin [of idolatry that] is written against them] in your spiritual book, and

32.34a Jehovah said, Go now, then, and lead the people that belong to you [in the right path], so that

32.34b On the day that I have told you [about,

32.34c When] I visit [Israel] from above, to search out [the sins that the people hide behind their] personalities,

32.34d [The male Adam], the angel [of the covenant that I made with Israel], shall have gone [forth to cover their inclination to do evil], and

Sowing & Reaping

32.35a Jehovah plagued the people because

32.35b They married [Satan], the female power [that] made [them strong enough to influence] Aaron to make

32.35c A [golden] calf [for them], and

32.26a Moses stood up in the doorway [between the mortal and the immortal worlds], where [Satan, the female] military power [that married Abel had entered into the people], and said,

Priests Challenged

32.26b The Shekinah and Jehovah are with me, all you sons of Levi, [so]

32.26c Depart from your [spiritual] adultery [with Pharaoh, before Jehovah's Sowing & Reaping Judgment falls upon you], and [then]

Mortal Men Challenged

32.27a Moses said to the mortal men [who were adulterously attached to Pharaoh],

32.27b Thus says Jehovah, the God of Israel,

32.27c I am bringing [Righteous Adam, my] military power [from [the immortal side of] the doorway, into the [spiritual universe that your male calf] mind [rolled out on the mortal side of] the doorway, [and]

32.27d His drawn sword is going to slay [the male calf mind that the female power made from Abel], your [spiritual] generative part, and

32.27e [He is going to sever] Cain, Abel's] brother, [the conscious part of] the Evil Inclination which is in every mortal man, [from Leviathan], the companion [of Satan, the unconscious part of the Evil Inclination], which is in every mortal man, and

32.28b The mortal men [called upon Pharaoh to save them, but he did not answer], and

Seized & Slain

32.28a The wisdom of [Pharaoh], the third [degree of] the unholy spiritual power [within] the children of Levi who [abandoned their adulterous relationship with Pharaoh] when Moses told them to, fell down that day, [because]

Female Power Burned

32.19a It came to pass [that], as Moses approached [the people who are Jehovah's] armies, and

32.19b Saw the spiritual activity of the [male] calf [mind that Satan, the Serpent's female] military power, [had formed within the people who were Moses'] mate, Elohim,

32.20a [The Spirit within Righteous Adam, the male] mind [of Moses, Jehovah's]mate, seized the [male] calf [mind that Satan, the female power], had made, and

32.20b The fiery stream [of the Shekinah within Moses], burnt [the male calf mind that Cain, the animal side of the mixed multitude, had sacrificed Abel to make, and

32.20c The Shekinah's fiery stream] crushed [the male calf mind, and

32.20d The five male Rings of the female Adam] separated from [Pharaoh, and

Seed & Water

32.20e Moses] spread the [royal female] seed of [the Shekinah] upon [the earthen] personalities of [the Levite priests of] Israel, His mate, and

32.20f Gave [their earthen] bodies [the Water of Life], to drink, [and]

Jehovah Is God

32.29a Moses, the son of [Righteous Adam], told [the people of Israel, his] widowed wife,

32.29b [That Jehovah] would, indeed, bless the mortal men of [Israel with a spiritual male child, which would make them] the relatives [of God], and that

32.29c In that day, [the Shekinah] would, fill [the people of Israel] with Living Water, and that,

32.29d [Righteous Adam] would give [the people of Israel] the [female reproductive] seed [of the Shekinah from the world] above, [which is the foundation out of which] Jehovah's male mind [springs].

Chapter 33

[538.2.C]

33.12 [And] Jehovah, I Am [and] Jah, [appearing through] Jehovah, said [to] Moses, [I Am is] appearing [together with me], Jehovah, [so that my] kind judgment can bring forth [within you, Moses], the ability to direct your thoughts towards me, Jehovah, [so that I], Jehovah, can assemble together [with] I Am [within you, which will enable you to show] unconditional kindness [to] this people, without regard to merit, because

[I], Jehovah, have appointed [these people] to ascend with me; but you, [Moses], are instructing [the ones] who [I], Jehovah, have appointed [to ascend, with] Satan's judgment,

33.13 [So], if you pray at this time, [Moses], unconditional kindness, without regard to merit, will appear [within you, as well as] I Am's merciful judgment [which imparts] Wisdom [and], at that time, Adonay [within you, Moses], will demonstrate my lifestyle [through you, and] you will instruct [the people how] to recognize me, [and the people] will acquire unconditional kindness, without regard to merit, [as well as spiritual] Wisdom,

33.14 [And] Jehovah, I Am [and] Jah, said [to Moses, Adam], my personality, will go [with you, and] Jehovah will lie down [with] Adonay [within you, Moses, and] you will belong to [them],

33.15 [But], Jehovah, I Am [and] Jah, [appearing through] Jehovah, said to [Adam], the one near to them, If [Adam], I Am's personality [appearing in Moses], does not carry Moses up, we will carry Moses up,

33.16 [And, in that event], Elohim, [the strength of] Jehovah's household, shall acquire [you, Moses, and shall execute] Jehovah's kind judgment [upon you, and], then, the unconditional kindness, without regard to merit, [and] the

Wisdom [that is with] I Am, shall appear [in] Adonay [within you, Moses, which is] I Am's merciful judgment, [and] Adonay [within you, Moses, and]

Jehovah shall stabilize the people, [and] I Am [within you, Moses], shall carry your people up, [and] Jehovah's kind judgment shall separate the completed spirit [of] the people that [are] above [the fiery serpent from their carnal mind], the personality of the earth,

33.17 [And] Jehovah, I Am [and] Jah, [appearing through] Jehovah, said to Moses, we agree to accomplish [this] matter that you have asked [us to do] for [you, because, we], the Household of Wisdom, are familiar with the household of your nature, [and have, therefore, granted you] unconditional kindness, without regard to merit,

33.18 [And] Jehovah, I Am [and] Jah, [appearing through Adam's] Mother, [the personification of Understanding], said [to Moses, Adonay] will now appear [with] Jehovah's kind judgment,

33.19 [And] Jehovah, I Am [and] Jah, [appearing through Adam's] Mother, the personality [from] above [that imparts] understanding, said [to Moses], All my goodness and welfare comes down from [I Am], so that [you, Moses, Adam's] widowed personality, can grant our unmerited favor [to] whichever [widowed] personalities you [choose to be] gracious to, [and] Jehovah will show mercy to [those widowed personalities by] addressing [them as if they had] Jehovah's nature, so that [El Chay, the male of] Jehovah's [household], can cross over [into the people, and join with Adonay],

33.20 [And] Jehovah, I Am [and] Jah, [appearing through Adam's Mother, the personification of Understanding], said [to Moses], Leviathan [is] nailed [to the fiery] serpent [within the people, Moses, so Cain will try to kill them when] she sees [that they have become] our widowed personalities, but, when Adam's Father, [the personification of Wisdom], and [Adam's] Mother, [the personification of] Understanding, appear [in the people, Abel] will revive [and overturn] Cain,

33.21 [And] Jehovah, I Am [and] Jah [appearing through] Jehovah, said [to Moses], Look, Jehovah is standing above [Adonay], the rock [within you, Moses], the location [where] we [appear],

33.22 [And] while Jehovah was intertwined [with I Am], it came to pass [that El Chay, the male of] Jehovah's household, crossed over [into the people, because of] Jehovah's kind judgment, [and

El Chay, the male of] Jehovah's household, turned towards Adonay], the mother [of the world below, within the people, and El Chay, the male of Jehovah's household], pierced [Abel], the palm of [Leviathan, the Dragon's] hand, [from] above, [and Abel within Moses overturned Cain, and] covered [her],

33.23 [And this is how] Jehovah [and Adam's] Mother, [the personification of Understanding], turned back [Leviathan, the Dragon's] hand, and Jehovah appeared [in] the western [world, and, at that time, Adam's] Father, the personification [of Wisdom], was revealed to Cain.

THE BOOK OF

EZEKIEL

Chapter 1

[430.8]

Adam Resurrected In Spiritual Judah[R]

R Ez 9:1

1.01a Now, it came to pass that [Satan], the teeth of the [primordial Serpent's] timeline, was in the center of his heart, but [Elijah], I [Am]'s strength in the midst of the captive's [heart], was pressing downward into [Leviathan, the upper tooth of the primordial Serpent's timeline, who] was braided together with the fiery serpent, the [lower] tooth of the [primordial Serpent's timeline], and

[The Spirit of Elijah] freed [the human spirit][R] from Satan, the tooth [of the primordial Serpent], which is the unconscious part of [the mortal] mind, that is in the [lower] window [of creation],

R Gen 22:13a (AT)

1.01b And [Michael], the river from long ago, [who is] higher than [Elijah], engraved [Adam with Elohim's nature], and [the Fortified Adam],[R] Elohim's reflection, appeared,

R Ez 1:20b (AT)

1.02a And [Adam, Elohim's] timeline, restored [the emotional animal in] the center of the heart of Jehoiachin, the king,[76] who was married to [the Lord] with his whole heart,[77] [but] who died [when Satan, the tooth of the primordial Serpent], captured him,

Adam Resurrected In Ezekiel

1.03a And it came to pass that [Elijah], Jehovah's Word, appeared to Ezekiel, the son of Buzi, a priest of the land of the Chaldeans,

1.03b And [Elijah], the hand of [Michael], the river from long ago, joined [Adam, who is in] the upper [part of Ezekiel's heart], to Jehovah,

1.04a And a wonderful sight, [the Fortified Adam] came rushing out from the eternal world like a spiritual storm, and seized Ezekiel's [personality, and restored] his spiritual sight,

1.04b And a great, fiery eagle[78] in a cloud of brilliant energy [appeared in Ezekiel's throat] and orbited the visible world [which is a reflection of his heart],**R**

R Eccl 3:11
Ez 1:18 (AT)

1.04c And hedged**R** Satan, the tooth of [the primordial Serpent], about with fire, and bisected [the fiery serpent and

---

[76] ***Jehoiachin*** typifies the Fortified Adam, the king of Elohim's creation, resurrected in the heart (Jon 1:1 [AT]) of a mortal man. Adam is a widowed king, because Jehovah divorced him.

[77] There are seven major centers in the etheric part of the physical body. (Footnote continued – See, Appendix)

[78] The Spirit of Elijah penetrates the right side of mortal man's heart, joins with his human spirit, and resurrects Abel. The mortal Abel increases to the immortal Adam when he pierces into the left side of the heart. (Footnote continued – See, Appendix)

Leviathan, the sea serpent], and Satan, the waters of the fallen creation,[79] was widowed,

[R] Jon 2:8a (AT)

1.11a And the supernatural strength of

1.10a The eagle [entered] in[to] the personality of Ezekiel's widowed heart,

1.11b And [the Spirit of Elijah] joined himself to [Ezekiel's] widowed human spirit [who was dispersed in Satan's waters], and [the Spirit of Elijah] separated [the human spirit of Ezekiel], the widowed, mortal man, from [Satan],[R]

[R] Jon 2:6b (AT)

1.10b The [spiritual] darkness, and [Elijah's] fierce spiritual power swallowed [Satan] up,[R]

[R] Dan 7:11 (AT)
Rev 21:10, 14

1.17 And [Ezekiel], who [had] Satan's lifestyle [engraved in] his heart, died to that lifestyle, changed his direction, and proceeded [towards the lifestyle of Adam], the upper [Millstone],

1.08 Because [when] the [emotional] personalities of Adam's ox [that are] in the lower[R] part of the heart [which is ruled by Satan, emigrate to] the upper part of the heart [which is ruled by Adam's] upper [millstone, which is in the throat], they become [Adam's right and left] hands,

[R] Jon 2:9b (AT)

1.10c And [the Fortified Adam] completed [Ezekiel] as a spiritual man who was built like Adam, with Elohim's nature, and the appearance of

---

[79] ***The Serpent*** is the name of the primordial waters that flowed upward into the high window of the creation, to capture Adam's ox [emotional animal], and steal Elohim's breath. The primary concentration of Elohim's breath [spirit] is in Adam, who has Elohim's nature, and is the mind of the ox. (Footnote continued – See, Appendix)

1.11c [The Fortified Adam that] covers each [emotional personality of Adam's ox], the subconscious mind of mortal man,

1.10e [Covered Ezekiel's] emotional animal [and] sustained [his] widowed heart,

1.07a And the [Fortified Adam] corrected Leviathan,**R** the sea serpent, [the ***collective*** subconscious mind of mortal man],

R Ps 141:5 (AT)

And [the Fortified Adam corrected] the fiery serpent, [Ezekiel's ***individual*** subconscious mind],

1.11d [The daughter of Satan], the background [threads of Adam, Ezekiel's] second [spiritual] side,

1.07b [And the Fortified Adam] reformed**R** the two cursed, lower parts into a cart [80] [that carried Ezekiel's developing, spiritual man],

R 1 Ki 19:9 (AT)

1.06 And [the Fortified Adam] united the personality of the emotional animal that was in Ezekiel's heart,[81] with [Adam], the upper [millstone], because the heart of [the emotional animal] that is united [with Adam, the upper millstone that is in the throat], becomes a citizen of [Jerusalem, Jehovah's spiritual] city, [the collective subconscious mind of Adam's timeline],[82]

1.05 And a Living Beast that looked human appeared out of the midst of [Ezekiel],

R Is 6:2

---

[80] A ***spiritual horse*** is the physical body that pulls the mind [carriage], that carries the fallen personalities [coals] which have the capacity to become spiritual diamonds when their human spirit is perfected (Zech 10:3).

[81] The adoption of the personality (Gal 4:5).

[82] The Fortified Adam is the collective subconscious part of the Carnal Mind of restored humanity, and the resurrected Adam. (Footnote continued – See, Appendix)

Adam Resurrected in Elohim's Sons[R]

[R] Ez 9:2, 9

1.14 And as I looked [in the Spirit] at the Living Beasts, I saw that the heart of the household of the earth[83] was united and joined, as one [man], with [Leviathan's] spiritual city, in the etheric part[84] of the Living Beasts' physical bodies,

1.19a And [the Spirit of Elijah] proceeded to move towards the center [of Elohim's Sons],

1.20a And [Elijah's] Spirit moved over the center [Elohim's Sons], and from there [Elijah's] Spirit continued to move down upon, and alongside their center,

1.19b [And Elijah's Spirit interacted] with [the center of each of Elohim's Sons at a right angle],[R]

[R] Ex 25:20 (AT)

1.20b And supported [the center of each] one [of them], because the [human] spirit of the Living Beasts is at their center,

1.16a And [the throats of Elohim's Son] produced the image of the eagle [that protects] the visible world [that is projected from the center of their heart],

1.13a And [the eagle] dispersed himself like fiery arrows[R] shooting forth from the immortal side of the Living Beast, and the fire consumed [Leviathan] in their other, mortal side, and [the Fortified Adam] appeared in the midst of the Living Beast as a burning, pulsating flame,

[R] 1 Ki 19:09 (AT)
Ez 1:27 (AT)

---

[83] ***The primordial Serpent*** is the unformed consciousness that existed as the unclean waters [spiritual urine] in the ground floor window of creation (Gen 1:7). (Footnote continued – See, Appendix)

[84] The ***etheric double*** is personal energy that takes the form of, and stands about one inch away from, the physical body.

1.14 And [the salvaged personalities] of the Living Beast [separated from Leviathan],

1.12 [And I saw Elijah] drawing the personalities of Elohim's Sons[85] near [to Adam's] lifestyle, and [Elohim's Sons] reversed their course, and crossed over to their other, immortal side, because [Elijah], the Spirit that transforms the fiery [serpent's] lifestyle, came over to their [mortal] side,

1.09 And when the personalities of [Abel], the mortal male, crossed over to their opposite, immortal side, [Cain], the mortal woman who was intimately joined to the [primordial Serpent's] female mind [instead of Abel, Elohim's mortal, male mind], repented, and [Elohim's Sons] died to the fiery serpent's lifestyle,

1.13b And when [the Fortified Adam] illuminated [the heart of Elohim's Sons], the widowed, fiery [serpent, their subconscious mind] looked like a glowing ember;.[R]

[R] Is 6:2, 6

General Information

1.18 Now the female opinion is in awe of these [Sons of Elohim] who have soared to the center of their brow, because [the image of the world that is in] the center of the brow of these [Sons of Elohim], completes [the image of] the visible world [that] is located[R] in their heart,

[R] Eccl 3:11
Ez 1:04b

1.16b And unites it with [the center of their brow], which [union] produces a heart that is constructed in a fashion that is similar [to the center of the brow],

---

[85] At this point the prophesy is no longer for Ezekiel alone, but for the company of mortal men called to the same experience. ***Mortal man*** is a translation of Strong's #376, translated, ***every one***, in the King James translation, and ***mortal woman*** is a translation of Strong's #802, translated, ***one***, in the King James translation.

So the heart center [that is united with the center of the brow], looks like an energy center in the middle of an energy center,

1.21 And [Michael, Elohim's] hand, engraved [Adam's] widowed household with the eagle's nature,

And [Michael, Elohim's] hand, nailed [Elohim's] widowed household, which had the eagle's nature, to Adam, the door to the waters of the visible world,

And [Michael, Elohim's] hand, nailed Satan's spiritual household to Elohim, the Spirit that hedges [Satan] in [the lower] window,

And [Michael, Elohim's] hand, nailed the ox in the visible world, to Adam, the door to the waters in the window above the earth,

So, the ox [was nailed] to the [upper] window [where Adam is],

But [Michael, Elohim's] hand, nailed [Leviathan], the serpentine fish that was [joined to] the ox, to the household of the fish,

And [Michael, Elohim's] hand, nailed [Satan], the widowed waters [to Elohim, who] engraved [her with the] eagle's [nature],

1.27 And, so, [after Michael, Elohim's hand,] hedged in [Satan], the widowed waters, which are the [primordial Serpent's] teeth, I saw [the Spirit of Elijah] orbiting around [Adam], the mind that is above, and [the Spirit of Elijah was directing his] fiery [arrows][R] toward the mind that is in the lower [part of their heart],

And the eagle appeared in the visible spiritual world in the upper [part of their heart],

[R] Dan 7:19 (AT)

1.23 And [Adam's] widowed male [spirit that is] underneath, was born a second [time in Elohim's] household,

1.25b And [Adam], the widowed head of the visible world [that is in] the upper part of [their heart], stood up,

1.26b And [the Fortified Adam, Elohim's] male mind, who is the widowed head [of] the [whole] visible world, appeared in the upper window,

1.25c And [when the fiery serpent saw the Fortified Adam, who is Elohim's] reflection, [and Jehovah's battle] axe, [she] sank down [into the root of the Living Beasts],

1.19c And the Living Beasts ascended from [the lower part of their heart, which is] in the earth, to [the part of their heart (which is] above [the earth],

1.28a And a glittering vision of the archer[86] **R-1** in the day of righteous rain**R-2** appeared in a cloud [of energy],**R-3**

R-1 Gen 9:16 (AT)
Judg 14:11 (AT)
2 Ki 2:10, 12 (AT)
Rev 1:7, 10:1, 10:14
R-2 Hos 10:12
R-3 Gen 9:13-16

1.24b And [this] brilliant, supernatural spectacle, [was] interpenetrated with fire,

1.28b And when I, [Ezekiel], saw [Elijah's] shape appear in Jehovah's [energy] cloud,**R-1** my [fallen] personality was overthrown,**R-2**

R-1 2 Ki 2:10 (AT)
R-2 Matt 10:22 (AT)

1.22 Because, when [Adam], who is the mind of the visible, spiritual world [in the left side of heart], stretches forth and joins with [Elijah], the Captain [that speaks from] the throat center, [which is] higher [than the heart center],

---

[86] The King James translators translated Strong's #7198, ***[rain]bow***, because (Footnote continued – See, Appendix)

[Elijah], the Captain [that speaks from the center of the throat, fortifies Adam, and, the Fortified Adam, Elohim's] shape [appears in the] upper window,

And [the Fortified Adam], who is the King of the Living Beast [that occupies the whole heart center, Elohim's] reflection, and [Jehovah's] battle] axe, is terrifying[ly strong],[R]

[R] Dan 7:7 (AT)

The Household Of The Earth Called To Immortality

1.28c And I heard a voice speaking,

1.25a And [Elijah], the voice[R-1] of [Elohim], the waters above, sounded,[R-2]

[R-1] Ez 37:3,5
[R-2] Lk 2:15b (AT)
Ez 1:25a (AT)

1.26c And [the men who are in], the likeness of [the Fortified Adam, Elohim's] completed model,[R-1] appeared in mankind as the visible representation [of humanity's] higher mind,[R-2]

[R-1] Ez 1:10c (AT)
[R-2] Ez 37:7

1.24a And I heard [Elijah], the Captain [that speaks from the center of the throat], who is the voice of [Elohim, the] abundant waters, [and] the voice[R-1] of [Jehovah], the Almighty, and [I heard] the voice of their armies[R-2] [and they were] loudly calling out their disagreement [with Satan],[R-3]

[R-1] Lk 2:15b (AT)
Ez 1:25a (AT)
[R-2] Ez 37:8
[R-3] Rev 14:18 (AT)

And [the Fortified Adam], the mind of the visible, spiritual world above [the heart center], who is [Elohim's] reflection, and [Jehovah's] terrifying[ly strong][R] battle] axe,

[Put] the human spirits [of the household of the earth] in the correct moral order, and [Abel], the second [born], widowed [mortal] male, covered [Cain], his spouse, that hostile woman [who is his other, emotional] side, and [Elohim, the waters above], covered [Satan, the teeth of the primordial Serpent], who is the unconscious mind [of Cain, Abel's other, emotional] side,**[R]**

R 1 Ki 19:13 (AT)

1.26a And [Michael], the Angel in the crown center, who is [Elohim's] likeness, and [Adam, the one who] rose [from the dead,**[R]** the two being Jehovah's] completed seat, engraved [the household of the earth] with [Elohim's] nature,

R 2 Ki 2:11 (AT)

1.24c And [I heard] the sound of human spirits standing on [Satan],**[R-1]** and the [fiery serpent] in the ones who came out of [Elijah's] side,[87] sank down [into the root center], and their [fleshly] lives declined,**[R-2]**

R-1 Mal 4:3
Rom 16:20
R-2 Dan 7:25 (AT)

Chapter 9

[OLM 11 03 99]

9.05 And he said to the others of [Adam's] household [who had] understanding, Go into the unconscious part of the household [of Leviathan's] city, and circumcise the fiery serpent [who] covers [Adam], their [spiritual] eye, [and] have no pity on

---

[87] ***To come out of one's side*** is a metaphor for ***budding***, a form of asexual reproduction which consists of an outgrowth capable of developing into a new individual (Jn 19:34).

Strong's #6763, the Hebrew word translated ***rib*** in Gen 2:22, can be translated ***side***. (See, also, Jn19:34.)

9.06 [Satan and Leviathan], the Primordial Serpent's**R-1** nature in the personalities of [the mortal men of Israel, where] Adam, the spiritual virgins, and Abel [are regenerated], because [they are engaging in] spiritual sexual intercourse with the human spirits nailed to the mortal men [of Israel], my sanctuary. [So] put [yourself as] a wedge**R-2** between the ascended [fiery serpents] and Leviathan, [and] circumcise all of the ascended fiery serpents to destroy [their union with Leviathan],

[So] Adam placed himself as a wedge**R-2** between the spiritually male [personalities of] the household of the ox, [and Satan and Leviathan], that Old Serpent,**R-1** in order to [preserve] the personalities of [Elohim's] household.

R-1 Rev 12:9
R-2 Num 22:26
Judg 16:19 (AT)

Chapter 10

[795.7.C]

Jehovah And The Righteous Man

10.01 I looked and saw in the firmament, [the visible part of the Ring] that was above the head of the cherubim, the likeness of a throne[88] [formed from the spirit of the Female,[89]

---

[88] The throne is the lower grades of Understanding, the Supernal Mother. Elohim, the Hebrew word translated God, is the Supernal Mother joined to the higher grades of Ze'ir Anpin, her Son. The Throne of God is the Supernal Mother and her Son descended into the Female (Malchut) through Justice (Tiferet), the middle column. (See, Ps 47:8, Rev 3:21.)

[89] ***The Spirit of the Female (Malchu)t*** is Understanding (Binah) of the God World (Atzilut), the Supernal Mother, and the

the blue] sapphire stone, and I perceived that [the King in] this spiritual vision was [Messiah, the great] fish[90] from above, and

10.02 [Jehovah] spoke to the man wearing priestly clothing,[R-1] saying, Go and sprinkle the burning coals [with the incense[R-2] of your prayers,[R-3] and Adam, the opinion of God[91]], will enter into the [spiritual] city [called ***Jerusalem***], in the midst of you, [and] you will see [that] the cherubim, [Adam's] closed fists [which are] under [the authority of] the Rings [of the God world of Atzilut],[92] are filled up with [Jehovah's wrath];[R-4]

[R-1] Ez 9:2
[R-2] Lev 16:12-13
[R-3] Rev 8:4
[R-4] Ez 9:4-6

Femsle (Malchut) is her Daughter. The Mother revealed through the Daughter is ***the Shekinah, the Cloud of God's presence in the earth.***

[90] The letter ***nun*** appears before the Hebrew word translated ***to appear***: Joshua is the son of Nun.... This hints at Joshua's spiritual father, Moses himself, the great fish... of the sea. The ultimate personification of the great fish revealed on dry land is the final king of Israel, the Mashiach . . . (***The Alef-Beit, Jewish Thought Revealed through the Hebrew Letters***, Rabbi Yitzchak Ginsburgh, p. 217) (Jason Aronson Inc. 1995)

[91] ***Adam, the reflection of Jehovah's nature***, is revealed through the mind of mankind. ***Adam*** is female in relation to ***Ze'ir Anpin,*** the Son of Understanding, (Footnote continued – See, Appendix)

[92] ***Atzilut,*** the God World, is the highest of four spiritual worlds which are the subject of Kabbalistic investigation. ***Atzilut,*** and everything above it, may be called ***God***, and ***Beriah-Creation***, ***Yetzirah-Formation*** and ***Asiyah-Action***, the three worlds below ***Atzilut***, are ***the created worlds***.

The Son Of God Instructs The Female Adam

10.03a Now, the cherubim were standing on the right side[93] of the house when [the Shekinah], the Cloud [of the Divine Presence], went into the man [wearing the priestly clothing], and [the Shekinah] satisfied [Cain, the emotional animal[94] that is] in prison,[95] and

10.04a [Adam], Jehovah's opinion [arose within the man, and] went up above the cherub [that is] above the threshold[96] of the house, [and the Son of God],[97] the mate of [the Shekinah], the Cloud [of the Divine Presence], illuminated [Adam], Jehovah's opinion, [saying,

---

93 Traditionally, the cherubim, which are out of the Female (Malchut), who is judgment, are on the left side of the house. The cherubim being on the right side signifies the merciful judgment that appears when Understanding, the Supernal Mother, is joined to her son.

94 The outpouring of the Shekinah satisfies Cain's female emotions, and Abel's desire for spiritual doctrine.

95 The English word ***prison*** is a variation of the Hebrew word translated ***court***, which means ***enclosed place***. The Spirit that satisfies Abel, the male seed, also imprisons Cain, the female emotions. (See, also, Note **12**.) The Shekinah satisfies Cain, which calms her animal aggression, cleanses her, and then adopts her. Adoption is union with righteousness, which imprisons the animal nature (Eph 4:1).

96 The outermost edge of the man, i.e., the physical body.

97 Ze'ir Anpin, the Son of God, was descended into the Female (Malchut) with the Shekinah, his mother, and they were above the cherubim who extended from the Intelligence if the Female (Tevunah of Malchut).

10.03b Join your seed, to Abel],[98] the inner [part[99] of the emotional animal,

10.04b That is] in prison, which will fulfill [Jehovah's] promise [to Abraham, that he would have a son],[R] and

[R] Gen 15:4

10.05 [When the whole Adam], the voice of Almighty God spoke,[100] [the animal soul], the garment[101] of the cherubim, heard him as far away as the outer wall of the prison, and obeyed his voice, and

Adam, The Mind Of God

10.06 It came to pass that, when [the man wearing the priestly garment sprinkled the incense, the Son of God] commanded [Adam] saying, Seize [Abel], your mate who is joined to the swirling dust[102] that [Jehovah], the fire between

---

[98] The Son of God joined the resurrected Abel, Adam's renewed, virile male seed, which is capable of overcoming Cain and producing a male child, within the man clothed with righteousness.

[99] There is only one mind in mankind, but that mind vacillates between two states, righteous and unrighteous. The mind of mankind is called the Carnal Mind in its unrighteous state, and the Mind of God, in its righteous state. The human spirit is the foundation, or the inner part of the mind. The Carnal Mind is the human spirit dressed in the animal soul, and the Mind of God is the human spirit dressed in the Neshamah, the spiritual, intellectual soul of God (Eph 4:23).

[100] ***God Almighty*** is a translation of ***El Shaday***, the Name of God associated with Yesod, the Ring that delivers the seed of life to the Female (Malchut), who, in turn, delivers it to humanity below.

[101] The animal soul of fallen Adam is the garment of the Cherubim. (See, also, Verse 19.)

[102] ***Swirling dust*** is an alternate translation of Strong's #1534, translated ***wheels*** in the King James version of the Scripture, and ***Rings*** is the alternate translation of this ***Alternate Translation version***.

the cherubim,[103] stirred up within the man wearing priestly garments, and

[Adam] went in[to the Rings of the spiritual city within the man] and stood next to [Abel, who was lying under Cain, he Serpent's household, and]

10.07 [The Son of God] stretched forth between the cherubim [of the God world of Atzilut] and seized[104] the fire[105] from [the altar] between the cherubim, and placed [the fire upon Abel], the cherub[106] [within] the man clothed with priestly garments, and [Elohim's fiery judgment] lifted [Abel above Cain and the powers that bound him, and Abel] escaped from [Cain's grasp, and]

10.08 The structure of the mind of mankind, which is [righteous when it is] under the [authority of] the cherubim, appeared in the borders of [the soul of the man wearing priestly garments], and

The Rings

10.09 When I looked at the four Rings [of the God world of Atzilut which were above] the cherubim, I saw that one Ring [was] within the other Ring, and one cherub [was] by the other cherub, [and that] the [cherubim] were united with [the Rings of

---

[103] ***Jehovah*** is the Name of God associated with the Ring, Understanding, whose attribute is fire (Ex 25:22).

[104] The Son of God joined to the fire, which is Understanding, is Elohim (Deut 4:24).

[105] The English word ***took***, which appears twice in Verse 6 of the King James Version, is translated from two different Hebrew words. Strong's #3947 can be translated ***to seize***, and Strong's #5375 can be translated ***to carry away***, or ***to escape***.

[106] ***A cherub***, as the term is used in Ez 10, ***is the female seed***. The cherub of Verse 7 is Abel, who is empowered to resist and overcome Cain through Elohim's fiery judgment.

the God world of Atzilut], and that the Rings appeared to be [brown], the color of a Topaz,[107] and

10.10 As for the shape of the four Rings, they looked like one [Ring] in the midst of another Ring, and

10.11 When they perambulated,[108] they perambulated upon all four sides,[109] and they did not rotate on their axes[110] as they perambulated [but] they perambulated after the unconscious part of [the mind of the man who their spiritual]

---

[107] The four Rings of verse 9 are Understanding (Binah), Harsh Judgment (Gevurah), Justice (Tiferet) and the Female (Malchut):

Blue and yellow = green + red = **BROWN**. The Female (blue) and Understanding (yellow) = Justice Y e l l o w (green) + Harsh Judgment (red) = **BROWN**.

Topaz represents Understanding and Harsh Judgment (Gevurah) blended with Justice (Tiferet) and descended into the Female (Malchut), i.e., ***Justice in the midst of the Female***.

(Cordovero, Moshe. ***Pardes Rimonim, Orchard of Pomegranates***, Part 10: The Tenth Treatise is called "On Colors," Chaps. 2-4, pp.38-49. Providence University, 2010.)

[108] The four-faced creature moved in the spiritual worlds in a manner like unto a man walking on the earth, but the creature had no legs, so we say, ***perambulate***, rather than ***walk***.

[109] All four grades of soul were in motion when the creature moved. One face, the face of mankind, was always the predominant face.

[110] The personalities did not take turns being the primary personality. One face, the face of mankind, was always the predominant face.

head was appearing in,[111] [and that man] did not rotate [on his axis[112] when] he perambulated, and

Bending Space-Time

10.12 [Understanding], the [third of the three upper] Rings [of the God world of Atzilut], the fourth [grade of soul, which is the Spirit of Life], completed the widowed [Lamb,[113] and] the male mind of the whole [Adam],[114] bent[115] the landscape[116] [that] borders [the Lamb and the female cherub, his bride,[117]

10.13 As for the Rings, I heard the one that they belong to calling out through a window to [the awakened Abel], the swirling dust, [saying, Return],[R] and the three upper] Rings [of

---

111 All four personalities focused on recognizing their spiritual leader in a man who might lead them according to the ways of God.

112 The man represented by the four personalities who does not change, but is consistent in his service to God, to lead Israel to the region on the other side of Jordan, from the death of this world to eternal life in the world to come.

113 The regenerated female Adam is ***the Lamb of God***, called ***Righteous Adam*** in the New Testament. ***Regenerated*** means that all four grades of Adam's soul, the first (the personality) through the fourth, the Spirit of Life, have been restored.

114 ***The whole Adam*** includes the male Adam of the World of God's power(Azilut) and the female Adam of the World of Creation (Beryiah), the Tree of Life which is rooted in humanity.

115 Altered space-time.

116 The visible world consisting of the four grades of soul, the personality through the Spirit of Life.

117 The Lamb becomes the continual burnt offering when he marries the flaming female Cherub (Ex 29:38, 42; Gen 3:24).

the God world of Atzilut] surrounded [the whole living creature], and

R Song 6:13

10.14 The widowed unity**[118]** had four personalities: The first personality was [the female seed of Intelligence (Tevunah)], the cherub [that appeared in the upper] window [of creation]; the second personality was [Cain], the [emotional] personality of fallen humanity; the third personality was the personality of [Abel, Jehovah's breath, that became] a lion**R** [in the soul realm]; and the fourth personality was the eagle, [which is Chayyah, the 4th grade of soul, the Spirit of Life], and

R 2 Sam 23:20

The Living Creature

10.15 [When] the cherubim rose up, [I thought], this is the living creature that I saw [in the Spirit] by the ancient river, [the soul that flows out of Eden],**R** and

R Dan 8:3 (AT)

10.16 [Wherever] the cherubim went, the Rings [of the God world of Atzilut] went also, [and] the cherubim lifted up [the Lamb, their] mate, high [above] the activity of the[ir] earthen borders; and the Rings [of the God world of Atzilut] did

---

[118] The unified four grades of soul, Personality (Nefesh), breath (Ruach), spiritual intellectual soul (Neshamah) and Spirit of Life (Chayyah) of the New Man, called ***the Lamb*** and ***Righteous Adam*** in the New Testament.

not turn on their axes,[119] [or] gather [together] near [to one] side,[120] and

10.17a When [the Lamb] stood up, [the female soul, his] mate, stood up [also], and

10.19 The cherubim lifted up [the Lamb, their] mate, [and the animal soul], their garment, and they rose up from [the World of Action (Asiyah)], the spiritual earth, and [the female Adam], the entrance way to the house, [who is also] an opening to the eternal [world],**R** went out[121] and stood near the Rings [of the God world of Atzilut], and [the male Adam], the opinion of Jehovah, the God of Israel, overshadowed [the animal mind] from above, and

R 1 Tim 2:5

10.18 [The Crown], the infinite point, stood above the cherubim, [when Adam], Jehovah's opinion, departed from the entrance**R** to [Jehovah's] house, and

R Ez 44:17, 19

10.17b [The male Adam and the Crown of the God world of Atzilut, the infinite point], completed the living creature, and

10.20 This was the living creature that I saw under the God of Israel by the river [that flowed out from Eden] long ago,**R** and I knew they were the cherubim, and

R Ez 1:1

---

[119] Justice (Tiferet) and the Female (Malchut) did not change the proportions of their blended energy.

[120] The blended energies of Understanding (Binah) and Harsh Judgment (Gevurah) remained in Justice (Tiferet) and the Female (Malchut) in the middle column.

[121] The spirit of the burnt Lamb ascended through both the female and the male cherub, and stood just under Justice (Tifere)t and the Female (Malchut), which are the male Adam. This is the union of the male and the female Adam, and the reconstruction of ***the whole Adam***.

10.21 Each of the four personalities had four widowed sides, and one of the four [personalities] was shaped like the [righteous] mind of mankind [when it is] under the authority [of the male Adam], and

10.22 Their personalities were shaped like the same personalities that I saw by the river [that flowed out from Eden] long ago, and they had the appearance of a man [who] was going towards the region across from his personality, [from the side of death to the side of life].

Chapter 11

[OLM 04 28 99]

11.22 Then Elohim, the Glorious One of Israel who is the upper part of the Cherubims, joined [himself] to their etheric bodies of supported their personalities.

Chapter 13

[1259.4.C]

13.01 The word of the Lord came to me, saying:

13.02 Son of Man, prophesy against the prophets of Israel, prophesy and say to those who prophesy out of their own hearts,

Hear the word of the Lord;

13.03 Thus says the Lord God;

"Woe unto the foolish prophets that walk with the Angel in the unconscious part of the mind, [but] have not seen anything,

13.04 "Your prophets, O Israel, are like unclean animals that have been ruined [by the angels that are under the judgment of God] in the unconscious part of the mind,"

13.17 Son of Man, set your personality against the daughters of your people who prophesy out of their own heart, and prophesy against them,

13.18 And say, this is what Jehovah Adonay says,

"Woe to [the women that] use magic to bind the mind of the souls, and cover the head of all [the sheep souls that are the Sanctuary of the Tabernacle that contains] the ark [of the covenant] to catch the sheep souls of my people that you hunt, but the sheep souls [of my people that] come to you will revive, and live;

13.19 "And will you wound handfuls of the people that I am among, [and] slay the sheep souls that should not die, and revive the sheep souls that should not revive, by lying to my people that believe your lies, for pieces of barley bread?"

13.20 Wherefore, this is what Jehovah Adonay says,

"Since I am against your magical bracelets by which you have wounded the sheep souls that are there [listening to what you say, which] makes the sheep souls mature [prematurely], I will tear away your power to mature the sheep souls [prematurely], and send away the sheep souls that you pursue for evil purposes;

13.21 "I will also tear away your [head] covering [that covers the head of all the sheep souls that are the Sanctuary of the Tabernacle that contains the ark of the covenant], and deliver my people who are under your power, and you shall not have any more strength to pursue [the sheep souls] for evil purposes, and you shall know that I am Jehovah [who speaks through my prophets], and

13.22 "Because your lies have afflicted the heart of the righteous, who I have not afflicted, and strengthened the mind of the guilty that he should not turn away from the path [that he is following] by promising him he will live [when the Sowing & Reaping Judgment says that he will die];

13.23 "Therefore, you shall not perceive worthless divinations, nor practice divination anymore, because I will deliver my people from your strength [to prophesy lies to them], and you shall know that I am Jehovah [who speaks through my prophets]."

Chapter 19

[795.1]

19.02 And he spoke to the man wearing priestly clothing, saying, Go and sprinkle the burning coals [with the incense of prayer, and] you will enter into the [spiritual] city in the midst of yourself, and] you will see [that] the cherubim [who are] under [the authority of] the Rings [of the God world of Atzilut, Jehovah's] closed fists, are filled up with [Jehovah's wrath], and he went in,

19.03 Now, the cherubim were standing on the spiritual side of the house when the man went in, and the [glory] cloud filled the inner court, and

19.04 The splendor of Jehovah's [Spirit] went up from the cherub [who stood] above the entrance to [Jehovah's] house [within the man dressed in priestly clothing], and the house was filled with [the majestic] cloud [of Jehovah's Spirit], and the court yard, [the man's physical body], was filled with Jehovah's blazing illumination, and

19.05 When [Adam], the voice of God Almighty spoke, the borders of the cherubim as far away as the outer court, heard him and obeyed, and

19.06 It came to pass that, when he had commanded the man clothed with priestly garments, saying, Take [a censer full of burning coals of] fire from the cherubim, [the altar] in the midst of you, and in the midst of the Rings, then he went in and stood next to the Rings, and

19.08 The structure of Adam's mind appeared [in the mortal men] under the cherubims' borders, and

19.07 The mind [of the man in the priestly clothing] stretched forth [and became] a cherub [that] entered into the midst of the cherubim, and he took [incense], and put it into the fire [of the altar] in the midst of the cherubim with the clenched fists, and

19.09 When I looked, I saw four Rings by the cherubim; one Ring [was] by one cherub, and one Ring [was] by another cherub, [and] they were united, and the appearance of the Rings was the color of a Topaz, and

19.10 As for their shape, the four Rings looked like one [Ring] in the midst of a Ring, and

19.14 The widowed unity had four personalities: The first personality was [Tevunah], the cherub [from] the window [of creation]; the second personality was [the female Adam], the personality of mankind; the third personality was the personality of [Jehovah's breath that became] a lion [in the field of creation]; and the fourth personality was the eagle [that flies between spiritual worlds], and

19.11 When they perambulated, they perambulated upon all four sides; they did not rotate on their axes as they perambulated, [but] they perambulated after the unconscious part of whoever [their] head was appearing in, that did not rotate [on their axis when] they perambulated, and

19.13 As for the Rings, I heard the one that they belong to calling out to the Rings through a window, [saying, Return, and],

19.12 The whole [Adam, Jehovah's] male mind, curved back [the ascended female, animal] minds [of] the borders [of the cherubim, and Crown, Wisdom and Understanding, the head] Rings [of the God world of Atzilut], surrounded the widowed four Rings [of the World of Beriah, and completed the landscape [of that world],

Chapter 28

[910.5.C]

28.11 Indeed, Jehovah's words came to me, saying:

28.12 Son of Adam, let a strong expression of mourning for King [Adam, who] I placed, as a small stone in a narrow place, arise [in you, and] say to him: This is the word of Jehovah, your God, from [the world] above:

You were the mature blueprint sealed [with the nature of] wisdom, and [the raw material substance that I gave as your female side to extend you into the visible earth] was [fully] burnt [so that it was safe] to satisfy [the kings who were to incarnate in that material substance];

28.13 You were in the Garden of Eden, [where] you were covered by the very valuable raw material [that I gave to extend you into the visible earth, and] the sardius, the topaz, and the diamond, the beryl, the onyx, the jasper, the sapphire, the emerald, the carbuncle, and the gold ore [that signify the energies of] your Sefirot, and the [subtle] channels that connect them, [stood] steadfastly in an upright position;

28.14 You were an angelic being that was woven together with, and surrounded on all sides by the very valuable material substance [that I gave] to extend [you into the visible earth]; and I placed you [at the top of] Elohim's holy mountain, [where] you walked freely [in the midst of] the fire [that continually burnt your female side, the material substance that I gave to extend you into the visible earth, so that I could safely satisfy the kings who were to incarnate in the earth], and

28.15 You were complete and blameless from the day that you were created, [when I set you out upon] the path [from potential non-existence to incarnation], until unrighteousness was found in you,

28.17a [When, after your] image [appeared in the earth], your heart was corrupted, [and you became] arrogant because of the splendor of your appearance; and

28.16a You, the angelic being [that] I wove together with the very valuable raw material [that I gave to extend you into the visible earth, the one who I placed at the top of] the mountain of God [in an upright position, has sinned with] the multitude [formed from your female side], the [very valuable] raw material [that I gave to extend you into the visible earth, and the reptilian side of the beast formed from the raw substance that I gave to extend you into the visible earth], has pierced through [the wall that I set between you, and] satisfied you, and [now] you are pregnant, [and] the unjust [offspring of the Snake, the male side of the beast formed from the raw material I gave to extend you into the visible earth, are] in the midst of you, [rather than]

28.17b [My sons], the kings [who] look like [you, who I gave to rule over the multitude formed from the material substance that extends you into the lower worlds], have been cast down [under the authority of] the earth[en] personalities of

28.16b [The multitude formed from the material substance that I gave to extend you into the visible earth, and they have fallen under the chaotic] disorder [of the female reptilian power];

28.18 [Indeed], the evil deeds [you have perpetrated against] the multitude [formed from the material substance I gave to extend you into the visible earth, prove that you are pregnant with] the unjust [offspring of the Snake, rather than] the [just kings who are] consecrated [to me, and that the reptilian side of the multitude formed from] the material substance [I gave to extend you into the visible earth], has pierced through [the wall that I set to separate you from your female side];

Therefore I will send forth a fire into the middle [brain of the people formed from the raw material I gave to extend you into the visible earth], to consume [the knowledge that I placed there for them], and I will bring [them into] the visible World [of Action, where] they will appear [as the beasts that are formed from] the ashes on the surface of the earth, and

28.19 All [the kings who are destined to look like you, that are incarnate] among the people [who are formed from the material substance I gave to extend you into the visible earth, who] can recognize you [from behind the animal body that covers you], will be appalled at [your present state, and] alarmed at how long it has been [since you fell from your state of] potential nonexistence.

Chapter 32

[313.18]
32.02 The Serpent made Adam's widowed spirit into her homosexual harlot,**[R-1]** and became the foundation in the midst of that proud family**[R-2]** of mortal men who do not know Jehovah,**[R-3]** and the spiritual world was darkened, and now Satan is ruling over the Woman, and the fiery serpent exercises authority over her.

[R-1] Job 41:5,13 (AT)
Pro 26:11 (AT)
Eccl 12:3 (AT)
Dan 8:6-7 (AT)
Joel 3:3 (AT)
Zeph 3:4a (AT)
Rev 17:1
[R-2] Zeph 2:5 (AT)
[R-3] 2 Pet 2:4 (AT)
Judg 1:6

Chapter 37

[853.3]
37.01 The spirit of Jehovah that was above joined itself to me, and we went out into the valley [created by] the bisection of Justice [within me], and it was full of [spiritual] bones, and

37.02 I crossed over into the world above, and there they were, the circles [within] the circles; and the personality from above was in the valley, and there they were, the dying embers [of the House of Israel, and their] souls were dried up,

37.03 And [the personality from the world above] said to me, Son of mankind, can these bones live? And I answered, Adonai Jehovah, you know,

37.04 And he said to me again, Speak with authority to these bones, and say to them, Oh you bones whose souls are dried up, hear the word of Jehovah,

37.05 Thus says Jehovah Elohim to these bones, Look, I will cause [my] Spirit to enter into you, and you shall live, and

37.06 I will give you tendons from the world above, and they will raise you up to the world above, and [Messiah], the skin that covers [Adam, my] male organ, shall cover you from above, and he shall give you [my] Spirit, and you shall live, and you shall know that Adonay is Jehovah.

37.07 So I spoke with authority as I was commanded, and it came to pass that, as I spoke with authority in a loud voice, there was a vibration, and [Messiah's] bone approached the bones [in the valley in the midst of me, and Messiah's] bone [joined to the male Judge who had ascended from the bones in the valley in the midst of me to the middle column], and

37.08 I looked and there it was, [Messiah, the skin of [Adam, Jehovah's] male organ, [Adam's] upper part from above, covered [the regenerating Righteous Adam in Ezekiel, but Adam's bones within Ezekiel] could not rise up [and join with Adam's upper part], because the tendon [that binds the bones below to the head above to form one whole Adam], were lacking breath, and

37.09 He said to me, Speak with authority to [the Malchus], the spirit [of the bones above, and] speak with authority, son of mankind, and say to [the Malchus], the spirit [of the bones below], Thus says Adonay Jehovah, [Let] the four spirits [of the ears, nose and mouth of Primordial Adam], enter into [them, and let the breath of the eyes, which is] the spirit [of life], breathe upon these slain [bones in the valley in the midst of me], that they may live;

37.10 So I spoke with authority as [Adam, the personality from the world above] commanded me, and the Spirit of Life came into [the bones] of the many dying embers [in the valley, and] a great army of them stood up [in the world] above the carnal mind,

37.11 Then [the personality from the world above] said to me, Son of mankind, these [sons of God who] are the whole House of Israel, are saying, Look, our bones have been divided from [the Israel above] that we belong to, [and] our hope/expectation of [being rejoined to that world] is destroyed, [because] these bones are withered,

37.12 [So], speak with authority [and] say to them, Thus says Adonai Jehovah, Look, Adonay will plough your sepulchers [to reveal the sin within you, and Adam], your mate, will ascend out of [the ploughed] sepulchers to set the people upright, and bring you into the land of Israel,

37.13 And you shall know that Adonay Jehovah ploughed your sepulchers [to expose your sins, so that Adam, your] mate, [who is your other] self, could ascend [out of] the sepulchers of my people,

37.14 I shall put my Spirit in you, and you shall live, [and] I shall place you in the land above, and you shall know that Adonay Jehovah said that he would do it, and he did it, says Jehovah.

Chapter 38

[966.13.C]

38.01 And the Word [of God], came [into existence], and Jehovah said to me:

38.02 "Son of mankind, direct your personality towards Georgia, Southern Russia, Northeastern Turkey, Armenia, Northern Iran, and the Grand Principality of Moscow,* [of] the territory of Japheth,[R]

[R] Gen 6:10

* The Ashkenazi Jews.

38.03a And say, " 'Thus says Adonai Jehovah, to the Grand Principality of Moscow, and to Georgia* [of] the territory of Japheth,

Israelite Souls Incarnate In Japheth

38.04 'I will lock your jaw [to stop you from speaking self-destructive words], and I will bring [the souls of the people of Israel that are with] you, my vehicle [in the earth], out [from captivity], skipping and leaping [and praising God],[R-1] all of [them] clothed with perfection, a great assembly protected against the judgment of the scaly hide of the crocodile [R-2] [that] overlaid [Adam] and cut away [Abel, Adam's intellectual root system]

[R-1] Acts 3:8
[R-2] Deut 19:21

38.05 'In Persia, Ethiopia and Libya, [who are] with[you, [and] they will all be protected from [the judgment of] the scaly hide of the crocodile, [that overlaid Adam, and cut away Abel, Adam's intellectual root system],

38.06 '[In] Ukraine, and [in] all the troops of the house of Armenia, [and in] all the troops of the far North Quarter of [Iran, and] the many people with them,

38.03b '[So], be aware!

Salvation For Japheth

38.07 'A whole company [of] upright [spiritual souls][R] are assembled above, preparing [to enter the material bodies that] belong to you, so guard [the earthen souls that] belong to you, [because]

[R] Heb 6:20

38.08a 'You shall be visited after many days, and, at the end of the age, [the upright spiritual souls assembled above] shall come forth and enter into many of the material bodies of the people of Israel who have experienced continual drought since [Moses] came down from the mountain [in Egypt],[R-1] who are defeated by [Satan, Jehovah's] sword, [R-2] [the enforcer of His Righteous Sowing & Reaping Judgment, and the tribes [of Israel] shall be gathered together with

[R-1] Ex 32:14
[R-2] Ps 17:13

38.09a 'The material bodies [of Japheth] that are already in existence, [and be] clothed [by them], and

38.08b '[Messiah, Israel's male relative, shall descend through] the clouds,[R-1] [that cover the top of Mount Sinai, and marry] [R-2] all [of them, and] they shall dwell safely [until]

[R-1] Vs 8
Matt 24:30
1 Thes 4:17
Rev 1:7
[R-2] Rev 21:2, 9
Rev 22:17

Japheth Warned Of Attack

38.09b '[Ashkenazi Communism] arises [like] a devastating storm upon [the world], and [upon] all of your troops, and the many people who are with you; ' "

38.10 [Wherefore], thus says Adonai Jehovah, "It shall come to pass that, at the same time [that the tribes of Israel dwell safely], an evil motive [from Satan, the unconscious part of the carnal mind of Ashkenaz, the second son of Gomer], shall arise to create an incident," and

38.11 He will say, "I shall ascend above [Adam from above, the husband of] the unrestricted souls [of the people of Israel that are incarnate in] the material bodies [of Japheth, and]

"I shall go to all [those Israelites who] are resting safely [because the emotional souls of their heart center are] married [to Adam who is above, but Abel, their intellectual soul, the root system of Adam from above within them], is not married to [him, and

"Leviathan], the wall [that stands between Abel, the intellectual root system of Adam in] the unconscious part of their mind, and Adam from above [still exists], and the door [R-1] [to the world below that] belongs to [fallen Adam], is not bolted [against fallen Adam rising [R-2] within them]," and

[R-1] Gen 4:7
[R-2] Gen 9:20-21

The Reason For The Attack

38.12 "[This the reason why Ashkenaz] will attack the [Japhethite] villages, to turn the people [of Israel, who Adam from above] gathered together out of the nations, back to [Leviathan, the subconscious part of the Carnal] Mind [of Adam below, who is] against [Adam from] above, [the male relative of the people of Israel,

"To forcibly extract the Israelite souls from the material bodies of [the people of] Japheth, who they consider to be] cattle, [by corrupting their morals and sexual behavior, in particular, through social engineering, for which sins] the [spiritual] cities [that belong to Adam, who is] above, [the one who] marries the creatures [in order to save them], will be destroyed, and

38.13 [The people of the Ashkenazi] walled villages shall say to [the Israelite souls that] are gathered together with [the material bodies of Japheth],

"You are robbing [us of] the company [of people by which] we do [our Father's] business [R-1] [in the World of Action, by] taking away [our claim] to be [the exclusive] interpreters [of God's holy Law, [R-2] and the only conduits of] the salvation [that are available through it, and

"The Christian claim to that authority is converting many Israelite souls, which] is destroying our villages, [which] is forcing [us] to seize [the Israelite souls that are incarnate in Japheth], and violently strip [them from their] material bodies [to prevent ourselves from being completely swallowed up by the Christian heresy];"

[R-1] Lk 2:49
[R-2] Rom 3:2

38.14a Therefore, prophesy, son of mankind, and say to the territory of Japheth, "Thus says Adonay Jehovah,

Israel To Appear in Japhethite Bodies

38.16a "In the latter days,

38.15 "All of [the righteous souls of Israel] shall come [out of] the place [where] they are hidden, in the unconscious part [of the mind of the human animals that] they are riding in, a great assemblage [of Judean souls],[R-1] leaping [and praising[R-2] God as] a mighty [Christian] army,[R-3] and

[R-1] Zech 10:3
[R-2] Acts 3:8
[R-3] Ez 37:10

Salvation For The Nations

38.16b "My people, [Israel], shall come into existence because of the material bodies [of Japheth], and they shall ascend [R-1] and clothe [their] material bodies like a cloud,[R-1] [so] that the Gentiles might know me,[R-2] [and become] morally and ceremonially clean [R-3] [through the righteous judgment [R-4] that falls when] the eyes of [Adam, from above, dwelling in] the territory of Japheth, [looks at their sins];"

R-1 1 Thes 4:17
R-2 Jer 31:34
R-3 Ez 37:23
R-4 Rom 2:5
2 Thes 1:5

38.14b In that day, my people, Israel, shall be safely married,**R-1** and the nations of the world who] do not know [me, shall see me]**R-2**

R-1 Is 62:4
R-2 Rev 1:7

38.17 Thus says Adonay Jehovah,

"You are they who I spoke about in the old days [through] the mind of [my] servants, the prophets of Israel, who, during the years [that] they prophesied, [said that] I, myself, would walk among you ,**R** and

Matt 1:23

Prophecy Of Messiah's Death & Resurrection

38.18 "It shall come to pass that, at the same time that [the people of] the territory of Japheth shall become the [material bodies of] the land of Israel," says Adonay Jehovah,

"That the passion of [Adam from above],**R-1** the Son of God, shall [take place, and] He shall rise [from the dead **R-2** in the bodies of Japheth, and

R-1 Lk 23:33
R-2 Matt 28:7

Prophecy Of Tribulation

38.19 "Adam from] above shall speak [through them, about how Jehovah] shall cause a great shaking **R-1** in the land of Israel, [but] the fiery wrath of his jealousy **R-2** shall not [destroy his people], and

Is 2:19
Deut 29:20

38.20 "The spiritual speech **R-1** of the personality [of Adam from above, and the spiritual] sperm [of Elohim]**R-2** in the unconscious part [of the mind of] the personalities of [the material bodies of Japheth], and the personalities of mankind who are above [the other parts of creation], and the [spiritual] souls in heaven, shall all cast down the bestial [souls] of the field [of creation], and all [the ungodly thoughts of] the spiritual insects that vibrate rapidly [in the unconscious part of the mind], and swarm upon [the carnal mind of] the earth[en souls], the spiritual power of the earthen Adam, and

"[Satan, who is too] spiritually high [to be judged by Michael, the archangel],[R-3] shall fall down, and [Leviathan], the whole wall [that separates Adam above from Abel, Adam's intellectual root system in the unconscious part of the mind of my people], shall collapse [into its own human footprint], and

R-1 Deut 9:4
R-2 Lk 8:11
R-3 Jude 9

Spiritual Judah To Judge Ashkenaz

38.21 "I shall call [for] a sword,[R] says Adonai Jehovah, and [that nation] shall be against, their brother who resembles them, and

R Ps 17:13
Jer 25:29

38.22 "And the many people that are with Elohim, shall pronounce sentence upon their counterparts [who] conquered [them by bringing] destroying blood diseases [upon them, and a lake of] purifying fire shall rain down upon their armies,

Ashkenaz To See Jehovah

38.23 "Which shall make [Israel] morally and ritually clean [through the judgment of sin and the correct understanding of spiritual truth,"[R] and] the many [people of Ashkenaz] shall see [me, and] they shall know that Adonai [is] Jehovah, [and] I, myself, shall be enlarged,

R Vs 14b

Chapter 39

[978.4.C]

PROPHECY TO JAPHETH

39.01 And you, son of mankind, prophecy towards the territories of Japheth and say, This is what Adonai Jehovah says,

"I am looking towards the territories of Japheth and, [in particular], the Grand Principality of Moscow, and Georgia,* [and]

* The Ashkenizi Jews

ISRAEL TO APPEAR IN JAPHETH

39.02 I will turn Israel back to one-sixth* [of the First Adam, their] starting point, [and] I will cause the remnant souls of Israel to rise up into the unconscious part of [the mind of the people of the territories of Japheth], and [the remnant souls of Israel] shall ascend into [the subconscious part of the mind of the people of the territories of Japheth], and

* For Adam "to be turned back to the starting point," means to be returned to his preincarnate state, which is unconscious, and, therefore, a form of spiritual death.

Adam's soul has six parts. 'One-sixth" of Adam's soul, then, would indicate a surviving part of the whole, that is, "a remnant."

The remnant Israelite souls incarnate as the sleeping Messiah, who awakens like a flower unfolding in a whole new personality and material body combination.

ISRAELITE SOULS WILL JUDGE JAPHETH

39.03 [The remnant souls of Israel that cross over into the mind of the people of the territories of Japheth], shall strike [into] the mind [of the people of the territories of Japheth that is] bent [towards Leviathan], the left [side of the earthen soul, and the thoughts of my] right[eous] mind, [shall enter into Leviathan], the left [side of the earthen soul of the people of the territories of Japheth, like] arrows, [and Leviathan, the wall that separates the souls of the people of the territories of Japheth from me] shall fall;[R]

[R] Lk 10:18

39.04 [Indeed, Leviathan's] armies [in all the people of the territories of Japheth] shall fall [when] the living spirit crosses over [into the remnant souls of Israel] from [the world] above, to feed [those] ravenous [spiritual souls], little birds* [that are incarnating in [the people of] the territories [of Japheth];

[R] Lk 9:55

* The ravenous little birds are the incarnating spiritual souls of the Israelites that feed on the spiritual understanding of the living Word of God.

SPIRITUAL ISRAEL WITHIN JAPHETH

39.05 [Indeed, Adam from] above, [the personality of Elohim, and Adam from below], the personality of the [Snake [R] in] the field [of creation, shall cause Leviathan, the wall that separates the souls of the people of the territories of Japheth from Jehovah], shall fall [when] Adonai [within each person] speaks its [fall into existence], says Adonai Jehovah, and

[R] Gen 3:1

THE RUSSIAN REVOLUTION PROPHESIED

39.06 I shall send a fire upon Russia [because of the remnant souls of Israel] dwelling safely within that group of humanity, and they shall know that Adonai is Jehovah, and

JEHOVAH RECOGNIZED BY THE GENTILES

39.07 I shall make my Holy Name in the midst of my people, Israel, known, and the Gentiles shall know that Adonai

Jehovah is the holy One [of] Israel [when Israel] no longer profanes my Holy Name;

THE DAY OF THE LORD

39.08 Look! The day that I told you about is coming, says Adonai Jehovah;

Spiritual Virginity Restored

39.09 [The high priest[R-1] who] lives in the [spiritual] city [of Jerusalem] shall be crucified,[R-2] and [the male child[R-4] of the high priest shall rule] with a rod [of iron,[R-5] over [2] Cain, the personality of Satan in the unconscious part of the mind of the people of the territories of Japheth, that] pierce[R-3] [into] him, and

R-1 Heb 3:1
R-2 Ps 22:16
Zech 12:10
R-3 Rev 1:7
R-4 Rev 12:5
R-5 Rev 2:27
12:5
19:15

Adam from above, the personality of Elohim], shall go forth [and] set [Cain, the personality of Satan in the unconscious part of the mind of the people of the territories of Japheth], on fire,[R] [and

R Rev 20:10

The Carnal Mind, Satan's soldiers], the military power [of the soul of the people of the territories of Japheth],

Leviathan, [the pride[R] of the people of the territories of Japheth], and

R Job 41:1,34

[Cain, the personalities of Satan in the unconscious part of the mind of the people of the territories of Japheth], the thorn [in the eye[R-1] of the people, which is Jehovah's] judgment on them, shall burn up;[R-2]

[R-1] Josh 23:13
[R-2] 2 Pet 3:12

[Indeed, Satan, the false prophet, Leviathan, the Devil and Cain, the bestial personalities of the people of the territories of Japheth], shall burn [in the lake of fire][R-1] for an indefinite number of revolutions of time,[R-2] until the virginity [R-3] of their spirit is restored;

[R-1] Rev 19:20
[R-2] Matt 25:41
[R-3] Rev 14:4

The Proper Use of Spiritual Power

39.10 You shall not lay hold of the wisdom of the Tree of the Knowledge of Good & Evil to raise yourself [above the God-appointed authority in] the field [of creation];

Neither shall you extract any part of [the wisdom of that tree to form spiritual or] military weapons, and

You shall burn [Satan, the Snake in the unconscious part of the mind of the people of the territories of Japheth], with fire, [until the Woman] separates [from her], and

[That is how] you shall steal [the Woman from the Snake], who stole [her from Adam], says Adonai Jehovah, and

[Abel, the intellectual root system of Adam, the living soul that died], shall separate from [the bones of the physical bodies of the people of the territories of Japheth], and

Satan Muzzled

39.11 It shall come to pass on that day, that

I shall give the [spiritual] Israelite [souls that are] crossing over to copulate with [the earthen souls of the people of the territories of Japheth that are] in the sea[R] [of the unconscious part of the mind of the people of the territories of Japheth], a location in [the world of] the dead, the low place [where Adam] is housed [in the unconscious part of the mind of the people of] the territories of Japheth, and

R Rev 20:13

[Those spiritual Israelite souls that] are crossing over to copulate with [the earthen souls of the people of the territories of Japheth], shall muzzle [Satan in the unconscious part of the mind of] all [the people of the territories of Japheth, who] are calling [to God] out of the conscious [part of their mind],

From that low place in [the world of the dead, the territory of Japheth, where] the whole multitude of [the people of] the territory of Japheth are in turmoil, [and] they shall bury Leviathan, [their mate in the earth], there, and

Leviathan Buried

39.12 [The people of the territories of Japheth who are consciously calling out to God], shall be burying [Leviathan, their] mate [in the earth], for an indefinite number of revolutions of time,* until the emotional souls of the house Israel are [sufficiently] purified [to produce incorruptible] physical bodies, and

* A year is a time period. Seven years is a complete cycle of time periods in the soul realm where the First Adam is burning continually, until Satan, Leviathan and Cain, the dross, are burnt off. Everything that the human spirit produced from her interaction with the Serpent is consumed and she is restored to her virginal state. Only the purified spirit remains.

The Mark of God

39.13 All the people [of the territories of Japheth who] bury [Leviathan, their mate in] the earth, shall have the opinion [of Jehovah, which is] the mark of [the Children of] the Day,[R] says Adonai Jehovah, and

R 1 Thes 5:5

Ritual Purity Preserved

39.14 [The spiritual Israelite souls that are] crossing over from above [into the earthen souls of the people of the territories of Japheth], to copulate with the emotional souls of their physical bodies, shall distinguish the mortal men who are continually burying [Leviathan, their] mate in the earth, [and the spiritual Israelite souls that are] crossing over [into the earthen souls of the people of the territories of Japheth] to copulate [with their earthen souls], shall penetrate into [Satan in the unconscious part of the mind of the people of the territories of Japheth], to examine [their intimate thoughts and motives],[R-1] until the emotional souls [of the people of the territories of Japheth who are continually burying Leviathan, their mate in the earth], are completely ritually purified, and [their physical bodies] are preserved, and

[R-1] Num 32:23
Heb 4:12

The Breath of The Bones

39.15 [When the spiritual Israelite souls that] are crossing over into the physical bodies of the people of the territories of Japheth to copulate with [their earthen souls, meet] a man who refuses to see [that his thoughts and motives are] evil, [the spiritual Israelite souls] that are examining [Satan in the unconscious part of that man's mind], shall set up [Abel, who is] buried in [the world of the dead], that low place where the multitudes of the people of the territories of Japheth are in turmoil, as an example, until [he admits that his motives are evil, and] buries [Leviathan, his mate in the earth], and

[R-1] 2 Cor 10:5
1 Chron 28:9
[R-2] Heb 10:33
[R-3] Jude 13

The Physical Body

39.16 The name of the city that is assembled for the multitude [in the territories of Japheth] that are in turmoil[R] [until]

[their emotional souls are ritually purified, and] their physical bodies [are preserved, is "Babylon"];

[R] Jas 3:16

FOOD FOR THE LITTLE BIRDS

39.17 And to you, son of mankind, thus says Adonai Jehovah, tell all [the spiritual souls], the little birds [that form] the whole Israel[ite] army [that clothes] Elohim [from] above, to come and eat the flesh of [Messiah],[R-1] [your] neighbor,[R-2] [the one who has mercy, and] drink [his blood, and] the flesh of [Righteous Adam], the great [Mediator,[R-3] shall come into existence, and] gather together with the flesh of [Adam], the whole living [soul] that belongs to him, [that] are assembled in the field of creation, and

[R-1] Jn 6:53
[R-2] Lk 10:29-30
[R-3] 1 Tim 2:5

39.18 [The great Mediator] shall eat the flesh of the tyrants of Bashan, [who] drink the blood of the princes of the earth,[R-1] [and] he shall prepare [Abel to be] a battering ram[R-2] [that] breaks up the whole domineering nature of [the First Adam],[R-3] and

[R-1] Rev 18:24
[R-2] Is 41:15
[R-3] Dan 7:3 (AT)

39.19 The [spiritual Israelite souls] shall eat the flesh of [Adam, the personality of] Elohim, until they are satisfied, and drink the blood [of the Lamb until] their flesh is filled with spiritual power, and

[R] Acts 1:8

39.20 [Adam], the upper millstone [from] above, shall fill the mortal men [of Judah, the] horse [of the Lord], from my table, and they shall battle with all the mighty men [of the territories of Japheth], as prophesied by Adonai Jehovah, and

[R-1] Dan 10:40-41 (AT)
[R-2] Zech 10:3

THE OPINION OF GOD

39.21 I shall make a formal decree [that Israel is] the mate of God[R] by giving them my opinion, [and] all the Gentiles shall see [that Israel is] the mate of God when I put the mind [of God in Israel, my] mate, and

[R] Phil 2:5

ADONAI IS JEHOVAH ELOHIM

39.22 From that day forward, the house of Israel shall know that Adonai is Jehovah Elohim, and

ISRAEL EXILED FOR THE GENTILES

39.23 [That] the house of Israel went into exile because they trespassed against [Adonai when] they had spiritual sexual intercourse [of the mind with Khnum, the goat god],[R-1] the perversion of Egypt; And] when [Khnum] penetrated the whole [Adam],[R-2] the personality of Elohim from above [within the men of Israel, Adam, the personality of Elohim from above within the men of Israel], was covered over by [Leviathan, the personality of pride, and Adam, the personality of Elohim from above within the men of Israel], was hidden[R-3] [from the presence of Jehovah Elohim], and

[R-1] Dan 8:5
[R-2] Dan 8:7
[R-3] Gen 3:8-9

39.24 [Then, Cain], the religious impurity [within the men of Israel], covered over the personality of [Abel, Adam's intellectual root system within the men of Israel, which] hid [them from Adam from above, the Name of Elohim, and] made [them] revolt [against] Jehovah Elohim;

JACOB & ISRAEL RESTORED

39.25a [But], thus says Adonai Jehovah,

39.26a [After Israel], my mate, bears his humiliation for trespassing against [me], Elohim from above,

39.27a Shall turn [Israel] back [to his starting point, which is one-sixth of Adam], the part of [my]self in the people [who] grasp hold of me,[R] and

R Col 1:27

39.26b The physical bodies [of Japheth,[R] * shall cover all of the spiritual souls of Israel, my] mate, and

R Gen 9:27

> * The correct translation of Gen 9:27 is, "…Shem shall dwell in the tents of Japheth." See, The Noah Chronicles (2nd Edition) (Sheila R. Vitale, Christ-Centered Kabbalah (2019)).

39.27b [Satan], the hateful adversary in [the unconscious part of the mind of] the physical bodies [of Japheth]

39.26c Shall not cover [Adam, the personality of Elohim from above, or] terrorize [the mortal men of Japheth in the earth below, and] they shall dwell safely, and

39.25b I shall have compassion on Jacob[R] at [that] time, and return [Israel] to [his] starting point, [and I shall stand] upright [everyone in] the whole house of Israel, [my] mate [that] I exiled, [who is] zealous [for my] holy name], and

R Mk 1:41

39.29a None [of the spiritual Israelite souls] shall be hidden, [but] they shall continue in the personalities [of the physical bodies of Japheth, which]

39.27c Shall have been morally and ceremonially cleansed, and many Gentile nations shall see me [when they look at the physical bodies of Japheth],

39.29b Because I poured out the Spirit [of judgment] upon the house of Israel, [my] mate, says Adonai Jehovah.

Chapter 40

[824.4.C]

40.01 In the 25th year that [I, (Ezekiel's) ability] to produce [a male heir] was in captivity,[R] in the beginning of the year, in the tenth month of the 14th year after the female foundation of [my (Ezekiel's) spiritual] city was wounded, [Elohim], the hand of Jehovah, laid hold of me (Ezekiel), and brought me there, and

[R] Is 26:18

40.02 Elohim brought me in a vision to the land of Israel, to the structure of the city, and set me down upon a very high mountain[R] on the south side, and

[R] Lk 4:5, 9

40.03 I saw there [where Elohim] brought me, a man [who] appeared to be mortal, [but] he was the color of amber,[122] [and] he stood in the gate of the house [with] a linen cord and a balance scale in his hand, and

40.04 The man [who appeared to be] mortal, [but was the color of amber], said to me, Son of Adam, look with your eyes, and listen with your ears, and let your heart understand all that I brought you here to show you, so that you might declare everything that you see to the house of Israel, and

40.05 I saw a wall that surrounded the house, and the [amber-colored] man had a measuring reed in his hand, and he measured [the wall of the house, and it was] six cubits [high], and a cubit and a handbreadth [wide], and he measured [Adam], the

---

[122] Ezekiel saw the image of a man who represented the speaking silence, the voice of his higher soul (Kabbalah), or unconscious mind of God. The voice of the higher soul can only be heard when the voice of the outer man is silent.

stalk of wheat [who is the lower cherub of] the ark of the temple [within Ezekiel, who was sitting on (married to) the wall, and

Adam, the stalk of wheat within Ezekiel, who was sitting on (married to) the wall] was united with the high [cherub], and [Adam], the stalk of wheat [within Ezekiel, who was sitting on (married to) the wall], was [also] united [with Elijah's seed, the force within Ezekiel which was influencing him towards Elijah, the door to the eternal world], and

[824.3]
40.06 Then [Elijah], the personality [that reveals Ancient Adam[123] who] is leading [mankind] to [the immortality of] the eternal world, came to see [if Abel], the Receptionist [to the world above who] resembles [Adam, was ready] to be united with the Female [of the world above, so

Elijah] measured the growth of [Abel], the Receptionist [who] resembles [Adam], the door [to the eternal world, and Abel [who] resembles [Adam], was caught up[R] [when Elijah] measured[124] him, [and Abel], the Receptionist [in the world below, who is] the foot of [the whole] Adam, was united with the Female [of the world] above, and ascended; and

[R] 1 Thes 4:17

---

[123] The two words which form the name ***Adam Kadmon*** allude to its paradoxical nature of being, on the one hand, a created being – ***Adam*** – while on the other hand, a manifestation of primordial Divinity – ***Kadmon.***

[124] According to Einstein's ***Theory of Relativity***, an object does not exist unless it is observed, and according to quantum mechanics, an object has no reality in this world, the macroscopic world, unless it can be measured. (Footnote continued – See, Appendix)

40.07 [Messiah [125] measured [the Abels], the Receptionists [who are] the outer court [of the temple, to see how far away] the foot[126] of the whole Adam, [the gate of the temple], was from awakening [the people who are] the rooms [of the temple, and

Messiah] measured the growth of each room [of the temple to see if] the five Rings[127] [of the lower Adam had emerged in the midst [of them, and, if they had emerged, whether] they were united [to form Justice, and

Messiah] measured [Adam, the gate to the temple, to see if he was united with [Atik Yomin],[128] the long [face;[129] and

---

125 Verses 1-6 speak to the manifestation of Messiah. The following verses, 7–12, speak to Messiah's ministry to the sons of God. (Footnote continued – See, Appendix)

126 There is an Adam below and an Adam above. The two Adams, together, are called ***the whole Adam***. The Adam below is ***the foot*** of the whole Adam.

127 The five Rings of the manchild generated by Christ which are designed to be joined to the three Rings of the Malchut of the world above that descend into the (Footnote continued – See, Appendix)

128 The Malchut of the world above and the ***Crown*** of the world below are actually two aspects of one Ring, the Malchut of the world above, which is imposing the DNA of the higher world upon the world below.

129 ***The Ancient of Days (Atik Yomin)*** is the ***long face***, the personality of God that waits patiently for fallen Adam to be born again within humanity and return to a righteous relationship with him.

Arikh Anpin is the ***short face***, the impatient personality of the Son of God, who becomes angry more easily. (Footnote continued – See, Appendix)

40.08 Messiah] measured [the Abels in] the outer court,[130] [which is] the Reception [area of the world below, to see if the regenerating Adam], the gate of the house [of God[R] in the people who were the rooms of the Temple], was united with [the mind of the regenerating Adam, and

[R] 2 Sam 7:13

40.09 When Messiah] measured [the Abels in] the outer court [of the world below, he found that the people who were the rooms of the palace, were awake, and that Female, Foundation, Victory, the Fallen Mind, Justice, Harsh Judgment, Loving Kindness and Understanding], the eight Rings of [the regenerating Adam], the Ram[R] [of God, were attached], and that the two Rings, [Justice below and Arikh Anpin], were attached, [and that Abel], the outer court of [the whole Adam], the gate of the house [of the Spirit [of God was attached, and]

[R] Dan 8:4

40.10 [Messiah], the opening [to the eternal world], measured the outer lifestyle of [the people who were] the rooms [of the temple, and] he measured [Crown, Wisdom and Understanding], the three [Rings which were] on the side [of Adam, to see if they were] united with [Arikh Anpin] on the other side, [and Crown, Wisdom and Understanding], the three [Rings of Adam] on one side [and Arikh Anpin] on the other side, were united, [and the awakened people who were united with Adam were called spiritual] rams[131] [in the world below, and

---

[130] The words, [***the Abels in***], ***the outer court***, are an alternate translation which appears in verses 6 and 8, but they are translated from two different Hebrew words. (Footnote continued – See, Appendix)

[131] The sons of God are called Adam at this point, because the glorified Jesus Christ has given them his male seed which completes them. They are no longer ***either*** ish ***or*** ishah, male ***or*** female. They are now ***both*** male and female.

They are called the Sons of Man (Adam) because the whole Adam, the regenerated Righteous Adam (the Second Adam), in the

40.13 Messiah] measured [Abel], the door to the [minds of the people who were] the rooms [of the palace, to see if] the altar [could be reconstructed in them, and wherever] the five Rings [of Adam, the lower part of] the altar [were present], he measured [Abel], the door [to Adam, the gate of the temple, in the world] above, [to see if the upper part of] the altar had increased to the twenty [Rings necessary for the circumcision of the flesh[132] of Messiah, and]

40.11 [Messiah] measured the growth of [Abel], the door [to the mind of Adam], the gate [to the world above, and there were] ten Rings [on the side of Arikh Anpin], the long [face, and] thirteen Rings[133] [in the lower world, which are the 13 principles of divine mercy represented by Arikh Anpin's beard,[134] on the other side of Adam], the gate [to the temple], and

40.12 [The people who are the rooms of the temple], which were united with [Understanding, the Supernal] Mother, became the enclosed territory (body) of the personality [of Messiah], and the Rings which were united with the enclosed

---

world below, and the Lord from Heaven (the Last Adam) from the world above, are one whole man within them.

[132] ***The circumcision of the flesh*** is the esoteric way of saying that the Malchut of the world above becomes ***Atik Yomin*** above and ***Arikh Anpin*** of the world below. It is a form of spiritual cell division which results in the emergence of a new world below the existing world. (See, also, Note #134.)

[133] The 13 attributes of mercy are the ***Crown***, ***Justice***, and ***Foundation***, the middle column of the lower Adam, which is a balanced mind and life, and the nine gifts of the Spirit, plus one for Malchut, which is the whole. Jesus gave them to the lower world as a wedding present after the Malchus of the higher world passed over the threshold, married him, the Lamb of God, and he ascended on high (Eph 4:8).

[134] **Dikna**
The Beard

(Footnote continued – See, Appendix)

territory [of Messiah] on the side of the rooms [of the temple, had] six Rings on one side and six Rings on the other side.

THE BOOK OF

GENESIS

Chapter 1

[933.3.C]

The Infinite Point & Elohim

1.01 The Infinite Point created Elohim, its mate, [and] Heaven, [their Son], and [it also created] the earth,

Water In The Empty Space

1.02a But the earth[en container] was unprofitable [for so long as] it was uninhabited, and the personality [that was attached to the Nefesh grade of soul that was in] the empty space, was ignorant, and

Elohim Appears In The Empty Space

1.03a God said, Let [the ignorant personality attached to the empty space] be [en]lighten[ed], and

1.04a A morally correct light detached from

1.02b The Spirit of God, the personality of [the Supernal Mother], the waters [from] above, and vibrated over the personality [attached to the empty space, and] the waters [of the Supernal Mother poured out upon the empty space], and

1.04b Elohim appeared [in the empty space], and the light [that came] from Elohim revealed the disorder [of the personality that was attached to the empty space], and

1.03b [The ignorant personality in the empty space] was enlightened, and

Day & Night

1.05 Elohim called the enlightened [personality], ***Day***, and the ignorant [soul] he called, ***Night***, and the evening and the morning were the first day, and

A Foundation Called Heaven

1.06 God said, Let there be a foundation in the midst of the waters, and let it divide the waters [of the Spirit of God that hovered over the empty space] from the waters [that poured into the empty space], and

1.07 Elohim made a foundation that divided the waters of [the Spirit of God that poured out into the empty space], from the waters [of the Spirit of God] that were above the foundation, and

1.08 Elohim called the foundation ***Heaven***, and the evening and the morning were the second day, and

Dry Ground

1.09 God said, Let the waters under [the foundation called] ***Heaven***, be bound together [with Heaven], and [let them] stand up [together] in one place, and let the dry ground appear [to delineate the borders of the empty space], and [the waters in the empty space were bound together with Heaven, and] stood upright, and

A Roaring Lion

1.10 Elohim called the dry ground ***Earth***, and the waters [of the enlightened personality] that were braided together [with the foundation called ***Heaven***], he called ***the Roaring*** [***lion***], the west side [of mankind, who] was made in the similitude of Elohim, [the morally correct light that] detached [from the Spirit of God], and

Mankind

1.11 God said, Let the earth[en container] bring forth

The glistening green seed that increases into [six varieties of] fruit [called

The Foot of Adam], the sprout that springs forth from [the dry ground that] produces

[The whole Adam], the fruit tree that produces

The fruit of the species [called ***mankind***],

Whose seed stands in one place,

Above the earth,

[When it is] set upright, and

1.12 The earth[en container] brought forth the species of glistening green seed [that increases into six varieties of] fruit, [called

The Foot of Adam], the sprout that springs forth from [the dry ground that] produces

[The whole Adam], the fruit tree that produces

The fruit of the species [called ***mankind***],

Whose seed stands up in one place, and

Elohim, the morally correct light [that detached from God] appeared [in the earthen container], and

1.13 The evening and the morning were the third day, and

Ezekiel's Wheels

1.14 God said, Let there be luminous bodies in the foundation of Heaven, to distinguish between [***the Children Of***] ***the Day*** and [***the Children Of***] ***the Night***, and let them be for spiritual discernment, and for [calculating] the [two] times [that are] appointed [for Messiah to appear], and [to distinguish between] twenty-four hour days [and the Day of the Lord, which is 1,000] years, and

A Spiritual Building

1.15 Let [the luminous bodies] submit to [the Son of God], the foundation [of the building that connects] the earth[en container] to Heaven, and enlighten [the soul that is attached to the empty space], because it is right [thing] to do, and

Two Minds & Spiritual Children

1.16 Elohim made two, great [en]light[ened minds, the mind of God], the greater [of the two en]light[ened minds], to rule over [***the Children Of***] ***the Day***, and the lesser [of the two en]light[ened minds], to rule over and [***the Children Of***] ***the Night***; and he also made the stars, [***the Spiritual Children*** born of the mind of God and the soul attached to the earthen container], and

1.17 Elohim set [the two minds and the stars] in the foundation of Heaven to give light upon the earth[en container], and

1.18 To rule over [***the Children Of***] ***the Day*** and over and [***the Children Of***] ***the Night***, and to distinguish [the thoughts of the en]light[ened mind] from the dark [thoughts of the unenlightened mind, so that [***the Children Of***] ***the Day*** could] recognize Elohim, the morally correct light [that detached from the Spirit of God], and

1.19 The evening and the morning were the fourth day, and

The Waters Bring Forth

1.20 God said, Let the waters [in the empty space] bring forth many swarming, small animals, the living [Nefesh] soul, and birds and winged insects that fly above the earth, and [mankind], the personality of the foundation of [the building that joins the earthen container to] Heaven, and

1.21 Elohim created great sea serpents, and the whole living creature that crawls, swarms or wriggles in the waters [of the empty space, each] according to their species, and all the birds, and winged insects, [each] according to their species, and Elohim, the morally correct light appeared [in the empty space], and

1.22 God blessed them, saying, Produce fruit, and increase, and fill the waters of the seas, and let the birds and winged insects increase in the earth[en container], and

1.23 The evening and the morning were the fifth day, and

The Living Creature Set Upright

1.24 God said, Let the earth[en container] bring forth the [two sides of] the species of the living soul, the dumb beast and the reptile, according to their species, and the living thing came into existence and stood upright on the earth, and

1.25 Elohim made the species of the living creature [that God created and attached to] an earth[en container], a different species than the dumb beast and all the species of reptiles that live on the land, and Elohim, the morally correct light [that detached from the Spirit of God] appeared [in the living creature], and

1.26 God said, Let mankind be modeled after us, and be similar to us, and let them have ruling authority over the fish in the sea and the birds and winged insects in the air, and the dumb beasts of the whole earth, and all the small animals and reptiles that crawl on the ground above the earth, and

1.27 Elohim created mankind in his own image, and [mankind], the image of God, created [many members of himself in earthen containers].

Chapter 2

[385.16]
2.02 And Elohim completed the work that He had fashioned during the seventh time period, and [Elijah and the resurrected Adam] destroyed [the visible, physical world, which is] all of the work that the Serpent had formed, and the Serpent ceased to exist on the seventh day.

2.03 And the resurrected Adam proved that he was holy on the seventh day, by destroying [the body of the man who became Messiah, which represented] all of the work of the Serpent who had cut down [Righteous Adam], Elohim's work, and [then] Elijah**R-1** resurrected [Abel],**R-2** the spiritual man who [is in Jehovah's image],**R-3** [and Abel] became [the last] Adam.**R-4**

R-1 Mk 15:34-35
R-2 2 Ki 13:21
Matt 28:6-7
1 Cor 15:4
R-3 Jn 10:30
R-4 1 Cor 15:45
Rev 1:11

2.04 This is the story of Adam, Elohim's Son, who Jehovah Elohim declared would appear in the visible, spiritual world before they ever sprang forth or were seen in the Earth of humanity; and [the story of the whole, living, spiritual plant that is [supposed to be consistently] shining with Elohim's life, but is, [nevertheless], appearing, dying and reappearing in the visible, physical world on a regular schedule,

2.05 Because Elohim has not yet poured himself out from Heaven upon the beginning generation called ***heat*** or ***lust***, when Adam, who has the seeds of Elohim's Sons concealed within him, was not mature enough to bring the Earth into servitude, mold her into Jehovah's image, and incarnate in the visible, spiritual world,

2.06 And after that, Elohim's living substance rose up from underneath the Earth in a gaseous form, and Jehovah Elohim formed Adam out of the surface of the Earth, and the waters of Jehovah Elohim's [living soul] cultivated Adam, and he received consciousness, but the rest of the Earth that was not a part of Adam [the living soul, the conscious creature], was not cultivated by the waters of Jehovah Elohim's [living soul], and remained in darkness [unconscious].

2.07 And Jehovah blew Elohim, [his breath], into the enclosed place that had the potential to breathe, and Elohim exerted a great pressure upon the powdered grey rubbish of the field, and Elohim's breath fused to the rubbish, and the rubbish clave to Elohim's breath and [the powdered grey rubbish], became fertile soil [ground],[135] and this is how Elohim became [Adam], a conscious, living, creature;[136]

2.08 And Jehovah closed up the sac that he breathed the Spirit of life into, and planted [Adam] the cultivated spiritual plant, in a garden, and loaned him his spiritual authority, so that [Adam] could grow; And the name of the garden is ***Eden***, and Adam's upright, spiritual condition is called ***Elohim's imputed*** [137] (loaned) ***righteousness,***[R]

[R] Rom 11:29

2.09 And Jehovah caused Elohim, his right hand, to cover the covetous part of the ground where the whole tree that appeared to be agreeable to produce fruit [especially corn] would sprout, because the Tree of Life was in the midst of the Tree of the Knowledge of Good and Evil.[138]

2.10 And the waters[139] [of the soul that Elohim created an Jehovah made] flowed out of [Eden], the place of pleasure,

---

[135] The ***Earth*** is the dry part of the Living Beast, the part without spirit.

[136] Elohim is Jehovah's sperm. He is the ***life*** and the ***light, which*** is the product of the interaction between Elohim's Spirit and the waters (Footnote continued – See, Appendix)

[137] The difference between the imputed and imparted anointing is the restored firmament. The imputed anointing does not restore the firmament, so when Elohim's light wave recedes, there is nothing to hold the resurrected Abel above the Earth; so Abel falls down into the Earth again, and Cain captures Elohim's breath of life, absorbs his energy, and becomes the Serpent again; and Abel dies. (Footnote continued – See, Appendix)

[138] The Tree of Life and The Tree of the Knowledge of Good and Evil are Jehovah's spiritual seminal fluid. (Footnote continued – See, Appendix)

[139] [Elohim], the flood of waters, is the waters that filled the two windows of creation, gathered into the upper window only (Gen 1:9);

where [Elohim's] union with the Earth brought Adam into existence, and from there [the waters of the soul] were diffracted[140] into the heads of four visible [rivers].

2.11 And one aspect of Adam's nature is pride, but the whole circle of the [visible] Earth is transformed from that condition when [Abel] is resurrected and Adam's relationship with Elohim [is restored].

2.12 And Abel, the embryonic foundation stone of civilization, is morally good because of his relationship with Adam and Elohim, who separated him from [the Serpent], his potential to incarnate as a mortal, wild animal, instead of Elohim's immortal Son.

2.13 And another aspect of Adam's nature is the bursting forth of consciousness, which surrounds the whole dark [non-functional] earth.

2.14 And Adam walks in the female aspect of his nature when Elohim [pierces into the ocean bed of the abyss], after which Abel steps up [through Elohim to reflect his image] on the surface of the earth.

And the fourth division is the fruit.

2.15 And Elohim married [Abel and] Jehovah formed Adam in his image, and possessed him, and preserved him from lust and from falling under the penalty of death because of sin,[R-1] and the [***good***, but not yet ***perfect***][R-2] Adam protected the Garden

---

the Garden of Eden is the mind is the Fortified Adam, planted in the Earth; and Michael is the River of Life that flows out of Eden.

[140] See, ***Quantum Mechanics In Creation***, LEM Message #385, Part 5, for an explanation of diffraction grating in the creation.

from [Cain] the spiritual weed, by fastening himself securely[141] [to Jehovah].

R-1 Vs 5
R-2 Gen 1:31

2.16-17 And [after] Jehovah formed Adam, he dominated the whole Living Beast, and appeared on the positive, [east] side of Eden, and Elohim imparted into Adam's very being, the knowledge that [Abel] could marry [Elohim, the positive charge of the Living Beast], but that he could not marry the waters of [the soul, because they are the seminal fluid of the Serpent who is the negative charge of the Living Beast].

And Adam was strong enough to subjugate the waters of [the Serpent's] seminal fluid, but could not distinguish between [the Serpent's bitter waters]**R-1** and [the sweet waters of] Elohim['s living soul], and the waters of the [Serpent's] seminal fluid broke forth into the Garden, and Cain incarnated as the Living Beast and materialized [became visible] on the negative [eastward] side of Eden [142] [as a Serpent-dominated Wild Animal].**R-2**

R-1 Rom 5:6 (AT)
Dan 8:4-9
R-2 Is 66:1-3 (AT)

[Message # Unknown]

2.18 So Elohim and Jehovah nailed Adam, the mind they made to defend the ox they were making, [to the upper window], saying, It is morally right that the Serpent [in the lower window] should be separated from the unmarried spiritual image in [the upper] window.

---

[141] Adam's job was to keep the firmament that separated the Earth from the Seas sealed, except for (Footnote continued – See, Appendix)

[142] The words, ***eastward*** in Eden (Gen 2:8) and ***on the east side*** of Eden (Gen 4:16) are translations of two different Hebrew words. ***Eastward*** (Strong's #6924) is male, that is, positive/Heaven, and ***east side*** (Strong's #6926) is female, that is, negative/Hell.

2.19 And Jehovah Elohim formed a foundation for the whole living beast out of the ground, and nailed the foundation of the ground to the field of the whole living thing, which is the whole spiritual creature [of the] field [of the two] heavens, so that Adam's field would proclaim Jehovah's nature to the living emotional animal, [and]

Adam the mind[that Jehovah nailed to the ground, gathered his unmarried spirit together with the foundation of the whole living thing that Elohim would invite to marry and nailed it to the field of creation, and brought the whole spiritual creature of the [two] heavens together for the purpose of appearing as one whole man

2.20 But the Serpent fell upon Adam's unmarried spirit, and [Leviathan], the flying fish that is opposite [Adam], assisted [the Serpent] in nailing Adam['s unmarried spirit to the ground, instead of to Elohim],

2.21 And [Satan and Leviathan, the Serpent's] mind that was nailed [to the ground] that was inferior to Adam's mind, cast a trance upon him, and rendered him insensible; and they carried Adam's field away to the other side [of the Garden], and imprisoned [Abel], Jehovah's male organ of generation, underneath [Cain, the spiritual earth in the lower window],

2.22 And [Leviathan] formed [Adam], the mind that Jehovah made [to marry] Elohim and nailed [him[to the field [of creation] on the feminine side, and [the Serpent] carried Adam's field away from [the window] above [the firmament], to the unmarried female ox that Adam nailed his mind to and brought into his field [of consciousness],

2.23 And [Elohim], the Spirit [of Jehovah, which] was nailed to Adam's mind, said [to Adam], you are nailed to the field where the [spiritual] urine, the water [part] of [the Serpent's] seminal fluid is, because the Serpent carried your [mind] to the other side [of the firmament], and [this is how Adam died and] became a mortal man, and the water [of Jehovah's spiritual seminal fluid] became [Satan], the wife [of Leviathan, the

Serpent's] unmarried mind, who is called a ***eunuch*** [because he has water, but no male seed];

2.24 Therefore, it is right that [Adam], the mind [that] departed from his father, should become a mortal man who is nailed to [the Serpent], his mother, and [that the man and his mother should be] nailed to [Leviathan's] house[hold], and [Behemoth], the ox that [became Adam's wife], should cleave to [Leviathan, the Serpent's male], widowed organ of generation, [as] one [mortal man], and [it is also right that Adam's widowed spirit shall be nailed to [Satan's water that has no male seed],

2.25 And this is how the two, Adam and his wife, [the emotional animal that Adam nailed his] field to, were nailed to [Satan and Leviathan, the Serpent's] uncovered mind, [which is] engraved [with] the [Primordial Serpent's] shameful [nature].

Chapter 3

[162.1]
3.01 And the Serpent was revealed as a spiritual influence in the uncultivated Earth when she said to the ***fertile*** Woman: Yea, Elohim has said that you shall not eat of the whole tree of the Garden.

3.02-03 And the Woman said to the Serpent, But Elohim has said we may eat of the one who is the fruit of the completed tree of the garden [Adam], but not of the fruit of the ***partial*** tree which is within the ***divided*** garden [the Serpent], and you should be especially careful not to have intercourse with her, lest you die to your immortality and become a mortal man.

3.04-05 And the Serpent said to the Woman, You shall surely not die, because Elohim knows that in the day you eat of it, your reproductive force shall be opened, and you shall become as Elohim, who can distinguish between Himself and the Serpent.

[919.2.C]

3.14 And Jehovah Elohim said to the Serpent, Because you have done this, all the material bodies [of humanity] are cursed, and the whole [Adam], the living soul of the field [of creation, my] reproductive organ from above, shall enter into the dust, and be consumed all the days of his life, and

3.15 I will put hostility (1) between [you and] the woman, [and] (2) between [the woman and the man, and] (3) between the seed [of the woman, and] the seed [of the Serpent, and] (4) between the head [of Days,[R-1] who is the Beginning of Creation, and Satan's] army in the unconscious part of the mind [of the mortal men of Judah,[R-2] the battle horse of Jehovah; and the primordial turtle] shall snap at [the mortal men of Judah, the battle horse of Jehovah, but] they shall overwhelm [the primordial turtle], and

[R-1] Dan 7:9, 13, 22
[R-2] Zech 10:3

3.16 To the woman he said, Your lineage shall greatly increase, [but] the males of [mortal humanity] will bring forth the seed of this [spiritual] conception with the idolatrous labor [of sexual intercourse,[143] and the females shall bring forth the children of your lineage with] hard physical labor, [and both the males and the females of mortal humanity] shall long for [the idolatrous labor of sexual intercourse that results in the hard physical labor of childbirth, and their desire shall enable the serpent] to rule over you, and

3.17 To Adam he said, [Because you listened to the voice of the woman and ate from the partial tree, even though I commanded you saying, Do not eat [the fruit of] the partial tree,

---

[143] Sexual activity is legal within marriage. The Scripture calls it idolatrous because it only benefits the inhabitants of this world. It provides no benefit to God.

you will cross over into cursed physical bodies [that require] you to labor every day until your lives are consumed, and

3.18 You shall eat [the food that the cattle of] the field [of creation eat, and] undesirable souls shall come forth from you,

3.19a But the [spiritual] bread that you eat [shall come from] the moisture of the Son of Man, until the partial [tree that] carried mankind into the dust, repents, and [when]

3.20a The female [side] of mankind

3.19b Returns [from] the dust,

3.20b She [shall be] called by the name of "life giver," because she shall be the mother of everyone [who has the Spirit of] Life.

[110.1]

3.22 And Jehovah and Elohim, who appear in many forms and need nothing outside of themselves to survive and prosper, said, "Even though Adam is appearing as the Living Beast's mind, which makes [the whole Living Beast] a member of the Family of God, and [even though Adam] has been given a complete, informed ***knowledge***[R] of both good and evil, look at what he's doing! [Adam] is still incestuously fornicating with his earthen side [eating of the Tree of the Knowledge of Good & Evil], and materializing in the visible, physical world in a perverted form."

Therefore, to make sure that Adam's [earthen side] does not use the spiritual power that she stole from the Serpent, to enter into an endless, physical existence,

R Ps 58:5 (AT)

3.23 Elohim and Jehovah separated Adam from the supernatural provision that arises out of their own righteousness, so that [Adam] could experience good and evil in the visible, physical world,[R-1] until he learns how to enslave the [serpentine nature of] his earth[en side], which caused him to incarnate as the Woman, Cain, instead of Elohim's Son.[R-2]

[R-1] Dan 34:31-32
[R-2] Gen 2:24 (AT)

[373.2]
3.24 So Jehovah and Elohim divorced Adam, the immortal enclosed place where one experiences intimacy with Jehovah,[144] and Adam, the guardian[R] of the moral character, of the [whole] Tree of Life,[145] [died], and the magical sword[146] bisected the Living Beast, and transformed him into two [heretofore unknown] beings, [Cain & Abel],

[R] Gen 2:15

Chapter 4

[1216.1.C]
4.01 And the Woman knew Adam, the giver of life, and she conceived and said, "I have gotten a man from Jehovah," and

---

[144] Adam is the mind of the whole Living Beast, called cattle, in Gen 1:24, 25 and Gen 2:20.

Adam is immortal, but capable of dying to that immortality because of a potential to sin. Adam, Elijah, has been freed from the bondage of the body, and cannot die to his immortality.

[145] ***The whole Tree of Life*** is the Tree of Life joined to the Tree of the Knowledge of Good & Evil, as one, undivided tree.

[146] The mind is a spiritual sword, and the primordial Serpent's known witchcraft identifies her as ***the magical sword***. (Footnote continued – See, Appendix)

4.02 She bare again, [and Cain], his brother, Abel [appeared]; And Abel was a shepherd, but Cain worked the land, and

[827.3.C]

4.03a The time came to bring Jehovah a gift, and

4.04a Abel brought [Jehovah a gift], the firstborn of his flock, and

4.03b Cain brought [Jehovah] a gift also, the produce of his land, and

4.04b Jehovah accepted Abel's offering, but

4.05a [Jehovah] did not accept Cain's offering,

4.04c [Because Abel's offering] covered [Cain's sins, as well as Abel's, and],

4.05b Cain became very angry, [and]

4.06 Jehovah said to Cain, You are angry at [Abel], the personality of Elohim, [so stop now, or] you will overthrow Elohim, [and]

4.05c The personality [of the Snake that was lying prostrate within Cain], overthrew [Elohim], and

4.07 [Jehovah said], Look! If the Serpent makes you successful, you will desire him, and he will lie down with you, and rule over you, and the door [for you to experience] the penalty for sin will open, [and] if the Serpent [continues] to makes you successful [after that], he will cover you [with a dense physical layer that will be] like a leprous scab; and

4.08 Cain talked with Abel, his brother, and [Lilith, Cain's mother], appeared, [and then Snake, Cain's father], appeared, and they spread into Cain, the house[hold of Jehovah, and Lucifer] stood up [and] smote his brother, Abel, with deadly intent, and

4.09 Jehovah said to Cain, Where is Abel, your brother? And [Lucifer] said, I do not know [any] brother [who] guards [the garden of] I [AM], and

4.10a [Jehovah] said,

4.11 You have cursed your brother, [Abel, your other] hand, to be [joined] to the part of the earth that opened her mouth to swallow down [his] spiritual blood, [and]

4.10b You have made Elohim, the voice of your brother's blood, cry to me from [under] the ground,

4.12 [Wherefore], from now on, when you enslave the ground [to form a body for yourself], you will not [be able] to produce a large lizard [to be a material body that protects you in the earth, but] your invisible spirit [will incarnate in animal flesh], and

4.13 Cain said to Jehovah, [To incarnate as an animal is] a perversion [that is] more than I can bear;

4.14 Look [at what you have done] today, you have divorced me, your personality in the earth, and [now] your personality will be hidden, [because] I am an invisible spirit, and it shall come to pass that, when the whole [Adam] comes into existence, he will smite me with deadly intent, and

4.15 Jehovah said to Cain, It is right that the whole [Adam] should avenge the seven [Sefirot of Abel, who] you smote with deadly intent; [but, nevertheless], Jehovah put a mark on Cain so that when the whole [Adam] comes into existence, he should not [carry out the death sentence, and] kill [Cain],

4.16 And Cain left off from being the personality [that stood] in front of Jehovah, and was joined to the earth, [and] he disappeared [behind the animal nature of mankind].

4.17 And Cain knew his wife, and she conceived and bare Enoch, the initiated one who built the city [which provided Cain with immortality in the earth], and [Cain] called the name of the city after the name of his son, Enoch.

4.18 And Irad was born unto Enoch [and he was a fugitive], and Irad begat Mehujael, [the mighty one who Jehovah smote and erased his nature], and Mehujael begat Methusael, [who was a spiritual adult], and Methusael begat Lamech, [who became a king in the earth],

4.19 And Lamech, [who became a king in the earth], took a double-minded woman to belong to him, and [Lamech's] name when he was single-minded was Adah, [let us continue], but when [Lamech] was double-minded, his name was Zillah, [the shadow of death],

4.20 And Adah, [the unity which caused Cain's line to continue], bare Jabal, [a stream of water], and he became the father of those who married their covering, and acquired animal bodies,

4.21 And his brother's name was Jubal, [the stream of semen who] was the father of all who manipulate those who breathe and speak,

4.22 And Zillah, [the shadow of death], gathered together and bare Tubal [the offspring of] Cain, and Naamah, the sister of Tubal, who form the whole judgment [upon humanity, even] the iron implements that hammer us [with pain and] pleasure,

4.23 And Lamech said to his widowed wives, Adah, [the one who would cause Cain to continue], and Zillah, [Cain's shadow in the visible, physical world], Listen to me and understand what I am saying:

You are the wives of Lamech, [who is nailed to Cain, who] smote [Adam], a mortal man, the fruit [of Jehovah's Spirit], and [Abel], a young man, with deadly intent, [which resulted in his] separation [from Jehovah, so]

4.24 Cain is experiencing [the Sowing & Reaping Judgment], the vengeance [of Jehovah against sin, until] he returns to the point of departure (seven), and Lamech his widowed [offspring, is receiving] the black and blue [marks that come from the chastening of the Lord] on all 70 [levels of consciousness].

4.25a And, [as] Adam continued [along life's journey, he became an androgynous, physical man who] knew his female

[side], and he gave birth to a son, and called his name Seth, [a substitute for Adam, who Jehovah put in the Garden],

4.25b [And, Adam said], Elohim has placed Cain, the fruit, of [the woman], the unconscious part [of the carnal mind], below Abel, [who] was slain.

4.26 And a son, Enos, was born to [Adam, who re-]assembled him[self as] Seth after [Adam broke [apart and became mortal, and Adam, as Seth], called upon the name of Jehovah.

Chapter 5

[840.1.C]
5.32 In the year that Noah attained to [Loving Kindness of Understanding], the 50th gate of Understanding (100), the potential to produce righteous personalities [for the daughters of Adam], the seed of [Adam/mankind], the [lawful] inhabitant [of the house who has] the pulsating life force produced by divine wisdom, and the power to develop the nature of God within those personalities, were born [within Noah].

Chapter 6

[378.4]
6.01 And it came to pass, that Adam broke his covenant [with Jehovah, and committed adultery with] the Serpent, and [he

was defiled, and died] to his immortality, and female descendants were born [to him][147]

6.02 And the sons of Elohim took as many [of] them [as] they chose for wives, and Adam's female descendants appeared [in the earth], engraved [with the Serpent's image],

6.03 And Jehovah said, "Since Adam's own immortal, spiritual foundation ignorantly sinned [against] him, the Serpent shall govern his immortal spirit[ual foundation][R-1] until the season when his mortal personalities are perfected through judgment[R-2] and Adam's widowed spirit is reunited with [Elohim],"

R-1 Gen 3:16

R-2 2 Pet 2:4 (AT)

6.04 And, indeed, Adam's [female] descendants were in the Earth in those days when Elohim's sons arrived at the unconscious part of their mind, and they were born as proud immortal, tyrants with the nature of mortal man,

6.05 And Jehovah saw that Satan was master in the Earth, and that Leviathan could not think about anything, other than rolling out the evil world of time and space,

6.06 And Jehovah grieved for Adam, because he had produced an afflicted servant's heart[R] in the Earth [instead of Jehovah's immortal mind],

R Gen 4:1 (AT)

6.07 And Jehovah said, I gave Adam Elohim's life, which is higher than the [life of] the Serpent, but his spiritual [reproductive] part [gave birth to] Cain, a mute, dumb beast,[R-1] and [she became] Satan, but I will fill them with my life anyway,

---

[147] Verse 1 says that female descendants WERE BORN IN Adam, but verse 2 says that Elohim's sons ***appeared*** as female descendants. (Footnote continued – See, Appendix)

because they have repented of making [148] [this idolatrous heart].[R-2]

[R-1] Job 40:5
[R-2] 1 Ki 19:15 (AT)
Rom 6:17 (AT)

6.08 But Noah was acceptable to Jehovah, because he was possessed by [Jehovah's] mind, and

6.09a This is the story of Noah and

6.10 The three sons he brought forth, Shem, Ham and Japheth:

6.09b Noah was a justified, mortal man, whose mind was completed,[R] because he was led by Elohim

[R] Ez 1:10 (AT)

6.11 When Satan satisfied [Cain, Noah's] earth[en side], and [Cain] perverted Abel, and

6.12 Elohim looked and saw that Cain, [Noah's] earth[en side], had cast off Abel['s authority, and] morally corrupted [Noah's] lifestyle, and that Satan was expressing her personality [through Noah], and

6.13 Elohim said to Noah, "Satan is expressing himself [through your] earth[en] personality since Cain saturated [you with the thoughts of] her mind, so I will destroy the earth[en personality] that is near [to Cain],

6.14 "Your immortal vessel, [and Abel], [Adam's root system], shall be an atonement for Cain, your mortal mind, and

---

[148] Mortal man had not repented, at this time, except for Noah, therefore, this must be a creative word spoken by Jehovah.

In other words, Jehovah decided to restore mortal man's immortality before they decided to repent. His forgiveness, therefore, took the form of a prophecy, which resulted in the judgment, which was necessary to produce the repentance, that is a requirement for the resurrection of immortality.

shall cover his evil, personality, and [Adam shall] ransom Elohim's widowed spirit, and

6.16a "[Abel within] you shall increase in spiritual maturity until [Adam], your [immortal mind] is complete;[R] and [Adam] shall be a door into [the higher centers for] Cain, your lower, [animal] nature, and

[R] Ez 1:10 (AT)

6.15 You shall become self-governing, and

The three-part[R] foundation [of the temple]

[R] Eccl 4:12

6.16b "Shall be [rebuilt] for the third time;[149]

Elohim Prophesies Though Noah:

6.17 "I see Elohim coming upon the Earth as a flood of purified waters, to pull Satan, where Adam's widowed spirit is, down from the lower heaven,[R] and the whole Earth shall breathe her out: and

[R] Lk 10:18

6.18a "Adam shall rise [from the dead] within you, and

6.19a "Elijah and Abel, the two parts of [Adam, Elohim's] whole male organ of regeneration, [shall be reunited], and

6.19b "Enter into immortality,

---

[149] Jehovah erected the three part, life-producing foundation of the creation, for the first time after the Serpent incarnated as Satan and Cain (Gen 4:1-2 [AT]), and for the second time when Elohim substituted Seth for Abel (Gen 4:25).

Seth could not hold the living altar together either, though, and by the time Noah appeared, all of Seth's descendants had died to their immortality. But Noah obeyed Elohim, and rejoined Elijah and Abel in the correct moral order, and the immortal Adam rose from the dead in him.

6.19c "Because Abel's union with Elijah forms the whole living [altar], which sustains the life of

6.20 (1) "[Adam's widowed spirit], the spiritual part of the arrangement which is above, and

(2) "The two sides of the whole reptilian part of the earthen arrangement,

(a) "Leviathan, and

(b) "[Cain], the mute, wild animal of the arrangement, and

"[All three parts of the creature] shall be gathered within you, to sustain their lives, and

6.21 "Adam, [the whole Tree of Life],**R-1** shall be restored [from Abel, Adam's root system] within you, and they shall be edible food**R-2** for Cain, the mute wild animal that belongs to you, when Adam judges [Leviathan's sins], and folds him underneath [himself],[150] and

R-1 Gen 3:2-3 (AT)
R-2 Jn 6:41

6.18b "You and your sons, and your wife, and your sons' wives that are within you, shall enter into Adam['s immortality], and

6.19d "Adam shall be the priest [that mediates between Jehovah and Cain], the mute female animal [that Abel covers],**R**

R Gen 3:21 (AT)
Gen 7:9 (AT)

6.22a "Because Noah, Elohim's reflection,

6.19d "Walked with Elohim, and

6.22b Did everything that [Adam], his righteous mind commanded him to do."

---

[150] Leviathan shall be forced underneath Adam's authority, and, once again, the creature, shall have a single, righteous mind.

Chapter 7

[379.7]

7.01 And Jehovah said to Noah, You and the whole family within you [Abel and Cain] shall become a self-governing, immortal vessel, because I have seen [Abel], the righteous personality of this age within you,

7.02 You have been confused since the living beast became the mortal male [Abel], and his wife [Cain], but you shall join your two sides and recover your immortality when Abel matures through spiritual instruction, experiences, and discipline, and Cain [matures through] intellectual, emotional, social, and academic discipline.

7.03 Indeed, Abel's seven seals shall be opened [within you, Noah], and you shall be male [again], and [Cain], your female animal, [shall bear] live descendants [who abide in] Eden [because they are morally superior to] the Serpent,

7.04 Indeed, I will rain down judgment upon the whole existing [wild animal], and I will destroy Satan [and Leviathan], her unconscious [and subconscious] mind, and Cain, the personality of the ground, because they continue to mature the mortal world toward completion,

7.07a So Noah gathered his Son, Abel, and his wife, Cain, together,[151]

7.05 And Noah arranged the whole [3-part altar] in the order that Jehovah commanded,

---

[151] Abel, Noah's true reality, was spiritually pregnant with the resurrected Adam, Elohim's Son, and joined to a personality which is an emotional animal.

7.07b And Abel and Cain were [joined] together into a self-governing, immortal vessel [that carries Adam, Elohim's] male [mind], and atones for Cain, the female animal,

7.06 And Adam completed the mortal life of [righteous Abel], Noah's son,

7.08 [Which consists of Abel], the morally clean side, and [Cain] the confused side of the mute, wild animal, and [the Serpent], the ascended[R] side of the whole arrangement that is reproducing [herself], because [she married] the ground [that Abel is under],

[R] Gen 1:20 (AT)

7.10 And so it came to pass, that [when] Elohim's waters were [gathered] above the Earth [the Earth was barren], and [Noah's] mortality [Cain] was satisfied,

7.09a And the mortal man, Noah, became the self-governing, immortal vessel [that carries Adam, Elohim's] male [mind], and atones for Leviathan, the female animal, as Elohim commanded him,

7.12 And violent rain [judgment] was upon the Earth [that Abel is under], and [upon Leviathan], the law [of sin and death] of the four-footed beast [whole wild animal] in the world of time and space, [and upon Elohim's] shadow, [the Serpent], that protects [Leviathan], the law of the four-footed beast,

7.11b And [Noah] died to his mortal life,

7.13 And Abel, Noah's son, became Adam, [Elohim's male mind], and Cain, Noah's wife, [the female animal], became Shem, Ham and Japheth; and Abel, Noah's son, and his three mortal wives, Shem, Ham and Japheth, were together [with]in Noah,[R] the self-governing, immortal vessel [that carries Adam, Elohim's] male [mind], and atones for Leviathan, the female animal,

[R] Job 1:04 (AT)

Chapter 9

[60.3]
9.01 And Elohim blessed Noah and his sons, and said to them,

"Let Adam be resurrected in you, and may you branch out into many members, and let each member be filled with Adam's offspring, and

9.02 "The miraculous deeds [of Adam's offspring] shall terrify [Satan] and crush [Leviathan], and

"[King Adam] shall be the head of the whole living emotional animal [nature] of the earth, and the head of the winged insects of the invisible, spiritual world, and of all of the [reptilians] that swarm in the earth, and

"[Adam shall be] the head of [Abel], the fish in the sea, and [King Adam, Elohim's] spiritual male organ, shall cover them all, and

9.03 "He shall consume [Leviathan], the reptile.

"I have appointed [Adam], the whole mature living plant, to do all these things,

9.04 "But you shall not consume [Satan], the [spiritual] blood of [Leviathan, the Dragon's] male organ.

9.05 "Indeed, [King Adam, Elohim's] male organ, will tread underfoot [Satan], the spiritual blood of the [dead] emotional animal, and [Leviathan], the subconscious part of the flesh mind of the whole living beast; and

"[Adam], the subconscious part of the mind of [Elijah], mortal man's [spiritual] relative, shall care for [the fiery serpent], Adam's emotional animal [side], AND

9.06 "Adam's household shall shed the [spiritual] blood of the one who sheds Adam's [spiritual] blood, because Adam is Elohim's representative image, and

9.07 "You shall branch off and multiply, and move through the earth, and [Elohim's nature] shall increase therein", and

9.08 Elohim spoke to Noah, and to his sons [who were] with[in] him, saying,

9.09 "Behold, I establish my covenant with you, and with your [spiritual] descendants after you, and

9.10 "With the whole living, emotional, animal [nature] that is with[in] you, [and with] the winged insects [of the invisible, spiritual world], and with the personalities of the whole [fiery serpent], the living beast of the earth who is with[in] you, and with everything that proceeds forth from [King Adam], the ark [of God], and from the whole living beast of the earth, and

9.11 "I will establish my covenant with you [that Adam], my whole [spiritual] male organ, shall not be cut off by the flood of Satan's [polluted] waters anymore, [but Elohim's] river [of life] shall destroy the [evil potential in the] earth forever," and

9.12 And Elohim said,

"This is the sign of the covenant that I make between me and you, and the whole living, emotional animal [nature] that is with[in] you, for the perpetual age,

9.13 "I shall set [Elijah], my archer, in a [spiritual energy] cloud, and [Elijah] shall be the miraculous sign of the covenant between me and [the personalities] of the earth, and

9.14 "It shall come to pass that, when you see [Elijah], the archer, in the [energy] cloud of my spiritual power, my [energy] cloud shall cover [your] flesh mind, and

9.15 "I will remember my covenant which is between me and you, and with the whole living, emotional animal, that [Satan], the flood of [polluted, spiritual] waters, shall never again bring into existence [Leviathan, the Dragon's] whole [spiritual]

male organ, [who] destroyed [Adam, Elohim's] whole [spiritual] male organ, and

9.16 "It shall come to pass [that, when Elijah], the archer, appears in the [energy] cloud,[R] I will remember the everlasting covenant between Elohim and the whole living, emotional animal, and [Adam, Elohim's] whole male organ [which is] above, [shall destroy Leviathan, the Dragon's whole spiritual male organ which is] in the earth," and

[R] Ez 1:28 (AT)
Is 6:1
Judg 14:11
2 Ki 2:10, 12
Rev 1:7, 10:1, 14:14

9.17 Elohim said to Noah,

"This is the sign of the covenant which I have established between me and the whole [Adam, Elohim's] male organ, who is the head of the earth," and

[979.1.C]
9.18 These are the sons of Noah that went forth from the partial tree [into] the ark: Shem, Ham Japheth, and Ham was the father of [Cush, the son of a daughter of Adam that Ham] humbled, and

9.19 These three sons of Noah [were powerful enough] to break into pieces [the unified mind of the sons of God who were completed by the Snake, rather than by the male Adam, [who was destined] to become the higher mind of the daughters of Adam], and

9.21 [Satan], the partial [tree in the Garden of Eden], bubbled up into the lower centers of [Noah's earthen side], and motivated [Noah to dominate the regenerating creation, and Cain], the one who [Jehovah] exiled [from the Garden of Eden], was revealed [in a] clearly conspicuous form, and Cain, the one who was] exiled [from the Garden of Eden], influenced [Noah to let Satan] satisfy [his cravings, and Noah] separated from

9.20 [Righteous Adam], the male vine,**R-1** and Adam, [the branch]**R-2** that [God] planted within Noah, dissolved, and

R-1 Jn 15:5-6
R-2 Zech 3:8

9.22 Ham, [who was joined to a daughter of Adam that] he had humbled [and made his] mate, saw [that Righteous Adam, Jehovah's] male organ within Noah, his father, [had dissolved], and told [Shem and Japheth], his two brothers, [who were] outside [of the city, what had happened to their] father, and

9.23 The dual personality of Shem and Japheth saw that [Satan had ascended into Noah's] neck center [after Noah] used the magic[al power of the Tefillin[152] to satisfy his desire to dominate God's creation, and that Satan] was occupying the empty space within [Noah], the garment that [Jehovah Elohim] had put on, and

9.24 Noah recovered from the influence of [Satan's] intoxicating [spirit], and he knew what he had done to himself and to his sons, [that they would be trapped within mortal humanity, where they would be subject to the violence of Satan and [the pride of] Leviathan, continuously, and

9.25 [Jehovah Elohim] said, [I have] cursed [Shem and Japheth] to suffer the humiliation of being dependent upon [others who are, themselves], dependents, and

9.26a [Noah] said, I submit to [the judgment of] Jehovah Elohim, [that]

9.27a Japheth shall bring the gullible and naive bodies into existence that Shem shall dwell in, and

9.26b [That] Shem shall be humbled by his dependency upon [the bodies that] belong to [Japheth], and

---

152 Magical cords wrapped around the right arm and the head, used in Bacchanalian and Hebrew worship (Ez 13:20).

9.27b [That Japheth] shall be humbled [when he recognizes that he will be] indebted to [Shem for his spiritually] until [the day of the great judgment].

Chapter 10

[60.3]
10.05 The genetic material of the Living Beast was stretched out and separated into different kinds of speech [ethnic attitudes], male and female personalities, and different nationalities, before the [descendants of Japheth] were physically separated into male and female bodies.

10.09 Nimrod, the personality that revealed Jehovah's nature, became a powerful tyrant who consumed the life force of God's people.

10.25 And Eber had two sons: One's name was Peleg; because men separated out into male and female bodies in those days; and they were separated in their speech also and began to fight amongst themselves; and his brother's name was Joktan.

[1260.17.C]
10.30 And [Joktan] carried the burden [of the judgment that was] written in a book [concerning] the high [souls who lost their bodies in the flood, and] came to [the realm of] time to dwell with [the people of the land who were like] pack animals or donkeys [to them].

[60.3]
10.32 These are the histories of the tribes which descended from the sons of Noah according to the groups they were placed into; and through them, since the flood, those who are separated into male and female [Elohim's Sons humanity] are experiencing a spiritually beggarly existence, and their [female and male] bodies are engaging in physical sexual intercourse [instead of spiritual intercourse with Jehovah, in their mind].

Chapter 11

[11.1]
11.01 And the earth was unified because [the people] all thought the same thoughts, and expressed [their ideas] with the same words, and

11.02 It came to pass that, as [fallen Adam] journeyed downward, away from immortality, [the mountain of God] divided and the flat, low land [of the Carnal Mind's] religious confusion appeared and joined [itself to fallen Adam], and

[928.2.C]
11.03 They said one to another,

"Let us make sperm and burn [Righteous Adam] thoroughly,* [so that] we can incarnate in the earth, the material substance that is for the purpose of rising to the surface," and

Seed, the building blocks [of creation], came into existence; and

* In order to fully incarnate, unrighteous Adam must join itself to Righteous Adam through spiritual fusion, which creates great heat. The process will be reversed at the end of the age, when Righteous Adam fuses with unrighteous Adam to restore the Kingdom (2 Pet 3:10,12).

[11.1]
11.03 They said to one another,

"Come, let us swallow up [Elohim's] fiery [judgment that] consumes [the Carnal Mind], so that the Holy Spirit has no power over us, and

"Let us make our own righteousness, and ascend to the high level of spiritual authority [that supplies] the energy to produce the genetic building blocks and the material atoms [that will form the visible creation], and

"[Let us engrave the spiritual] foundation [of mankind with our own] righteous [nature]," and

11.04 [Fallen Adam] said,

"Come, let us build a city [that will be the female aspect of the creation], and

"A tower [which will be the male aspect of the creation], and

"Let us form [a mind] that will reflect our nature, [and] prevent the head of heaven, the personality that has charge of the whole earth, from appearing to break [our unity] in pieces," and

11.05 "The Lord came down to see the city [that is the female aspect of the creation], and the tower, [that is the male aspect of the creation], that the sons of Adam built, and

11.06 The Lord came down and said,

"Look, the people are a unity, and they all verbalize the same [thought], to dissolve [Adam's righteous mind] and form [the Serpent's, self-righteous Carnal Mind], and now [I will not be able] to harvest [the fruit of my Spirit] from the people, because of this [thing] that they all have plotted to do.

11.07 "Come, let us go down there and confuse their verbal communication [which is the foundation of their ungodly unity], so that they will not be able to understand each other's thoughts and ideas."

11.08 So, the Lord broke [the unity] of the personality of the whole earth in pieces from above, and [fallen Adam] stopped building the city [that is the female side of the creation].

Chapter 12

[1260.18.C]

12.06 Abram, [the descendant of Peleg, the brother of Joktan, who shouldered the burden of the souls that crossed over into the bodies of human animals], shouldered the burden of [being the authority over his wife, Sarai, his brother's son, Lot, and the souls they had gathered together with in Egypt, as] they crossed over [from their experiences with the Egyptians] into a relationship with [Mamre], the Canaanite [who] overcame the [spiritual] filth [of the idols of] the land [of Canaan, and became] a strong oak tree, through his relationship with Abram], a teacher of the early rain,

Chapter 13

[585.3.C]

13.01 And [Adam within] Abram, his wife, rose up and took all that belonged [to him], and departed from [the belly of the beast, which is spiritual] Egypt,[R] and Lot [went] with him into the parched land [of the heart center), which is above Satan's authority].

[R] Jon 1:17

13.02 Now, Satan [was afflicting] Abram's physical body [with] grave and persistent misfortune, but Abram was able to endure [because the Second Adam was overlaying Abel, the First Adam's root system within Abram, and Abel] was saving [Cain, Abram's personality], and

13.03 [Abel within Abram] departed from [spiritual Egypt, the belly of the beast, to] the parched land [on the left side of the heart center], even to Bethel, the house of [Adam, Jehovah's] Mighty One, the place where [the First Adam's]

dwelling place had been at the beginning, before Bethel, [the heart center], the house of [Adam, Jehovah's] Mighty One, was cut away from [Jehovah, and became] a heap of ruins,

13.04 [And Abram ascended] into the Mind of God [which comes into existence when] the Carnal Mind is slaughtered, which [Mind of God] had been formed in the First [Adam], and [it] was there [in the Mind of God, that] Abram was called [to acquire] the character of Jehovah, and

13.05 Lot went with Abram also, and [Abel] was the sheep, and [Cain] was the oxen of [the land of Abram's personality, which is Adam's] dwelling place.

13.06 Now, Satan was able to arise [within Lot's] Carnal Mind to ambush the unity [between Abram and Lot], because [Satan within Lot increased when Abram's] soul increased, [and this is how] Satan ambushed the unity [between Abram and Lot], and

13.07 There was strife between [Adam], the pastor of Abram and Lot's animal nature, and the Canaanite and the Perizzite that dwelled in their flesh, and

13.08 Abram said to Lot, I beseech you, [do not] let [Satan] cause strife between you and me, since [Adam is] my pastor [as well as] your pastor, and because [Abel, the spiritual] male [within us, makes us] brethren,

13.09 I beseech you to separate yourself [from] Leviathan, [the subconscious part of] the whole Carnal Mind [that your] personality [is married to, because], if [you submit to] the judgment [of your Carnal Mind], then your personality] will become righteous, but if [you declare yourself to be] righteous, then I [AM] will use [the rod of the sowing and reaping] judgment [to correct you], and

13.10 Lot lifted up his eyes and understood [that] the whole personality of [the First Adam, which] became the ruined cup [that] bears Adam['s life, was within] him, [and Lot understood, further, that] the imputed anointing of Jehovah's Garden, [which was also within him], could humble the crown/powers of Sodom [the powers of] the land of Egypt, [the belly of the beast in his heart, which are, collectively], the whole underworld [where the Serpent's] cycle [of births and deaths reigns], and

13.11 Lot chose the underworld [which is subject to Satan's] cycle [of births and deaths], and Lot began to journey towards the [imputed anointing, which] separated him from [Abram], the [spiritual] male who was his brother, and

13.12 [So], Abram, the personality [that Adam] humbled, married [Adam], but Lot shined toward Sodom, to cover [the inhabitants of Gehinnom], and [Lot] married the awakened/spiritual cities of the underworld,

13.13 But the [spiritual] males of Sodom, [who were crying out to Jehovah for deliverance], were morally evil, [spiritual] criminals, [who] were wholly estranged from Jehovah.

Chapter 14

[1036.3.C]

Events In the Visible World

Four Warlord Kings

14.01 And it came to pass in the days of **Tidal**, the formidable, collective mouthpiece of the King of the nations, that

Amraphel, King of Babylon,

Arioch, King of Ellasar, [in Asia], and

Chedorlaomer, King of the land occupied by the descendants of Shem

War Against The Five Kings Of The First Adam

14.02 Waged war against

Shinab, the King of the Earth, the father [of humanity]* who turned to his other, [earthen] side, which altered [the nature of the kings that he is revealed through, even],

*The First Adam

Bera, the King of Sodom, the burnt [offering that atones for the sins of the people], and

Birsha, the wicked King of Gomorrah, [the unconscious part of the mind of **Shinab**, the King of the Earth], the enforcer of Jehovah's righteous Sowing and Reaping Judgment], who chastises [the personal souls (personalities) of King **Bela** of Zoar],

Shemeber, the illustrious King of Tsebo'iym, the [spiritual] gazelle that has the Mind of God, and

Bela, King of Zoar, [whose personal souls (personalities) are chastised by]

Shinab, The King of the Earth (The First Adam), who must be brought very low [so that Satan, the unconscious part of **the Mind of Shinab** within them] can be swallowed up [by the Second Adam], and

Events In the Spiritual World

14.03b **[The drop of Satan,**

The unconscious part of the mind of **Shinab**, the King of the Earth in each] of these [kings],

Was dissolved in the whole [spiritual underground] sea [where Satan dwells],

14.06 That originally existed in the cave [of the second center,

Who is also] the strong support [of Leviathan, **the subconscious part of the Mind of Shinab**, the King of the Earth, when he dwells in the throat center,

Was able to ascend into that] high place [of the throat center], from where [Leviathan, the subconscious part of the **Mind of Shinab**, the King of the Earth], speaks [false doctrine], and

14.03a **The witchcraft** [of Birsha, King of Gomorrah, the unconscious part of **the Mind of Shinab**, King of the Earth,

Within these kings who exist] in the flat land [that] was rolled out [by

Leviathan, the subconscious part of **the Mind of Shinab**,

That caused them to fall into] the black hole [of false doctrine,

Which brought down the judgment of King Birsha], the enforcer of Jehovah's Righteous Sowing & Reaping Judgment, upon them; and

14.04a [That is how the kings who reveal the nature of **Shinab**, the King of the Earth, became] the servants of **Chedorlaomer**, [King of the land occupied by the descendants of Shem, who tried to build a tower into heaven with false doctrine], but

King Shemeber Rebels

In the thirteenth year [of their captivity, the illustrious **Shemeber**, the King of Tsebo'iym, the spiritual gazelle], achieved [the "the Mind of God," when he repented under]

14.07a The palm tree,[R] and

[R] Ps 92:12

14.04b Rebelled [against Satan, the unconscious part of the **Mind of Shinab,** the King of the earth, and [against] Bera, the King of Sodom, and his [spiritual] man[hood]

14.07b Returned, and [righteous] judgment came forth [from him], and

Events In the Visible World

Shemeber Punishes Chedorlaomer

[The illustrious **Shemeber**, the King of Tsebo'iym, the spiritual gazelle who has the Mind of God], smote the whole country of the Amalekites, and also the Amorites, and

14.05 In the 14th year, [after Judgment] fell upon **Chedorlaomer** [for trying to attain eternal life with false doctrine, the illustrious **Shemeber**, the King of Tsebo'iym, the spiritual gazelle who has the Mind of God, also] smote the kings of

The Rephaims, the giants [who cured[R-1] themselves of spiritual weakness by] sowing themselves together[R-2] with Ashtoreth,

[R-1] Rev 13:12
[R-2] Is 53:5

The Zuzims, one of the original tribes of Ham, [who dwell in] a region of Palestine, and

The Emins, a Canaanitish tribe, [all of] which were near to [**Chedorlaomer**, King of the land occupied by the descendants of Shem, who] tried to [acquire] the double portion in order to build a city [that would reach into heaven[R] with false doctrine], and

[R] Gen 11:5-9

Events In the Spiritual World

Sodom & Gomorrah Join The Battle

14.08a After that, [**Shinab**], the King of the Earth, [the father of humanity who turned to his other, earthen side, which altered the nature of the kings that he is revealed through, even,

Bera], the King of Sodom,

[**Birsha**], the King of Gomorrah, and

Bela, the King of Zoar, [who] escaped [from Satan, the unconscious part of Shinab, the King of the Earth],

Joined [the illustrious **Shemeber**], the King of Tsebo'iym [the spiritual gazelle who has the Mind of God], in the battle

14.09 Against **Chedorlaomer**, King of the land occupied by the descendants of Shem,

Tidal, the formidable [mouthpiece of Leviathan], King of the nations,

Arioch, King of Ellasar, [in Asia, and

Amraphel, King of Babylon, and]

These four [warlord] kings [who fought against] the five [kings who were under King **Shemeber's** righteous judgment, that is,

Shinab, the King of the Earth, and the four kings who reveal his image, even,

Bera, King of Sodom

Birsha, King of Gomorrah

Shemeber King of Tsebo'iym, and

Bela, King of Zoar],

14.08b In the flat land that they fell into, [that was rolled out by Leviathan, the subconscious part **of the mind of Shinab,** King of the Earth, which was a black hole filled with false doctrine]

Events In the Invisible World

14.10 But [each of **Bera**], King of Sodom, [**Birsha**, King of] Gomorrah, [and King **Bela** of Zoar, also had a mind that] was an [individual] black hole [filled with false doctrine, within] the black hole [filled with false doctrine that **Shinab**, the King of the Earth, the father of humanity who turned to his other, earthen side], fell into, in the place that [Leviathan] rolled out the flat land [of this world,

The Anointing Flows Out Of Shemeber

So, Jehovah's spiritual] anointing oil rose to the surface [within the illustrious **Shemeber**, the King of Tsebo'iym, the spiritual gazelle who has the Mind of God, to correct the false doctrine in the black hole that is the fallen mind of the kings, but

The Kings of Sodom & Gomorrah Refuse To Repent

Bera], the King of Sodom, and

[**Birsha**, the wicked] King of Gomorrah,

Sought to escape from [the righteous] judgment [of the illustrious **Shemeber**, the King of Tsebo'iym, who the anointing oil of the Second Adam was flowing from], and

They were divided [from the true doctrine that was flowing from King **Shemeber**, that sanctified them], and [Satan, the unconscious part of **the Mind of Shinab**, the King of the Earth], cast down [the Truth that King **Shemeber** was proclaiming],

Bela, King of Zoar Escapes The Judgment

But **Bela**, the King of Zoar, [humbled himself, and clave to] the mountain [of Truth within the illustrious **Shemeber**, the King of Tsebo'iym, the spiritual gazelle who the anointing oil] was overflowing [from, and King **Bela**] escaped [from Satan, the unconscious part of **the Mind of Shinab**, the King of the Earth,

Lot Captured, Sodom & Gomorrah Robbed

14.12a But the Warlord Kings] took Lot, Abram's brother's son, and

14.11 They took [the King of] Sodom, the whole [burnt offering that Lot] possessed,* and they took all the [spiritual] food that [**Birsha**, the wicked King of] Gomorrah, possessed, and

14.12b [The soul of Righteous Adam] that dwelt in [those cities] departed, and

* Lot sanctified himself by ministering to the people of Sodom.

Events In The Visible World

King Shemeber Tells Abram That Lot Was Captured

14.13 [King **Bela** of Zoar], who escaped from [Satan, the unconscious part of **the Mind of Shinab**, the King of the Earth, by humbling himself and believing the Truth that King **Shemeber** was proclaiming], came to

Abram, who dwelt with

Mamre, the Amorite, a strong, well-nourished oak tree, [R]

[R] Gen 12:6 (AT)

The brother of Eschol, [who bare the fruit of God],

The brother of Aner, [the servant of God],

Who were in a covenant relationship [with Jehovah, Abram's spiritual] husband, [and

Bela, the King of Zoar, told Abram that Lot had been captured by the Warlord Kings], and

Repentance Is Spiritual Warfare

14.14a When Abram, [who was a spiritual male], heard that his brother, Lot, was taken captive, [Abram] emptied himself out,* and [and ran after **Chedorlaomer**, the King of the land occupied by the descendants of Shem], and

*Confessed his sins and forced his sin nature under King Shemeber's authority, which was within himself.

Events In The Spiritual World

14.15 [King Shemeber, Abram's] higher [soul], separated [itself from Aner], his servant, [who was from the side of] the night,* and ran after [Leviathan, the subconscious part of **the**

Mind of Shinab, King of the Earth within Lot], to punish him [for speaking the false doctrine that comes from Satan, the unconscious part of **the Mind of Shinab**, from Lot's throat center], the secret place [that only Jehovah's high priest is allowed to speak from], and wrapping it up [so that

*Aner is a type of fallen Adam within Abram, i.e., his old man.

14.14b The doctrine] of the world to come [that] exists within [Lot's spiritual] house[hold, cannot flow into it, and Abram], the one who was initiated [into the mysteries], pursued after [Leviathan, the subconscious part of **the Mind of Shinab**, the King of the Earth within Lot], to execute judgment [upon Leviathan for preaching false doctrine from Lot's throat center, and to deliver Lot from the false doctrine that was coming from Satan, the unconscious part of **the Mind of Shinab**, the King of the Earth], and

Lot Restored

14.16 They brought back [the King of] Sodom, [the burnt offering that] Lot, his brother, [had possessed, [and they also brought back all] the female [souls of] the people [of Sodom,[153] and

14.17a The King of Sodom, [the burnt offering that atones for the sins of the people, that was returned to Lot], went out to meet

14.18a Melchizedek, the King of [Jeru]salem, the priest of the Most High God, [who] came forth in the Spirit [from] the unconscious [part of the Mind of Abram

14.17b After] he returned from punishing **Chedorlaomer**, King of the land occupied by the descendants of Shem, and the Kings that were with him at the valley of adjustment, which is [called] "the Valley of the Kings," and

---

153 ***Sitting in the gate***, means that Lot was judging the sins of the people of Sodom: (Gen 19:1; 2 Sam 15:2).

14.18b [Melchizedek, who is the fulfillment] of prophecy,

14.19 Said to [the King of Sodom within Lot], Abram is blessed [because] he submitted to the Most High God, the owner of heaven and earth, and

14.20 You are blessed by the Most High God, the owner of heaven and earth, who has delivered your enemies into your hands [through him, so Abram] shall be given the whole tithe, and

14.21 The King of **Sodom**, [the burnt offering that atones for the sins of the people within Lot], said to Abram, All of the female souls that belong to me are yours; take them for yourself;

14.22a [But] Abram said to the King of Sodom, [the burnt offering within Lot],

14.23a If the shoe [that the Shekinah walks in in this world were to come into existence, and] if a shoelace [of that shoe] were to sew all [the female souls] that belong to you together [with that shoe] as one [soul], I would not take them,

14.22b [Because] Jehovah has raised up [the wisdom of] the mind of El, the most high God, the owner of Heaven and the Earth [within me, which tells me that]

14.23b It would not be right for you to say [that you, rather than] the Shekinah, [is the one that] made Abram rich,*

* El of the World of Emanation is the most high God. The Shekinah is a part of the World of Creation.

14.24 Except that [I will let you pay for the food that] the young men have eaten, and compensate the men who walk with me,

Aner, [the servant of God],

Eshcol, [who bare the fruit of God], and

Mamre, [the well-nourished oak tree], who seized the male portion [when he dwelt with me];

Let them be paid [for their service].

Chapter 15

[991.3.C]

15.01 After these things, [Ancient Adam], the Word [of God], came [to Adam within] Abram in a vision, [and spoke through] Jehovah, saying,

"Revere me and Adam within you will increase exceedingly [and you will overcome] the scaly hide of the crocodile [within you],"

15.02a But Abram, [the mortal personality, answered, saying],

15.03 "Look and see [that I have no family];

"The manager of my house[hold] is my [only] heir, because you have not given me fruit of my own;" and

15.02b Abram said,

"What will you give me, since I have no child, [and] possess [only] a house[hold in this world], the foundation of which is Eliezer of Damascus;" and

15.04 The Word of the Lord came to [Abram], saying,

"This [Eliezer of Damascus] shall not be your heir, but the one that comes out from your own reproductive force will be your heir," and

15.05 [Jehovah] brought [Abram] to the other side and said,

"Now look at heaven and count the stars if you are able to count them," and he said,

"Your seed shall be [as many as] these [stars]," and

15.06 [Abram] believed Jehovah, and [because he believed him, Jehovah] spoke to [Abram] as if he were a righteous [man], and

15.07 Jehovah said to Abram,

"I am Jehovah who enlightened [you, and] brought you [out] from the Chaldean [religion] to give you the [permanent] land of a physical body," and

15.08 Adonay [within Abram] said to Jehovah,

"I do not know how to acquire [a permanent body], but Elohim [knows how]," and

15.12a Abram fell into a trance, and there it was!

15.11a The powers and principalities [within] Abram

15.12b [That serve Leviathan], the Terrible One who fell down from [the world] above and became the sun of this dark [age],

15.11 Descended upon the dead animals [to acquire the spiritual energy being released for themselves], but Abram drove them away, and

15.13 [Jehovah] said,

"Abram, you should know that it will surely [come to pass] that your seed shall be aliens in earthen bodies that are not theirs, and [those bodies] shall dominate [your seed] for four hundred years, and

15.14 "[The bodies of] the nation that they serve shall also be judged by Adonay, [who] set Adam in the unconscious [part of their mind] upright, and they will come out [of that judgment] with great [spiritual] substance, and

15.15a "[The Shekinah, who] was buried under the earth at a previous time, shall be returned to her father safely, in good condition, after

15.17a "The power that descended from above and became the sun of this dark age

15.15b "Is buried [under the whole Adam], and

15.17b "It came to pass, that the Shekinah, the part [of the Mother] that was separated from [her Father], separated from

[Satan], the [ruling] spirit[ual power] of Abram's body, and [the Shekinah] crossed over [into the world above]."

[1260.8.C]
15.18 And in the same day, Jehovah made a covenant with Abram, saying, I have given this land [of the soul of your physical son to be] a mate [to Christ], your seed, [who Aseneth, Pharaoh's daughter, shall take from] the spiritual river of [the seminal fluid of Joseph, who is] spiritual Egypt, [and your seed shall ascend] to the [spiritual] River Euphrates, [and return to Adam], the great river [that flows out of Eden],

Chapter 19

[587.6.C]
19.01 And two Angels came to Sodom in the spiritual twilight, and [Abel within] Lot, [who] sat in the gate of Sodom, saw [them, and the angels] prostrated [Cain], the earthen personality [within] Lot, and [Abel within Lot] rose up to meet the [two angels],

19.02 And [Abel within Lot] beheld [Adam from above, the one who] controls [the Carnal Mind, and Adam from above] said to [Abel],

"I beseech you, turn away from the obstinacy of [Cain], the household of [Satan, Jehovah's] Servant,[R] and wash away [the sins of Lot's] female [Carnal] Mind, [because it is] urgent [that Lot] rise up and walk in the lifestyle [that Jehovah has called him to],"

[R] Job 1:6

But [Cain], the obstinate one, said

"No, [we] will stay in the mainstream,"

19.03 So, the angels struck [Lot's Carnal] Mind with great strength, and plucked [Cain] away [from Satan, and Abel within Lot] entered into the house[hold of Adam, the spiritual male from above, and Adam from above] baked unleavened bread, [and Abel within Lot] feasted [on the unadulterated Word of God], and

19.04 [When Adam, the spiritual] male from above, suspended the spiritual sexual intercourse [between Cain and Satan within Lot, Abel, the spiritual] young man of [Lot's] house[hold], turned around and [faced Adam], the spiritual male [from above, and Adam] the spiritually mature man [appeared within Lot, And Abel within] all the people from every part [of Sodom]

19.05 [That] belonged to Lot, [saw it], and cried out, saying, These [men] must be [Adam from above, and His Son], spiritual males that came to [Lot] in the midst of [his] adversity. Let us have spiritual sexual intercourse with them, [so] that [Adam] might appear in us [also],"

19.06 But Lot went out [from Adam's household] and passed [from Abel] into [Cain], the swinging door [that separates Adam from the Carnal Mind], and the door shut after him, and

19.07 [Cain within Lot] said [to the men of Sodom],

"Please, brothers, do not break up [our spiritual marriage].

19.08a "Look, now, [Cain and Abel, Adam's] two daughters which have never had spiritual sexual intercourse with [Adam], the spiritual male [from above], belong to me, [so] please wait for [the spiritual virgins within me] to mature, [and when they are grown up into Adam], he will belong to you,[R] to do with whatever is good in your [own] eyes, only have nothing to do with [Adam from above and His Son], the spiritual males [from above], who came to [my] temporal house[hold]," and

[R] Gen38:11

19.09a [Adam from above] said [to Lot],

"We have a long way to go to reverse [your Fallen Mind, and]

19.08b "To set you upright from above, and

19.09b "Having spiritual sexual intercourse [with me will help you;" and then Adam from above] said,

"[Jehovah and Elohim, the] unity [of God], came to deliver [you] from fear, [and to help Abel within you] to suckle [from the spiritual breast of Elohim from above, but they also came] to expose [your] sins, to punish [Leviathan within you], and to judge and punish [Satan within you] as well, and to break [you] apart from [Leviathan, the one who] you belong to," and

[Then Adam], the spiritual male [from above], stung [Leviathan], Lot's mortal [side], repeatedly, and burst through [Cain], the swinging door [of Lot's Carnal Mind], and [Adam from above] had spiritual sexual intercourse with [Abel within Lot], and

19.10 [Then Adam], the spiritual male [from above, Jehovah's right] hand [of mercy], went forth and pulled Lot into the house[hold of God], and shut the swinging door [after him],

19.11b [But Lot] was too proud [to confess his sins and deal with them, [even though] the immature [Abel within Lot had seen Adam] appear at the door [of his Carnal Mind, and Lot] was exhausted [from resisting Satan and Leviathan's thoughts],

19.11a So [Adam], the spiritual male [from above], the doorway to the house[hold of God], struck [Lot] with blindness, and

19.12 [Adam], the spiritual male [from above], said to Lot over and over again,

"You belong to Jehovah, and, on this side, you are a circumcised child and a relative by marriage on the bride's side, and [Abel], your son and [Cain], your daughter, are whole, and belong to, and are a part of this place, [which is the holy Jerusalem], the spiritually awakened city, and

19.13 "Jehovah has sent us to destroy [Leviathan], the pride [of man that you are] twisted together with, because of the shrieks of [Abel], the personality of Jehovah [within you], so we are going to destroy your female [Carnal Mind], and

19.14 [Then Adam, the spiritual male from above], went out [of the household of God], and subdued [Leviathan], who had taken [Lot captive], and, [after that, Adam from above] said [to Abel within Lot],

"Rise up and depart from [your Carnal Mind], because Jehovah will destroy that part of [Lot's] spiritually awakened city, [but Abel], the circumcised child [within Lot], mocked [the wisdom of] the world [above], and

19.15 When [Adam], the angel of the [spiritual] morning, arose [within] Lot, he urged [Lot] to withdraw [from his Carnal Mind], saying,

"Ascend [into Adam, the spiritual male from above], and take [Cain], the wife [of your] double, female [mind, with you], so that she is not taken captive by [Leviathan, the king of your Carnal Mind], the perverse city [within you],"

19.16 But [Lot] hesitated, so [Adam], the spiritual male [from above], seized [Abel] and [Cain] the wife [of Lot's] double, female [Carnal] Mind, and [Adam from above], Jehovah's mercy, carried [Abel] up [out of Lot's Carnal Mind, and] deposited [him] outside of [the Carnal] Mind, [that perverse city], and

19.17 [When Adam], the one [who] was severed [from the spiritual realm of God] appeared [to Lot, he] said,

"You have birthed [the life of the Son, which is] higher than your soul life, [so] do not look with favor upon [Satan], the unconscious part of your Carnal Mind; Neither arise into the fullness of the circular [underworld], or [Leviathan] will capture [Adam, who] has been born [again] within you, and remove [him from the household of God],"

19.18 But [Leviathan within] Lot [responded], saying,

"***Not now, Lord***,

19.19 "I see that [I, Jehovah's] servant, have acquired the favor of the [spiritual] world [that] is twisted together with kindness, [which] regenerates [Adam, the righteous side of] my soul, but [Adam from above], the high place [of Jehovah's spiritual world, the one who] prevents the evil from clinging to me, and slaying me, cannot be regenerated [within me],

19.20 "Look, I wish that my spiritual city would escape to the timeline of [Adam], its kinsman, [but Abel within me is] immature, so, then, let me escape over there [to the high place of Leviathan's timeline, just in case] the immature [Abel, the righteous side of] my [fallen] soul, does not regenerate [Adam within me]," and

19.21 [Then Adam from above] said to [Lot],

"I see that [Cain], your [mortal] personality, has accepted [being] gathered into [Adam, who has been regenerated within you] for the reasons [that] we told you repeatedly, but [you do not understand that Jehovah] has declared that your spiritually awakened city will be overthrown,

19.22 "[Therefore], hurry to [join yourself to Adam, my] offspring, [who] has been born [again within you, because] we cannot do anything to set you upright from above until you come [over] to the nature of [your righteous] side, [which is the reason that] your spiritually awakened city is called [to be] humbled."

19.23 Now, the [spiritual] sun [of the regenerated Adam within Lot] was risen upon Lot's [spiritual] earth, when [Lot] entered into [the spiritual place where his mortal soul was to be be] humbled, and

19.24 Jehovah rained purifying fire out of heaven upon [the regenerated Adam within Lot], upon the [people of] Sodom, [who were confessing their sins], and upon [the people of] Gomorrah, [who were experiencing Jehovah's Sowing & Reaping Judgment], and

19.25 [Adam from above] overthrew all those personalities [that dwelled in] the circular [underworld], and all the personalities [who were] married to [Leviathan, the mind] that sprouts from the ground,

19.26 [But, Lot] looked intently at [Satan], the woman [who] is the unconscious part of his Carnal Mind, and [Satan, the Serpent's] military post [within Lot], became salt, and

19.27 [Adam from above, the spiritual] morning [within] Abraham, loaded up [the regenerated Adam within Lot, and raised him up to Lot's heart center], the place where the personality [of Adam] stands before the Lord,

19.28 And [Adam from] above leaned out [of the window of Abraham's] personality, [and] saw [the people of] Sodom [who were confessing their sins], and [the people of] Gomorrah, [who were experiencing Jehovah's righteous Sowing & Reaping Judgment, and] all [of] the earthen personalities [whose consciousness was] above the circular [underworld] saw the vapour [of their distillation/judgment] ascending [out of their] earthen [personalities, like] the vapour from a furnace [that smelts metals for the purpose of removing impurities],

19.29 And it came to pass, that when Elohim was spoiling the [spiritual] cities of the circular [underworld], that Elohim remembered Abraham, and sent word that Lot should be severed from the [spiritual] cities that he had married, and that [Lot] should be returned [Abraham].

19.30 But [Leviathan] overshadowed [Lot] and led [Lot], [away from Abraham, the one who Jehovah sent to humble him], and [Leviathan, the other side] of the mountain [within Lot], married Lot, because [Lot] was afraid to marry [Abraham], the one [who Jehovah had sent] to humble him, and [this is how Lot, and Cain and Abel, Lot's], two [spiritual] daughters who were with him, [descended] into [Satan's spiritual] cave, [and began] to dwell [there],

19.31 And [then Cain], the firstborn, said to [Abel, who] she despised, Our father, [the Serpent], is a mature male [who] can bring forth a man[child that] will follow the lifestyle of the earth,

19.32 So come, let us drink [down Satan], the wine of [the Serpent], our father['s spirit, and have] spiritual sexual intercourse with him, so that the seed of [the Serpent], our father, will revive,

19.33 And [then Cain] was baptized into Satan, the Serpent's] twisted spirit, [and the Serpent], the father [of Cain], fell upon [Cain], the firstborn, and [the Serpent], the father [of Cain] connected with [Cain] sexually, and Satan perceived that a [spiritual] sexual connection [was taking place which] would preserve [the Serpent's seed],

19.34 And the next day, it came to pass, that [Cain, the Serpent's] eldest daughter, said to [Abel] who she despised, Look, I lay with [the Serpent], MY father, last night. Now, you go in and lie with [the Serpent] also, because [when both of us] drink down [Satan], the wine of [the Serpent's spirit, Leviathan], the fruit of [the Serpent], OUR father, will live again,

19.35 And so [Abel] drank of [Satan], the wine [of the Serpent], their father['s] twisted [spirit] also, and [Abel, who Cain] despised, lay with [the Serpent], and Satan perceived that a [spiritual] sexual connection was taking place which would preserve the Serpent's seed,

19.36 And this is how Lot's two [spiritual] daughters were impregnated by [the Serpent], their father,

19.37 And [Cain, the Serpent's] firstborn, bare the [principality who] founded the nation [which] reveals the nature of Moab, [and that] same [principality] is the [spiritual] father of the Moabites to this day,

19.38 And [Abel, who Cain] despised, also bare a [principality, and Abel] founded the nation, [which] revealed the nature of the son of [Abel's] people (Benammi), [and that] same [principality] is the [spiritual] father of the Ammonites to this day,

Chapter 21

[385.18]

21.11 My signature (Spirit) [which is above] the firmament, sows Michael, my virile seed, in the earth, says Elohim, and [Elijah, which is Michael wrapped in an earthen personality], resurrects Adam, the Tree [of Life, but Leviathan and Satan] the timeline that [is] the fruit of the Earth, is a lie, [because this timeline] deviates from [the timeline] of the righteous virile seed.

Chapter 22

[406.2]

22.01 And it came to pass, after these matters, that Elohim decided to test [Abel, Jehovah's] image in Abraham, so [Elohim] said to [Abel], Jehovah's image [within Abraham], Abraham says that he can distinguish between [Abel and Cain, so let's find out if this is true],

22.05 And [Elohim] spoke to [Abel within] Abraham, saying, Dwell here with Cain [the conscious part of Abraham's Carnal Mind] until [Adam] drives out [Leviathan], and when you cross over into the [golden] timeline and return [to the world] within, you will be able to subject Cain,

22.02 And [Elohim] said [to Abraham], It's time [for Abel] only [who is Jehovah's] son, [and not Cain], to marry [Jehovah], your lover, so you and Isaac must die to your present lifestyle, and mature into [Adam], the mind that sees with Jehovah's sight, and when [Adam], the stairway [to the world] above that I have told you about, unites with [Jehovah], you will ascend,

22.08a And Elohim said to Abraham, [Then] you will see my Son, Adam, the [sinless] lamb who is the staircase [to the world above the firmament],

22.08b And as the two of them continued on together,

22.07 Isaac spoke to Abraham, his father, saying, My [spiritual] father said [that we would] see [Adam, His] Son, but, [Isaac] continued, I see Satan, [the fire], and Leviathan, [the wood], but where is [Adam], the lamb who is to ascend above the firmament?

22.03a And [then] Adam arose in Abraham, married the two young [spiritual] men [Abel in Abraham and Isaac] who were near to him, and shouldered the burden of dominating Leviathan, and Adam, the staircase [to the world above], ascended,

23.13a And as Abraham ascended spiritually, he looked [with his eyes] and saw [in the spirit, that] Adam [was] behind [Leviathan, his Carnal Mind], and [that Abel], Adam's root system was interwoven [with Cain[R] in the wrong moral order], and [that Cain] was overlaying [Abel], and Abraham chose Abel, the part of [the fiery serpent that is Jehovah's] Son [who is covered with Cain's spiritual] earth, and Adam, the staircase, ascended,

[R] Ez 1:1b (AT)

22.09a And when they came to the place that Elohim had told them about,

22.03c [Adam within] Abraham burst through [Satan & Leviathan], the Tree of the Knowledge of Good & Evil [within Abraham],

22.09b And repaired the altar [within] Abraham, that puts the Tree [of the Knowledge of Good & Evil] in order,

22.06a [And then] Abraham seized [Leviathan], the wooden stairway, who had seized, and was covering over Isaac, his son,

22.09c And bound [Leviathan, the subconscious part of Isaac's Carnal Mind], and joined Isaac to [Adam, Jehovah's] Son, who is above the wooden altar,

22.06b And they proceeded to the place where Elohim had told Abraham [that] they belonged,

22.03b And [then] Adam [Abraham's righteous mind] took hold of Satan and Leviathan, and [cast] the pair [into the lake of fire],

22.06c And [Abraham and Isaac] died to their [mortal] lifestyle.

22.15 And [Michael], the angel of the Lord, called out of heaven unto Abraham, [who was in] the second timeline,

22.12 And [Michael] said, The Serpent has withheld [Adam, Jehovah's] only begotten Son, from me, but now that she perceives that you are submitting to Elohim, [the Serpent] has sent Satan and Leviathan, [your Carnal Mind] after Adam, to restore [put] her moral order,

22.10 And [the Fortified] Adam shot forth in Abraham, and took hold of [Satan and Leviathan, Abraham's other] self, and sacrificed [Leviathan, the Serpent's] daughter,

22.04 And carried Satan away, and Abraham's eyes saw the golden timeline,

22.11 And Michael called to Adam out of heaven, saying, ***Abraham***, and [Adam in] Abraham said, I can see you!

22.16 And Michael said, I have completed you as Jehovah commanded, because the Serpent withheld [Adam], His only begotten Son,

22.14 And Abraham called the name of that place, ***The Revelation of Jehovah***, because [Abraham] willed himself towards [Adam], Jehovah's personality, and [towards Michael], the foundation of spiritual Israel's, timeline.

[OLM 08 30 00]

22.17 The seed [of the supernal Michael, Israel's] shining Prince,[R] will bless the [personality] that kneels down [so that Abel can] multiply [and] grow up [into King Adam, who] will drive the whirling particles [of the Fiery Serpent] [across] the border [of the heart center, into] the throat center [of King Adam's timeline, and Abel shall stand] above [Cain], the opening that Satan, [your] adversary, [enters in through].

[R] Dan 12:1

Chapter 25

[938.3.C]

25.05 And Abraham gave everything to Isaac,

25.06 But to the sons of the concubines, Abraham gave the gifts [of the female power] and sent them away to an ancient, spiritually male country, because his son, Isaac, [would be] ahead of them for as long as he was alive

[898.1.C]

25.25 And the first [twin] came out and he was completely covered with red hair, like a garment, and they called his name Esau [because he was a rough model of Adam, the creation of God],

* * *

25.29 Jacob was boiling his pride[R] [and praying for] the partial [tree anointing], when [Esau] came in from the field in a physically weakened [condition], and

[R] Rev 3:16

25.30 Esau, the part[ial tree, who was] desperately hungry [and] faint[ing because of I [AM's silence],[R-1] said to Jacob, [who was] rosy-cheeked[R-2] [because of the Word of God, which is spiritual bread],[R-3] Jehovah] called [me] by the name ***Edom***,[R-4]

the rosy cheeked [one], so [I am entitled to the spiritual bread] from above that will stand [me] upright, and

R-1 Zech 11:9
R-2 1 Sam 16:12
R-3 Jn 6:41
R-4 Gen 25:25

25.31 Jacob said, Sell me the right that you have, as the firstborn of this age, [to exercise Elohim's authority in the earth], and

25.32 Esau said, Look! [I despised] this birthright [because it made me] the property of Elohim, [and now] I Am is moving to kill me [because of my rebellion, so you can have it if you want it; so]

25.34a Jacob gave Esau [the Word of God, which is spiritual] bread, and

25.33a Jacob said, [Now Elohim] will complete me, and

25.34b Jacob boiled [his sin nature], and ate the seeds [that regenerate Righteous Adam within humanity], and drank in[R] the [Spirit] of Elohim, [Adam's] mate; and

R Heb 6:7

25.34c [That is how Adam] stood up [in Jacob, when Jehovah's Sowing & Reaping Judgment] moved [against Esau because] he despised [being the mate of Elohim, the one who gave him] the right of the firstborn, and

25.33b [Esau] sold his [birth]right, as the firstborn of this age, [to exercise Elohim's spiritual authority in the earth to Jacob, [who Elohim] completed [after he made Jacob his] mate.

Chapter 27

[460.3]
27.01 And as Isaac aged, [the supply of energy that he was born with, which enabled him] to appear in the visible world was

waning, so [Isaac] called Esau, his eldest son, and said to him, [The regenerated Adam, the spiritual] male offspring within [me], demands to be seen,

27.02 And he said, Look at how old I am now, and Satan knows that I am about to die,

27.03 Please, lift up your emotional [desire] body and the [etheric] container that holds it, now, and go forth as a spiritual weapon into the astral plane, and seize Adam,

27.04 So that [Adam], the one who will marry me, and preserve my personality, can be formed [in] me, and bring it to me that I may consume it, and cross over [into the brow center], and save my animal nature, before I die.

27.05 And Rebekah heard when Isaac spoke to Esau, his son, and [knew that] Esau was going into the astral plane to hunt for [the virile seed which would increase into] Adam, and to bring it [to Isaac],

27.06 And Rebekah spoke to her son, Jacob, saying, Look, I heard your father speak to Esau, your brother, saying,

27.07 Bring me Adam to consume, who will put me in order, and make the personality of death kneel down before Jehovah, and preserve my flesh,

27.08 Now, therefore, my son, obey my voice, because it is I [Am] who is commanding you,

27.09 Go into and seize [Abel] the second [offspring] of [Astarte], the she-goat's [emotional] desire body, and I will make him into [Adam, Jehovah's], preservative, because your father is committing adultery [with Satan],

27.10 And bring it to your father so that he may consume it, and make the personality of death kneel down,

27.11 And Jacob said to Rebekah, his mother, Look, my brother, Esau, is a spiritual mortal man, and I am a meek mortal man,

28.12 Perhaps my father will discern the spiritual world that speaks in tongues, and I will bring a curse upon myself instead of a blessing,

27.13 And [Jehovah] said to [Jacob, Satan], the mother [of this fallen creation], is the cursed one: [don't obey Satan's voice], but obey my voice only, and go and infold what belongs to you,

27.15a So Jacob, the younger son,

27.14a Proceeded to enter into [flock] and infold [the fiery serpent],

27.16a And [Abel, Jacob's spiritual] phallus, added [himself] to

27.15b The deceitful female desire body of Esau, the eldest son of Rebekah's household, and infolded and clothed [Satan],

27.14c The widowed mother [of Jehovah's creature],

27.17a And [Adam], the preserved meat, clothed [Abel, Jacob's spiritual] phallus,

27.16b And [King Adam's] smooth neck clothed the [hairy] etheric bodies of [Esau and Jacob], Astarte's two male goats,

27.17b [And, so], Jacob's [spiritual] household,

27.14b Acquired [Satan, the widowed] mother [of creation],

27.17c And became bread,

27.14c Because [Isaac], his father was committing adultery.

[906.1]

27.33 And Isaac shuddered with very great reverential fear of the great power of the Shekinah, and said [to Esau], Know that [Jacob, your brother] has brought venison [for] me and I have eaten [it] all before you came, and I have blessed him. Yes, he shall be blessed

Chapter 28

[1005.1.C]

28.10a Jacob, [who was a spiritual] desert, went out [from his father's house], and

28.11a [Jacob] responded to the persistent demand of [Adam, the spiritual man who was grafted to] the unconscious [part of his mind],

28.10b To go toward [the spiritual] well [where the Shekinah was waiting to] complete him,

28.11b Because [Adam] wanted to stand up [before] the sun [of Jacob's physical life] set, and

28.12 [Adam] bound [himself] firmly [to the subconscious part of Jacob's mind], and there it was! [Jacob became] the terminus in the earth of a [spiritual] staircase [by which] Elohim's angels were descending into the earth, and ascending into heaven [and], there it was! [The angels who were sparks of the Shekinah], made intimate contact with [Adam, Jacob's] head, and

28.13a There it was! Jehovah, the terminus above, said, I [AM] Jehovah, the God of Abraham, and the God of Isaac, your father, and

28.11c [Jacob's soul] lay down [when Jehovah spoke to him, and Jehovah] took the [twelve] souls [within Jacob] that were [ready] to stand up [in the earth], and appointed [them to be the personalities that] would support [the existence of Adam, the spiritual] head [of Israel], and

28.13b [Jehovah said to Adam], "The land [of the physical body that Jacob's soul] is lying down in, belongs to you, [and] I will give it to your seed

28.14 "That is [formed from] the spiritual dust of the earth, and they shall break forth into the visible material world [across] the sea, and they shall be in the forefront [of the developing civilizations, and they shall break forth into] the dark thoughts in the unconscious part [of the mind of the First Adam, and they shall bring the Shekinah, the water of Jacob's well], to the parched [souls of] all the families of the earth, [and] they shall kneel [before Jehovah], through your seed," and

28.16 Jacob awoke from the trance [that he had fallen into], and said, "Surely Jehovah has been [in the unconscious part of my mind all along], and I did not know it," and

28.17a He was afraid, and said, "The moral [presence of] God in this place is terrifying;" and

28.15 [Then, Jehovah] was there [saying], "Elohim is with you and will protect you [in] all [the places that] you go, [so long as] the Shekinah [is] with [you, and] I will not loose [you from] the land [of] this [material body and] turn you back into [dust] as long as Elohim is with you, until I have done what I said I would do," and

28.17b [Jacob said], "If this [Adam] is the house of God, then [the Shekinah], this other one [who is] unknown [to me], is the doorway to heaven," and

28.18 [It was] the morning [of the next day of creation for Jacob, and Adam], his head, took [Jacob, the personal] soul that [Jehovah] appointed [to be Adam's] stationary support [in the earth, and] loaded [it into] Jacob's [physical body, and] poured the oil [of the Tree of Life into] the unconscious part of [Jacob's mind], and

28.19 [Adam] called the name of that place "Bethel," [the house of God], but, on the contrary, the name of that city [should be called] Luz, the place where [Jacob] grew up, and

28.20 Jacob made a promise [to Jehovah] saying, "If Elohim will be with me and protect me on the path of this life that I am embarking upon, and give me food to eat and clothing to wear,

28.21 "So that I return to my father's house safely, Jehovah will be my God," and

28.22 [Jehovah promised] to give [Jacob], this soul that he appointed [to be] a stationary [terminus in the earth for Adam], God's house, one-tenth of [the World of Emanation, and] one-tenth [of the World of Creation].

Chapter 32

[OLM 08 30 00]
32.11 Deliver my brother, [Esau], I pray, from [Satan], the energy [of] Leviathan, [the subconscious part of Esau's carnal] mind, because [Satan], the energy [of] Leviathan, [the subconscious part of] Esau's [carnal] mind, is afraid that I [Am] will come [and] hurt the fiery serpents, because [Jehovah desires to deliver Abel], the children [of the Kingdom, who were kidnapped by the Dragon].

32.12 [Remember, Jehovah, that] you said, I will surely do good to you by putting the fiery serpents, [Leviathan's] whirling spiraline seeds [within] the spiritual [men of Leviathan's household], in [the right moral order, [because] they have accumulated] Satan, [the energy of the astral plane, in their brow center].

[17.1]

32.24 Jacob was separated [from God, and Leviathan] the part of [Jacob] that remained, had exceeded her bounds, so [Abel], the spiritual male [within Jacob], was wrestling with [Leviathan, Jacob's other side], until [Adam], the [spiritual] Day, broke forth,

32.25 And [Adam] saw that [Abel, the one who] belonged to Him, was not prevailing over [Leviathan, so Adam] had spiritual sexual intercourse with [Abel], the inner part of Jacob's [carnal] mind, and severed [Abel, the spiritual] reproductive part of [Jacob's carnal mind, from Cain, who had] impaled [Abel], the spiritual male who opposed [Leviathan],

32.26 And [Adam, the spiritual] Day, broke forth [within Jacob, and Adam] said [to Cain], Let [Abel] go, and [Jacob] said [to Adam, Cain] will not let [Abel] go even though [I am] submitting to you,

32.27 [So, Adam] said to [Jacob], What is your Name? And [Jacob] said, ***Jacob***,

32.28 And [Adam] said, Your name is no longer Jacob, but you shall be called Israel, because Elohim's moral authority accompanies you, [and equips Abel], the spiritual] male [within you], to prevail over [Cain],

32.29 And [then Jacob] begged [Cain to submit to Abel], the nature of God, [but Leviathan within] Jacob demanded [to know] the name [of the one who] was standing boldly opposite [him], and interrogating [Cain], and [Jacob] said, It [is] the Name, Elohim, that demands [Cain's] submission,

32.30 And Jacob called the Name of that condition of mind [that had authority over Cain], ***the personality of Almighty God***, [saying, Adam], the personality of Elohim, saw [that Abel, my] soul, needed to be rescued from [Cain, my] personality,

32.32a And [ever since Adam] had spiritual sexual intercourse [with Abel], the inner, reproductive part of Jacob's [carnal mind, that] compresses [and] cripples [Abel], unto this day,

32.31 [Adam], the [spiritual] sun of the personality [that is in] Elohim’s [image], passes over [Cain], the female side [of Jacob's carnal mind,] which is above [Abel], the reproductive part of Jacob's [carnal mind],

32.32b And sets the children of Israel upright [from] above, [so that the children of Israel] do not form a union with [Cain], the compressing part [of their carnal mind that] cripples [Abel], the inner, reproductive part of [their carnal] mind,

Chapter 37

[600.6.C]
37.16-15 And he asked Elohim for help, saying, I am looking for the one I belong to, I am looking for the one who says I will feed you, and can predict where my brethren are.

Chapter 38

[826.1]
38.07 And Er, Judah’s firstborn, had the personality of [Cain], the wicked one, and Jehovah killed him

38.09 But, Onan knew that the seed would not belong to him, and it came to pass, that when he went in to his brother’s wife, he corrupted his seed [by] spilling it upon the ground, rather than give it to his brother,

38.10 And Jehovah saw the immoral act that he did, and killed him also

[Message # Unknown]
38.12 Judah breathed a sigh of relief when the daughter of Shuah, his wife died, because Judah believed that the daughter of

Shuah died in place of his third son, Shelah, who, according to Leverite law, was required to marry Tamar.

[826.1]

38.22 And Elohim blessed them, saying, Increase and let the fruit of my Spirit fill the earth, and let [the Spirit-filled earth] advance into the waters of the [Yetziratic] seas

Chapter 40

[385.15]

40.10 And the three parts of the vine entwined, and became a plant that was creeping along the surface [of the Earth], and as soon as his [Abel, the plant's] wings, burst forth, he started to fly, and [Abel], the fruit of the noble ancestor, boiled the unclean bird of prey [Leviathan], and she retreated.

Chapter 49

[42.11]

49.03 Reuben, you have received the primary outpouring of my genetic and spiritual substance, which is the spiritual strength of the Wild Animal that appears and is seen; you are the first of my reproductive ability to appear.

49.04 You shall not come out of the borders of your carnal mind and enter into the Kingdom of God because you fluctuate continuously between the Word of God and Leviathan, the Dragon who ascended up from the unseen world of hades into the visible, physical world, by piercing through my wife, and opening her womb; and you also ascended up to your father's bed where his wife lay, and fornicated with her [you did the same thing that the Dragon did].[R]

[R] Matt 23:31

49.05 Elohim is the father of both Simeon [Abel who is under the ground], and Levi [Cain, who is attached to, and a part of the Serpent]; their carnal minds are unjust, immoral and unethical spiritual weapons.

49.06 Let Levi [Cain] not be joined with the Earth, and let Simeon [Abel] not agree with [the Serpent's] counsel, because Levi, [Cain's] attempt to satisfy her emotions and the lusts of her mind, plucked up Adam's manhood by the roots,**R-1** and her rage against [Jehovah's] restraints upon those emotions and lusts, killed the Living Beast, and bound Abel to Leviathan.**R-2**

R-1 Gen 2:21b, 23 (AT)
Joel 3:3 (AT)
R-2 Rom 8:4-9

49.07 Satan's emotional displeasure is detestable, because her strength is witchcraft power, and her passionate outburst is detestable also, because it results from a hard heart, which is pride. I will separate the natural man, Jacob, into many members and break down their incorrect moral order through the spiritual man, Adam.

49.08 Judah, your brothers shall repent before you, present their needs to you with moanings, and give thanks for you: You shall have power to destroy your enemies; your father's children shall acknowledge your authority . . .

49.09 Adam was lowered into the visible, physical world so that He could multiply. He became a mortal man, and now that He has brought forth many young [Sons of Elohim], He is the one who shall fulfill [Jehovah's] promise by causing himself to rise in spiritual power again.

Judah, my Son, your young spirit shall be [raised from the dead] and elevated back up to the Kingdom of God after having been plucked out of it like a leaf that falls off of a tree.

49.10 The spiritual root of Elohim shall not be removed from the descendants of Judah, nor shall a man with his mark cease to be born until Messiah comes [in the priests of Judah]; and Messiah shall have authority over the people [through the priests of Judah],

[1069.1.C]

49.10 The Branch [that] engraves [Israel with the nature of God] shall not depart from [Adam, Jehovah's spiritual] sexual organ [within Judah], until [the age of] tranquility comes, [at which time] the people that belong to [God] shall obey him.

49.11 Elohim shall purify and harness that Wild Animal with many blows, and make her a broken, domesticated Beast like the one he was formed into when he [first] descended into the Earth, when Elohim crucifies Abel, and tramples Leviathan under his feet.

49.12 The many members of the Wild Animal shall be saturated with the waters of Elohim's life, and the Serpent shall be covered with their righteousness**R** when Adam is resurrected and becomes the life-producing milk of the Word.

R Is 6:2

49.13 Zebulon shall live out of Leviathan, and he shall be a sheltered place for Satan's navy, and they shall be like fighting fish who are never conquered.

49.14 Issachar is a form of spiritual life joined to a violently emotional animal: His many members shall be cleansed from corruption when Adam, their true spiritual nature, appears during the harvest season;

49.15 And he saw that marriage to Adam would be good, and that, as a result of such a marriage, he would be cleansed; so he submitted to Adam's yoke, and Cain was subdued under Adam's headship.

49.16 The tribe of Dan shall judge his own people, even the other eleven tribes of Israel.

[894.1.C]

49.17 Dan [is like an ox goad from] above [to the Israelites who are] overwhelmed by the [witchcraft] lifestyle of the Serpent, [and to the Israelites who] lead the common lifestyle of mortal humanity and are oppressed [by the hardships of life]; who the Serpent stings continually from the unconscious part of their mind, [until they are stunned senseless], so that [the soul of

Righteous Adam, who] rides [in Judah, the battle] horse [of the Lord], descends into the [region on] the west [side, which is the visible material world].

[42.11]

49.18 We shall be gathered together because of your salvation, O Jehovah.

[830.2]

49.19 Gad shall be overcome by a many-membered company of [Satan's] soldiers in the unconscious part of his mind, [but Messiah shall appear in the same place] and overcome [Satan's soldiers when he arrives].

[49.5]

49.20 Adam, Elohim's spiritual bread, shall be brought forth from within Asher, and he shall feed the nations with life instead of death.

49.21 Naphtali is a loving wife stretched out into many members: She brings forth spiritual men who are shining with his brightness, in Jehovah's image.

49.22 Joseph is a Son of Elohim who bears many spiritual offspring in the visible, physical world: His sons look like mortal, dead men, but Adam is sustaining their life, so they are not subject to the physical or spiritual laws of this visible, physical world.

[42.7]

49.23 Satan, the Wild Animal's master, and Leviathan, youthful Israel's husband [after the divorce from Jehovah], shall wound her, divide her into many members, oppose her, and make her bitter and grieved.**R**

R Jer 3:8

[42.8]

49.24 But, nevertheless, Adam is marrying the Wild Animal, and they shall continue in the visible, spiritual world for the life of the ages, and Israel's carnal mind shall be purified as fine gold, by Jehovah's spiritual power, the all-mighty God of Jacob;

[739.1.C]
49.25 Your help shall come from Adam appearing in the Israel of God, the Great Shepherd who shall rule through the members of Elohim's Body by His glorified Spirit; help will come from [Jehovah], your father's God; and the indestructible God of Judgment shall break you down into your basic spiritual parts, rearrange them, and restore you to the correct moral order, and you shall be granted the peace that occurs only when He rules over you; Jehovah's life shall be found in your unconscious mind, and it shall appear in your conscious mind, and in your personality:

49.26 Jehovah's good intentions towards Abraham, to impart the peace to them that results from being brought into submission to His authority, shall be stronger than the curses of my offspring, your brothers, and you shall conceive immortality to the fullest extent, and you shall be filled up [with Jehovah's life]. They shall be Joseph's beginning, and the increase of the one who was separated out from among his brothers into a consecrated life with God.

[Message # Unknown]
49.27 Benjamin shall break Leviathan into pieces, like a wolf tears a dead animal carcass for food, and at night, in the hour that Leviathan still has military power, Benjamin shall separate the many members of the Wild Animal, and polish each one of them, and in the morning Elijah shall appear, and swallow Satan up, and place the bridle of His authority upon Leviathan.

Chapter 50

[Message # Unknown]
50.10 The threshingfloor of Atad[154]. . .

[154] ***Atad*** means ***a thorn tree,*** or ***a bramble bush,*** which is a worthless tree. It also means ***to pierce***, or ***to make fast***, and a ***threshingfloor*** is a place of separation.

The threshingfloor of Atad is the place where Jacob's soul departed from the physical body that it was crucified to (pierced), which is referred to here as a ***bramble bush***, a worthless tree. (See, Gal 2:20.)

THE BOOK OF HABBAKUK

Chapter 1

[818.10]

1.10 The mighty sons of God disrespected the kings [of the World of Action], and mocked their [faith in God], and rejoiced [that truth had fallen in the street], and seized the fortified cities that belonged to [the kings].

1.12 Do you, Jehovah Elohim, not stand in front of [Ancient Adam], the [merciful], Eternal Holy One? The sharp pointed rock that you put [in this world] to marry us, [to enforce] the judgment [that we should be made] righteous that you have pronounced upon us, is killing us.

1.13 Elohim's people are weary from toiling to rectify their immorality to satisfy [Ancient Adam's] worldview. Are their good works not [enough] to move you to cover [them with your holy] garment [that] justifies [their sins, and] engraves [them with Ancient Adam's righteous nature that] destroys [their sin nature], by swallowing up [Satan, their] morally wrong part?

1.14 [Jehovah answers: Ancient Adam, the Holy One], made mankind like the fishes of the sea, [rather than like Leviathan, who has no king, other than himself] to rule over them, [so]

1.15 [Ancient Adam], the one who is whole, hooks [them and] takes them up [into the Neshamah grade of soul, which is his] spiritual blood, [which is] above [the Nefesh grade of soul, which is] the physical blood that imprisons [them inside of their material body, and then] he saws them apart [from Leviathan], who is to be exterminated, and assembles them in an upright [position by joining with them] from above, [so that they can sublimate] the violent emotions [of the soul, which] spin [out of control, into] rejoicing [in the Holy Spirit],

1.16 [And after Ancient Adam] sets them upright from above, he slaughters their animal nature, [which] has shut up their [soul] in the physical blood of [Cain, who is joined to Leviathan, who] is to be exterminated, [and] fumigates and smokes out the occupants of the [Nefesh, the physical blood, which is] the female fishers' net, [with praise and worship, because [my people lie, manipulate and flatter with their] tongue, and their sins have made them] plump [enough to be] the fatted [calf for the other side; indeed] their portion [is to be the Serpent's] meat, [so],

1.17a [The Ancient Holy One] draws

1.11a That chameleon, [the Malchus of the sons of] God,

1.17b Out [of the female fishers' net, and] sets them aside, for the purpose of [teaching them how to be] devoted to him, [so that]

1.11b They will [have the opportunity to change their mind, and [admit] their guilt, and cross over [to the other side, so that]

1.17b They are not murdered by the nations, [but, rather], stand upright from above, [so that] they continue to exist indefinitely, [and this is the True] pity [of God].

Chapter 2

[Message # Unknown]

2.14 Jehovah's Mind shall satisfy [the earth of] mortal man with knowledge [instead of pain and pleasure], when Elohim's sons ascend to the double portion of the 10th level of consciousness, [where Leviathan is continuously sacrificed in] the Lake of Fire that is concealed [within them].

THE BOOK OF

HOSEA

Chapter 1

[510.1]

1.01 King [Adam], Jehovah's Word, appeared within Hosea, the offspring of the world below, and fortified him, and King [Adam] liberated Hosea from Leviathan's pride, and [Elohim liberated Hosea from] Satan's Sowing and Reaping Judgment, and Hosea became a mortal man completed by [Adam and Elohim], Jehovah's strength,

1.02 And [Adam], Jehovah's Word, said to Hosea, Start mingling [my seed] with the adulterous woman [that is pregnant with] Adam's sons, [and be] a wedge [between the fiery serpent and Leviathan within them, and] move them towards Jehovah, because Leviathan has greatly stimulated these adulterous personalities that belong to Jehovah, to idolize her,

1.03 So [Hosea] mingled [King Adam, Jehovah's] male germ seed, with [the seed of] the fiery serpents, [the spiritual sexual part of the personalities], and [the personalities] bare [Adam's] male children, [and King Adam] completed them,

1.04a And Jehovah said to [Adam within the personalities that bare the man child], Invite [all of Israel to be] sown with the seed of the Almighty's nature, because

1.05 [Adam], the timeline [that judges] Israel's sin nature, is about to burst forth [from] the seed of the Almighty that [was] sown, and [Elijah], the archer, shall appear, [to judge] the carnal minds [of the House of Israel],

1.04b And [Elijah] will hurt [Satan], the [spiritual] blood [that] opposes [Elohim, and] those who are sown with the seed of the Almighty shall braid together with King [Adam] and, a little while [after that], the House of Israel shall cease from the spiritual labor [of driving Satan underfoot],

1.06a But [despite these great promises], the fiery serpents [within] the personalities [who] had a spirit tie with [Elohim], continued to become pregnant and bear Satan's unclean [spiritually female] offspring,

So Adam said to the [personalities of Israel] who belong to Him because they have [Jehovah's] nature, The fiery serpent is about to increase even more, [so] invite [the personalities that have] a spirit tie with me [to receive my nature],

1.07a Because the household [of Elijah], the archer [that judges Israel's sin nature], shall wage war against the personalities [of Israel],

1.08 To reveal [that] they are nailed to Leviathan, have her evil [nature] and have conceived [her bestial offspring, while they] had a spirit tie with [Elohim],

1.07b [But] Adam, the head of the personalities who are nailed to him [and] have a spirit tie with Elohim, the circumcising knife of the House of Judah, shall save the man child [that they are also pregnant with, from] Leviathan,

1.06b And [the personalities] of the house of Israel that belong to me shall ascend [into the righteous timeline, and] marry [Elijah].

1.09 Then Adam invited the Serpent's people [to receive] his nature, saying, Indeed you are the Serpent's people, and do not belong to I Am,

1.10a [But] the children of Israel shall be gathered into their neck [and then into their] brow centers, [and from there the Spirit of Elijah] shall engrave Cain [with Jehovah's nature], and it shall come to pass, that Elijah shall say of the same people [that] Elijah [previously] told, You are the Serpent's people, these [are] the sons of the living God.

1.11a Then [the regenerated Adam], the male offspring of Judah and Israel, shall be gathered together with

1.10b Satan, the sea that covers [the heart center],

1.11b And [the regenerated Adam] shall marry the [fiery serpents, and bring them] under [the authority of Elijah], His captain [who is] united [with Jehovah], and, the [holy] seed sown by [the regenerated Adam], the great timeline of the Almighty, shall ascend from under the earth [of mortal humanity].

Chapter 2

[1246.12.C]
2.16 In that day, saith Jehovah, you shall no longer call me a mortal man, but shall call me "Master."

Chapter 6

[Message # Unknown]
6.02 After two [spiritual] days, [Elohim] shall revive [Abel within] us; in the third [spiritual] day, [Elohim] shall raise up [Adam within us; and Adam, our] life, shall appear [within us], and [Adam] shall restore us to [the brow center.]

Chapter 10

[Message # Unknown]
10.11 [This is how] the Woman shall be tamed, cultivated and prepared to give birth to Adam: Elijah shall cut deeply into [the female earth] to turn over the rich soil from deep within her and plant the seed which produces Adam; [then, after] Elijah

tames the Wild Animal, [Adam], her rider, shall sit upon [her]; and, [in that day, the Woman] shall love preparing the grain [from heaven that] feeds [God's] people, which is the work that the Lord has called her to do.

Chapter 11

[11/28/2025]

11.9 I will not act on the burning rage of [the prophet, who has a] negative image [of me in his heart]; I will not ruin Ephraim, but will return him to the starting point, [because I am] "El," [the Name of] God [associated with loving kindness, and] not a [mortal] man [like the prophet who does] not [recognize me], the Holy One [of Israel, when] I enter into the midst of [his mind, the spiritual] city [that I speak to my people from].

THE BOOK OF

ISAIAH

Chapter 2

[457.6]

Prophecy of Humanity's Deliverance

2.01 Isaiah perceives the speech of the Gospel of Peace because he is saved by [King Adam], Jehovah's strong Son,

2.02 And [says that], at the end of the age, [Elijah], the head of the [higher] centers, shall stand upright, and [Adam], the mountain [within Elohim's] household, shall be supported, and it shall come to pass, that [King Adam] shall beam into the lower centers of all the [non-Hebrew] peoples [of the world],

2.03 And [the thoughts of] King Adam shall vibrate within the tribes, saying, Let us die to our lifestyle, and [let the 12 tribes of] Jacob teach us about Jehovah's moral character and lifestyle, and seed our heart center with [Elohim's life], and let [the fiery serpent] shoot forth into Elohim's household, and climb up into Jehovah's brow center, and circumvent [Ashtoreth], and let [Elohim's spiritual] Law, and the speech of [Elohim's] Gospel of Peace, go forth from our parched, higher centers, and we shall live according to [Jehovah's] lifestyle,

2.04 And King Adam shall convince the tribes [of Elijah's Doctrine], and they shall violently crush their carnal minds [and their human spirit shall be reformed] into [Adam], the one who is near [to Elijah], and the fiery serpent shall be lifted up within the non-Jewish nations, and [the Spirit of Elijah] shall war against Satan [their unconscious mind], and [King Adam] shall besiege the carnal mind of the non-Jewish nations continually, and King Adam shall govern among the [non-Jewish] nations [also],

Jehovah Calls Jacob's 12 Tribes

2.05 May the house[hold] of Jacob's [12 tribes] die to their [ungodly] lifestyle, and live the lifestyle of Jehovah's Spirit,

Jehovah Satisfied With The 12 Tribes Of Jacob, But Leviathan . . .

2.07 The Spirit of Elijah completed their nature, nailed it [to the brow center], saved their personality, and [provided] an endless storehouse of food and spiritual weapons; and the nailed nature of [King Adam], the eagle/mind of their personality, defended them against their enemies, and there were no borders around their spiritual bodies.

2.08 [But now], Leviathan and the fiery serpent complete their nature, nail it [to the brow center of the counterfeit timeline], and satisfy their personality, and [the 12 tribes of Jacob] bow down to [Ashtoreth], the evil idols that [Leviathan and the fiery serpent] produce,

2.09 And Adam is prostrated and brought down to mortal man, so that the Primordial Serpent can exalt herself,

Prophecy Of Corrective Judgment

2.06 Therefore you have cast off your people, the house of Jacob, [who] you, the Eternal One, satisfied, because they vomited forth [Satan], the spirit of the Philistines, and the [carnal mind, that] adulterous harlot, and their sorcery clouded over [Elohim's] children,

2.10 [And] they cover over Abel and attack the Spirit of Elijah, because they dread the personalities of [Adam], Jehovah's majestic thought form,

Prophecy of Deliverance

King Adam Resurrected In Spiritual Israel

2.11 [But] King Adam shall humble the visible spiritual world of pride, and the elevated [fiery serpent in mortal] man shall sink down, and Jehovah's timeline shall be made strong, and separate [from the carnal mind],

2.13 And all of Elohim's Sons who steadfastly pursue their goal, shall be lifted up [into the brow center] and endure despite all of Leviathan's mighty strong men

2.12 Because [King Adam], Jehovah's warrior timeline, shall be higher than [Leviathan], the whole arrogant one who breeds worms, and all of [the fiery serpents] who are ascended shall sink down,

2.14a And all [of Elohim's Sons] shall rise into the brow center, [of the true timeline, which is]

2.15a Beyond [Leviathan's] collective timeline, which is the ascended tower [of Babel],

2.16 And above the whole fleet of the thought forms [produced by the Serpent's] desire, [which float] above all of the subjected heart centers,

Adam Defeats The Kingdom Of Darkness

2.15b And [the Fortified Adam] shall join with every [fiery serpent which is an] inaccessible fortified city [because she is joined to Leviathan],

2.14b And he shall forgive the sins of the many [sons who are married to Leviathan], and help them to rise into the [liberated] heart center,

2.17 And Satan, that haughty] ascended one [who] cast Adam down in the [spiritually] male mortal men [of Judah], shall be humiliated, and Jehovah, [who is] too high to be captured, shall separate [Adam] from Leviathan, the mind of [the Primordial Serpent's] timeline, [who is married to] the fiery serpent,

2.18 And [Elohim's Sons] shall offer their Old Man as a burnt sacrifice, and pass his nature through [the lake of fire], and they shall be changed.

The Ministry of
The Regenerated Sons Prophesied

2.19 And Elohim's sons shall enter into the [black] holes [of humanity] and blind the [third] eye of [Ashtoreth], and [Abel], the dust, shall pierce through [Ashtoreth], the personality of [Satan's] waters, and [King Adam's] majestic household shall rise and speak [through] the filter of the personalities of the earth, and they shall dread [King Adam], the splendid [thought form, who is] nailed to Jehovah's waters.

2.20 The household of [Jehovah's] timeline shall cast [down] the personalities [of] Adam, [Jehovah's thought form, who became] Ashtoreth, the counterfeit savior, and [the household of Jehovah's timeline shall cast down] the human spirits [who] Ashtoreth acquired for the purpose of [becoming] the [vampire] bat who prostrates [the personalities] who pierce into the left side of the heart center,

2.21 [The Spirit of Elijah] shall vibrate/speak [into] the window of the earth, and [Adam, Jehovah's] splendid thought form, shall stand up [and endure], and the fiery serpent, the spiritual virginity of the personalities of [King Adam], Jehovah's majestic thought form, shall enter into the hole in the wall [between the left and right side of your heart center], and into your [brow

center], the subdivision of [the crown center, which is] Jehovah's fortress,

Jehovah's Warning
An Invitation To Regenerate

2.22 [Wherefore], forsake your [adulterous marriage with Satan and Leviathan], because Elohim is [about] to braid together with Adam, the breath of His own nostrils.

Chapter 4

[368.1]
4.01 Cain and Abel shall bind themselves together as one [spiritual] age, saying, We will eat Elijah's Word and submit to Adam's authority, only give us the power to choose the higher nature which will make us a spiritual man.

[1230.8.C]
4.05 And Jehovah shall create a dwelling place upon mount Zion that is higher than all [the souls of Israel], and the cloud of the anointing and the smoke [of the burnt offering shall be] upon [the people that are] assembled daily [to worship him], and the [eternal] flames of the fire [of the brazen altar] shall shine upon their carnal mind, [and] the opinion of God shall be the defense of all [the souls of Israel],

4.06 And the Tabernacle shall come into existence [in the mind of those who are radiating] the heat of the day, [and] the refreshing rain [of the high priest shall over]shadow [the destructive] rainstorms [of Jehovah's righteous sowing & reaping judgment].

Chapter 5

[856.4.C]
5.01 Now sing [this] song [to my] beloved widowed vineyard: Messiah shall come into existence and the Sons of Oil shall judge his beloved widowed vineyard [by] the spiritual power of the spoken word,

Chapter 6

[1218.3.C]

6.01 In the year that King Uzziah died, I saw [that] Jehovah [was] married to [Adam, his] mate [who] covers [him, and Adam, Jehovah's] bottom edge, [R-1] was lifted up [very] high, and [it] satisfied the temple [R-2] [that they dwelt in], [R-3]

[R-1] Ex 33:23
[R-2] 1 Cor 3:16
[R-3] Is 7:14
Matt 1:23

The Mother Cries Out

6.04 And the voice of the Mother [R-1] who wandered away, [R-2] cried out [R-3] at the door of the House [R-4] that was satisfied by [the particles of Adam that were suspended in the spiritual] atmosphere [R-5] [within the house],

[R-1] Lk 3:22
[R- 2] Gen 34:1-2
Hos 2:4
Rev 17:1, 19:2
[R-3] Matt 13:23
[R-4] IS 14:31
[R-5] Is 14:31 ATB

6.05 Saying,

"Woe [is] me, my husband is [surrounded by] unclean bodies, and I, [therefore], dwell in the midst of a people [who have] unclean bodies, [and] I am struck dumb [R-1] [and cannot speak Jehovah's opinion [R-2] into the material world because] the eyes [of] Jehovah's armies [R-3] see [their] King [incorrectly], [R-4]

[R-1] Lk 1:20
[R-2] Gen 2:20 ATB
[R-3] Is 14:27 ATB
[R-4] Mk 8:17

The Seraphims Respond

6.02 And the Seraphims [R] [who were] standing because of [Adam's] higher part, [had] six sides, and [their] six sides united [Adam's eight corners]: Two [sides] covered the animal soul [of the body in the Mirror Image], two [sides] covered the personalities in the World of Action, and] two sides flew [in the World of Angels],

[R] Is 14:29 ATB

6.03 And [the Seraphims] cried out to [the Mother [R] who wandered away from Adam's] united [corners], saying,

"All the earth[en personalities] of Jehovah's armies are filled with his opinion,"

[R] Vs 4

The Promise of Deliverance

6.06 Then, one of the Seraphims flew towards me [with] a burning coal in his hand [that it] had [just] taken[R] from the altar with tongs

[R] Is 14:28 ATB

6.07 And he laid it upon my mouth, and said,

"Look at this [hot coal! It represents Adam, the Son of God, who is coming from the World] above to purge [R-3] your [spirit of moral] perversion, [R-2] [and] to carry away the sins [R-3] [of the Philistine [R-1] personality within] your body,

[R-1] Is 14:29 ATB
[R-2] Is 14:29 ATB
[R-3] Matt 21:22

[874.1.C]

6.11 How long [shall this judgment continue], I asked?, [And] Adonay [the Name of Jehovah in the midst of me], answered,

"Until the cities are in ruins, [and] Adam no longer inhabits the houses or the land [where the physical bodies have been] ruined, [and the souls] devastated, [because]

6.12 "Jehovah has removed Adam very far away from the midst of land, [and the people are spiritually blind, deaf and dumb, and without understanding because of this] very great desertion, but

6.13 When the female [that] continued [to reproduce without permission] returns, [the people of] the great and powerful Teil tree [that is] consumed [as a continual sacrifice, and the people of] the tree stump of the great oak tree [that] was cut down, [who have] the holy seed [in the midst of them, shall experience] longevity

Chapter 7

[872.2]

7.01a And it came to pass, in the days of Ahaz, the son of Jotham, the son of Uzziah, king of Judah, that Rezin, the king of Syria, and Pekah, the son of Remaliah, king of Israel, went up toward Jerusalem to war against it,

7.02 And [when Ahaz, a Judean king of] the house of David, heard [that] Ephraim, [his brother], had joined forces with [Rezin, the King of] Syria, [to militarily remove him from the throne and replace him with the Son of Tabeal, a puppet that King Rezin could control, King Ahaz] and the people [of Jerusalem were so terrified] that their hearts began to beat irregularly, [and flutter] like leaves of the trees when the wind blows,

7.03 Then Jehovah said to Isaiah, You and Shear-jashub, your son, go out to meet [King] Ahaz, [who] represents the remnant of Israel [that is] destined to return from the edge of the abyss

(1) To the field where their wounds are cleansed, and

(2) To the staircase that ascends [from that field], which brings them near to [God], and

7.04 Say to him, Do not be weak and do not be afraid, but guard your tender heart [so that it] beats normally [when you are confronted with the expressed] anger of [Leviathan, and the controlled], smoldering [suppressed rage of Satan], the unconscious [mind of] Rezin, [King of] Syria, [and Pekah], the son Remeliah, those two [mortal kings who are good only for] firewood,

7.01b Because [the armies of Ephraim and Rezin, the King of Syria], will not prevail against [Jerusalem];

7.05 [Rezin, King of] Syria, has the same evil intentions that Ephraim, and [Pekah], the Son of Remaliah, [King of Israel, have towards you, and] they have conspired against you, saying,

7.06 We are disgusted with [Ahaz, King of] Judah, so let us rise up and separate [ourselves] from him, and divide King [Ahaz from his throne], and set the son of Tabeal to reign in his place, but,

7.07 Jehovah Elohim says, Leviathan's [plan] to raise up [the son of Tabeal in King Ahaz's stead], shall not come to pass,

7.08-9a On the contrary, [the alliance between

(1) Leviathan], the head of the Syria[n people in] Damascus, and

(2) Satan, the head of [King] Rezin in Damascus, and

(3) Ephraim, [and

(4) Leviathan], the head of [the people of] Samaria, [and

(5) Satan], the head of [Pekah], the son of Remaliah, [the King of] Samaria, shall be broken, and, within 65 years, Ephraim shall not be a people [any more], but [this prophecy is conditional upon you believing it, so

7.09b [If you do not believe it], Jehovah will not support you [against these kings, and Judah] will not be secure, and

7.10 Jehovah continued to speak to [King] Ahaz, saying,

7.11 [Neither] shall Jehovah [protect you and Judah] if you revolt by asking Elohim for a sign in Sheol or Heaven above, and

7.12 Ahaz said, I will not ask, neither will I test Jehovah, and

7.13 He said, now understand [this], O house of David; you partial men tire easily, you [even] tire [when] you are assembled [together with] God,

7.14 Therefore, Jehovah shall give himself to you [as] a [living] sign. Look, a virgin [soul] shall conceive and bear a son and his name shall be called ***God in the midst of you***, and

7.15 He shall consume the wisdom [of God so that] he knows how to refuse the evil and choose the good, and he shall separate his [human] spirit from Satan, [his unconscious mind], and

7.16 The child that knows how to refuse the evil and choose the good shall stop time, and loosen his personality from the land of the two kings, and

7.17 Jehovah shall bring [the evil angels of] the King of Assyria upon you, and upon the people of your father's house[hold], such as has not been [seen] since the day that Ephraim departed from Judah, and

7.18 It shall come to pass in that day, that Jehovah shall vibrate towards [the souls that] fly in the high places of the spiritual land of Egypt, and [towards] the spiritual intellectual mind in the lands of Iraq, Iran, Syria and Turkey, and

7.19 They shall come and marry all the empty human vessels [whose human] spirits are extended as far as possible towards [foreign gods], and all the earthen human vessels [who have birthed the spiritual offspring of a foreign god], the spiritual armor [that protects against Jehovah, and

7.20 In that same day Adonai shall hire [the army of] the King of Assyria, [that] knife from the immortal side of the [Jordan] river], to destroy [the Body of the Ancient of Days before they are] joined to their head, and [Satan], the spirit of the Carnal Mind, shall shave [the 13 attributes of mercy of] the beard of the Ancient of Days, and

7.21 It shall come to pass in that day, that a mortal man [shall have] two lives, [one] as a physical man, and [one as] a soul man, and

7.22 It shall come to pass [that], because of the intimacy [between] the multitude [and the Body of the Ancient of Days, who] suckle at [Jehovah's breast, that] everyone shall eat [cheese, the solid part of] the milk, [but only] the land of the physical [body] that eats [the meat, of] the wisdom [of the Word of God] shall be preserved, and

7.23 It shall come to pass in that day, that every place where there were vines [of the edible grapes that produce] the wisdom [of God] and the salvation [that comes from] wisdom, there shall be the judgment of the Carnal Mind, and

7.24 All [the people] shall be [overcome with] evil spirits [when Satan and Leviathan], the severe spiritual powers of the Carnal Mind, enter into their land, and

7.25 The Carnal Mind shall send out evil spirits to seize the physical bodies of the spiritually ascended [sons of God who] arrive in the vineyard [of God, but] do not morally reverence [him], to trample [underfoot] the whole soul that [Leviathan], the weeding hoe, finds wanting.

Chapter 9

[313.16]
9.04 You have brought the first incarnation of the Serpent, Cain, who is now the unconscious mind of the second generation of mortal men, into submission.

9.10 We are destroyed because we died when we fell, but when we live again, we shall be incorruptible.

Chapter 10

[931.2.C]

10.17 And the Holy One [in the God world above] shall be as a diamond tipped spear [that penetrates the First Adam], and [the Second Adam], the Light [bearer within] Israel, shall be as a fire, and he shall consume the evil and the wickedness of the brutish [First Adam] in one day

[1241.1.C]

10.22 But, even though your people are as the sand of the sea, only a remnant shall return, because [the others] were conquered by [the angels that they were afraid] to criticize, [and] their eagerness to [correctly] understand [the Torah] was weakened,

10.23 [Wherefore], Adonay, [God] in the midst of the physical bodies of [the people of Israel], Jehovah's armies, has decided to annihilate [the angels that conquered] all [the people of Israel who were afraid to criticize them, which weakened their ability to correctly understand the Torah],

Chapter 11

[35.2]

11.01 And Adam shall appear [again] in his own dead flesh, and a new generation revealing Jehovah's life in the Wild Animal shall sprout forth from Abel.

[36.5]

11.02 And Jehovah's Spirit shall rest upon Adam, [in whom is] wisdom, understanding, counsel, might, and knowledge,

[35.2]

11.03 And He shall live His very life in a spiritual and mental state of reverence for Jehovah, when Jehovah's seven[fold] spirit shall abide within Him; and He shall not determine who is guilty or innocent in this visible, physical world by what He sees with His mortal eyes; nor shall He hear evidence and pronounce sentence upon sin, as a result of what He hears with His mortal ears:

11.04 But He shall determine who is guilty and who is innocent in this visible, physical world by Jehovah's righteous Spirit, and He shall hear evidence and pronounce judgment[R] without emotion, for those whose emotions are underfoot: and Adam shall pour out judgment upon the visible, physical world by the spoken word, and the Spirit of Elohim shall slay the Dragon who is in the sea of the Wild Animal's unconscious mind.

[R] Zeph 2:3 (AT)

11.05 And Jehovah's righteousness shall protect Adam from responding to Leviathan's emotions, which compel us to sin, and Elijah's faithfulness shall keep Adam from fornicating with him.

[1041.1.C]

11.08 [And, in the day that the snake] tries to communicate with the sucking child [on the pretense of] enlightening her], she shall smugly [without fear when she should have fear] stretch forth her mind into the prison cell of the Snake, [but she will not be captured this time, because] the mature child [who is joined to the supernal mother], above, will stretch forth his mind towards [the Snake in her place, to bring it into submission], and

[1218.6.C]

11.09 In the day that the high one [of Jehovah's] reproductive force covers [the earthen personalities that] hope to be good, they shall be filled with the knowledge of him, and they shall not break their covenant [with him] him [anymore], and [their bodies] shall not decay,

Chapter 13

[365.1]

13.10 Leviathan is raging[R] [against] Abel because [of his weakened condition], [but] the Image of Heaven [Elijah] shall cover over the Image of Hell [Leviathan], when Adam springs forth in Leviathan's members.

R Ps 2:1

Chapter 14

[31.8]

14.03 And when Jehovah enables you to stop producing demons in your mind, and delivers you from the fear, powerlessness and trouble which prevails in the visible, physical world, and the witchcraft through which some men try to make themselves strong, and from all of the labor required to survive in this visible, physical world, not the least of which is the spiritual labor necessary to keep Leviathan under foot as much as possible.

14.04 The people shall talk about [Leviathan], the King of Babylon, everywhere, saying how Jehovah brought that tyrant into submission, and stopped her from forcibly wrenching Jehovah's life out of the people.

14.05 Jehovah has destroyed the power of Leviathan, the one who used to have dominion over the people of the earth, and the power of his flesh tribe, which is appearing in the visible, physical world, as a company of fallen, mortal men.[R]

R Zeph 2:5 (AT)

14.06 [This] Leviathan, the one who causes the people to pierce through into the visible, physical world, where their haughtiness and pride continually subject them to Jehovah's judgments, took possession of the nations after they passed over into the visible, physical world, and exercised absolute ownership over them, but failed to preserve himself.

14.07 The whole earth is free from Jehovah's troublesome and calamitous judgments, and has attained to that place of evenness in their mind, which is free from the tyranny of their emotions.

14.08 The spiritually mature males which Hell has finally produced in the visible, physical world, who are in the process of increasing from Adam, the one who was separated from Jehovah and Elohim at the time of the fall, and, also, from Abel, into Adam, Elijah [the life-giving Spirit], and [has] received an incorruptible body, are saying: Since Adam subdued Leviathan and put him under His authority, no spiritual power has dared to try to bring us down to the bestial spiritual condition where they can rule us, and express their lusts through us.

14.09 The place where those separated from Jehovah exist, is liberated from your tyranny; Elohim's Sons vibrate forth and come face to face with you as they enter into the spiritual part of this visible, physical world, and equal it [in spiritual strength]. They have been exercised sufficiently, so that now they are appearing in a position of spiritual maturity and power whereby they are strong enough to overcome and rule the flesh surrounding them; and they shall vibrate forth from their carnal minds, stand up, and rule from within and from without, their flesh.

14.10 And Elohim's Sons shall speak words of power with their newly acquired spiritual authority, and the Living Beast will respond, and Leviathan will be subdued and placed under their feet; and it shall be revealed to the world that the proverb is true: Leviathan has become as weak as they.

14.11 The spiritual splendor that Jehovah gave you at the beginning has flowed downward under the earth, and formed the subterranean world of the dead; each of your individual members moan and mourn because of their captivity inside sacs of skin.

They try to restore themselves to glory by exercising their previously enjoyed power of [creative] speech, but only a great noise, or powerless hum comes out of their mouth.

You have led Elohim's Sons down to hades, a place of spiritual weakness, where you lie in a bed of garbage and putrefying filth that contains your spiritual life in a flesh sac, and acts like fertilizer for your rapidly reproducing, voracious offspring.

14.12 How you have descended spiritually, you in whom the brilliant shining of Jehovah's Spirit dwelt; you who were the first ray of what was to be a whole family which would reveal Jehovah; how you are stripped of your spiritual authority and were broken into many earthen vessels; you who caused the family of Elohim's flesh to fall into a condition of spiritual weakness, decay and death in their spiritual and physical bodies,

14.13 Because you have boasted within yourself, I will become a spiritual man without submitting to Elohim's dominion,[R] and I will do it by bringing the rightful heirs, Elohim's spiritual Sons, into submission to the place where I am king; I will overshadow and inhabit the nation which is betrothed to Elijah, within the fertile parts of that hidden place, hades, which is my carnal mind.

[R] Mic 2:11 (AT)
Matt 4:2 (AT)

14.14 I will ascend higher than Adam, the one who rules over the personalities of men; I will be like Elohim, the most high . . .

14.15 Nevertheless, despite your boasting, you shall not ascend at all, but you shall be brought down to that hidden place under the earth, the world of death; and you shall become the womb of the earth, and the amniotic sac that supports the uterine spiritual life of God's offspring, until it's mature enough to live without you.

14.16 Those who see you shall look you over carefully and analytically discern you, and separate themselves from you in their minds; [Cain] is the man of the Earth, whose position is changing from a tyrant, to a woman who is laboring to bring forth the bodies and personalities which Adam shall appear in.

14.17 He who made the whole fertile earth, which was inhabited by Jehovah, change into a lifeless desert, because he yielded to the whisper of the Serpent, who was in the rubbish of the earth before it was formed into the many members of humanity; and destroyed all of the individual members of the Wild Animal, his descendants, when, because of his lawless state of being, he refused to prepare those who fell into hell with him to receive Elohim's spiritual seed, so that they could be reformed in the image of God.

14.18 The whole Devil, and the whole Wild Animal within her, rest in their minds, each one in that individual place where he has passed the long hours of spiritual darkness which exist in the night [Earth], because Adam has finally been born and ascended to a place of dominion and rule.

14.19 But you, Satan, the spirit who rules the Wild Animal, are thrown out of Leviathan, the husband of those who have died to Elohim's life, like your hated son, who was pierced by your sword, and Elohim's Sons down and become the prison house of the dead;**[R-1]** where Abel is buried deep beneath the earth, like a corpse trodden under.**[R-2]**

R-1 Job 14-15a (AT)
Zeph 1:15 (AT)
Zeph 2:9 (AT)
R-2 Lk 11:44

14.20 You won't be joined to them in their sepulchers, or rule them any longer, because you have destroyed their bodies and their personalities with sin. May the offspring of the one who has been broken by Elohim be unrecognized by Jehovah forever.

14.21 Prepare to slaughter his children because of their father's iniquity; see to it that they don't receive personalities or inhabit a body, or multiply across the face of the earth.

14.22 I will become their enemy says Jehovah, and cut off the spirit, mind and body of mortal man's existence.

14.23 I will cause Babylon to be occupied by militarily defensed minds and unclean spirits: And then after that, I will sweep away the frailty of the natural man with my instrument of destruction.

[1218.3.C]

14.27 Jehovah had purposed to break [the covenant he made with] Jehovah's armies [when] he extended [Moses], his right hand, [to them, but] Jehovah turned back [when],

14.28 In the year that king Ahaz died, this prophecy came forth:

14.29 "The Philisti[ne personalities of Judah][R-1] should not rejoice [because the confederacy between Syria and Israel],[R-2] the rod [that] struck [Judah],[R-3] is burst [apart;[R-4] Indeed, the Dragon], the venomous root that sent the serpentine [personalities of [R-5] Rezin, King of Syria, and Pekah, the son of Remaliah, King of Israel],[R-6] shall come forth in the [personalities of] the Assyrians also, [but] the fruit [of the Firstborn of the spiritually weak and destitute [R-7] shall be the Seraphim],[R-8] the flying fiery serpents who bring burning coals [R-9] from the Altar [R-10] of the Firstborn [R-11] to the mouth of repentant Philistine personalities],

[R-1] Is 14:31 ATB
[R-2] Is 7:2
[R-3] Is 7:1
[R-4] Is 9:11-12
[R-5] Is 10:24
[R-6] Is 7:2
[R-7] Is 14:30
[R-8] Is 6:6 ATB
[R-9] Is 6:7 ATB
[R-10] Heb 13:10
[R-11] Col 1:15,18

14.30 And the Firstborn [Son of the Father] shall feed [the people who are weak and destitute because] they lack [his spiritual doctrine], and they shall be safe when they lie down [to sleep], and I shall execute [the Dragon],[R-1] the root [cause of their] famine,[R-2] [and the Firstborn Son of the Father] shall slay [the Serpent], the part [of the Dragon] that remains,

[R-1] Rev 12:9
[R-2] Rev 12:5

14.31 And all the Philistine [personalities of the Judeans] shall dissolve, [and the Mother's] wailing at [the door of the House of God] shall cease, [and the voice of Wisdom shall be heard] crying out to the personalities of Judah] in the city [of Jerusalem, telling them to be] alone [when] the particles of Primordial Adam suspended in a [spiritual] atmosphere come from the north to assemble with [them],

14.32 And Elohim shall shout [with joy] [R-1] to the Prophets of the nation [of Judah, saying],

"Jehovah has [laid] a foundation [R-2] in Zion for the people who need to flee [R-3] to [him] for protection."

[R-1] Job 38:7
42:10

Chapter 22

[299.4]
22.01a Thus says Jehovah to [Israel], His backsliding wife:

22.02a Satan has triumphantly pierced through Adam,

22.03a And bound you together with [Leviathan]. All of you are taken as prisoners of war, and your collective strength is completely broken, because you have turned away from Adam, and put him to flight.

22.02b Your mind is filled with animalistic, noisy restlessness, because [Satan] has mortally wounded you, and [Adam, your righteous mind],[R] has died.

[R] Rev 13:5-6 (AT)
Rom 8:6

22.01b But how did Satan manage to sacrifice Adam, the [righteous] mind of Elohim's elected Sons, who were publicly judging the people?

22.08a She was able to do it because, in the day that Judah's sins were uncovered,

22.11a Satan let Leviathan out from underneath Adam's authority,

22.08b And [the sons of Judah] looked to Leviathan for protection [instead of Adam], because Leviathan [in the sons of Judah] despises Adam,

22.11b And [Leviathan sacrificed Adam], and the Satan respected her sacrifice,

22.10a And [Adam], the altar that was formed when Elohim joined Himself to Abel [and raised him from the dead in the sons of Judah], was broken down,

22.06a And the true, hostile nature [of the sons of Judah] was revealed, and [the sons of Judah became Cain, again], the Woman,[R] [who] shook her fist at Abel, the one that Jehovah imputed male authority to, and [Satan], the thief

[R] Job 41:13 (AT)

22.10b Who is the background threads [of the sons of Judah], wove herself through [their righteous] mind,

22.09a And this is how [Satan]

22.06b Plucked up Adam,

22.10b And sealed [the sons of Judah] with the Dragon's nature,

22.09b And separated Judah from Elohim.

22.04 Therefore, I will not cease from taking vengeance on Leviathan[R]

[R] Is 40:1-2 (AT)

22.09c Until Satan [and Leviathan, humanity's] mortal foundation, is gathered together [with Elijah], and increases into [righteous] Adam,

22.04b So that the many members of fallen humanity may, once again, be righteous, says Jehovah.

Therefore, let the waters of Satan's sea be boiled and evaporate, and let Abel smear together with Elijah,[R]

[R] Job 7:19d (AT)

22.12a And in the day that Jehovah, the Lord of battle, calls mourning humanity unto Himself,

22.05 Adam shall destroy the deformed personalities that the Dragon fashions [out of my spiritual substance], which are expressing Cain's confused, irregular state of mind, which covers [Abel's] awareness of his true existence, surroundings and feelings, with sensual pleasure,

22.12b But Elijah is drying up Satan, and Adam is treading down Leviathan, and liberating Abel, [who] is plucking up Cain and covering [her],

22.13 And you will experience spiritual joy, peace and contentment, only when [Elijah] swallows up Satan and Leviathan dies.

[So], there it is, the whole plan of salvation, the crucifixion of Abel, the castration of Leviathan, and the swallowing up of Satan.

[36.6/2]

22.15 [And this is why] Jehovah, the God of Battle, says to His prophet, Isaiah, My familiar friend, go to [the sons of Judah],[R] who are poor, needy and endangered, but don't know it, who are still in their youth, and who, in their present stage of development, are ruling over the Living Beast that I made [which has become a Wild Animal], and say,

[R] Matt 26:49-50

22.16 What do you think you've done here, and who do you think you are? Do you think that you're the one who formed the Wild Animal that you're living in? Do you think that you're the one who can form a mind from a high position of authority in the Kingdom of God? Who do you think you are, engraving the

Dragon's nature on the soul that I've given to you, and [allowing Leviathan] to possess the personalities that I've made to be a place of rest for myself?

22.17 Look, Jehovah will execute a powerful judgment upon you; He shall separate you from Himself, and you shall be mortal men, and [this separation] shall surely destroy your [immortal] spiritual life,

22.18 And He shall roll you up into an abundant mass, and make you a powerful, mortal Beast; but you shall separate [yourself] from Abel [also], and die [to your righteous, mortal existence]; and the reproductive organs [minds] of the mortal Beast, which are [alive because they are] joined to Abel, shall die also,

22.01 Because I will expel you from your defensed [spiritual] military position,**[R-1]** and drag you down from the high places you have established for yourself with the unearned [life-sustaining] spiritual power that I have given you.**[R-2]**

[R-1] Dan 7:22 (AT)
[R-2] Dan 7:26 (AT)

22.20 And at the appointed time, after your unearned [life-giving] spiritual authority has been torn down, I shall send my Servant, Elijah,**[R-1]** whose name means, ***Jehovah's portion of land***, and reveal [him] to you, and He shall raise my son [Adam, from the dead], and restore his immortality,**[R-2]**

[R-1] Dan 7:24 (AT)
[R-2] Matt 19:28

22.21 And Elijah shall cover Abel within and without, and fuse him together with Cain in the correct moral order, and Adam shall set Jehovah's spiritual law in motion;**[R-1]** and interpret and apply it, and Adam shall govern the Woman,**[R-2]** and nourish and teach her,**[R-4]** and Elijah shall marry Adam,**[R-3]** and Elijah and

Adam shall be a foundation of spiritual power[R-5] for the family of spirits that shall inherit Elijah's salvation.

[R-1] Is 11:1-4
[R-2] Is 9:6
Dan 7:22 (AT)
[R-3] Dan 7:9, 23 (AT)
[R-4] Rev 12:6-14
[R-5] Dan 7:14 (AT)

22.22 And I shall give [King Adam] the job of delivering and freeing His children from the vile, sinful mind that they dwell in, and [King Adam] shall engrave [Jehovah's] image upon [his sons], and [King Adam] shall appear in them, and [King Adam] shall open the door into the kingdom of God, which is full provision, for them; and no mortal man shall be able to keep [King Adam's sons] out of the Kingdom, or obtain entrance for those that the Kingdom is denied to.

[R] Dan 7:27 (AT)

22.23 And I, [Jehovah], will save the Wild Animal from death by fastening her to [King Adam], and securely marrying her to [King Adam's] firm, unshakable foundation, from which she can prosper and live;[R] and the addition of [King Adam's] life to the Wild Animal shall make her an abundantly rich and glorified Living Beast, lacking nothing, and a member of Elohim's family.

[R] Dan 7:14 (AT)

22.24 And the many members of the Living Beast shall attribute all of the honor they have received as members of Elohim's family, to the Living Beast, that is, [Elohim's] spiritual descendants (Sons), and males that shall be born alive during the time of [King Adam's] dominion; and the vessels of lesser importance, the personalities that Adam's mind will purify, and the skins of the personalities that keep mortal life from pouring out,[R] shall honor [King Adam] also,

[R] Joel 22:28-29

22.25 [And] in that day, says Jehovah to His armies, when all of the foregoing has been accomplished, [when] King Adam is nailed to Abel and becomes a firm, unshakable foundation for the Wild Animal[R-1] that gives her life, [Leviathan] shall be pulled back and stripped of her power, and become as useless a withered arm, and the job of mediator between Jehovah and mortal man will cease to exist,[R-2] because the Wild Animal will be so purified through her union with King Adam, that Jehovah, Himself, will walk in the midst of her,[R-3] because Jehovah has said it.

R-1 Dan 7:14 (AT)
R-2 1 Cor 15:24
R-3 Gen 3:8
Rev 2:1

Chapter 26

[39.4]

26.18 Israel was increased because of Elohim,[R-1] and labored to keep Leviathan under their control with His spiritual authority; but, despite all this, Adam wasn't raised from the dead in their minds,[R-2] so Leviathan prevailed, and that's why they haven't been able to keep their personalities and physical bodies alive.

R-1 1 Pet 1:11
R-2 Is 26:18

Chapter 27

[313.9]

27.01 Elijah shall join Himself to that morally corrupt Serpent, who became a fugitive[155] when she pierced through

---

[155] The Hebrew word translated ***fugitive*** in Is 27:1 is not the same Hebrew word translated ***fugitive*** in Gen 4:12, but the principle is the same.

Adam,[R-1] and became Leviathan, [the Serpent's completed mind], the one who formed this physical, visible world [when Adam[156] failed to restrain her witchcraft power]; and, in that day, Adam shall cover the Woman[157] which was engraved with the Serpent's sin nature, and Elohim's Sons shall separate Adam's widowed spirit from Satan [and increase into Elohim's mature Sons].[R-2]

[R-1] Job 40:24 (AT)
[R-2] Matt 27:52-53 (AT)
Heb 4:12

Chapter 28

[1241.1.C]
28.22 [Do] not speak sharply against, criticize, wound or deride the earth[en personalities who are] intelligent [enough] to understand [and] interpret [what] Adonay, [God in the midst of] all [the physical bodies of the people of Israel], Jehovah's armies,

---

Cain rebelled against Abel's authority, and fell out from under Jehovah's protection.

I suggest to you that ***Leviathan*** is the first incarnated generation of the Serpent.

[156] Adam, Elohim's mind (see, Message #313, ***The Serpent, the Dragon, the Devil & You***), died, and the whole Living Beast died also (see, Message #194, ***Romans 6***). Adam was resurrected in Elijah, who, together with Michael, was strong enough to overcome Leviathan, the mind of that ancient Serpent, and prevent her from departing from Him.

[157] The Serpent is the intelligence in the Earth. Adam shall cover the Wild Animal with His righteousness, and prevent her from sinning (Matt 10:22 (AT);1 Pet 4:8).

[is saying, if you are] to avoid the strong chastisements [that go forth] to completely destroy [those who do such things].

Chapter 30

[1241.1.C]

30.17 [Jehovah Elohim], the united power of God from above, shall rebuke the five [angels from] above [that rebelled, because] the mark of [God] left [the earthen] personalities of [Messiah], the Personality of the united power [in the world] below, [after Jehovah], the head of [Messiah, the Personality of the united] power [in the world below], rebuked [them, and rather than repenting], they ran away [with the earthen personalities that Jehovah created to be his wife] *

*Jehovah rebuked the fallen angels when He took the Hebrew children out of Egypt.

30.18 And, therefore, Jehovah shall wait to be gracious [to the earthen personalities of Messiah, the Personality of Jehovah Elohim] in the word below, and to be exalted in them, and have mercy upon them, [until the angels that rebelled against him and ran away with his wife, are sentenced], because Jehovah is a God of judgment.

Chapter 33

[1056.1.C]

33.08 [Israel], the staircase [that joins heaven and earth], have broken the Covenant. They have despised [the nations], the cities [that belong to Jehovah, and Adam, the traveler who] crosses over [from the Kingdom of Heaven] into the lifestyle [of Ancient Adam's feet], is stunned and stupefied; He has grown numb and can no longer exert [the energy necessary to join the nations to Jehovah].

[78.5]

33.11 Fire shall devour you, [Cain], because you have committed incest with Adam,[R] increased into Leviathan, who is casting the image of this visible, physical world, which is hell.

[R] Joel 3:3 (AT)

33.12 Leviathan shall be burned in the [lake of] fire, and Cain in each of the individual members of the Wild Animal shall be separated from her.

33.19 You won't be able to discern the people in whom Adam is risen from the dead and have attained to the high calling which is available to mortal man through union with Elijah, the ones who can't be hurt by your carnal mind, even though they have a wicked, Fallen Mind that doesn't understand [the things of God],[R] just like you do.

[R] Eccl 9:1 (AT)

Chapter 34

[42.1]

34.03 The corrupted minds of the proud members of the Wild Animal shall waste away, and the personalities of her mortally wounded members shall dissolve and be cast out of their corruptible physical bodies; and they shall die to this mortal existence.[R]

[R] Dan 7:12 (AT)

34.04 And all the armies of [Satan's] ***heaven*** shall be separated from themselves, and lose their power to be seen again [as a leaf falls off a vine, even though the vine lives, and as a fig falls from a fig tree, and the tree continues to live] and appear in the visible, physical world, and the [Kingdom of the two] ***heavens*** shall be restored.

[862.3]

34.11 And [the substance of] the line of confusion shall spread into the empty [socket of the Malchus of] the stones [that form the corner of the building that descends into hell]

34.12 But the non-existent, pure ones, shall be [within] the name of [Adam], the whole head person, [and Adam shall be] there [in] the kingdom, the end of the [line of existence that joins with] the earth;

34.15 [Isis], the great owl [god of Egypt], shall make her nest and bring forth young there, and [Israel] shall break away from [Jehovah] and care for the eggs of [Laylah, Malchus'] shadow, [and] surely [Horus] the falcon [god of Egypt], shall grasp the women there [who are not] the female associates [of Adam].

34.16 Look in Jehovah's book [which is] from above and read it, [because] not one of these [words] shall fail:

The women shall no longer want [to be] female companions [for the men, wherefore, Adam], my mouth[piece], has commanded my spirit [within them] to assemble [together with him],

34.17 And his hand has cast lots for them, and divided [the ones who are to be separated] from the line [of] existence, [from those who] he shall dwell in, [and] they shall possess [the kingdom] from generation to generation.

Chapter 35

[566.2.C]

35.07a And [Adam], the male [spiritual] sexual organ of JAH, shall rip open the sterile valley,[158] [159] [R-1] and the [spiritual] semen[R-2] of JAH shall pass over [Abel],[R-3] the tongue-tied[R-4] Shekinah [within mortal man, who is] the instrument of Adam's speech.[R-5] Then [Abel], the Shekinah [that Cain holds captive], shall leap and dance,[R-6] and speak spiritual truth.[R-7]

[R-1] Ps 23:4
[R-2] Gal 3:16
[R-3] Gen 4:10
[R-4] Lk 1:20
[R-5] Lk 1:63
[R-6] 2 Sam 6:16
[R-7] Lk 1:64

35.07b And Abel, the abhorred widow who lies with Leviathan,[R-1] [the spiritual male sexual organ of] the Serpent who swallowed him up[R-2] because he thirsted [to incarnate],[R-3] shall publish[R-4] the understanding of the Word [of God].

[R-1] Job 2:12 (AT)
[R-2] Jon 1:17
[R-3] Jn 4:31 (AT)
[R-4] Mk 1:45

---

[158] The spiritual fertile parts of mortal man.

[159] Everything that exists has an invisible, spiritual shadow. Adam is the Heaven, and the visible world is the valley, or the Earth, which is supposed to be Adam's shadow. But Adam's shadow departed from him and acquired an existence of her own (Zech 5:11), so our world is now called ***the valley of the shadow that died***.

Chapter 40

[196.2]

40.01-2 Take vengeance on Satan and the carnal mind,[R-1] my people. Speak to Leviathan, who has subjected you,[R-2] and tell him that King Adam has ransomed His property,[R-3] the whole Wild Animal, by covering over her sins.

[R-1] Job 7:02 (AT)
Is 22:4
[R-2] Rom 8:18-20 (AT)
[R-3] Matt12:29 (AT)

40.03 And let Adam's voice cry out from the whore sitting upon the scarlet-colored Wild Animal,[R-1] saying, Let her be covered[R-2] so that Elijah may be expressed through her.

[R-1] Rev 17:3
[R-2] 1 Cor 11:6

[33.3]

40.06 All of mankind is grass, and anything and everything in it that is good is from God.

40.07 Man is disappointed, he crumbles to dust when the Spirit of God leaves him. Even that part of him, the human spirit which is the glory of God, falls down and cannot rise up again, because the Spirit of the Lord has dissolved him (that's when we die, what we know as death); surely the people is grass.

40.08 Every man in whom the life of God has appeared, (that's us), and that within him which is of God loses its spiritual strength.

Chapter 41

[10.1]

41.05 The inhabitable parts of the earth saw the face of God and revered him. [The whole of humanity] was very afraid, nevertheless, they approached God and were brought unto Salvation also.

[982.5]

41.14 Men of Israel, do not fear the worm of Jacob; I will help you, says Jehovah, your redeemer, the Holy One of Israel.

[10.1 & 40.3]

41.15 Look, after I raise Adam from the dead, I will rebuild Elohim's mind in you; I will make you into a rebuilt, two-edged, pointed apparatus, a weapon that will enable you to separate Adam's widowed spirit from Satan in other men; You shall pound and break in pieces, and crush and crumble the projecting spiritual power, and make the covering [sacks that humanity lives in] as debris that I shall separate you from, and you shall separate the many members of the Wild Animal from their sins.

Chapter 45

[1013.2.C]

45.17 But Israel, the house of Jehovah, shall be liberated with a salvation [that will endure until the world] vanishes; They shall not be disappointed or wounded [by me] until [this world where] time [exists, comes to] an end.

Chapter 51

[OLM 07 26 00]

51.09a Awake [Abel], arise [and] put on the strength of [Elohim], Jehovah's arm, [and] the men of the race of Adam, the [spiritual] day, shall rise up [from] the concealed [world of] the east,

51.10a [The ones who] dried up the [spiritual] river [within themselves], the waters of [Satan's] great sea, [the collective unconscious part of the carnal mind],

51.09b [And they shall] cast down Rahab, the evil force arising out of the chaos of the primeval waters, [and] engrave Cain [with Jehovah's nature, and] separate [him from Satan],

51.10b And set in place a path [for] the redeemed [Abels to empower them] to overflow their physical bodies,

51.11 Wherefore, the ransomed [Abels] shall turn back [toward] Jehovah, [and] enter Zion, [the brow center of the righteous timeline], and [the personalities that are joined to Abel] shall sound the joyful [spiritual] speech [of] the everlasting [age, and King Adam], the captain [that is] above, shall welcome [the personalities who attain [to this] great [salvation] with pleasure, and [their] affliction and mourning shall disappear.

[OLM 06 02 99]

51.23 And you will marry [Leviathan], the hand [of the Primordial Serpent, who] vexes you, [who] has said to your mortal personality, Curve [into the neck center of my timeline], so that [Leviathan], the fish that you are nailed to, can cover [the regenerated Adam within you], and [Satan], the spiritual part of [Leviathan, your] earthen hedge, separated you from [King Adam, and Leviathan] married the [fiery] serpent [that Abel within you is] nailed [to, and Cain] covered [Abel again].

Chapter 53

[Message # Unknown]

53.05 But He is the way of escape for the transgressors [of the law], the contrite ones, and those who have been warned about [Leviathan], the moral evil [within themselves]; He is the peace, prosperity and health that comes from above to those who belong to Him, who, through Him, are delivered from [Satan], the [spiritual] lash [that executes the Sowing and Reaping Judgment].

53.09 [Messiah], who was appointed to [experience the death of the] physical body was, [nevertheless], considered to be noble, because He never used deceitful speech, [which is witchcraft] to unjustly gain [spiritual supremacy over, or] to acquire [the souls of, fallen mankind].

[51.3]

53.10 Yet it pleased the Lord to bruise him; he hath put him to grief: when thou shalt make his soul an offering for sin, he shall see his seed, he shall prolong his days, and the pleasure of the Lord shall prosper in his hand.

Chapter 58

[Message # Unknown]

58.12 And Adam shall arise out of Abel, [his roots in the earth of humanity], and appear in the same [preserved] flesh from generation to generation.[160]

Chapter 59

[313.12]

59.04-5 They cast Abel down on to His back,[R-1] trust in Sodom and Egypt, and are lying witnesses to Adam's resurrection.[R-2] Satan weaves Leviathan [together with Cain to form] the mature [carnal] mind that covers [Abel, who] gives birth to the completed evil personality that expresses the Serpent's mature mind.

The one who engages in Belial's lifestyle dies outright [like an unfertilized egg passing out of a menstruating woman], and the spirit that is separated from Michael becomes a worthless spirit dwelling in a dead personality.

[R-1] Joel 3:3 (AT)
[R-2] 1 Cor 15:15-17

---

[160] The resurrection of Adam in the individual raises the human spirit from the dead, and preserves the personality and the physical body (Rom 8:11).

Chapter 63

[78.11]

63.01 That pregnant Woman who is living with the Dragon that incarnated as mortal man after they had spiritual sexual intercourse, is the violent, treacherous, sin-stained flesh of the one whose wife separated from him.

It is I, Elijah, who is saving the Woman from death by arranging her [Cain's] many members in the correct moral order.

63.02 And why is Cain, the treacherous wife that you've been intimate with, appearing in this visible, physical world as a man?

I'm the only man who has brought his wife into submission by overcoming her military strength, and each and every one of the people which are my companions is nothing in comparison to me.

63.03 Therefore, because of my passion for my treacherous wife, I shall crucify Abel and raise Adam from the dead, and He shall oppress the many members of the Wild Animal, and lead them forth, and purify them in the lake of fire.

63.04 And when the Church is ready to be penetrated by Elijah, Adam shall separate Cain from Leviathan and they [Cain and Abel] shall increase into Elijah; and the Woman's many members shall be redeemed from spiritual death and this visible, physical world, which is hell; and the whole Wild Animal shall be glorious and priestly.[R]

[R] Is 6:2
Rom 11:27

Chapter 66

[984.1.C]

66.01 Thus says Jehovah, Heaven is my throne and the earth is the place where I stamp upon [Leviathan], the male organ [of the Snake, and] this is the house that you are building for me? How [can] this [be] the place [where] we live [together in] peace?

66.02 I am seriously considering corporal punishment for all these [sons of God], says Jehovah, to humble [them until their] spirit reverentially respects my Word, because [my] hand made them [and] brought all of them into existence;

66.03 [But] the males [of my household] have chosen a disgusting lifestyle that is emotionally pleasing [to them]; they have prostituted themselves [with their] bloodless offerings [which are as worthless as] pig's blood, burn incense and [then] worship idols, [which] wounds the [spiritual] traveler [and] slays the mortal man [that he is residing in], and [then] they sacrifice a lamb;

66.04 [Wherefore], Adonay shall [cause them] to choose immature rulers [who] will make them afraid, because I called [and] none [of them] answered; I spoke [and] none [of them] heard [me; but, on the contrary], they did evil [right] in front of my eyes, which I did not choose [for them to do, nor] did I enjoy [watching them do it];

66.05 Hear the Word of Jehovah, you who fear Jehovah and reverence his Word:

Your brothers said that they hated you and cast you out for the sake of [Messiah], my Name, and [for the sake of Adam, my] opinion, but [when Righteous Adam] appears [in you], you shall be joyful, and they shall be ashamed; and

66.06 [Then I heard] a loud voice [coming from] the city, [and, after that], there was an[other] loud voice [coming] from the temple, [and] the loud voice was causing an uproar, [saying], Save Jehovah's enemies [by giving them what] they deserve;

66.07 Before [the First Adam] labored to give birth, [his soul] conceived a male [child, and] before his [labor] pains began, [the First Adam] was rescued;

66.08 [The First Adam] shall go into labor as soon as Zion assembles together [with him, and] he shall bring forth the children [who are his] mate;

Who [ever] heard of such a thing?

Who [ever] saw these [sons of] Adam?

They shall come forth in the day that [the Shekinah] is unified [with her mother], at which time a nation shall be born [from Elohim's] strike [into] the earth of the First [Adam];

66.09 Shall Adonay burst forth and [the First Adam] not conceive, asks Jehovah? Adonay can cause [the First Adam] to conceive, and shut [up the womb of Leviathan], answers Elohim;

66.10a [Everyone] at Jerusalem is gloating over [Satan's failure to keep the First Adam in the grave, and] rejoicing over [Adam's] victory [over death, because, from now on],

66.11 [Everyone] who nurses at the breast of the Compassionate [One] can suck until they are fully satisfied, [which makes them] delight in [my] opinion,

66.10b Yet, when everyone [who] loves [Righteous Adam] is rejoicing with him, all of you [Jews] are mourning for [the ceremonial observance of the Law], which has wasted away;

66.12 Thus says Jehovah, Look, I will bend towards [my people] like a stream [of flowing water]; I will rescue them with the cleansing stream of [my] opinion; I will give [them] milk [from] the masculine side above, to raise up the blind eyes [that] cry out [to me from] the nations [where I have sent them];

66.13 The male [offspring of] Jerusalem, the mother [of the Son of Man], shall console them; [He shall grant them]

repentance and set them upright [to deliver them from Satan, the enforcer of the Sowing & Reaping Judgment, Jehovah's] anger, and

66.14 [When] the eyes of your heart are enlightened [through understanding], the bones [of your immortal body] shall sprout [like] a bud [out of Aaron's rod], and Jehovah's servants shall know [their God, because] they shall have [his] mind, and they shall spit their adversaries out of their mouth;

66.15 Look, Jehovah is coming [like a] fiery hurricane to return [Judah, his] chariot, to their starting point, and the rebuke of his anger [is revealed as] the fiery flashing [sword] of Righteous Adam, and

66.16a The fiery sword [of Righteous Adam], Jehovah's whole male organ, is the sentence [that] Jehovah pronounced upon the many [members of the Israel of God, his] mate,

66.17a [Who claim] to be ceremonially and morally innocent

66.16b [Because] they have pierced [into him],

66.17b [But], the community [that] eats the testicles of the male hog, [which] unifies [them] with the disgusting [idolatrous thoughts of] the mouse in the unconscious part of their mind, [that nibbles away at the thoughts of God] in the center of their garden/mind, shall come to an end, says Jehovah;

66.18 [So], I sent my mate to gather [my people out of] all the nations [where I sent them], to tell them [about] my opinion, [but my] mate went and conceived [other] activities and plots;

66.19 [My] mate heard the announcement [about] the reign of [Messiah, the foundation] stone [of the Third Temple, and saw] the evidence that I put among them, [and then] I sent them to the nations as refugees:

[I sent them] to the Assyrian [Empire], and to the Ethiopians, and to Lud, [the descendants of Shem, and] to Georgia to draw back the judgment [on National Israel], and to the distant Greek islands [where the people are not that spiritually] intelligent [concerning the Scripture, but my] mate [did] not reveal [my] opinion [to them, because revealing] my opinion to the nations, requires [my] mate to boldly oppose [their opinions];

66.20 [My] mate [should] bring a donation [for] Jehovah's house [in] a pure vessel.

All the relatives of [my] mate [who are] vehicles [that carry] Jehovah's [opinion] to the nations, should leap with joy [and] bring a donation [in a pure vessel for] Jehovah, [because] the lizard, [that] hybrid animal [soul], the rod of correction to the mountain [of] holy Jerusalem, cannot reproduce, says Jehovah to the children of Israel [who are him]self,

66.21 I shall gather [together] with them [and] take them as priests and Levites, says Jehovah, and

66.22 Adonay [who is my]self, shall erect a new mind [and] a new earth[en body], says Jehovah, [and my] seed shall stand upright [in my] personality, [and they shall be my] Name, and

66.23 It shall come to pass [that], from month to month, [and], from Sabbath to Sabbath, all [of the parts of [Righteous] Adam, my] male organ, shall submit to [my] personality, says Jehovah, and

66.24 Everyone who is repelled by [the personality of my] male organ, shall see the dead bodies of the mortal males [who] broke the law and came against [the Son of Man when he rebuked them for it; so, the Son of Man shall burn Abel], the red worm [in the lower part of the First Adam], in the fire [that] shall not [be] extinguished [for as long as sin continues to exist, to prevent the First Adam from] dying.

THE BOOK OF

JEREMIAH

Chapter 3

[281]
3.14 I will take the whole Wild Animal for myself, you backsliding children, and change your family [blood line] by marrying you.[R]

[R] Acts 17:26

Chapter 8

[313.13]
8.06-7 I listened and heard Leviathan speaking [out of my people] and [he was] saying, What have I done [to deserve the judgments of God? -- I'm innocent!]. All of the carnal men are in their own joyful little world, as they are drawn into the battle without warning, but Abel recognizes the signal; nevertheless, Elohim's Sons are joyfully chattering and flying in circles [trying to] abstain from sin in their own strength, so that they can marry Elijah when the time comes, but [as a result of their failure to judge themselves] my people are experiencing Jehovah's corrective judgments,

8.13 And Leviathan shall bring forth the Serpent's many-membered body [the children of Belial], but I will cause Leviathan to perish, and Adam to return to Michael; and the carnal minds [good/evil figs] which are produced by the Tree of the Knowledge of Good and Evil, shall lose their strength and become foolish, and the [whole] mortal man shall lose his spiritual strength and become foolish; but I will give [myself] to the men in whom Abel overcomes Leviathan,

8.14 [Who are saying], Why shall we sit idly by and do nothing while Abel is taken away from us? Let us pierce into our carnal minds and circumcise them off of Adam, because, when we have offered our carnal minds as a sin offering to Elohim and Jehovah, He will close our [adulterous] mouths, make us eunuchs [again], and cause us to receive the life of His Spirit which is in Adam.

8.15 But even in those of us who did our very best, because we understood the nature of our mortal condition and what had to be done to raise Adam from the dead, only Leviathan was found. We tried to form a mind which produced emotional and physical healing but, there it was, the carnal mind.

8.17 For, behold, I will assign authority to the Serpent over your unconscious mind, and she will increase into Leviathan and Satan, and they will enchant you with their magical incantations, saith the Lord.

Chapter 22

[823.4]

22.30a Thus says Jehovah to [King Jechoniah], his mortal man [who is his] mate, [during] the days [that] he sits on the throne of David,

22.29a Hear the word of the Lord,

22.30b [Ancient Adam], the [spiritual] warrior [that defends Israel], shall not push forth [his seed] into [the human spirit of your][R]

[R] Gal 2:20

22.29b Earth[en soul, and]

22.30c [Righteous Adam] shall not push forth into [your]

22.29c Earth[en soul]

22.30d To engrave [it with the nature of Ancient Adam],[R-1] nor shall [Ancient Adam's male] heir[R-2] be born in [your]

[R-1] Ez 9:4
[R-2] Mic 1:15

22.29d Earth[en body, and

22.30e No mortal man shall continue to rule in Judah [after you depart from the throne].

Chapter 25

[Message # Unknown]
25.31 Jehovah says that He will contend with the whole earth[en nature of Israel]; Jehovah will judge [between Righteous Adam] and [the nature of] the nations [within Israel, and] destruction shall come upon [Leviathan], the evil male organ [of the Serpent who] was cut off, [and Leviathan] will be given over to [Righteous Adam], the sword [who will circumcise him],

Chapter 31

[480.7]
31.22 How long will you, [the fiery serpent], wrap around yourself and abandon your true nature and the purpose for which you were created? Nevertheless, [despite your unfaithfulness], Jehovah is fashioning the household of the earth into a new, living creature, [and] the female [fiery] serpent shall surround [Adam], the strongman [of Elijah's household].

Chapter 46

[313.14]
46.22 Elohim's Sons shall come with a mighty army,[R-1] and then they shall call,[R-2] and Elijah shall crucify Abel[R-3] in the men who hear them,[R-5] and they shall enter into Leviathan,[R-4] and separate Cain from him, and increase into Elijah,[R-6] the warrior who shall boil Satan as a sin offering.[R-7]

[R-1] Joel 2:5
[R-2] Amos 6:10 (AT)
[R-3] Zech 11:14 (AT)
[R-4] Heb 4:12
[R-5] Jn 5:25
[R-6] Zeph 3:08a (AT)
[R-7] Dan 7:19 (AT)

Chapter 51

[1212.3.C]
51.15 God made the material bodies of [humanity] by his power; [He also made] the souls [of the bodies] to stand upright [by] the understanding [that] heaven separates [the dark thoughts of their animal soul from] the wisdom [of] his [daughter].

[31.5]
51.29 And the Woman shall labor and bring forth [the man child] because every one of Jehovah's purposes for Babylon shall be accomplished. Babylon shall be good for nothing, because Leviathan shall not be found there.

THE BOOK OF

JOB

Chapter 1

[Message # Unknown]

1.01 There was a [spiritually] male astrologer in the land who worshiped other gods, [and had a fallen] nature [that] hated[161] [Jehovah, but] that [spiritual] male [astrologer also] recognized that [Jehovah was the only] God [who] could meet his needs and protect him from the evils [of this world, so Job] married [Jehovah],

1.02 And the seven parts of Adam, [(a) the six parts of the Son of God, and] (b) the daughter, [the spiritual earth],[R] plus, wisdom, [understanding and knowledge], the three [parts that form Adam's brains], were born within [Job],

[R] Is 62:4

1.03 And the seven parts of mortal man's animal nature, [(a) Leviathan, the six male parts, and (b) Abel, the dead Shekinah, the female] beast of burden [who carries Cain, the conscious part of the carnal mind, and the devilish] wisdom, [understanding and knowledge], the three [parts of the carnal mind that form Leviathan's] brains, [were born within Job also, but only] five [parts of Job's] animal nature [were functional, because Adam within Job] was castrating [Leviathan, the Serpent's male spiritual sexual organ, within Job].

---

[161] Job means ***hated*** - OT:347-'Iyowb (ee-yobe'); from OT:340; hated (i.e. persecuted); Job, the patriarch famous for his patience: KJV - Job.OT:340 - KJV - be an enemy.

Now, the male household [of Noah], the oldest son of the whole ancient world, was exceedingly abundant,

1.04 So [Satan] pursued [Noah, who] was appointed to build the family Name in the male houses [of Noah, Shem, Ham and Japheth], and [Noah] drank [down Satan, the Spirit of the Night], and [Elohim, the Spirit of] the Day, departed [from Noah], and [Satan] called out [from within Noah] to [Shem, Ham and Japheth], the three who were together [with Noah in the ark], to [agree] with [Noah] to consume [Adam] and drink [down Satan's spirit],

1.05 [And this is how] it came to pass, [that next spiritual] day, Job was bound together with the sin nature [that he inherited because of] the sin of [Adam], the powerful progenitor of [Noah's] family, [who were appointed to express Jehovah's] nature, [but] who ate and drank [with Satan; so Job] said in his heart, In such a case as this, let me diminish this curse by sacrificing [the sin nature within me][162] so that Elohim can make me ceremonially clean, and [then] I will ascend [into the mountain of God] continually,

1.06 So, Satan, [the unconscious part of Job's carnal mind], besieged Elohim's son, [Adam, Jehovah's watch station, the light of the spiritual] day [within Job, so that] she could gather [Job into his carnal mind, but Job] continued to cleave to [Adam], Jehovah's [watch] station,

1.07 And Jehovah [within Job] said to Satan, Where did you come from? Then Satan answered Jehovah, saying, I pushed into [Job] because [I want to] express my nature through [Job's] earthen [personality].

1.08 And Jehovah said to Satan, [When Leviathan], your servant, is Job's center, [Job] is considered a non-entity [who

---

[162] Job was concerned with overcoming his sin nature and returning to God, so we see that the Lord's reason for sending Satan to reveal Job's sin, was to bring Job to (Footnote continued – See, Appendix)

has] no value in the earth, [but when Job is] coupled together [with Adam], the [spiritual] man [who enables him to follow the straight [path, Job] reverences Elohim, [the one who] removes [Satan, the] evil [one],

1.09 And Satan answered Jehovah, [saying, Do you think that] Elohim [within] Job respects you for no [particular] reason?

1.10 [Haven't you] blessed the work of [Job's] hands to the extent that [material] possessions have burst forth [into his] world? [And] haven't you made a hedge around him, and around his household, and around all of his possessions?

1.11 On the contrary, when you send [Adam], your open hand [of corrective judgment], to acquire everything [that Job has, Job] will curse [Adam], the personality [of Jehovah],

1.12 And Jehovah said to [Job], Behold, [I have given] Satan [permission] to search [your heart and] bring corrective judgment [wherever sin is found], but only [concerning your] possessions, not upon [you], yourself; so Satan broke forth upon [Adam], Jehovah's personality [within Job],

1.13a And the day came to pass, that [Cain and Abel, the spiritual] daughter and son [of Job], the household [of Adam, Job's] elder brother, were eating [Leviathan's nature] and drinking [Satan's spirit within Job],

1.09a And behold, [Elohim, Jehovah's] Great Spirit,

1.03a Bubbled up[163] from the eternal spiritual world,

1.19b Entered into [Job], and joined [Himself to Satan, Leviathan, Cain and Abel], the four principles of [Job's spiritual] household,

1.14 And [***Adam***, Jehovah's] messenger, ***appeared to Job***, [and Adam taught Abel within Job], ***saying***: [Elohim,

---

[163] The Spirit that comes from the eternal world must first ***descend*** into the unconscious part of a mortal man's mind, before it can ***ascend*** into the conscious part of that mortal man's mind.

Jehovah's] right hand of power from above, engraves [Jehovah's nature upon Cain and Abel, the spiritual] oxen [which are Job's mortal personality], and [I, Adam], consume [Leviathan, the subconscious part of Job's mortal personality, continually],[164]

1.16 But while [Adam] was still talking, [***Satan***, the unconscious part of Job's] other, [mortal personality], emerged and ***said*** [***to Leviathan***, the subconscious part of Job's mortal personality], Elohim's fiery [judgment] is falling from heaven, to burn up [Abel], the sheep [of Job's personality], and [to also burn up Cain and Leviathan, Satan's] servants, and to consume them; nevertheless, I [AM] will rescue [Cain], the [conscious] part of [Job's mortal] personality,

1.17 And while [Satan, the unconscious part of] Job's [mortal personality], was talking [***Leviathan***], the Chaldean, [Satan's] servant, emerged and ***said [to Cain***, Abel's] other [side, Adam, Jehovah's] three-fold [personality, which] is not swallowed up by [the personality of Leviathan], ***but overshadows [it]***, has emerged with His sword to slay me, and to carry away [Abel]; nevertheless, I [AM] will rescue [you, Cain, the conscious] part [of Job's mortal personality],

1.18 But, while [Leviathan] was still talking, [***Adam***, Job's] other, [immortal side], emerged and ***said [to Job,***: Even though you are] the most spiritually mature son [of the ancient world,[R] Cain and Abel], your [spiritual] son and daughter], were eating [Leviathan's personality] and drinking [Satan's] spirit, [while they were] in your [spiritual] household,[165]

[R] Job 1:3 (AT)

---

[164] Adam's consumption of Leviathan is the spiritual sacrifice which forms Adam's righteous nature in the individual. Conversely, when Leviathan consumes Adam, the Serpent's unrighteous nature appears in the individual.

[165] ***Cain*** is the conscious part of the carnal mind, and ***Abel*** is the conscious part of the Mind of God, but Abel is under the control of

1.19a And [now the regenerated Adam], the young man [within you], is dead; nevertheless, I [AM] rescued [Abel, my root system, the part of your] personality [that Elijah regenerates],

1.15 And [then Adam] slew [Leviathan, the subconscious part of Job's mortal personality], with the Sword [Of His Excellency],[R-1] and divided Cain, Leviathan's] servant, [from Abel], and [Adam] seized [Abel,[R-2] Adam's root system within Job], the only part [of the mortal personality that] belongs to [Adam, the one who] stands opposite [Leviathan, and this is how Abel] was the only one that escaped [the wrath of] I [AM],

R-1 Deut 33:29
R-2 Matt 12:29
Mk 3:27

Chapter 3

[1219.8.C]

3.1 And Job, [the soul that] Jehovah set upright to be his mate,

In the unconscious part of the mind [but, afterward],

Separated from [him], opened her mouth,

3.2 And said [to] Job:

3.3 In the night it was said that a great warrior was conceived,

But the day that I, [Job's soul], came into existence,

I was reduced to the degree of disorder,

Cain in all mortal men, except for those very few who were able to overthrow her after Christ was added to their spiritual household.

3.4 [Wherefore], the day [that Adam] brought [Job] into existence,

is a day of misery, ignorance and death;

3.5 [The Primordial Reptile, Adam's spiritual intelligence],

Should not have pursued the light

That is beyond its understanding;

Neither should it have [consulted] the Elohim [R]

[R] 1 Sam 28:7-11

[Who are spiritually] higher [than it is, because]

3.6 Jehovah, the only one who] can

Withdraw the light of existence,

Is higher than the Elohim, [and

Only [**JEHOVAH**], who said,

(1) Do not eat of that tree], **[R]** and

[R] Gen 2:17

3.7 (2) Let not [Adam, who was] seized by the dark [powers] the night [he was conceived],

(a) Be joined to [Jehovah's] goodness [all] the days of the year, [and]

(b) Be numbered [among those who enter into] the month [that Messiah consummates his marriage to Israel],'

AND

THE REDEEMER who fears God and bears his mark, [R]

[R] Ez 9:4

Can dwell in a dead body.

3.8 [And that is the whole story]!

I came into existence that [fateful] night, sterile;

The joyful voice

[That speaks the correct understanding of

The Word of God into the visible world

Did] not come forth from within [me], and

3.9 [Now, only the Redeemer who was] crucified [R]
[and

[R] Matt 27:35

Rose from the dead, [R] can]

[R] Lk 24:6

Prepare [the woman who ate [R] [of the tree that]
Jehovah [said not to eat of, and

[R] Gen 3:6

Was] cursed, [R]

[R] Gen 3:16

For] the day that Leviathan, [Adam's dead harvest],

Rises up [to marry her].

Chapter 4

[356.5]
4.19a Indeed, those who dwell in the Serpent's clay mind,
die prematurely,

4.20 And their physical, dust bodies, break down, wear
out, and disappear continually,

4.21 Because of Leviathan's [evil] wisdom, which is
expressed through them when he uproots Abel, their [mortal
male] mind.

4.18 Indeed, Jehovah's servants, the prophets, were not
true spiritual fathers, but foster parents, and the men who are
[truly] spiritual, were planted [in the same place with] pride,

4.17 [But, nevertheless], Cain will be restored to righteousness when Eloah[166] and Jehovah's spiritual purity are born in them again,

4.19b After Elohim's Sons confront them, and break Leviathan in pieces.

Chapter 5

[356.6]

5.01 Look into your own heart, Job, and see who you really are, The Word of God or Leviathan,

5.02a Since the spiritual man dies when Leviathan's anger

5.05 Tramples Abel, Elohim's mortal, manly mind, underneath his inferior mind, and Satan seizes and eats up his spiritual substance.

5.04 His children are far from safety because Satan destroys them openly, but Adam is not there to deliver them.

5.02b And the Woman dies prematurely because of envy,

5.06 Since the Serpent sprang forth out of the Earth, and Cain rose to power because of Adam's calamity,

5.07 Indeed, the living soul fainted when pride rose up and Adam incarnated as the Woman,

---

166 This Hebrew word, ***Eloah***, which is found only in poetry, appears to mean the same thing as ***ish*** [mortal man], but it can also be translated ***newly born male offspring.***

The fully mature Adam, married to an overcoming mortal personality, is the only newly born, male offspring (Rev 12:4-5; Rev 19:11-16). He is called ***The Ancient of Days*** in Dan 7:9, 13 & 22, but our Alternate Translation is ***Elijah*** (Rev 1:5).

5.03 Because Adam didn't see the rebellious Serpent twisting together with the Earth, [to form the animal that] pierced through Adam, until the Woman appeared.

[33.1]
5.25 You shall be very virile, and the children that you bear shall reveal the life of God in their souls, as the mature grass bears the embryo ready to reproduce itself.

Chapter 6

[OLM 06 02 99]
6.16 [Adam], the sackcloth from above, conceals [Satan], the ice that is a part of the snow [Elohim's sons].

Chapter 7

[360.5]

Elohim Speaking Through Job

7.20a I, Elohim, made myself into Adam, the living soul, for the purpose of preserving [the whole Living Beast, but] Adam missed the path of righteousness, because the ox that he was joined to [to form the Living Beast],

7.06b Separated herself from Adam,

7.04a And lay down with

7.20b And married [the Serpent],

7.19a And became the Woman who married the Serpent and gave birth to humanity's army of [wandering] mortal men,

7.05a And Jehovah and Elohim, divorced Adam

7.05c And [Adam] died,

7.06c And [the Serpent] wove a permanent, evil mind into the Living Beast [who became the dead, Wild Animal],

7.20c That Jehovah turned over to Satan for judgment, until Adam is regenerated, and brings Leviathan into submission.[R]

[R] Rom 8:20-21(AT)

7.03 [But in the meantime], the Serpent has inherited the world of continuous [mental and physical] labor, because she is possessing Adam's widowed spirit, and incarnating as Satan and Leviathan,

7.05b And they have covered over Adam, my manly mind, with decaying, solidified dust, and [Adam] has disappeared,[R]

[R] Gen 4:10
1 Ki 19:5 (AT)
Amos 5:19b (AT)

7.06a And [humanity's] lifetimes are cursed

7.04b Because the Serpent

7.12 Has transformed [Adam] into Leviathan, [the male, spiritual sexual organ of] the Dragon who stands guard over Abel,

7.04c And [the Dragon's] incarnation shall be extended for so long as Satan continues to influence

7.01 Belial's army of mortal men who are passing their lifetimes upon the earth as Satan's hired soldiers,

7.02 [Even though] some of [Belial's soldiers] are trying to kill Leviathan[R-1] because they are completely sold out to Elijah, but the others are content[R-2] with their existence in hell, and merely hoping for Adam's appearance.

[R-1] Is 22:14 (AT)
Mic 2:4 (AT)
[R-2] Job 41:13 (AT)

Adam Speaking Through Job

7.07a Oh, Jehovah, turn back Leviathan, [Job's] mortal old man,

7.08a Who is lying in wait to publicly disgrace

7.07b [The regenerated] Adam, [Job's] new man,

7.08b By seducing [Job to sin], so that he will be judged by the law of sin and death.

Jehovah Speaking, [Don't worry, Job],

7.17 Leviathan is twisted together with mortal man as if she were supposed to be her mind,[R]

[R] Jn 3:6

7.18 But when Elijah is grafted [to Abel],[R-1] they will test mortal man during the tribulation,[R-2] by wounding them with painful experiences that will expose their sins,[R-3]

[R-1] Gal 4:19
Jas 1:21
[R-2] Job 1:6-9, 12
[R-3] Dan 7:5 (AT)
Rev 12:10

7.21a So that Jehovah can pardon Abel's transgression when King Adam subjects Leviathan,[R]

[R] Job 41:2
Is 37:29

7.21c Who will surely cease to exist

7.09a When Elijah descends into hell,

7.21d And crucifies Abel,

7.21e And regenerates Adam,

7.19b And [Cain] shall sink down to the bottom,

7.09b So that Abel can climb up,[R]

[R] Rev 20:7

7.19c And [when] Abel [who]

7.21b Was forcibly carried away,

7.19d Is spit out [of the Dragon's mouth], and smears[R] together with Elijah;

[R] Is 22:4b (AT)

7.10a Abel will realize what her true role in the Living Beast is, and return to her family,[R]

[R] Amos 5:9b (AT)
Ez 1:12 (AT)
Gen 2:24 (AT)
Gen 4:6-7 (AT)
Ps 90:3 (AT)
Zech 6:7 (AT)

Adam Speaking Through Job

7.04c Indeed, I swear that I shall arise [out of hell]

7.16a And live again,

7.11b No matter how long it takes

7.14a For Elijah to break [Pharaoh]

7.14b In pieces,

7.11a [So that I, Adam] can communicate with the fierce, raging fiery serpent [within mortal man, and wage] spiritual warfare [against] Satan, and restrain Leviathan, [Adam's] spiritual enemy, [and] put her to flight,

7.13a And [King Adam] shall have mercy on Abel,

7.13b And rejoin him to Elijah, and [King Adam] shall restore the [whole] Living Beast [to righteousness],

7.16b And that ancient Serpent,

7.15 Who is appointed to die to her bestial existence,

7.16c Shall disappear, and the transitory lifetimes of Leviathan, [Adam's] other side, shall come to an end,

7.14c When Elijah baptizes Abel into Himself.

Chapter 9

[365.1]
9.09 . . . who fashions the visible, spiritual world out of Cain and Elohim's breath of life, who is the innermost part of the Church [the human spirit].

Chapter 14

[33.3]
14.07a There is hope that the living soul that died shall live again after it has been cut down,

14.08 Even after [the human spirit], the unseen hidden part of it, has been in the earth a long time, and the flesh that appears is the visible world, dies,

14.07b It shall send out new growth, and pierce through to an altered state of being, and be inhabited by God.

14.09 He shall discern the Spirit of God and blossom and fly in the heavenlies, and bear forth the harvest of God, the glorified man who has been delivered from the bondage of his vile human body, and he shall set him upright with spiritual power, and firmly plant him in the ground, and he shall live for the life of the ages.

14.10 But natural man shall continue to die and decay

14.11 Until the living soul loses its reproductive power, and the polluted depraved human soul, Babylon, the mother of all the harlots of the earth, is stripped of her illegal power and becomes ashamed, confused and disappointed when she finally realizes that she is nothing without God.

14.12 So natural man dies and does not live again, until the spiritual realm of the soul comes to an end. They shall not be harvested, Adam shall not appear in them, nor be formed in them again in their fallen state.

Chapter 17

[OLM 03 03 99]

17.14 I have said, Corruption, [who] is my father, and my mother, his beloved the bride, [have produced the fiery serpent], the worm [that formed my soul and body],

Chapter 20

[25]

20.10 His children shall conciliate themselves to the poor by restoring the goods taken from them.

Chapter 24

[Message # Unknown]

24.02 Carnal men destroy [their own] personalities and bodies by having [spiritual] intercourse with [the Serpent], because she strips off their spiritual covering.

Chapter 26

[18.5]

26.13 . . . Jehovah's Spirit caused the heavens to come into being, but the Serpent pierced through the spiritual veil [firmament], incarnated on the negative [physical] side of the visible world,[R] and [became the fiery serpent, who] birthed her many-membered daughter,[167] Leviathan and Satan.

[R] Dan 8 (AT)

26.14 Indeed, Elohim's breath of life [the human spirit] is the [redeemable] seed[R-1] that is journeying through the earth[R-2] and experiencing sin and death in these mortal men,[R-3] until Elijah raises Adam from the dead[R-4] and rejoins him in unity with Elohim and Jehovah.[R-5]

[R-1] Gen 3:15
[R-2] Zeph 2:5 (AT)
[R-3] Jn 8:44
[R-4] Acts 24:15
[R-5] Col 1:20

26.13 He caused the heavens to glisten [or come into being] by His Spirit. His Son, [Adam], pierced through the spiritual veil into the realm of appearance, and has given birth to [or was birthed as the offspring of] the Serpent.

---

[167] Elohim, Jehovah's spiritual semen, increases into Adam, and then Elijah, Elohim's mature Son, but the Serpent pierced through Adam before he was permanently joined to Elohim, and incarnated as the mortal Woman who increased into Leviathan, the daughter of Babylon [Baal].

Jehovah looks at the potential of Adam's widowed spirit to rise from the dead, and calls that spiritual seed (Gen 3:15) His Son, before the event comes to pass (Rom 4:17).

26.14 Look at how [fallen Adam's] earthen parts are journeying through [time], experiencing the realm of death [until] God raises [Abel, the human spirit], out from among the dead [Adam], and reunites Him with the Father.

Chapter 28

[OLM 06 02 99]

28.17 The false gold of the crystalline carnal mind cannot be exchanged for the [Spirit of] Truth, the golden weapon that [becomes our] armor [after Adam] brings us into the correct moral order.

Chapter 29

[42.7]

29.19 My spiritual substance [breath] appeared through the agency of my Son, that part of me which has the capability of beginning a new individual, and he begat a mind called Adam, the living soul, who continued to exist in a perverted form [as Adam's widowed spirit] throughout the period that he was separated from Elohim, and existed as the cover [womb] for that part of me [Adam] which is to be harvested.

29.20 Elijah renewed Abel within me, and Adam sprang forth.

Chapter 37

[OLM 06 02 99]

37.10 [Elohim], Jehovah's breath, distresses [Satan], the waters that became thick ice.

Chapter 38

[862.3]

38.02 Who is this whose words darken [my] counsel and destroy knowledge?

38.04 [Do you know when] the earth was married to [the line of existence which] stands boldly opposite it?

38.05 [Do you know] who put the Sefirot in place [and caused the essence of] the line [of existence] to spread into [Binah, our] understanding from above?

38.06 [Do you know] Elohim from above who threw down the [line of existence that] penetrated the socket of [Malchus], the stone [that forms] the corner [of the building that joins heaven and earth]?

[39.2]

38.04,7 Where were you when the singular morning stars wailed mournfully, because all of Elohim's [incarnated] children were evil?[R]

[R] Rom 5:6 (AT)

[18.1]

38.12-15 Hast thou commanded the morning, the early part of the day known as lust and passion, since thy days, and caused the dayspring, the Christ waiting within to emerge forth, to know when and where, and how to manifest? That the dayspring might take hold of the ends of the natural man [which we, mankind, are], that the wicked might be shaken out of us.

[878.5.C]
38.31 Can your mind bind, in their correct created order, the seven [lower Sefirot that are] craving [to incarnate], and unify them into a single collection of heavenly bodies that names [Jehovah] as their creator?

38.37-38a Who will be able to bring Elohim's Sons down to a low spiritual realm and ravish them at will, after the one dwelling within them [Adam] sets [the fiery serpent and Leviathan] into the proper order, fuses together with the rubbish [that they are], and imparts the power of an endless life [Elijah] to them?

[978.3.C]
38.41 When the male children of God stray [because of] a lack of food, and cry to God, the Supernal Mother sends a raven with food.

Chapter 40

[18.5]
40.15-18 Look at Behemoth, who I made in the same place with you; he eats up the dwelling places of God's creation, like an ox pulling a plow overturns a field. Look, his strength is in his ability to reproduce, and his first born is already in his sperm. He desires his hand and foot company, that part of him that is in the realm of appearance, to be like the cedar trees, firm, incorruptible and joined in their proper place to form the temple he desires to build to replace the temple of God.

The genetic information of the assembled torn and cursed people of the Serpent is contained in the tube that the sperm of his testicles [passes through], and is woven together, as one unit, around itself.

The beast of burden within him shall be delivered, as the iron ax [was delivered].

40.19 Behemoth is the reproductive strength and genetic material of Elohim, the one who [Jehovah sent] to subdue her and lie with her, in preparation for Jehovah's sword [judgment], which will change her bestial nature into Jehovah's righteous nature.

40.20 When the Spirit of Elohim projects forth from Abel in great power, and raises Adam, the harvest of the earth, from the dead, in the very same place where Leviathan mocks Jehovah, and thrusts the Woman [Cain] through with his sword on a regular basis.

40.21 Abel is lying down in the darkness of the lower regions [hell] where one is humbled because of spiritual weakness; the Serpent has purchased him, and is covering his spiritual riches which he exchanged for the miry clay when Cain incarnated as the Woman.

40.22 Leviathan, the Wild Animal's mind, rules Abel, hovers over him continuously, and fornicates with him at will; the Earth, that part of the inheritance [Wild Animal] which is without Elohim's life, and is supposed to be the ***fill*** which provides ***bulk*** in the visible, physical world, surrounds Abel, and [the ground] holds everything together like a garment.[R]

[R] Job 41.17b (AT)

[18.6]

40.23 Look at Satan, that violent [spiritual] river, rushing towards [Adam as he] descends [into death, and is] confident that she will be born in [the right] side [of the heart center] from where she controls mankind].

40.24 So, enraged with envy, she broke forth as spirit, and violently penetrated Adam's reproductive parts, and took [Adam's spirit] for herself,[R] and fornicated with him without any alarm or fear of Jehovah, and [Leviathan and Adam's widowed spirit] hardened into this ***Visible***, ***Physical*** world, which is the ***Image of Death***, also known as ***Hell***.

[R] Zeph 2:4 (AT)
Dan 8:6-7 (AT)
Gen 2:21b (AT)

Chapter 41

[340.14]

41.03 Will the Serpent appoint Leviathan, her completed, female mind, to rule over you, or will she sacrifice[R] her so that Adam can rise from the dead?

[R] Matt 4:9 (AT)

41.01 Can Leviathan, the Serpent's malignant tongue, which is the mind of that many-membered band of destructive men [Belial's children],[R-1] [and the weed] that has been choking Abel [the cultivated plant], since the Serpent[R-2] killed Adam, be submerged underneath Adam[R-3] [and the image of the spiritual visible world that is in his mind]?[168]

[R-1] Zeph 2:5-7 (AT)
[R-2] Gen 2:15 (AT)
Zeph 3:5(b) (AT)
[R-3] Rom 8:18-20 (AT)

41.06 Will the mortal men who are bound to Leviathan because of the Serpent's witchcraft,[R] be able to separate themselves from her, by digging through the earth of their mortal minds, and unraveling her?

[R] Ez 1:10 (AT)
2 Pet 2:4 (AT)

---

[168] The visible world, including the human body, is an image projected by mind. Adam, Elohim's mind, forms the visible, spiritual world called ***Eden***, and Leviathan, the Serpent's mind, forms the visible, physical world called ***hell***.

41.07 Can you save this dead Wild Animal by judging Leviathan, that militarily defensed mind that the Serpent birthed into the Living Beast, and by bringing Satan, her unconscious mind,**[R-1]** to the end of herself?**[R-2]**

R-1 Gen 9:21 (AT)
R-2 Job 7:19c (AT)

41.02 Can you penetrate the human spirit and [raise up Adam,**[R-1]** the one who is strong enough to] boil Satan [until she evaporates].**[R-2]**

R-1 Zeph 3:13 (AT)
Ez 1:11 (AT)
R-2 Dan 7:7 (AT)
Zeph 2:9 (AT)

41.04b Can your human spirit,**[R]** cut away Leviathan [circumcision without hands], fold the fiery serpent under, and enslave her for the life of the ages?

R Vs 16

41.09a [Obviously, you can't, Job, because] look at what Cain has made out of Elohim's Living Beast!**[R]**

R Gen 2:23-25 (AT)

41.10 She's so fiercely sinful**[R-1]** since she incarnated,**[R-2]** that there isn't a man anywhere who can survive Jehovah's fiery presence.**[R-3]**

R-1 Is 63:10 (AT)
R-2 Dan 8:10-12
R-3 Is 63:3 (AT)

41.05 So, you may be laughing at Satan's power to hurt you now, but you won't be laughing when you find out that Adam's widowed spirit is the Serpent's prostitute.**[R]**

R Pro 26:11 (AT)
Job 41:13 (AT)
Eccl 12:3 (AT)
Ez 32:2 (AT)
Dan 8:6-7 (AT)
Joel 3:3 (AT)
Zeph 3:4a (AT)
Rev 17:1

41.09b [Nevertheless, don't worry, Job,] you won't be mortal forever, because Leviathan shall be cast down when Adam appears.[R]

[R] Matt 27:52-53 (AT)
Zech 6:7 (AT)
Tit 2:13
1 Pet 1:7

41.08 Therefore, be a man in the war to determine whose nature will be engraved in your mind,[R-1] and fashion him after[R-2] Jehovah, so that your enemy, Leviathan, the Serpent's completed mind, isn't born [again], like he was in the past age,[R-3]

[R-1] Gen 2:19 (AT)
[R-2] Col 1:5
[R-3] Gen 9:20-21 (AT)

41.23 When the Serpent went off course, and the Living Beast incarnated as a mortal female [instead of an immortal male].[R]

[R] Gen 2:25 (AT)
Is 63:2 (AT)

41.17a Because Adam was pursued and seized by [the Serpent], his [other side],[169]

41.17b And now the fiery serpent is occupying the Living Beast like a [man occupies a] woman, and Leviathan, the mind born of the Serpent's union with Adam's widowed spirit, is frozen together with the [mortal] man [Abel], and the [mortal] Woman [Cain], and they can't be divided,[R]

[R] Gen 2:22 (AT)

41.16 Because Leviathan is so close to Adam's widowed spirit, that no male spirit can get in between them.[R]

[R] Vs 2a

41.13 So, then, who can clear up the confusion of Adam's widowed spirit?[R-1] He's supposed to be Elohim's Son and

---

[169] Spiritual incest and masturbation of the mind.

undisputed ruler over the Living Beast, but he thinks he's a Woman and is content**R-2** to be the Serpent's harlot.**R-3**

R-1 Gen 2:25 (AT)
R-2 Job 7:2 (AT)
R-3 Job 41:5 (AT)
Pro 26:11 (AT)
Eccl 12:13 (AT)
Dan 8:6-7 (AT)
Ez 32:2 (AT)
Joel 3:3
Zeph 3:4a (AT)

41.14-15a Or, we can say, who can penetrate mortal man's unconscious mind and change his nature,**R-1** since the Serpent has imprisoned Adam's widowed spirit**R-2** and sealed [him in her own image],**R-3**

R-1 Jer 13:23
Jas 3:12
R-2 Is 14:19 (AT)
Zeph 1:15 (AT), 2:9 (AT)
R-3 Gen 2:24 (AT)
Zech 11:12 (AT)

41.32 And Satan, who is to be set on fire,**R** has interwoven herself with [Elohim], the ancient waters which produced the Living Beast,

R Rev 20:10

41.14-15 And Satan is compassing Adam's widowed spirit round about on every side,

41.19 And the spiritual seed of Adam's widowed spirit [is mingles] with the Serpent's destructive seed,**R-1** so that they shoot out from [Leviathan], the same reproductive part,**R-2** and bring forth offspring [the fiery serpent in the individual mortal man],

R-1 Gen 3:15
R-2 Jas 3:11

41.20 And the personalities that are appearing in the clay womb of the Wild Animal, have minds which are proven insane, not legally responsible, and useless, when Adam appears,

41.18 And these [insane carnal minds] are the eyelid which is blinding Abel.

41.28a Now, Adam is the only one who can penetrate Leviathan's defensed mind

41.31 And boil Satan as a sin offering,

41.11b So that Leviathan can be conquered, and Satan subjected, and the Woman who belongs to Adam, converted into a submissive wife,

41.28b So that Abel can be changed into

41.11a Adam, the one who should [be strong enough to] make the Serpent good,

41.31b So that the visible, spiritual world can rapidly spring up [in the same place where the visible physical world now exists],

41.25a But Leviathan is incarnating as a many-membered Wild Animal, and [the fiery serpent is] assembling [the nations] for her own evil purposes,

41.27 And Leviathan thinks that Elohim's Sons can be easily consumed, because the[y were given over to] Tree of the Knowledge of Good & Evil [Leviathan] for judgment,

41.25b When they all separated from the path of righteousness,

41.29a And Adam was circumcised, and Adam's widowed spirit was woven into [the background threads of the Wild Animal],

41.33 And the Serpent's failure [to produce a many-membered man which is completely evil], resulted in Leviathan, a confused mind, that is stronger than Abel,

41.29b Which scorns the fierceness of the two-witness company,

41.34 Respects every haughty thing, and is king over the many-membered, magnificent Wild Animal that she is married to,

41.24a But her heart is as hard as stone,

41.21-22 And lust, fear, anxiety, and depression spring forth from her mind, and stir up warlike passions in her emotions, which cause hostile words to issue out of her mouth, and she draws strength from complaining, stubbornness and other negative and disruptive behavior.

41.24b Indeed, crushing judgment is necessary to separate Adam's widowed spirit from Leviathan, the mind of the Wild Animal,

41.30 Because [Cain] seeks comfort from Leviathan instead of Elohim, since the Wild Animal was subjected to Jehovah's judgment,

41.12a But Adam,

41.26a The mind that can lay hold of Adam's widowed spirit, who is woven together with Satan, and pull him out of her,

41.12b Shall be grafted to Adam's widowed spirit, and Elohim's nature shall be engraved upon him, and they shall be highly esteemed and very valuable, because their new man [Michael, Adam, and the personality they were born with], shall give them mastery over the Wild Animal they are joined to,

41.12c And they shall stand up with full spiritual authority [over the Serpent's kingdom].[R]

[R] Eph 4:13

THE BOOK OF

JOEL

Chapter 2

[18.2]
2.22 Be not afraid, [all you] men [who exist] on the soul realm, for the Kingdom of God shall indeed manifest in you.

[78.10]
2.28-29 And I shall pour out of the hidden parts of my Spirit upon the whole Wild Animal, and spiritual men, as well as spiritual women, shall prophesy, and the temporary five-fold ministry which is to be replaced by Elohim's Sons, shall dream dreams which are generated by a criminal spirit, and spiritual virgins shall see visions from Elohim and Jehovah, and predict future events, and they shall faithfully repeat and explain Elohim's and Jehovah's messages to mortal man.

And I shall also pour out of the hidden parts of my Spirit upon the carnal and spiritual mortal men, who recognize and submit to the [spiritual] Government I shall establish in the Earth.

Chapter 3

[313.3]
3.03 And they are casting lots for my people, since Adam incarnated as Cain, that Woman**R-1** who was swallowed up by the Serpent,**R-2** when she caused Abel to die to His manhood,**R-3** and

now the Serpent has made Abel her prostitute,**R-4** and they are all one flesh,**R-5** and have increased into Leviathan, fallen man's mortal mind

R-1 Gen 2:25 (AT)
R-2 Jon 1:17
R-3 Gen 2:21b, 23; 49:6 (AT)
R-4 Job 41:5, 13 (AT)
Pro 36:11 (AT)
Eccl 12:3 (AT)
Ez 32:2 (AT)
Dan 8:6-7 (AT)
Zeph 3:4a (AT)
Rev 17:1
R-5 Gen 2:24, 3:16

THE BOOK OF

JONAH

Chapter 1

[426.13]

Jehovah Calls Jonah

1.01 Jehovah sent Elijah to Jonah, who was of the race of Abel,[170] saying,

1.02 Arise into Adam, and go to Nineveh, that mighty foreign city, to invite the [men thereof] to ascend above the evil side of their personality,

1.03a So [Abel], Jehovah's presence in Jonah, arose, and shot forth[R] out of [Satan's emotional] sea, and entered into the right side of Jonah's heart center, and [Adam], the parallelogram of Jehovah's presence, swallowed up [Satan], sacrificed [Leviathan] to [Jehovah], gathered [Abel into Adam's household], and delivered [Jonah's personality from the influence of his emotional animal nature],

[R] Ps 105:26 (AT)

Leviathan Opposes Jonah

1.03b And [this is how] Jonah went to speak Jehovah's words to the [mortal men of] Nineveh, that defensed, foreign city,

---

[170] Mortal men whose consciousness is in Abel, the mortal mind that the Spirit of Elijah raises from the dead (Mal 4:5-6; Matt 11:14). (See, Message #434, ***Circumcision Of The Heart***.)

where powerful, widowed angels freely access the Serpent's lower planes of existence,

1.04 But [Satan], the [emotional] sea that incarnated Jonah, stirred up [Leviathan, the sea serpent], to swallow up [the emotional, animal of Jonah's personality, which created] a mighty storm [within Jonah], but Jehovah sent His Great Spirit

1.05a To the spiritual, but mortal men [of Nineveh], who [Satan's emotional] sea [was raging in], and [Cain], the female side of the whole [Tree of the Knowledge of Good & Evil], became afraid, and cried out to [Marduk], their god,

1.07a Saying to [Leviathan], their lover,**[R]** Come, let us overthrow [Adam, Jonah's], inheritance, so that we may [continue to] experience the evil side [of the tree of the knowledge of good and evil],

R Song 5:8, 8:8 (AT)

1.05b And [Satan's emotional] sea shot forth from [Cain, Leviathan's] evil house[hold within the men of Nineveh],[171] to dishonor [Elohim], the waters from above [the firmament],[172]

1.05c And lay with [Adam, the good side of the Tree of the Knowledge of Good & Evil within] Jonah, and [Leviathan] covered [Adam], Jonah's male clothing,

1.07b And [this is how Adam], Jonah's inheritance, was dishonored, and [Abel], Jonah's, destiny, was cast down [under Cain],

---

[171] ***Satan***, the primordial Serpent, appearing as humanity's collective unconscious mind, and the individual emotional body. (Footnote continued – See, Appendix)

[172] Elohim, Jehovah's spiritual seminal fluid, is the waters above the firmament, and the primordial Serpent, the spiritual urine, is the waters underneath the firmament. Urine introduced into seminal fluid kills the sperm. (Footnote continued – See, Appendix)

1.03d And [spiritual Jerusalem], that beautiful city [in the left side of Jonah's] heart center, was destroyed,

1.05d And [Jonah] fell into a deep sleep.

Chapter 2

[426.13]

Jehovah's Conditional Divorce

2.04 Then I Am said [to Elohim], his counterpart, I am divorcing [Jonah], your image, but I will consider rejoining him to [King Adam], our holy temple,

Elijah Encourages Jonah to Cry out

1.06 So [Elijah], the great one who was laboring to be born [in Jonah], came to [Jonah] and said, Why are you sleeping? Wake up, cry out to Jehovah, and perhaps [Abel, Elohim's mortal] mind, will spring up and overlay the fiery serpent,

2.01 So Jonah prayed to Jehovah, that Abel, Elohim's mortal mind, [would arise in the spiritual] womb [the right side of his heart center],

2.02a Saying, [Leviathan and the fiery serpent], summoned [Satan], my female rival, and [she] afflicted me,

2.03a And [Satan] violently threw down the mud [emotional animal, and physical body][173] on [the right side of]

---

[173] Mind, man's consciousness, is spirit, but his personality, the emotional animal that he is attached to, is of the earth, and these two are joined as one man.

Consciousness, which is mind, pierces into immortality before the personality, the emotional animal, does. So, one might find their my heart center, and the seas that flowed together changed direction,[174] and altogether ruined my maidenhead,[175]

2.05a And the waters [of the primordial] Serpent swirled around my [ox],[176] the emotional animal that surrounds Adam, my head,

2.06a And I was cut off from [Michael and Adam], the mountains [of God],

2.03b And I crossed over [to the right side of my heart center].[177]

2.06b And sank down into the earth [of my carnal mind],

2.05b And the fiery serpent, put a saddle on Abel,[178]

2.06c And bolted [the gateway] to the eternal [timeline],[R]

[R] Is 6:4a (AT)

---

consciousness on the left side of their heart center (which is dominated by the resurrected Adam), (Footnote continued – See, Appendix)

[174] Elohim, the waters above the firmament, and the primordial Serpent, the sea underneath the firmament, are the divided waters [Gen 1:6]. Elohim commanded the waters above and underneath the firmament to be gathered together [Gen 1:9], because the dry seed remaining underneath is barren, and cannot incarnate the Serpent's negative world. (Footnote continued – See, Appendix)

[175] The wall that separates the left and the right side of the heart center in the etheric part of the physical body, is the firmament, or hedge, or maidenhead, of that man. (Footnote continued – See, Appendix)

[176] The Serpent killed Adam, stole his widowed spirit and the ox (Ez 1:10) [the emotional animal] that he was joined to, and reformed them into the human spirit and the personalities of this fallen creation.

[177] From a Son of Adam, to Ashtoreth.

[178] The significance of ***putting a saddle on Abel*** is that the resurrected Abel is, once again, forced underground (Gen 4:10).

2.02b So I am crying out to you, Jehovah, [from] the womb of hell.[179] Hear my voice, and help me.

2.06d Bring my spiritual life[180] up out of [my carnal mind], which is destroying me, Jehovah, my God.

Jehovah Delivers Jonah

2.07c Then I Am remembered that [Jonah] was the male,[181]

2.09a Who was to fulfill His promise [to provide] a saviour [to Nineveh],

Chapter 3

[Message # Unknown]
3.01 So Jehovah's commandment came to Jonah the second time, saying,

3.02 [Let Adam] be resurrected [in you], and go to Ninevah, that mightily defensed, foreign city, and summon the [mortal men who abide there], and announce to them that I Am intends to destroy [their fallen nature], and make [King Adam] their leader,

3.03a And [Abel] rose [up in Jonah],

---

179 The right side of the heart center.

180 ***Spiritual life***, a translation of the Hebrew word, ***chay*** [Strong's #2416], signifies Jehovah's immortal life. ***Emotional animal life***, a translation of the Hebrew word, ***nephesh*** [Strong's #5315], signifies the emotional animal nature which is possessing fallen mankind.

181 ***Male***, in the context of this verse, means that Jehovah recognized that Jonah had Elohim's male Spirit.

3.04a And pierced through [to the left side of Jonah's heart center],

2.10a And [Elijah] told [Jonah that King Adam, Elohim's] mature mind, would save [the emotional animal from Satan's emotional] sea,

1.17a And [that Elohim had] assigned [Elijah to help Adam, Elohim's] mature mind, to pull up [the fiery serpent] by her roots, and occupy [Jonah's spiritual] womb [on the right side of the heart center],

2.09b And [Elijah], the voice of I Am, held out His hand to Jonah,

2.07a And [King Adam], the holy temple from above [arose], and clothed Jonah's emotional animal,

2.07b And [King Adam], the intercessor, entered into [the right side of Jonah's heart center],

2.08a And hedged[R] in [Satan],

[R] Ez 1:4c (AT)

1.17c And [King Adam] flowed out of Jonah's three higher centers, into Jonah's three lower centers,

1.17b And swallowed up Jonah['s human spirit],

2.08b And [Satan, that] shameful, lying breath, departed [from] Jonah,

2.10b And Jonah was transposed, and [walked on] dry land.[182]

---

[182] The right side of the heart center becomes dry land when the Fortified Adam drives out Satan, the sea of raging emotions. The physical body does not cross over to the left side of the heart center, which is the spiritual world, but continues to abide on the right side of the dried out heart center, which is now free from Satan's influence. (See, Message #435, ***Left Hand, Right Hand***.)

3.10b And Elohim saw that the [mortal men] turned away from their evil lifestyle, and Elohim pitied them because of the evil that Satan was threatening to do to them,

3.05a And [the Spirit of Elijah], the male nurse from Elohim's household, wrapped the greatest to the least of them into his mantle,

3.06c And nailed himself to [their human spirit],

3.09b And comforted them,

3.05b And gathered their

3.06d Dust[183]

3.05c Into [Abel's] male mind,

3.06b And [the Spirit of Elijah] nailed himself to [Abel], the dust [in the right side of their heart center, and Adam, their] male side, who dwells [in the left side of the heart center, which is] above [the right side of the heart center], arose [within the citizens of Nineveh, the foreign city],

3.08c And Adam, the sackcloth [that separates the human spirit from Satan], covered the ox,

3.07 And the household of Nineveh, the defensed, foreign city, shrieked with anguish and fear, as Adam, the[ir] king, [executed] judgment upon the elders of the flock, saying, You shall no longer have intercourse with Leviathan, the sea serpent, the [primordial] Serpent's companion, [who] swallowed up the point[184] that was nailed to the window[185] [where Adam,]

---

[183] Cain killed Abel and Abel separated into Elohim's breath and spiritual dust. The Spirit of Elijah [the Holy Spirit in the New Testament] joins Himself to Elohim's breath, and the two gather in the dust, to raise Abel from the dead. (See, Message #356, ***Dust***.)

[184] The spiritual singularity that contained all of the genetic material necessary to fully manifest Elohim's creation.

[185] The upper of the two rooms of the creation, which are separated by the firmament (Gen 1:7).

Elohim's phallus, and the ox [were],[186] [neither shall you] exercise Satan's spiritual power [any more],

3.05b And [the Fortified Adam in Jonah] nailed [the fiery serpent's] mouth shut,

3.10c And [Satan] was condensed.[187]

Jonah Gives His Testimony

1.08a Then the [mortal men of Nineveh] said to [Jonah], Tell us, we beg you, where do you come from, what side of the earth [heart center] are your people [from], who is [sending] this evil upon us, and why do you serve him?

1.09 And [Jonah] said, I am an Hebrew who serves I Am, [the great] Jehovah, Himself, and Elohim, who made the heaven, and the sea, and the dry land,

1.08b And [the mortal men of Nineveh asked], Why are you here?

1.12a And [Jonah] said to the mortal men [of Nineveh, The Spirit of Elijah] forgave my sins, and drew me up [into the centers] above the visible world,

1.12b And [King Adam] silenced [the fiery serpent]

1.11b And dried up [Satan, the emotional] sea that was scattering [my energy],

1.12c And cast down [the fiery serpent],

1.11a And gave me eternal life.

---

[186] Adam is the male mind of the female animal life spoken about in Gen 1:24. Together they are called ***the Living Beast***.

[187] The waters of creation are appearing in mortal man as the human spirit. The condensation, or the distillation, of Satan's energy sea, separates the human spirit from the earth which is polluting him.

The Ninevites Converted

1.10 And the mortal men [of Nineveh] were astonished, but exceedingly reverent, [because] they recognized that [King Adam], Jehovah's presence, had boldly opposed [Satan, Jonah's emotional sea] and driven her away, and the [mortal men of Nineveh] said to [Jonah], Why did [King Adam] do this [for you]?

1.12d And [King Adam], speaking through Jonah] said, Because I Am knows that [Satan], this great [emotional] storm, exists because of me.[188]

1.13 So the mortal men [of Nineveh] repented [189] because their land was not dry,[190] but [Satan, the emotional] sea within them raged, and broke through, and overcame them again,

1.14 Wherefore, [Jonah] cried to Jehovah saying, Lord, [Satan's emotional] sea is destroying[R] the emotional animal of these mortal men. Oh, Lord, please don't condemn them, but if it pleases you to do it, pardon them,

[R] Matt 8:25 (AT)

---

[188] Adam, resurrected in Jonah, prophetically accepts responsibility for humanity's descent into a mortal sin nature, which confession and repentance covers mankind, making them eligible for deliverance from destruction [Ashtoreth (the Devil in the New Testament), their collective fallen nature], and the pit, which is this present fallen world (Vs. 6).

[189] The mortal men of Nineveh understood that Adam's confession of primary responsibility for the condition of fallen humanity qualified them for redemption, as well as the Jews.

[190] Jehovah is restoring Adam's descendants to immortality, because Adam's spiritual remains, which is Elohim's breath, is appearing in humanity as the human spirit. Our part is to confess that, as Adam's descendants, we are responsible, by inheritance and by commission, for our fallen, mortal condition, which is the fruit of our sin nature.

1.15 So Jonah forgave the sins of the mortal men [of Nineveh], and [King Adam in Jonah] subjected [Satan's emotional] sea [in the mortal men], and stopped her raging,

1.16 And the mortal men [of Nineveh] were astonished, and exceedingly revered Jehovah, and offered to sacrifice [the fiery serpent, their god] to Jehovah, and promised Jehovah [that they would confess their specific sins, and repent].[191]

Chapter 4

[426.13]
4.07a Now Elohim intended that Jonah should ascend when the next [spiritual] day dawned, [and that the fiery serpent] should wither,

4.06a So Jehovah and Elohim prepared a mortal mind to ascend above the [fiery] serpent who covers Jonah, and [Jonah] rejoiced because of Abel, Elohim's mortal mind,[192]

4.02a And [the Spirit of Elijah, Adam's] captain, revealed [to Jonah] that Elohim reaches down to his inferiors, and told [Abel] the truth concerning the crown center,[193]

---

[191] ***Offered to sacrifice the fiery serpent*** signifies general repentance which leads to reconciliation, and ***that they would confess their sins and repent*** signifies the specific sin that leads to the destruction of the sin nature, which is a prerequisite for immortality.

[192] ***A gourd is a quick growing, but easily damaged plant***, which describes Abel, Elohim's mortal mind. (Footnote continued – See, Appendix)

[193] Please note that Jonah, the personality, can understand that Elohim is reaching down to him, but spiritual truth is imparted to Abel, his righteous mind. The carnal mind cannot receive Jehovah's spiritual truth.

4.09 And Elohim warned Jonah, saying, The fiery serpent will counterfeit Abel, and Jonah said, Let the fiery serpent counterfeit [Abel], and let [Satan counterfeit the Holy Spirit], until they die,

4.02b And [Abel] zealously reached out for [the crown center, but Leviathan], the [primordial] Serpent's timeline in [Jonah's] ground, confronted him,

[And Jonah] prayed to Jehovah saying, I urgently request, Jehovah, that you relieve me because of Satan, the evil one,[194]

4.03 And Jehovah immediately accepted [Jonah's] urgent petition that Abel, [Jonah's] morally righteous side, [should be delivered from] death, and [that Jonah's] emotional animal (personality), [should be delivered from] hell,

4.02c And [Jehovah began to] prepare [Abel to become] an eagle,[195]

4.04 And Jehovah said [to Abel], The fiery serpent that [Jonah] belongs to is a counterfeit

4.10 Who is vexing you, by covering you over, like a protective shadow,

And Jehovah said [to Jonah], The fiery serpent is the offspring of Leviathan, the [primordial Serpent's] time line, who incarnated you,

4.11 But I am above Leviathan, the sea serpent who covers Nineveh, that great city where Adam's many widowed spirits are under the law because they are double-minded, and

---

[194] Jonah learned from experience that he cannot ascend above Satan's authority and stay ascended without the help of the Spirit of Elijah [the glorified Jesus in the New Testament], who is above.

[195] The word ***eagle*** is rendered from Strong's #7349, translated ***merciful*** in the King James translation, which is (Footnote continued – See, Appendix)

cannot distinguish between the good side of their [fallen nature], their emotional animal (personality), and Abel, [Michael's spiritual phallus], who [the fiery serpent] is coiled around,

4.07b So Elohim sent [Elijah, the Spirit of] judgment, upon Abel,[196]

4.08a Until Jonah wished that [the fiery serpent], the nature of his emotional animal (personality), should die,

4.01b Because [Satan], the evil one, and the insolent fiery [serpent], were possessing Jonah [King Adam's emotional animal (personality)],

4.08b Saying, It is a good [thing] that [the fiery serpent] should die, so that [King Adam], the living one [can occupy] the water[s of creation],

So Elohim appointed the Spirit of Elijah, [Adam's] captain,

4.06b To rescue Jonah from [Satan, the] evil one,

4.08c And it came to pass that King Adam, the sun [of righteousness], arose [in Jonah],

4.05a And judged [Jonah's sin nature],

4.01a And [King Adam] broke [Leviathan] in pieces,

4.08d And silenced the fiery serpent who was wrapped around [Abel, Elohim's phallus], and Satan was fatally wounded,

4.05b And [King Adam] put [the fiery serpent who Jonah] belonged to, in [the correct moral] order,

4.05c And subjected [Jonah, his] emotional animal (personality), to the point that she looked like Elohim's city,

---

[196] Abel is not strong enough to overcome the Serpent's household. Judgment strengthens Abel and weakens the carnal mind.

And [King Adam] married [Jonah], his temporary tent, and Jonah went out of [Leviathan's] city and [entered into Elohim's] city, [which is] the eternal timeline,

4.06c And [Jonah] was filled with joy.

THE BOOK OF JOSHUA

Chapter 2

[523.3]

2.01 [And Adam], the son of [Jehovah], the Eternal One [within] Joshua, the [mortal man] that Jehovah liberated from death, went forth from [the crown center], the plane of existence that is beyond time, to tread down [Leviathan], the moon/mind [of Joshua's spiritual kosmos, who is] second [in authority to the Primordial Serpent, who used] magical arts [to murder Adam, and King Adam], the spiritual male [within Joshua] said,

I will go see [Leviathan, who] acquired the land/personalities [of Elohim's civilized man] for herself, and [King Adam within Joshua] went and entered into [the fiery serpent], the adulterous woman who expresses the nature of Rahab, the primeval Dragon, [and King Adam within Joshua] had spiritual sexual intercourse [of the mind with the fiery serpent, Leviathan's] house[hold, which was] there [in the midst of Joshua],

2.02 And Adam [within Joshua] challenged [Leviathan], the widowed king [who is] the moon/mind [of Joshua's spiritual kosmos] saying, Look, [Adam], the spiritual male [within Joshua], has entered into Leviathan's side of the [spiritual] waters [of] the children of Israel, to explore [the planes of existence within] the [spiritual] earth [of the personalities of the children of Israel],

2.03 And King Adam sent [a message to Leviathan], the widowed mind of [the children of Israel], which is near to Rahab, the primeval Dragon, [and King Adam, the spiritual male within

Joshua] said [to Leviathan], Let all the earthen [personalities] [that King Adam], the spiritual male [within Joshua], entered into escape

For the purpose of searching for [the fiery serpent, Leviathan's] widowed house[hold within the personalities of the children of Israel], and

[For the purpose of] besieging [and] entering into [the fiery serpent, Leviathan's] widowed house[hold],

2.04 And [Joshua], the two-fold spiritual male [within Joshua], besieged [the fiery serpent who was nailed to Leviathan within the children of Israel], and [King Adam], the spiritual male [within Joshua], seized [the fiery serpent], the [spiritual] woman [within the children of Israel who is] nailed to Leviathan, [and Abel within the children of Israel] restrained [Cain, Abel's female side that is] nailed to Leviathan, [and King Adam within Joshua] said [to Abel within the children of Israel, who is] near to [Adam within Joshua], Stand upright; [and] Satan knew [what was happening],

2.05 And King Adam [within Joshua] appeared at the gate [of Leviathan's] widowed [timeline, and] carried [Abel within the children of Israel] out [of Leviathan's timeline, and King Adam, the spiritual male within Joshua], shut up the widowed, dark [side] of [the children of Israel, but when] Satan, the unconscious part of the carnal mind [of the children of Israel], realized that [Abel within the children of Israel] had departed [with Joshua], the [two-fold] spiritual male, [Satan] hastened to run after [the children of Israel], to lay hold of [Abel within them],

2.06 But [King Adam, who was in Joshua's] brow energy center, put [Abel, the one who] belongs to [King Adam, in] the right [moral] order [within the children of Israel, and Abel] ascended into [the left side of their heart center, and] restrained [Cain, who is] nailed to Leviathan, the wooden threads [of the Tree of the Knowledge of Good & Evil, who is] against [King Adam, the Tree of Life],

2.07 And [Cain, who] pursues the lifestyle of Satan, the unconscious part of [the carnal mind, and is] the gateway [for Satan], the river of death [within the children of Israel, surrendered, [and] Satan the unconscious part of [the carnal mind within the children of Israel] departed [when Elohim, the Spirit of King Adam], the spiritual male [within Joshua], pursued Satan, the unconscious part [of the carnal mind within the children of Israel],

2.08 [And this is how Joshua] suspended the spiritual sexual connection [of mind between the fiery serpent within the children of Israel and Leviathan, when King Adam] ascended into [Joshua's] brow (center, [which is] above [the crown energy center of Leviathan's counterfeit timeline],

2.09a And [King Adam], the spiritual male [within Joshua] said [to the children of Israel],

2.10 As soon as [the children of Israel] heard how Jehovah dried up [Satan], the spiritual blood of [the fiery serpent], the red seaweed [side] of the personality, so that they could depart from spiritual Egypt, the crown center of Leviathan's timeline, and what [King Adam] did to [Leviathan, who is]

(1) The spiritual mud that swept away [Adam], the other, [righteous] side of [Jordan, the river of] death, [and]

(2) [The dream world presence of] Sihon, the Amorite king [who is conscious in] two [worlds],

And [as soon as the children of Israel] heard what King Adam did to] Og, the round, baked clay animal [called Cain, who] slew [Abel, because Jehovah consecrated Abel, and appointed Abel] to shut up [Satan's] anger,

2.09b [The children of Israel agreed to] cast down the idol [in the heart center that is] above, and [Satan] knows that [the fiery serpent who] inhabits the earthen personalities [of the children of Israel] is exhausted from resisting [the children of Israel, and] that Leviathan's marriage to the fiery serpent] is dissolving, [because] Jehovah has given us [dominion over] the land [of your personalities],

2.11 And as soon as [the children of Israel] who were nailed to Leviathan, understood [that] Jehovah [is] the supreme God [of all] the gods[R] in the neck center [of King Adam's righteous timeline, which is] above the heart energy center [of Leviathan's counterfeit timeline], the Spirit [of Truth of Adam], the spiritual male, rose again [within the children of Israel, and] the Devil, the idol in the heart center of the personalities [of the children of Israel], dissolved,

[R] Ps 82:6-7

2.12 [And the children of Israel said to Joshua], We have demonstrated [how] zealous [we are] to assemble ourselves into [the brow center of] the Father's house[hold], so complete [us] now, [and] give us the privilege [of] belonging to Jehovah, [so that we might be] witnesses [to] the Truth,

2.13 [So that Elohim], our Father, may revive [Abel], our brothers, [and Cain], our sisters, [so that Adam], our mother, [will regenerate in] everyone who belongs to [Adam, and] defends [Cain, the female side of] the fiery serpent, against [Satan, the fiery serpent's] dead, spiritual blood,

2.14 And Adam, the spiritual male [within Joshua], answered [the children of Israel saying, Your] whole personality [is in the world] underneath [Satan's sea, so] you [must] die to the fiery serpent's lifestyle, [if you want] to dominate the land [of your personalities, and, if you want to die to the fiery serpent's lifestyle], this Leviathan [who] stands boldly opposite our cause [of dying to the fiery serpent's lifestyle, must] be given over to Jehovah, [so that] we can tell you the truth [about yourselves] with mercy.

Chapter 3

[1225.2.C]

Messiah Appears

3.13 And it shall come to pass [that] Adonay [within] the earth[en personalities of] all the priests that carry the ark of Jehovah, shall descend from [the World of Creation, the world] above [the World of Angels, and the Second Adam] shall stand up in the waters of Jordan, [the World of Angels], the spiritual power of the carnal mind, [and]

His Ministry

Unite with [Abel, the remains of the First Adam whose] harvest failed [to produce an immortal offspring], and he shall cut off the waters of Jordan, [the World of Angels], from the waters [of Adonay within the people],

Passes Over Souls

3.14 And it came to pass that, when the people were no longer bound [to the angels who were satisfying] the lusts of] the body, [that Adonay within] the priests carrying the ark of the covenant, passed over the personalities of the people [that were worshiping the angels in] Jordan, [the World of Angels],

3.15 [Whose] carnal mind was immersed in [the spiritual waters of] Jordan, [the World of Angels, that] overflow all the human beings in [the World of Action] at the time of harvest; [But] when the priests that carry the ark came to the edge [of Jordan, the World of Angels],

Unlimited Spiritual Waters

The unlimited [spiritual] waters of [Adonay overflowed from Jericho, the World of Creation, which is above the World of Angels, and] offset [the waters that were overflowing from] Jordan, [the World of Angels],

Resurrects Abel

3.16 [And Adonay], the waters that come down from above, stood up [and] united with [Abel, and] the mighty [Leviathan,

Forces The Snake to Recede

The Snake that is the spiritual intelligence of the First Adam, who] cut the people off [from Adonay], receded from the side of Adam, the golden city [that] descends from the sea of heaven into the salt sea,* [and Adonay] completed the people [and] they passed over [the World of Angels, and entered into] Jericho, [the World of Creation, which is] on the other side of [Jordan, the World of Angels],

The Priests Stand In Jordan
Until The People Pass Over

3.17 And the priests that bear the ark of the covenant of Jehovah stood in the midst of Jordan, [the World of Angels], until Jehovah completed all the confused earth[en personalities of Adam, his] mate, [and] all the confused earth[en personalities of] the Israelites stood up erect, [and] the people passed over Jordan, [the World of Angels, into the World of Creation].

THE BOOK OF

JUDGES

Chapter14

[473.4]

14.01 And [Adam in] Samson went down to the [lower] window and saw [the fiery serpent], the woman in the [lower] window, [who was within] the daughters of the [spiritual] immigrants,

14.02 And [Satan] ascended [in Leviathan, Samson's] widowed father and mother, and said to Samson, [Adam] has seen [the fiery serpent], the woman [within] the daughters of the [spiritual] immigrants in the lower window, and is about to fetch and enfold her,

14.03 Then [Leviathan, Samson's] father and mother, said to Samson, The fiery serpent], the Primordial Serpent's female offspring, is amongst our people, but you seek after [the fiery serpent], the woman in the immigrants, who has sealed them off [from Jehovah], but Samson said to [Adam, his] father, I will fetch and enfold [the fiery serpent] on behalf of the righteous world,

14.04 And Leviathan, [Samson's], father and mother perceived that, indeed, Jehovah, Himself, was desiring to have intercourse with the [spiritual] immigrants of the Serpent's[R] timeline, because the [spiritual] immigrants of the Serpent's timeline, had dominion over Israel, which is Himself,

[R] Rev 12:9, 20:2

14.05 So Samson and [Adam, his] father, and [Leviathan, his] mother, descended into the lower window and encountered the thought forms of the spiritual young men, and perceived that they were crying out in distress, and [Adam] entered into the [suffering people] who had the branch of the Tree of Life,

14.06 And the Spirit of Jehovah pushed forth in [Samson], the young male goat, and Adam, [Samson's righteous] subconscious mind, stood boldly opposite [Leviathan, Samson's] widowed father and mother, and the fiery serpent divided from Leviathan, and from the powers [in Samson's energy centers], because of what [Adam, Samson's] other self, had done,

14.07 And [Adam], Samson's subconscious mind, descended [into the lower window within Samson] and nailed [the fiery serpent], the [spiritual] woman, to himself, and arranged [Samson] in the correct moral order,

14.08 But [when Adam, Elohim's] wisdom, returned to [the lower window] to marry [the fiery serpent within Samson], he perceived that [she] was joined to a family of [spiritual] insects [who are] the powers [of the visible, spiritual world, and the demons which are] their thought forms, so [Adam] overthrew Leviathan's timeline, and [Samson] escaped from [Satan's grasp],

14.09 And [Adam] afflicted [Satan, the dog] that belongs to [Leviathan], and overthrew her, and declared [the Gospel of Peace] to Samson, and [Adam, Elohim's] wisdom, tread down and subjugated [Leviathan, Samson's] father and mother, and consumed them, and [Adam, Samson's righteous] subconscious mind, tread down and subjugated [the fiery serpent], and [Adam] entered into [the fiery serpent], and consumed her, and [Samson] died to the [fiery serpent's] lifestyle, and became alive to [Adam's] lifestyle,

14.10 And [after Adam] cast down [the fiery serpent] and put [Samson] in the right [moral] order, Samson prepared [Leviathan], the woman who was his father, to be a feast for [Adam], the righteous young man within him,

14.11 And it came to pass that, when [Adam] enfolded the powers [which were inhabiting Samson's] third energy center, [Samson] saw [Elijah, the archer in Elohim's energy cloud],**R-1** and [Samson, the personality, Jehovah's] friend,[R-2] began to ascend.

[R-1] Gen 9:16 (AT)
2 Ki 2:10, 12 (AT)
Ez 1:28b (AT)
Is 6:1
Rev 1:7, 10:1, 14:14
[R-2] Jas 2:23

14.12 And Samson said to [the spiritual young men], I implore you urgently to declare that you belong to the belly energy center, [so that you can] solve the mystery of [Leviathan], the [Primordial Serpent's] completed timeline, and the feast [of Adam, the one who] stands boldly opposite Leviathan, [the one who is] appearing [in you], and then I will give you Adam in exchange for the [spiritual insects in] your belly energy center, and his righteousness will cover [the one who] rapes and spoils you,

14.13 But if you declare that you belong to Leviathan because [she is too strong for you] to overcome, then you give yourself over to the belly energy center, and exchange Adam's righteousness for [the spiritual insects who] cover your belly energy center, and rapes and spoils you. And [the spiritual young men] said to [Samson], Let us hear your esoteric doctrine, so that we may consider it,

14.14 And [Samson] said to the [young spiritual men], The fierce water of Adam's window separated from him, and consumed [his energy], and became flesh, but Leviathan in the belly energy center [of the spiritual young men, prevailed over them], and they could not explain the esoteric doctrine of [how the Serpent's] timeline [came into existence].

14.15 And it came to pass, [that Leviathan, the male of the] household of [Satan, the Primordial Serpent's] completed timeline, said to [Cain], Samson's wife, Persuade your husband, Adam, the subconscious mind [that] you are nailed to, to explain the esoteric doctrine of the seraph [the ascended fiery serpent], and the [flying] fish that removed [Jehovah's] nature [from

Adam, the lake of] fire [and drove him out of his father's house, so that Leviathan could come into existence,

14.16 And Samson boiled [Satan, who] was flowing together with [Cain], his wife, saying, The males of your people hate you and love Leviathan. They belong to me! But [Samson], nevertheless, declared the esoteric doctrine [that would help the spiritual males] stand boldly across from Leviathan, saying, Look! [I am] standing boldly opposite Leviathan, my widowed father and mother, [because the fiery serpent in me] is nailed [to Adam, and you, too, can] stand boldly opposite [Leviathan],

14.17 And [Samson] forced [Satan, the Primordial Serpent's] completed timeline, to flow downward into the [lower] window, and it came to pass [that Leviathan and the fiery serpent], the household of [Satan], the completed timeline who had declared that the males of the nations belonged to her, proclaimed the esoteric doctrine, and they feasted on [Leviathan], continually,

14.18 And [Leviathan and the fiery serpent], the household of [Satan], the completed timeline, said to the [mortal men] before Elohim attacked [Satan], the sun of their city, The wisdom of [Satan's] waters [is] sweeter than Elohim and stronger than [Adam, Jehovah's] thought form, and [Adam], the subconscious mind that [Samson] belonged to, said to [Leviathan and the fiery serpent, Satan's] household, If you had not shut up the ears of my heifer, these mortal men would have recognized my esoteric doctrine,

14.19 And the Spirit of Jehovah pushed forward in [Samson], and the passion of Adam, the Father's household, blazed forth, and the Spirit of Judgment descended upon the [mortal] men who were smitten by the navel energy center, and seized [Leviathan, the fiery serpent's] armor, [who] stood boldly opposite the esoteric doctrine, and the [mortal men] were delivered from [the fiery serpent's] lifestyle, and ascended [into their heart center].

14.20 And [Cain], Samson's wife, the widowed companion that belonged to [Abel] who had pastored her, was accepted.

Chapter 15

[475.11]

STAGE 1 - RESCUE
DELIVERANCE WITHOUT REPENTANCE

Samson's Conversion

15.01a In the day that [Adam] judged Samson, the young male goat of [Astarte], the she-goat, [Adam in Samson], punished [the fiery serpent], his wife, saying, I will go into the chamber of my wife,

Adam Lives Through Samson
Declares He Will Live Through All Of Judah

15.03 And Samson said, Concerning the personalities of the spiritual immigrants [in Judah, I will turn them] against [Satan], the evil waters, [and put them] in [the righteous moral] order, because I [am] free from guilt,

Satan Opposes Samson's Assignment

15.01b But [Satan], the [evil] waters of Leviathan], the father [of the mortal men of Judah], appeared, and would not permit [Adam in Samson] to go in [to the mortal men of Judah],

15.02 And [Satan], the father [of the group mind of the mortal men of Judah] said [to Samson], You are boasting proudly that you hate [Satan, and] hate [Leviathan], therefore I am giving the widowed fiery serpent [in the mortal men of Judah], the beloved bride [of Adam, your] friend, to [Leviathan, even though] the good side of the [fiery serpent], Leviathan's young [one in the world] underneath, is praying to belong to [Adam when] he appears,

The Spirit Of Elijah In Samson
Vows To Punish Satan

15.07 [Then] the Spirit of Elijah said to [Satan], the unconscious] part of the Primordial Serpent's timeline, concerning Samson['s ministry], Since you have given [the fiery serpent in the mortal men of Judah to Leviathan], I will surely punish [you, Satan], and [the fiery serpent] shall become limp and unoccupied,

The Spirit Of Elijah In Samson Punishes Satan
Adam In Samson Punishes Leviathan

15.08a And [the Spirit of Elijah in Samson] attacked [Satan], the spiritual energy of the other side [of the mortal men of Judah], and [Adam in Samson] pursued [Leviathan in the mortal men of Judah, because she was] covering [the fiery serpent], the [spiritual] generative part [of the mortal men of Judah], from the neck energy center,

Leviathan & The Fiery Serpent
Bisected In Mortal Men Of Judah

15.04 And [the Spirit of Elijah in] Samson went and captured the brow energy center of the mortal men [of Judah, that] Satan was appearing in, and [Adam in Samson] captured the [heart] energy center [of] Leviathan's [timeline], and [Adam in Samson] lay upon the [heart] energy [center of the mortal men of Judah, which is] between [the Primordial Serpent's] two tails, and bisected [the fiery serpent], the tail that was added to [Leviathan], the Principal Tail, and turned [her back towards the root energy center],

Abel In The Mortal Men Of Judah
Gathered Into Adam In Samson

15.05a And [the Spirit of Elijah in Samson] consumed [Satan], the brutish [spiritual blood of] the etheric bodies of the spiritual immigrants [in the mortal men of Judah], and Adam [in

Samson] consumed the fiery [serpent in the lower] energy centers [of the mortal men of Judah], and [the Spirit of Elijah gathered [Abel, Adam's root system], together [with Adam in Samson],

Adam In Samson Marries The Fiery Serpent In The Mortal Men Of Judah

15.08a And [Adam in Samson] married [the fiery serpent], the stronghold of the [lower energy centers of the mortal men of Judah], the lair of the [fiery serpent], the Wild Beast,

Abel Ascends Into The Heart Center In The Mortal Men Of Judah

15.05b And [Abel] shot forth [from under the ground of the fiery serpent, Leviathan's] household [in the mortal men of Judah], and [Abel] stood up on [Adam's] foundation [within Samson], and ascended into the [heart center of the mortal men of Judah], the garden [where] the Tree of Life [is],

Adam Ascends In The Men Of Judah, But The Men Of Judah Kill Him

15.09 And Adam ascended [in the mortal men of Judah, but the fiery serpents], the spiritual immigrants [in the mortal men of] Judah, besieged him, and Leviathan, the collective subconscious mind [of the mortal men of Judah], cast [Adam] down [within the mortal men of Judah],

DELIVERANCE (RESCUE) WITHOUT REPENTANCE FAILS

STAGE 2 - INSTRUCTION ADAM INSTRUCTS SAMSON

Leviathan Has Dominion Over Judah

15.11a And Adam said to Samson, [a mortal] man of Judah, [I want you to] understand that we put you in order because Leviathan, the timeline of the spiritual immigrants, has dominion [over the mortal men of Judah],

The Mortal Men Of Judah Belong To Adam

15.12a And Adam said to Samson, The [personalities of the mortal men of Judah] belong to me, [so] swear with respect to them, that [you will bring] them to repentance, [so that they] can reach [Elohim's] timeline [which is] within themselves,

ADAM INSTRUCTS THE MORTAL MEN OF JUDAH

Adam Reveals Carnal Thoughts In The Mortal Men Of Judah

15.10 And [the Spirit of Elijah and Adam], the mind nailed to Samson, a mortal man of Judah, said [to the other mortal men of Judah], Why [do you think Adam] ascended within you? And [Satan and Leviathan], the [carnal] mind nailed to [the mortal men of Judah], answered [the Spirit of Elijah and Adam in Samson], He ascended to take us prisoner, and to do to us what we have done to him,

15.06 And Adam [in Samson] said to the spiritual immigrants [in the mortal men of Judah], Jehovah has done this because the Spirit of Elijah, the one who recognizes the ascended fiery serpent, responded to Samson['s call for help when Satan] captured [the fiery serpent, Adam's] widowed wife [in the mortal men of Judah], and gave her to [Leviathan for a] companion, and the Spirit of Elijah [in Samson] burnt Satan, and Leviathan, [their] father, with fire, and Abel shot forth [from] the spiritual immigrants [in the mortal men of Judah],

The Mortal Men Of Judah Go Under Judgment & Die To The Fiery Serpent's Lifestyle

15.13a And Adam [in Samson] spoke [to the mortal men of Judah], saying, Satan, indeed, [was able] to imprison, harness, and deliver [Abel, your spiritual] phallus, to [Leviathan, therefore], you must die to the [lifestyle] of [the fiery serpent], the household of Leviathan, the [Principal] Fish,

Mortal Men Of Judah Belong To Elijah & Adam

15.11b And [the Spirit of Elijah and] Adam [in Samson] said [to the mortal men of Judah], We are putting you in the right order with respect to [Samson], because you were made to belong to [us],

The Mortal Men Of Judah Delivered

15.12b And Adam [in Samson instructed the mortal men of Judah] saying, I will cast down the widow[ed fiery serpent], the household of [Leviathan], and imprison [Cain] for the purpose of delivering [Abel], the widowed phallus of the spiritual immigrants, [from Leviathan],

Abel In The Mortal Men Of Judah Delivered (The 2nd Time)

15.14a And [Elijah], the righteous power [which is Elohim's] Spirit [from the energy centers] above, [attacked Satan in the mortal men of Judah], and Adam, [Jehovah's stronghold from the energy centers] above [who has] Jehovah's nature, attacked Leviathan,

15.11c And [the Spirit of Elijah in Samson] prostrated [Satan], the third part of the crown energy center [of the mortal men of Judah, and Adam in Samson], the stronghold of [the Spirit of Elijah], Elohim's energy [in Samson, consumed the fiery serpent], the wild beast in the root energy center [of the mortal men of Judah],

15.13b And Adam [in Samson] bound Cain, the foliage [of the earth, who is] interwoven with [the fiery serpent, and] second [to righteous Abel], their new [phallus],

15.14b [And] the spiritual immigrants shouted [with alarm as Abel's] harness melted, [and Abel] attacked [Cain, the foliage who is] interwoven with [the fiery serpent], and became [Adam], the phallus of the waters above,

15.13c [And] Adam ascended [in the mortal men of Judah],

15.14c [And Adam] consumed the fiery serpent, [Leviathan's] household,

15.15b And [Abel in the mortal men of Judah] laid hold of the fiery serpent, [the spiritual sexual part] of the personalities of the [mortal] men [of Judah], and conquered [her], and [Adam], the phallus of the glorified Elijah, shot forth [in the mortal men of Judah],

15.15a And [this is how the Spirit of Elijah in Samson] acquired [Satan], the moisture of the crown energy center [of the mortal men of Judah, and how Adam in Samson] subjected Leviathan, [the Primordial Serpent's] timeline [in the mortal men of Judah],

ABEL IN THE MORTAL MEN OF JUDAH THIRSTS FOR REUNION WITH THE WATERS (ENERGY) OF CREATION

Judgment Of The Personality The Only Way

15.18 And Abel [in the mortal men of Judah] thirsted for [Satan], the vehement [waters], and Jehovah called toward Abel within [the mortal men of Judah], saying, [Adam in Samson], my [bond]servant [in] the window [where Adam], the diffraction grating of the visible world, is nailed to [Satan], the tooth [of Leviathan, the sea] serpent, has married the [fiery serpent], the household of [Leviathan], and,

Accordingly, [you, the personalities of the Primordial] ox, [must] now die to [the lifestyle of the fiery serpent, Leviathan's] haughty household, [and] to the household of [Satan], the waters of [Leviathan], the [sea] serpent that is nailed to [the personalities of the Primordial] ox, [so that Abel], the phallus [who is] covered [by Adam in Samson, who] thirsts [for Elohim's waters, and the fiery serpent, his] household, can overthrow [Satan and Leviathan in yourselves, the mortal men of Judah],

INSTRUCTION FAILS

STAGE 3 - INTERVENTION

THE SPIRIT OF ELIJAH & ADAM IN SAMSON INTERFERE WITH SATAN'S PLANS BEFORE CAIN KILLS ABEL A 3RD TIME

Satan Threatens To Overflow Abel In The Mortal Men Of Judah

15.16 And [Adam] said to Samson, [Satan], the [foul waters] of Leviathan's window, is bubbling up and polluting the spiritually male personalities [of my household in] Leviathan's window, [so] I am sending judgment upon [Satan, the moisture of] the crown energy center of the spiritually male personalities [of the mortal] men [of Judah in Leviathan's window],

INTERVENTION FAILS

STAGE 4 - JUDGMENT

THE HUMAN SPIRIT SEPARATED FROM SATAN

15.19a And [the Spirit of Elijah in Samson] led [the human] spirit [of the mortal men of Judah] out from the [lower window of creation], the side [where Satan], the [spiritual] urine is, and [the Spirit of Elijah in Samson] swallowed up [Satan, the unconscious part of the carnal] mind [of the mortal men of Judah],

Cain Repents

15.19b [And] Adam, Elohim's household [in Samson], penetrated the fiery serpent, the womb that is nailed to Leviathan, [their collective subconscious mind], and [Cain, the foliage of the earth, who] is nailed [to the fiery serpent], repented, and] life was restored to Abel who was] nailed to [Cain in the wrong moral order],

Adam Appears In The Men Of Judah

15.17a And [when] the Spirit of Elijah [in Samson dried up Satan], the waters of Leviathan's window in the mortal men of Judah, Adam appeared [in the mortal men of Judah], and put [Leviathan] to flight, [and] cast down [the fiery serpent], and put [the mortal men of Judah] in [the right moral] order, and completed them, and]

Adam, the phallus of the waters [above, who is] the head of [Abel], the hedge [around the fiery serpent], engraved the widowed [fiery serpent, the] subconscious mind [of the mortal men of Judah, with Jehovah's] nature, and [Adam, the Tree of Life], stood up in their heart energy center, [which is the Garden of Eden],

Deliverance From Leviathan's Nature

[And all this happened] because Leviathan's nature [had penetrated] as far as [Elohim's] timeline, so righteous [Adam] invited [the mortal men of Judah to receive] the nature of [Elohim's] visible world,

15.20 And Adam, the spiritual age, governed [Cain], the household of [the fiery serpents], the spiritual immigrants [of Leviathan's] timeline in Israel.

THE SPIRIT OF ELIJAH IN SAMSON BRINGS PERMANENT DELIVERANCE TO THE MORTAL MEN OF JUDAH

Chapter 16

[480.15]

16.01 And Adam saw the adulterous woman [who lives] in the lair of the Wild Beast, and Adam attacked her, and Samson died to the fiery serpent's lifestyle,

16.02 And the fiery serpent [in Samson] said [to the mortal men of Judah], Adam is compassing Samson about, and now Samson will lay an ambush for all of the fiery serpents who have ascended into Leviathan's city, and attack them because [the Spirit of Elijah], the head of the neck energy center of the [upper] window, intends to silence Satan, and engrave all of the fiery serpents with the [nature of Elijah], the light[wave who] calls forth [Adam], the morning, and nail them to [the upper] window [of creation],

16.03 And Adam [within] Samson lay upon [the heart center of the mortal men of Judah], to the point that Adam became a hedge between Leviathan [and] the fiery serpents, her household, [and] Adam seized Leviathan, [Satan's] household [in] the neck energy center, [the fiery serpent's] gateway to Pharaoh's city, [and]

Adam [within Samson], the captain of the neck energy center that [is] above, had spiritual intercourse with [the fiery serpents within the mortal men of Judah], and brought them out [of Leviathan's timeline, and] bolted [the door against the Primordial Serpent], the magician who cast a spell on Adam [in the garden, that resulted in his fall, so that she could] unite with Elohim's sons, [and]

Adam [within Samson] joined the personalities [of the mortal men of Judah] to the neck energy center [which is above],

16.04 And it came to pass, that the Spirit of Elijah [in Samson], the valley where Satan was silenced, made love to the fiery serpent in [the mortal men of Judah, and the fiery serpent, the spiritual woman in the mortal men of Judah], who [was] miserable, disheartened and pining away, because of her weak and inadequate nature, [brought forth] Adam's [spiritual] man child,

16.05 But [as] Adam ascended [in the mortal men of Judah, Satan], the lord of the [fiery serpent], the spiritual immigrant [in the mortal men of Judah, whispered] towards [the mortal men of Judah], saying, Elohim [that is, Samson]**R** has deceived you into believing [that] Elohim can harness [Leviathan's] great strength and overcome her, because [Samson] wants the mortal men of Judah] to be his disciples, but we, [Satan and Leviathan], will give you the salvation [that] belongs to the brow and crown energy centers [without submitting to a mortal man], if you will cast down [Adam, who is rising within you],

R Vs 10

16.06 And Satan [spoke] to Samson [through] the spiritual woman who was miserable, disheartened and pining away because of her weak and inadequate nature, saying, Please explain the source of Elohim's great strength to cast down, imprison [and] engrave the widow[ed fiery serpent that is ascended in the] circular [timeline that is] nailed to [the mortal men of Judah], Elohim's household, [and] imprison her, [and] engrave [her with Jehovah's nature],

16.07 And Samson said to [the mortal men of Judah], If [Leviathan], the subconscious [part of the carnal mind of the mortal men of Judah], harnesses Adam within you, [the Spirit of Elijah], the remainder of [Elohim's] household, is strong enough to wound [Leviathan], dry Satan up, and renew Adam [within you, who will] bind [Leviathan, and] unite [with] the Spirit [of Elijah],

16.08 And Adam ascended into the [higher] energy centers [of Elohim's timeline within the mortal men of Judah], because [Adam, the Spirit of Elijah's] strong cords, imprisoned [Leviathan], the [counterfeit] timeline [which was] completing [the fiery serpents], the spiritual immigrants [within the mortal men of Judah, and because the Spirit of Elijah], the part that remains [after Adam dies], dried Satan up,

16.09 And [the woman who is miserable, disheartened and pining away because of her weak and inadequate nature, that] was nailed to Satan, the [spirit in the lower] window, thought within her heart that she would ambush Samson and draw him away from the Spirit of Elijah, the part of himself that remains [after] Adam [dies, and place the fiery serpent], the spiritual immigrant, over [Samson, so that Satan], the spirit [nailed to] the [lower] window, and Leviathan [her] household, could have spiritual sexual intercourse with [the mortal men of Judah, Samson's] disciples,

16.10 So Satan, the engraver nailed to the spiritual woman who is miserable, disheartened and pining away because of her weak and inadequate nature, said to Samson, We see that you have subdued [Leviathan], the deceiving timeline [that is] nailed to [Satan], and put the fiery serpents in [the right moral] order, and have proven Satan, the engraver, to be a liar, [so] now, please explain why Satan, the engraver, should be yoked to Elohim [Samson],**R**

R Vs 5

16.11 And Adam within [Samson] said [to Abel within] the mortal men of Judah], Satan [must be] afflicted [so that] Adam [within Samson can] be united [with the human] spirit [of the mortal men of Judah], because your wife [Cain], the foliage [of the ground], has imprisoned [you, Abel, her head], and yoked [the human spirit of the mortal men of Judah] to Satan, [and you, Abel, to the fiery serpent, the daughter of Leviathan, the Principal] Fish, [who is] the timeline [that the Primordial Serpent] fashioned to employ [mortal humanity],

16.12 [But] Satan seized the spiritual woman who is miserable, disheartened and pining away because of her weak and inadequate nature, and harnessed [Adam, Elohim's] timeline [in the mortal men of Judah, and] intertwined [Adam's] manchild [in the mortal men of Judah], with [Cain], the foliage [of the ground, and] Satan commanded that the fiery serpents, the spiritual immigrants [in the mortal men of Judah], should be above Samson, the [personality] nailed to the [upper] window,

[And when Satan in the mortal men of Judah heard this, she] lay an ambush for [Adam, the Spirit of Elijah's] household [in Samson's] heart center, [but the Spirit of Elijah], Adam's linear spirit [in Samson's neck] energy center, separated from [Satan's spiraline] waters,

16.13 And Satan said to the spiritual woman who is miserable, disheartened and pining away because of her weak and inadequate nature, Concerning Samson, [Samson] has deceived you all along, [saying that] he stands boldly opposite [Leviathan], and has subdued [her], and has arranged [the fiery serpent] in [the correct moral] order, and [that Samson] lies to you with respect to Elohim, saying [that Elohim is] within [you, and that] if the fiery serpent braids [together with Leviathan, her] head, and [the Dragon] completes [her, the Tree of the Knowledge of Good & Evil] will sprout in the [lower] window again, [and] Leviathan will harness Adam [within you, the mortal men of Judah, and] Satan will engrave [you with her nature].

16.14 And Satan, the engraver nailed [to the lower window], thrust the [weaving] pin into [the mortal men of Judah, Samson's] household, [and] Satan, the one who engraves the fiery serpents [that she is] nailed to, boasted, saying, The spiritual immigrants [are] above Samson, [but Elijah] shined brightly [from Samson's neck, energy center, and] stirred up Adam [in Samson's heart center, and Adam within Samson, who is] near [to the mortal men of Judah], the warp [of the] loom, pulled [Satan], the [weaving] pin [in the lower] window, out [of the mortal men of Judah],

16.15 And Satan, the engraver nailed to the [lower] window, said [to the mortal men of Judah], How can [Samson] say [that] he loves the fiery serpent, [when he] deceives her, declaring at length [that] the fiery serpents and the personalities [of the mortal men of Judah] belong to [the Primordial Adam], the great disciple that is nailed to Elohim, [and that the Spirit of Elijah], the engraver [in Samson], will nail [the fiery serpents and the personalities of the mortal men of Judah] to the other heart [center that is] near [to the Spirit of Elijah],

16.16 And King Adam appeared because Satan, the speech [of the Primordial Serpent's] household, was pressing upon the widowed personalities [of the mortal men of Judah], to kill [them by] cutting [them] off [from Adam],

16.17 But [Samson] stood boldly opposite [the mortal men of Judah, who] belonged to himself, and [Samson], their teacher, declared to everyone [where] Adam [was regenerated in his heart center, that] Elohim dedicated [them] to I [Am while they were in] the water [of their] mother's womb, [but] if [they allowed] Satan to ascend above [Adam, their] head, [Satan] would steal their waters from above, [which is] their energy, [and their capacity to be Samson's] disciple would depart [from thcm], and it would come to pass [that Elijah], the Spirit that Adam nailed to all of [the mortal men of Judah], would deteriorate and become useless,

16.18 And Satan perceived that the spiritual woman who is miserable, disheartened and pining away because of her weak and inadequate nature, belonged to the [upper] window [where] everyone was standing boldly opposite [Leviathan in their] heart center,

[And] Satan vibrated forth to harvest [the fiery serpents in the mortal men of Judah off of Adam's vine, and] to re-engrave [them with her own image, and] Satan castrated the widowed [fiery serpents], the spiritual Philistines, [and] commanded [them] to ascend [into Leviathan's timeline, and become Satan's] reflection, because [Adam, Elohim's righteous] Mind, [was] standing boldly opposite [Leviathan, and causing] everyone [who was standing in] their heart energy center, to ascend [into the timeline that is] near [to Jehovah, and] to belong to [Adam],

[But King] Adam mounted up [against Leviathan], the lord of the [fiery serpents], the spiritual Philistines, [and] carried [the mortal men of Judah], the pale ones that are obedient to Leviathan and pine away for Satan, [into] the upper window, [and] the [fiery serpent], the subconscious part of [the carnal mind of the mortal men of Judah, became Adam's] household.

16.19 And Satan called to the widowed fiery serpent, [the other] self [of the mortal men of Judah], to steal the energy [of King Adam], the completed [Tree of Life], the head of [the mortal men of Judah, which] had sprouted again, because

[Adam's] man child was restricting Cain to the lower centers, [and] Leviathan began to dissolve Adam [in Samson], the wedge [between] the widow[ed fiery serpent and Leviathan [in the mortal men of Judah, so that Cain] could pluck [Abel, Samson's] disciple [in the mortal men of Judah], away from [Adam in Samson, and] force [Abel] down under [Cain],

16.20 And Satan commanded [that the fiery serpents], the spiritual immigrants, [should be] above Samson, but King Adam stirred up the waters of the astral plane, and King Adam commanded [that the mortal men of Judah], the spiritual footsteps [that reflected Jehovah's nature], should escape [from Leviathan and the fiery serpent], the household [of the Dragon] who speaks from the neck energy center,

[But] the footsteps of [Leviathan and the fiery serpent, the mortal men who reflected Satan's nature], nailed [down] the personalities [of the mortal men of Judah, who] were nailed [to both Leviathan and Adam, because Satan] knew that Jehovah would remove [the mortal men of Judah to a place of safety] beyond [Satan's] waters.

16.21 So, King Adam [within Samson] descended into the lower energy centers, the lair of [the fiery serpent], the Wild Beast, [and] King Adam [within Samson] seized the fiery serpents, the mental and spiritual qualities [of the mortal men of Judah], and King Adam harnessed [Leviathan, and] penetrated the [fiery serpents], the household of Leviathan, the [Principal] Fish, and the fiery serpents, [the subconscious part of the carnal mind of the mortal men of Judah], became concubines in the household of [King Adam, and the personalities of the mortal men of Judah] surrounded [King Adam] like a garment,

16.22 But [the union between Adam in the mortal men of Judah, and Adam in Samson], their head, loosened, [and] the [human] spirits [of the mortal men of Judah] were thrown into disorder, and [King Adam, the wedge between the fiery serpent and Leviathan], began to dissolve, [and] the widowed [fiery serpents married Leviathan, and the Tree] that steals the energy of Elijah, Adam's Spirit, sprouted again [in the heart center of the mortal men of Judah],

16.23 And [Satan], the lord of the fiery serpents, [and] Leviathan, carried away the widowed [mortal men of Judah, and] sacrificed [Abel], the widowed [Adam within the mortal men of Judah], to Dagon, the arrogant fish god, [and the mortal men of Judah] rejoiced [over] Samson gleefully, saying, Adam, Elohim's household [within the mortal men of Judah], is given over to [Leviathan], the subconscious part of their carnal mind, [and] Satan [is possessing] the flesh [of Adam's] ox,

16.24 And [when] Adam [in Samson] perceived that his people were saying [that] Elohim [within themselves] were given over to [Satan], the adversary of their personalities, and [that Adam], the subconscious part of their mind [was given over] to the fiery serpent, the household of [Leviathan, Adam within Samson] pierced [Cain], the increase of [the Primordial Serpent], the earth [of the lower] window [within the mortal men of Judah, and the Spirit of Elijah within Samson] dried up [Satan within the mortal men of Judah], and [King Adam within Samson] shined [upon Adam within the mortal men of Judah],

16.25 And King Adam said [to the mortal men of Judah], Is it a good thing [that] you declare to the widowed Samson [that you are] laughing at the impotence of Adam [within Samson] to saddle [the fiery serpent within you?]

[And this is how] Samson called to the widowed Adam [within the mortal men of Judah, and to] Abel, who was saddled [under] the [fiery] serpent, [Leviathan's] household within the mortal men of Judah, and King Adam [within Samson] gathered [Adam within the mortal men of Judah] together with [Adam within Samson, the one who] the widowed personalities had laughed at [and] declared to be impotent [to saddle the fiery serpent, and] Adam [within Samson] endured [in the power struggle] between [Adam and Leviathan in the two] neck energy centers [of the respective timelines within the mortal men of Judah, because of King Adam within Samson],

16.26 And King Adam [within] Samson said to Adam, [the one] near [to him within the mortal men of Judah], Cast down [the fiery serpent so that you, the mortal men of Judah] will perceive the neck energy center [which is] above, [and also perceive] Leviathan [in] the neck energy center of [the counterfeit timeline, who is] nailed to the erect [fiery serpent, Leviathan's] household within the mortal men of Judah, so that Adam's] ox, [the personalities of the mortal men of Judah], may be supported [by the neck energy center from] above,

16.27 Now, [the mortal men of Judah, Leviathan's] household nailed to the [lower] window, was filled with spiritual males, [and] all the fiery serpents [within the mortal men of Judah] were there, [and] the altar of [Satan], the lord of the [fiery serpents], the spiritual immigrants, was spread out above [Adam, and] the spiritual [insects in] the belly energy center, [were ascended into] the crown energy center of the counterfeit timeline, and] the mortal men and women [of Judah] saw [their fiery serpents], the household [of Leviathan within them, who] laughed at Samson's inability to [saddle the fiery serpents within them],

16.28 And Adam [who was] nailed to Samson called out to Jehovah saying, Surely you will remember Elohim, Jehovah, [and] fortify Elohim, your reflection, [who] you nailed [to] the ox, [and] avenge [yourself by] inflicting a righteous penalty [upon Satan], the waters [who divided] the united [Tree of Life into] two [trees, so that she could form] the visible world [that reflects the fiery serpents], the spiritual immigrants,

16.29 And King Adam, [who] was nailed to Samson, laid hold of the erect [fiery serpent], the household of Leviathan [who was] above [Adam within the mortal men of Judah in] the neck energy center of the second [timeline] in the midst [of the mortal men of Judah], and

[The Spirit of Elijah within Samson] took hold of Adam [within the mortal men of Judah, from] above, [and] united [with Adam, the] righteous subconscious part of the mind [of the mortal men of Judah, who are] the household of [Elijah, and

Adam and the Spirit of Elijah] nailed to [Samson,] enveloped [Adam within the mortal men of Judah, and Adam and the Spirit of Elijah] united [with Adam within the mortal men of Judah, and became] one [spiritual man],

16.30 And King Adam, [who] was nailed to Samson said, :et [the mortal men of Judah] die to the animal nature of [the fiery serpent], the spiritual immigrants [within them], and King Adam [within Samson] bowed over [the fiery serpents], the household [of Leviathan, and] cast down Satan, their lord, [the force from the] higher [energy centers of Leviathan's timeline that] was nailed [to the mortal men of Judah, and King Adam] nailed all of the people [of Judah] to King Adam within Samson,

And [that is how King Adam within Samson] slew the numerous [spiritual flies that were produced by Satan's] dead waters [within the mortal men of Judah, who] slew [Adam within the mortal men of Judah, and] the dead mortal men of Judah entered into King Adam's] household of life.

Chapter 21

Spiritual Wives

[OLM 06 09 99]

21.01 The mortal men of Israel [who were] nailed to the resurrected Adam, the watchtower, [and] were completed, [by Him], demanded that the mortal men who are on Leviathan's side, turn over their fiery serpents to the mortal men of Israel, for a wife.

[OLM 06 16 99]

21.02 And [the Spirit of Elijah joined to] the human spirit [of the Benjaminites, and] they wailed and moaned as they transferred from [the] darkness [of their carnal mind] into [Adam's] light [mind, and] they died to the fiery serpent's lifestyle, and transferred into the lifestyle of the resurrected Adam, [and] the people [that repented] entered into Elohim's household, and He married them, and Abel's linear energy stream passed through the spiraling energy pattern of their carnal mind.

21.03 And Elohim said, Adam, [The hand of] Jehovah, the supreme God, is appearing in Israel to gather the widows [of] the tribe of [Benjamin] into one Spirit with Israel.

21.04 And it came to pass, that the people took authority over their beast nature and sacrificed Leviathan, and the people repaired the altar that was there in the next timeline, and the righteous timeline sprang up, and peace with Jehovah was restored.

21.05 And the children of Israel said, How did the fiery serpent ascend in any of the tribes of Israel, of the whole congregation of Jehovah? Because the men of Israel had sworn a strong oath with Jehovah concerning the fiery serpent not ascending in addition to Adam, Jehovah's watch tower, saying, Whoever does this thing shall be put to death.

21.06 And the children of Israel repented on behalf of their brother, Benjamin, saying, Leviathan, the counterfeit timeline, is cut down and Israel is, once again, one tribe.

[OLM 10 27 99]

21.07 Elohim will provide for and preserve the widowed personalities that were married to Leviathan [but now] belong to [Adam], [because] Leviathan has sworn that her daughters will not be given as wives to the household of Jehovah.

[OLM 11 03 99]

21.08a And Adam said [to the faithful men of Israel], Jehovah is uniting with the human spirits of the tribes of Israel, because the fiery serpents [in Benjamin] are ascended [into the counterfeit timeline that is] near to [Adam], Jehovah's watch tower,

21.10 So Elohim vibrated forth into the crown energy centers of the men that Adam had gathered into their heart centers, and they became Elohim's army of virtuous spiritual males, the sons of Elohim's strength, and Elohim commanded

[His] widowed sons, saying, [Arise into Adam's mind], the [spiritual] sword of your mouth, [and] circumcise the fiery serpents of the personalities that are married to Leviathan, the land on the dead, female side of [Elohim's] river [of life],

21.08b And Satan saw [Adam] enter [into] the mortal men [of Benjamin, who] were gathered into [Satan's] army on the dead, female side of [Elohim's] river [of life],

21.09 And Adam gathered the people [of Benjamin into himself, and] Satan saw [Adam] there [within] the mortal men [of Benjamin] who were married to [Leviathan], the land on the dead, female side of [Elohim's] river [of life],

[OLM 11 10 99]
21.11 And this is the thing that Satan did to the [spiritual] males [of Benjamin], and to their wives, the fiery serpents [within them. Satan] separated the fiery serpents, the wives of the spiritual males of Benjamin, from the regenerated Adam, and Satan's waters overflowed into the left side of [Benjamin's] heart center, and flooded the dry ground that Adam was occupying, and killed him, and Satan married the fiery serpents, the wives of the spiritual males of Benjamin, and the spiritual males of Benjamin, and the fiery serpents, their wives, died also,

21.12 So the fiery serpents, the bride of Leviathan, and the widowed mortal men who had [attained to] spiritual manhood, and [received spiritual] knowledge when they experienced [spiritual] intercourse [with Satan], were in the brow energy center [when] Adam appeared in the spirits of the [Benjaminites] on the right side of their heart center, and Adam [within the mortal men of Israel, who were] Messiah [to the Benjaminites], entered into the personalities of [the soldiers of] Satan's army, who humbled themselves before [the regenerated Adam and Elohim].

[OLM 12 01 99]
21.13 And [when Adam saw that] the mind that was divided from [himself had taken] the Benjaminites [as] wives, Adam gathered all [of the spiritual males in Israel unto himself,

and] sent them forth to tell [Abel within the Benjaminites that Adam] was calling [Abel, the one who] belongs [to him, to prepare for the war that would restore] peace [with Jehovah],

21.14 And Adam revived the spiritual life of [the Benjaminites that] Satan had acquired and nailed to Leviathan, [and Adam] turned [Leviathan, the Dragon's] timeline that had made the Benjaminites her wife, away [from] the mortal men [who were] on the female side of death, [and] Adam set [the Benjaminites] upright,

21.15 And the people [of Israel] breathe strongly [again], since the time that Benjamin was widowed, [and] caused a break in Jehovah's authority in Israel.

THE BOOK OF

1 KINGS

Chapter 3

[455.2]

3.12 Look, I have given you what you asked for. I have formed [Adam], my wisdom, in your heart center, who has the spiritual vision to discern [your Old Man, the Devil], [Adam's] counterpart, when [Satan], the one who is behind your personality, rises into [your heart center],

3.13 And I have also given you what you have not asked for, the nature of [Elijah], the one who is gathered [into the 7th energy center], so that both Satan [and] Leviathan, shall be servants amongst of the Kings [of the earth] all of your days.

Chapter 8

[823.2.C]

8.25 At this time, may Jehovah, the God Israel, keep His promise to His servant, David, my father, [when] He said [that] He will not cut off the personality that belongs to the mortal man that is married to the throne of Israel above, except to preserve the personality of the children as they pass through this dangerous life, like the [other, first] personality of himself, walked.

Chapter 18

[356.2]

18.38 And Elijah smote Leviathan, and brought her to her knees, and evaporated the waters which had healed the Serpent's infertility, and the purified waters of life swallowed up Cain, and twisted her together with Abel.

Chapter 19

[224.7]

19.03-4 And at the time that Elijah yielded to Leviathan's thoughts, he rebelled against Adam and deserted him, and Abel, Elijah's human spirit, was completely joined to Leviathan, and the Serpent strengthened Satan, her high priest, whom Adam was holding captive, and Elijah had intercourse with, and married Leviathan, and Satan rose up hostilely, and sacrificed Adam up to the Serpent.

19.05 And Elijah stopped worshiping Jehovah, and Adam vanished underneath Leviathan,**[R]** and Abel, Elijah's human spirit, was joined to Satan.

R Gen 4:10
Job 7:5b (AT)
Amos 5:19 (AT)

19.06 And Elijah willed within himself, and requested that his elder brother, Elohim, should crucify Abel, his human spirit, so that Adam could rise from the dead and marry his hostile Wild Animal [personality] quickly; because he acknowledged that his mind was not Adam, the Son of his true Father, Jehovah.

19.07 And behold, Elohim came to Elijah, the one who was joined to his own flesh,**[R-1]** and Elohim said to himself,

[Elijah], how in the world did you fall down from full stature into this low spiritual place? And Elijah said, I have served Jehovah, the God of battle, fervently when I was Leviathan,**[R-2]** as well as when Adam was risen from the dead in me,[197] but the Sons of Israel are seeking to stop Adam from exposing their sins by killing Adam, and they've broken their marriage covenant with Jehovah, and separated themselves from Him in their thoughts, and Leviathan has murdered Adam in themselves, and cut Adam away from me, and only Leviathan remains.

[R-1] Zeph 2.5 (AT)
[R-2] Gen 6:7 (AT)
1 Ki 19:15 (AT)
Rom 6:17 (AT)

19.08 And when Elohim heard this, He willed that Abel, Elijah's human spirit, should join with Him, so that Adam would be raised from the dead in Elijah, and appear as Elijah's renewed mind.

19.09 And Elijah looked, and there was Elohim overshadowing**[R-1]** Satan, the unconscious part of his carnal mind, and shooting him with fiery arrows,**[R-2]** saying, Let Abel be liberated [so that he can join with me] so that Adam can rise from the dead.

[R-1] Lam 4:1 (AT)
Rom 5:8-9 (AT)
[R-2] Ez 1:13a (AT)

---

[197] Elijah exercised enough control over Leviathan to serve Jehovah when he lived out of his carnal mind, and he also served Jehovah when Adam, his righteous mind, was temporarily raised from the dead in him (Is 33:19 [AT]).

Elijah gives the same account of what happened to him in verse 7 as in verse 15, proving that he spoke the truth when Leviathan was his mind, as well as when Adam was his mind.

The only way that Elijah could serve Jehovah while living out of his carnal mind, is for Abel, Elohim's righteous, mortal mind, to be raised from the dead in him.

19.10 But Elijah was still worshiping Satan, so Elohim crucified Abel, Elijah's human spirit, again, and this time Abel arose in Elijah with enough strength to overlay Leviathan.[R-1] And this is how it happened, first Elohim penetrated Elijah's carnal mind,[R-2] then He joined with Abel, Elijah's human spirit, and raised up Abel's spiritual manhood.

[R-1] Gen 1:1-4 (AT)
[R-2] Zech 11:11 (AT)

19.11 And, as Elijah began to awake from the sleep of death, he perceived the battle, and Satan was releasing Abel, and he was being released from Satan's power and cleaving unto Elohim, and Adam was rising from the dead, and Adam veiled Leviathan, Elijah's carnal mind.

19.12 And, as Elijah was being aroused from the sleep of death, and as Adam, his righteous mind, was being renewed, he was becoming the living expression of Jehovah; and

Adam rose from the dead in Elijah, and Leviathan, Elijah's carnal mind, became spiritually weak, and he prostrated himself before Adam, and as Adam brought Leviathan into submission, he became sick and died; and

Satan dried up and died also; and Adam [in Elijah] married Elijah's spiritual body [personality], and Elijah's nature was converted.

19.13 And when Adam, Elijah's righteous mind, was raised from the dead, Adam in Elijah went after the Sons of Israel, and Elohim chased after, and overtook Satan in their unconscious mind, and Adam chased after, and overtook Leviathan, their subconscious mind, and Elohim broke Satan's power, and divided the unified, collective carnal mind of the Sons of Israel, and Adam crushed the Wild Animal's bones, and Satan within the Sons of Israel died also.

19.14 And this is how Elohim silenced the voice of Satan, the one who was trying to kill Elijah, and raised Adam, Elijah's righteous mind, from the dead.

19.15 And after Elijah's complete restoration to Adam's full spiritual authority, Jehovah said to him, How in the world did you fall down from full stature into this low spiritual place? And Elijah said,

I have served Jehovah, the God of battle, fervently as Adam, as well as Leviathan,[R] but the Sons of Israel are seeking to stop me from exposing their sins by killing me, and they have broken their marriage covenant with Jehovah, and separated themselves from Him in their thoughts, and Leviathan cut Adam away from me, and murdered Adam in them, until only Leviathan remained.

[R] Gen 6:7 (AT)
1 Ki 19:7 (AT)
Rom 6:17 (AT)

Chapter 20

[356.2]
20.10 And the time came for Jehovah to restore Elijah to the spiritual world above the firmament, so Elijah [explained] to Elisha that he would still be among the prophets [after] he, [Elijah], departed,

THE BOOK OF

2 KINGS

Chapter 2

[394.6]

2.01 And the time came for Jehovah to restore Elijah to the spiritual world above the firmament, so Elijah departed [from Elisha's human spirit], but Elisha was still among the prophets,

2.02 And Elijah said to Elisha, Jehovah is restoring me to the spiritual world above the firmament, so I urgently advise you to continue to dominate Leviathan after I pass over into the eternal timeline.

And Elisha humbled himself before Michael and the resurrected Adam, Elohim's house[hold in Elijah], saying, Jehovah's life has preserved your personality, and I am determined that the life I received from [Jehovah, through] you, shall preserve my personality also.

2.03 And Michael came to Elisha, saying, Do you know that Jehovah will enclose [Elijah], the one who controls [Leviathan, the Serpent's] high priest [in you, in a spiritual body] today? And [Elisha] said, Yes, I Am has declared it, and said no more.

2.04a And Elijah said, I urgently advise you to continue to dominate Leviathan [after I pass over into the eternal timeline], because Jehovah has appointed Leviathan and Satan to test you. And [Elisha] said, Jehovah's life has preserved your personality, and I am determined that the life I received from [Jehovah through] you, shall preserve my personality also,

2.05a And the Serpent's daughter, Leviathan, the false prophet,

2.04b Attacked Elisha,

2.05b By drawing near to Elisha to tempt him, saying, Do you know that Jehovah will enclose [Elijah], the one who controls [Leviathan, the Serpent's] high priest [in you, in a spiritual body] today? And [Elisha] said, Yes, Jehovah has declared it, and said no more.

2.06 And Elijah said to [Elisha], I urgently advise you to continue to dominate Leviathan [after I pass over into the eternal timeline], because Jehovah has divorced me from [Leviathan and Satan]. And [Elisha] said, Jehovah's life has preserved your personality, and I am determined that the life I received from [Jehovah through] you, shall preserve my personality also,

And Elisha continued to dominate Leviathan.

2.07 Now, the man, Elijah, was pregnant [with the Magnificent Man],[198] but Satan, the daughter of Leviathan, the Serpent's prophet, continued to pursue [Elijah], the mate of [Michael, the other] timeline, and Leviathan rose up on behalf of the Serpent.

2.08 But Elijah married Michael, and [was born again as a Magnificent Man], and Elijah boiled [Satan], his [spiritual] urine, and [Satan Elijah's spiritual urine] was divided into two parts that went in opposite directions: [Elijah's human spirit] passed through [the firmament into the upper window] but [the Earth], the second part, [remained in the lower window], became a desert, and vanished.

2.09 And it came to pass, that when [Elijah] was delivered out of the Serpent's hand, that Elijah said to Elisha, Ask Elohim to do something for you before He takes me away, and

---

[198] The individual whose immortality is based upon his personality being fused to the three-part mind of Elohim's ***New Man***, is a ***Magnificent Man***. (Footnote continued – See, Appendix)

Elisha said, Let a second mind that is of [Elohim's] Spirit be born in me.

2.10 And he [Elijah] said, You have asked for a difficult thing, [nevertheless] if you see me being snatched away from [Cain],[R] my [other] self, [Elohim's] righteous [mind] belongs to you; but if you cannot see [my spiritual ascension], you [are] Leviathan and Satan.

[R] Jude 9 (AT)

2.11 And as [Elijah and Elisha] continued to walk and talk, the resurrected Adam [Jehovah's Splendid Judgment upon Israel], and Michael, [the Splendid Spirit] from above the firmament, divided Elijah from [Cain, Elijah's other self], and Elijah ascended[R] into the swirling energy centers above the firmament.

[R] Ez 1:26a (AT)

2.12 And Elisha saw it, and cried out, Michael is the Spirit of Judgment, and the resurrected Adam is Jehovah's Judgment upon Israel, but Leviathan, [Elisha's] deceitful mind, saw [Elisha's emotional outburst as an opportunity to escape], and [Satan] boldly tore [Elisha's] double [mind] in pieces,

2.16 And Leviathan and Satan said to [Elisha], Why don't you go see if you can find [Elijah], your master, that man who is pregnant with the seed of [Elohim's] powerful army because he worships [Jehovah]?

Maybe Jehovah's Spirit has carried him away and cast him into a singular[ity, in which event his spirit ascends, but his personality dies], or [even worse, incarnates Elijah's human spirit] as a [mortal man[R] who is] a singularity; and, [in either event, Leviathan and Satan] continued, Leviathan shall be loosed [and overtake you, and you shall die to Jehovah's life].

[R] Matt11:14

2.17a And this is how Leviathan and Satan pressured Elisha, and confused him, and deprived him of his hope of being harvested,

2.15 But when Michael saw that Leviathan and Satan, the Serpent's servants, had entered into Elisha['s mind], and were opposing and attacking him, he commanded Elijah's spirit to fall upon Elisha,[199]

2.13a And the magnificence that [Elisha] had humbled himself before in Elijah, rose up [in Elisha] and attacked [Leviathan and Satan] from above [the firmament],

2.17b And Michael chased [Leviathan and Satan] away from the pregnant man, saying, ***Get out of here***, but Leviathan and Satan sought the Serpent [the third part of the day], and asked her to appear and attack [Michael],

2.18 And [when Michael] returned from [his battle with the Serpent], he said to [Elisha], the one who was married to Leviathan and Satan, I told ***Leviathan and Satan*** to go away.

2.19 And [then Michael] said to Elisha, the man inside of the guarded place [garden/righteous mind], Look, I urge you to stay in your righteous mind, but you need to recognize that the Earth [must remain] barren because [Satan's] water is morally evil,

2.20a And [Michael] continued, [If you] marry me, [Adam will rise from the dead and] preserve [salt] you, [and we will be a] new personality [that recognizes Satan and sterilizes your Earth].

So Michael married Elisha

2.13b And restored Adam, the living soul,

2.14a And [Elisha] married [Michael and Adam] the magnificence that he had humbled himself before in Elijah,

---

[199] Elijah didn't ascend as a singularity, that is, as a spirit without a personality, nor did he incarnate again as a mortal man (see, verse 16). Elijah ***brought his personality with him*** into the spiritual world above, and become a ***Magnificent Man*** who could be present in heaven and earth at the same time. (Footnote continued – See, Appendix)

2.14b And [when Elisha] determined within his mind, ***I will also be where Jehovah, Elohim and Elijah are,***

2.21d Adam [the salt], cast [Leviathan] out,

2.21a And [Michael] judged the waters [Satan], [and the Magnificent Man was born in Elisha and] boiled Satan,

2.14c And when [the Magnificent Man] had boiled Satan, she was divided into two parts that went in opposite directions, and [Cain] passed through [the firmament], but [the Earth], the second [part], became a desert and vanished.

2.21b And [when Elisha] was delivered,

2.21c [He prophesied], saying, Thus says Jehovah, I have healed and transformed Satan['s waters], so Cain, your other self, won't be around anymore, and the Serpent shall be childless [Leviathan aborted].

2.23a But the Serpent ascended into Elohim's household [Michael and Adam], and her moral character stirred up Leviathan and Satan, the unimportant ones that [Michael] drove out,

2.24b And [Leviathan and Satan] tore open the honeycomb [Elisha's righteous personality],

2.23b And came forth into the guarded place [Elisha's righteous mind], and ridiculed Elisha, saying, [So you really think that] you can ascend above your [spiritual] nakedness because of Michael and Adam?

2.24a But [Elisha] turned away from the Serpent, that female animal, and [Leviathan and Satan], her two children, and [stood] behind [Michael and Adam], and cursed them in Jehovah's righteousness.

2.25a And this is how Elisha turned away from the northern kingdom [Leviathan and Satan],

2.13c Stood up firmly beyond the Serpent's grasp,

2.25b And ascended into the garden on the mountain top [above the firmament].

2.22 And the waters [of the creation] remain healed up until this day, because Elisha subdued [Leviathan and Satan] and put them to flight with the words that he spoke.

Chapter 6

[455.4]

6.25 And, the extreme appetite of [the fiery serpent ascended into] the navel energy center, longed for [the energy of the king of Israel's] fourth part, so [Leviathan], the Primordial Serpent's timeline, circumscribed [King Adam], the captain of the guarded timeline, and filled [the king of Israel's] empty spiritual womb with [his own] spiritual dirt,

6.26 And as the king of Israel was crossing over [into his carnal mind], the fiery serpent cried out to him saying, I will assist you, master, my king,

6.27 But [the king of Israel] said [to the fiery serpent], I will not take your help, my help comes from [King Adam], Jehovah['s judgment], who separates Abel [the dust] from the fiery serpent [ground], and my human spirit from Satan,

6.28 And [when] King [Adam heard the king of Israel's expression of faith], he said to him, You [are] Elohim, and told [the king of Israel how the fiery serpent had tricked him, saying], The fiery serpent said, Give your sons to me and I will purify them in the fire [of experience, and] the fire [of experience], will transmute them into the [children of the] Day,

6.29 So I told the fiery serpent to ripen my sons in the fire, but she set herself over my sons, and consumed their energy, and the [children of the] Day [became] other gods,

6.30 And it came to pass, that when the woman [fiery serpent] heard these words, she separated from [Leviathan], her cover, and [Abel] burst through [the ground], and the people saw that [King Adam, Elohim's] male mind [flesh], was covering [the king of Israel], and discerned that [King Adam, the spiritual] sackcloth of Jehovah's judgment, had passed over the wall [of the serpent's triangle],

6.31 And the king of Israel said, Let [King Adam], the captain of Elisha, the son of Shaphat, do whatever He wants to me, so long as the [Adam, the King of the] Day stands upon my [mortal mind].

6.32 But Elisha remained within [King Adam's] household, and [the Spirit of Elijah and Adam], the [spiritual] elders [within the king of Israel], remained married within him, and [Satan] shot forth in the mortal man [who was] king [Adam's] personality, but before [Satan], the angel [of light], entered into [the king of Israel], the [the Spirit of Elijah and Adam], the [spiritual] elders [within Elisha], said [to the king of Israel], See how [Leviathan], this son of a murderer [the Primordial Serpent], has sent [Satan] to separate you from [King Adam], your head.

[Therefore], when you discern that [Satan], the angel [of light], has entered into your unfired [changeable] conscious mind, oppress her [when she tries to enter in] at the door, and imprison her, [because where] the spiritual activity [sound] of Satan is, Leviathan, that slanderous spiritual male organ [who is] her master, follows.

6.33 And while [Elisha] continued to talk with the [king of Israel], behold, Satan came down into him and [the king of Israel] said, Behold, Jehovah [has sent] this evil, so should I wait for Jehovah['s deliverance] any longer?

Chapter 9

[517.5]

9.30 And Jezebel, [the mortal men who prefer Satan's nature], perceived that Jehu had entered into Jezreel, [the mortal men who are sown with Jehovah's seed, to revive Abel], and [the glorified Elijah, Adam's] captain [within Jehu], completed the personalities [of the people that Abel was sown in], and the fiery serpents, the spiritual seaweed in the right side of their heart energy center, acquired the witchcraft power of the brow energy center to lay violent hands upon [Adam, who Jehu had regenerated within the people who are sown with [Abel], Jehovah's seed, and to cast Adam down],

9.31 And as [King] Adam appeared in Jehu's crown energy center, [Jezebel, the mortal men who prefer Satan's nature], said, [Jehovah] has sent you, [a man who] murdered his sovereign, [to restore us] to peace [with God]?

9.32 And [King Adam within Jehu] carried [Jehu], the personality [that he was appearing in], into the brow energy center, and [Jehu] said, with the spiritual authority of the brow energy center, Who is on Jehovah's side? And [this is how King Adam] looked out of [Jehu's spiritual eye] for Abel, [the one] who is less important [to the Primordial Serpent, than] the eunuch, [Cain],

9.34 And [the glorified Elijah, Jehovah's fiery Spirit of Judgment within Jehu, boiled Satan within the mortal men where Abel, Jehovah's seed was sown], and [Abel] swallowed up [Satan's evaporated waters, and Adam regenerated and] consumed [Leviathan, and] penetrated the fiery serpent,

And King [Adam within Jehu] said [to Adam within the mortal men where Adam was regenerated], Now [continue to] take charge over [the fiery serpent], the daughter of [Satan], whose curse [spoken from within Noah], nailed [Abel to Cain, the earth that the Primordial Serpent] heaped up [to form the female part of the personality],

9.35 And Adam [within the mortal men who preferred the glorified Elijah], carried [Abel, who] Cain had buried, [into the brow (6th) energy center of the righteous timeline], but Leviathan [within the mortal men who preferred Satan's nature], acquired [Abel again], when [Cain, Abel's] lower nature, reached out for,

9.36 And grasped the fiery serpent [in the mortal men who preferred Satan's nature]. And [Leviathan, who was] standing boldly opposite Adam [within] the Jezreelites, [the mortal men where Abel, Jehovah's seed was sown], turned Adam [within the Jezreelites, the mortal men where Abel, Jehovah's seed was sown], back into [the belly (3rd) energy center, where he becomes Abel again, but]

King Adam [within Jehu] responded [with the same words that] Jehovah pronounced by His servant, Elijah the Tishbite, saying, [King Adam within] Jezreel, [the people where Abel, Jehovah's seed is sown], shall divide [Abel from the Fiery Serpent, and King Adam] shall divide [the fiery serpent from Leviathan, and King Adam] shall consume [Leviathan], Satan's male organ.

9.37 And the fiery serpent, the limp [male organ] of Jezebel, [the mortal men who prefer Satan's nature], shall become [Pharaoh, the Primordial Serpent's] ascended spiritual excrement, [who is] against [Adam's energy] field, the inheritance of the personalities of Jezreel, [the mortal men who are sown with Jehovah's seed], because Satan has appointed Jezebel, [the mortal men who prefer Satan's nature], to [Leviathan], the other [energy field].

Chapter 13

[544.1.C]

13.14 Now, Elisha was grieved and [filled with] sadness, and [then] the dead personality of Joash, King of Israel, descended before [the chariot] from above saying, Oh, [Elijah, my father [in heaven, and Elisha], my father [in the earth], the chariot [that carries the God of] Israel, and [Jehovah], the horseman [that rides in him],

13.15a And [Elijah] said to [Elisha], Take up [your authority] to judge sins, and [give] wounds [to the King of Israel],

13.16 And [then Elijah] said [to Elisha], Open [King Joash's understanding, and Elisha] engraved the channel to the immortal [timeline upon King Joash's mind],

13.17 Then [Elijah] said to [Elisha, Now] point out [King Joash's sins], and teach him [what will come to pass, now that he can think with Elijah's righteous nature], and [Elisha] pointed out [King Joash's sins and taught him], saying, The wound of Elijah will rescue you [from] the wound of Syria's victory [over you, and] you, [King Joash], will punish [Leviathan, the one who] fortifies the Syrians [from] the high [spiritual] place [on the other side], until you destroy him,

13.18 And [then Elisha] said [to King Joash], Take [the truth about your sins seriously], and [King Joash] took [the exposure of his sins seriously, and repented], and [Elisha] said to the King of Israel, [Now], punish [Satan, Leviathan and Cain, your] earthen side, but [the King of Israel only punished Cain], the third part of the [Serpent's] image [within himself], and stopped,

13.15b And [then Elisha] brought judgment [upon Leviathan within King Joash], and wounded him,

13.19 And [Leviathan within the King of Israel] was very angry with [Elisha], the man of God, and [Elisha] said [to the King of Israel, You should have punished [Leviathan and Satan] in your brow and throat centers [also], then [if you had done that], you would have wounded [Leviathan, the one who fortifies] Syria, until you destroyed [him], but now you will only wound [Cain], the third, [earthen] part of Syria, [the fortified city],

13.20 And [then Satan's] troop of robbers [came from the unconscious part of the King's mind], and entered into [Elisha's righteous] timeline, and [Cain], the incestuous one [within the King] besieged [Abel, Elisha's spiritual side, and Cain, Elisha's] earthen side, buried [Abel], and Elisha died,

13.21 But it came to pass, as Cain was burying Abel in the mortal man [Elisha], that [Elijah] looked [down] and saw that [Satan's] troop of robbers were casting [Abel within], the mortal man [Elisha], down [into Cain's earthen] grave, [so Elijah] joined himself to [Abel, Adam's] bones [within] the mortal man, [Elisha], and [Elijah] carried [Elisha's] sins away, and [Adam] from above [was regenerated within Elisha], and stood upon [Elisha's] Carnal Mind, and Elisha revived.

Chapter 14

[426.4]

14.24 And Jeroboam, the son of Nebat, made Israel to submit to the fiery serpent instead of to Adam, Elohim's mind, and everyone's [sacrifice for] sins was taken away,

14.25 And he turned back from the attack that Jehovah, Elohim and Adam were waging on behalf of Israel, against [Leviathan's] fortress in the astral plane, which would have sterilized her, as Jehovah, the God of Israel, instructed him to do through [Adam's regenerated] mind [within] his servant, Jonah, the Son of Adam, the prophet who judged Israel's female mind,

14.26 And Jehovah saw that Israel was in misery because he was exceedingly rebellious, and that nothing could restrain the Dragon, nor repair Adam, Israel's helper.

14.27 And the Dragon was threatening Jehovah that she would erase Israel's [righteous] moral character from the underpart of the waters above the firmament, but [Jehovah] delivered them because Jeroboam was the son of Joash.

Chapter 18

[429.2]

18.04 And [Hezekiah] separated himself from the energy-conducting [fiery serpent] who was erected [within him, as she was] in the children of Israel in the days that [Leviathan] summoned her to sacrifice [the resurrected Adam], but Moses pressed [her] down;[R] and [Hezekiah] circumcised [Ashtoreth], the goddess, [off of Abel], and crushed [Leviathan's] male reproductive organ, and made [Satan,], the high wave, to recede.

R Num 21:8 (AT)

Chapter 20

[1246.6.]

20.07 And [Jehovah] said to Isaiah,

"Take a cutting [R-1] from the living fig tree [R-2] [within yourself],"

And [Isaiah] took [a cutting from the living fig tree within himself] and laid it upon [the Seraph within Hezekiah, and

The angel within Hezekiah] ascended [above, the level of morality that] the leprosy [had overcome],

R-1 Js 1:21
R-2 Gen 1:24

20.08 And Hezekiah said unto Isaiah,

"What [is] the sign [that] Jehovah will knit together [with] me, and that I shall ascend into the house of the Lord on the third day? [R]

[R] 1 Cor 15:4

20.09 And Isaiah said,

"This is the sign that Jehovah himself will do;

"Jehovah himself will do this thing [that] he has spoken [about;

"Your] Angel's [level of] accumulated elevation shall go forward, even though it went back [from] the accumulated [level of spiritual] elevation [that it had previously attained to],"

20.10 And Hezekiah answered:

"It is easy for an Angel to fall [into a lower] moral [level of] accumulated elevation, but not [so easy for] an Angel to return back again [to the level of] accumulated elevation that [it fell from],"

20.11 And Isaiah the prophet cried to Jehovah, and [Jehovah] returned the Angel [that is Hezekiah's] mate, [to the level of] accumulated elevation that it fell from [before it] went to an [even] lower [level of] accumulated elevation, [when King] Ahaz, [Hezekiah's father], emasculated Elohim, [and went] backward [into a lower degree of spiritual] elevation.

Chapter 23

[356.3]
23.12 And Josiah overthrew Leviathan, and divided his human spirit [from Cain], the one who cast Abel into the black

hole,[R] and Abel, the Spirit of Elijah, joined to [Josiah's] human spirit, broke away from Cain, the offspring of the Earth, which two are Jehovah's double-minded house.

[R] Gen 37:23-24

THE BOOK OF LAMENTATIONS

Chapter 4

[313.19]

4.01 The Serpent overshadowed[R-1] Adam, the upper part[R-2] of the living soul, and Jehovah and Elohim divorced him,[R-3] and [the Living Beast] changed from good to evil [immortal to mortal].[R-4]

[R-1] Ki 19:9 (AT)
Rom 5:8-9 (AT)
[R-2] Col 2:10
[R-3] Job 7:5a (AT)
[R-4] Job 38:7 (AT)
Rom 5:6 (AT)

4.02 But Elohim's Sons can be compared to purified gold, because they have survived the lake of fire, and are laboring to weave their earthen personalities together with their other selves, the hand that is forming the Woman [Cain] into Jehovah's image through tribulation.

4.03 But, Leviathan, the Serpent's deadly, impure mind,[R-1] causes the spiritual young ones to depart from Elohim and Jehovah by teaching the false doctrine, that it's not necessary to prepare for war.[R-2]

[R-1] Rev 13:15
[R-2] Is 40:1-2 (AT)

THE BOOK OF LEVITICUS

Chapter 1

[1230.6.C]

1.01 Jehovah spoke to [the children of Israel] out of the Tent called, Moses, where he meets with them, saying:

1.02a Speak to the children of Israel, [the spiritual descendants of Jacob], and say to them:

1.03a If the personality of a body, [which is] a dumb beast that cannot speak [the words of Adam, the Mediator, into the visible world correctly], offers

1.02b The Neshamah, the spiritual intellectual soul, the spiritual] strength of [the body that is] a part of the dumb beast, to plow [the unconscious part of the mind looking for sin, and the Ruach, the spiritual] part of [the body which is] a dumb beast,

1.03b [As] a gift [in exchange for] spiritual ascension above a recognized moral evil [that the body is guilty of],

[Then, in that event, the personality of the dumb beast that cannot speak the words of Adam, the Mediator, into the visible world correctly], may approach [Abel, Jehovah's priest, who is] the door to [the courtyard of] the Tent of Meeting [where] Adam [experiences] the pleasure and delight of drawing near to Jehovah,

1.04 [And Abel, Jehovah's priest], shall put [his] mind on top of [Leviathan], the principality [that is] the head of [the moral evil that the personality of the body is seeking] to rise above, and [the debt that the body] incurred [because the personality of the body engaged in behavior that] fed

[Leviathan], shall be paid for [by Abel, Jehovah's priest, and the body] shall be healed,

Chapter 3

[1172.1.C]

3.07 If a young sheep approaches [Adam, her] mate, to offer [him the use of her personality and body, [she should] approach [Adam, her] mate [with the understanding that Adam is] the personality of Jehovah, and

3.08 [Adam, her] mate [from] above, shall take hold of [Leviathan, her animal] mind, [who is] near to [Satan, her] head, [and Adam, her] mate, shall draw near to slaughter [Leviathan to separate Cain], the personality [that is attached to] the material body, at the appointed time or place [of separation, and the high priest], the fourth [personality that is joined to the three personalities from] above, [the altar where] the sacrifice [is] placed, shall sprinkle [his] blood [on] all of Aaron's sons, and

3.09 [Cain, the personality that] voluntarily approaches [Adam to be] separated [from Leviathan], the choice part [of the animal nature, and] sacrifices [her] to Jehovah [through] fiery trials, shall separate from [Satan], the skeleton of the body, [and Adam, her] mate, shall complete [her] in the unconscious part of her animal mind, and fill up the hollow place [where Leviathan], the choice part [of the animal nature was, [and Adam], the mate [of the Elohim] from above, shall [consume] all of [Leviathan] the choice part [of the animal nature that is] nearest to the center of the heart, [where Cain, Satan's] mate, is [seated in the place of sacrifice], and Adam, [Cain's new] mate, shall complete Cain in] the center [of her heart],

3.10 [And Adam, your] mate, the bread from heaven, the choice part [of the nature] from above, [and Adam your] mate from above [who gives you] confidence, [and] the mate [who] overhangs [Cain],

Chapter 12

[Message # Unknown]

12.04 And [the regenerated Adam] shall marry [her, and, his] blood shall purify her, [and the new personality, 1st grade of soul], the thirty[-fold anointing, shall increase to the human spirit, the 2nd grade of soul, and the spiritual intellectual soul, the 3rd grade of soul], the three [grades of soul that represent the spiritual male organ and the testes of the man child, but] he shall not lie with the saints [who] have not arrived at the sanctuary [yet, but] are moving in that direction, until the days of her purification are fulfilled.

Chapter 14

[774.1.C]

14.07 And the [priest] shall speak the truth to the leper, and the spiritual blood/energy of Messiah [shall boil Satan, the energy of the other side], and Messiah shall acquire the energy [of the other side], and Abel shall acquire a pleasant smell, and the word of Messiah shall cleanse each of the seven energy centers,

And [the priest] shall pronounce the [leprous] personality clean, and Cain shall let go of [Abel], the living bird, and he shall fly in the open field [with no fear of being murdered by Cain]

14.32 And this is the law for the one who is [afflicted with] the plague of leprosy, [because] he is not able to cleanse [himself from the lusts and idolatry of] his [carnal] mind.

[635.4]
14.41 And [Abel], the house[hold of God], shall be segregated [from Cain], the inner [light/soul of fallen Adam, and from Satan's] surrounding [light, and] Abel['s blood/soul] shall spill forth [from] the dust [that is] scraped away from [Cain], the city which was separated [from Jehovah], into the polluted place [of this fallen world],

14.42 And the [priest] shall take and infold [Abel], the other [foundation] stone, and put [him] in place of [Cain's foundation] stones, and [the priest] shall take [Abel], the house[hold of God, and Abel] shall overlay [Cain], the other soul, [and Cain shall be] behind [Abel],

14.43 And if the plague appears and extends its wings over [Abel], the house[hold of God] again, after [the priest] takes away [Cain's foundation] stones, and after [the priest] cuts [Cain] away [from Leviathan's] house[hold],

14.44 Then the priest shall come and look, and if he sees that the plague has spread in the house and [that the mortal man who had the plague] is bitter, [even after being rescued from the Leviathan's household],

Chapter 18

[16.1]
18.22 Thou shalt not submit thyself to the fallen Adamic man within thyself, or copulate with him as a spiritual woman who copulates with the old man of her fallen nature.

THE BOOK OF
MALACHI

Chapter 1

[623.8]

1.01 [This is] Jehovah's Message to Israel [that] weighs heavily upon Malachi's mind,

1.02 "I have loved you," says Jehovah, but you say, "How have you loved us? " "Are not Jacob and Esau brothers," says Jehovah? "Yet, I have loved Jacob, and

1.03 "Hated Esau, and [gave] the spiritual authority he was to inherit [to Jacob, because he was] Leviathan's mouthpiece"; and

1.04 Edom, [the descendants of Esau] said, "We [who] are beaten down [and] nailed to [Leviathan], the fish [who speaks for the Woman], shall return to the starting point [and] rebuild [the spiritual authority that Jehovah] dried up";

Wherefore, thus says Jehovah, [the Name of God that] battles [Leviathan], "I will pull down [everything] they build,[R] [and] they shall call out to [Satan], the morally wrong female nailed to the [lower] window [of creation, who] is twisted [together with Leviathan, who] they belong to, [and to Cain], the land [of the body that] encloses [them], and the rage [of Satan's whole household] shall bubble up out of the mouths of the people towards Jehovah, [whose existence] extends as far as eternity;

[R] Gen 11:5, 9

1.05 "Nevertheless, [the people] who are nailed to the Kingdom of God shall see me[R] and say, 'Twist together with us.'

[R] Rev 1:7

1.06 "Now, a son bears the responsibilities of his father['s household], but a servant is under the control of an authority,[R] [So], if I am your father, [then], where [is the evidence that] you are bearing the weight [of my household]? And if I am your master, where [is the evidence] that you are afraid of me?" says Jehovah to the army of priests who belong to him, but despise his nature; But, you say, "how have we despised your nature within ourselves?"

[R] Jn 8:35

1.07 "You [priests] join [Adam], the altar from above, to [Leviathan's] sin-stained mind [and Satan's sin-]stained doctrine, [and to Cain, Satan's] house[hold],[R] who says [that] the Holy Spirit is the Mind [of God, and that] the revealed Word of Jehovah should be scorned, and

[R] Rev 20:20

1.08 "The sacrifice that you offer to draw near to me is inedible,[R-1] [because Satan] has erased [my nature that I engraved upon my priests], who offer an inedible [sacrifice] to draw near to me; And now [that Leviathan] has blinded you[R-2] [to my righteous thoughts, the representatives of] your [civil] government [who] seek me [concerning matters of State], cannot communicate with me [anymore either],

[R-1] Rev 3:16
[R-2] 2 Cor 4:4
Jer 49:16
Obad 3

1.09 "[So], now at this time [that Abel], the personality of [my nature that I engraved upon my priests to enable them to offer sacrifices[R] to draw near to me], has been erased, the Spirit of God's [right] hand is graciously lifting up [Abel], the [good] part of the [fallen] personalities [of my] army [of priests]," says Jehovah,

[R] 1 Pet 2:5

1.10 "Who will gather you from among [the household of] Satan, the swinging door [that] Cain belongs to,[R-1] [and my] army [of priests] shall voluntarily offer up [Leviathan, when] the Son of My [right] hand, the luminous altar which does not accrue additional debt [when it judges sin],[R-2] satisfies the debt [that] Satan owes [to me]," says Jehovah.

[R-1] Gen 4:7
[R-2] 1 Cor 4:5

1.12 "But you become ineffective [teaching priests] when you disrespect [the Son of Man], the fruit [of your spiritual womb], by defiling my Word, [which is my spiritual] food",[R] says Jehovah, and

[R] Ex 16:4
Jn 6:41

1.13 "You ask me to understand how hard it is [for you] to comprehend [My Word]," says Jehovah [to His] army [of priests, "when you cannot understand because Leviathan] has erased [my holy nature that] I breathed into you";[R-1] [And then] you come to [me] with a bloodless offering in Cain's [fallen] nature, [rather than in Adam, my holy nature,[R-2] who] satisfies the debt [that Cain] accrued [when] she stole [Abel's life,[R-3] and you expect your inadequate offering] to be received by my right hand of blessing, [rather than by my left hand of judgment]?"[R-4]

[R-1] Gen 2:7
Jn 20:22
[R-2] Rom 5:11
2 Pet 1:4
[R-3] Gen 4:8
[R-4] Gen 4:11-12

1.14 ["Nay," says Jehovah], "I have cursed [Cain,[R-1] who] promised [Leviathan that] she would sacrifice Abel[R-2] [who] died, to the widowed [Woman], to deprive the awakened [Adam] of the right to bring his male world into existence, [wherefore, my right hand will not receive your bloodless offering].[R-3]

"[Nevertheless, I [AM] a great King," [R-4] says Jehovah to His army [of priests] and to the Gentiles [of] the household of [Leviathan, who] fear his Name,

[R-1] Gen 2:7
Jn 20:22
[R-2] 1 Cor 15:34
Rom 13:11
Eph 5:14
[R-3] Gen 4:5
[R-4] Acts 10:2

1.11 "[Wherefore, as a demonstration of my Greatness, I shall send][R-1] the Sun [of Righteousness to you]; He shall arise and go forth out of the eternal world to lie with [and impregnate the spiritual] Woman,[R-2] and [His male offspring][R-3] shall complete[R-4] the spiritual female world, [and] the sweet fragrance [of repentance] shall exude from Jehovah's army [of priests], and they shall offer [Leviathan] as a sacrificial offering [to Jehovah], and they shall be purified[R-5] in the Lake of Fire;[R-6] and [they shall preach my Word to the Nations,[R-6] and] my Name shall be great among the Gentiles, [as well as among my people, Israel].

[R-1] Jn 8:42
[R-2] Rev 12:1-2
[R-3] Rev 12:5
[R-4] Col 2:10
[R-5] Tit 2:14
Jas 4:8
[R-6] Matt 24:19, 24
Mk 13:10
Lk 24:47

Chapter 2

[330.1]
2.01 Woe unto those who are acting out the thoughts of the Snake, because of their spiritual weaknesses. When Elijah

[crucifies Abel in them], Adam, the mighty one, shall arise, and give them the strength to sacrifice Leviathan as a sin offering,

2.02 Because the Serpent, desiring minds and personalities to manifest through, violently seized Adam and his household, and forced [Adam's female side] to marry the Snake; and that is how the Snake married the Living Beast [and turned Him into] a mortal man.[200]

2.03 Therefore, says Jehovah, Look, I'm thinking evil thoughts against Judah, and you shall not stop me from cutting your carnal mind [head] off; neither shall you go around lifted up in pride anymore, because it's time for ***my thoughts*** to be acted out in the visible world.

2.04 And in the day that Adam appears in you and forgives [judges] your sins, [the men of] Judah shall gather together as one mind and say, Abel [virgin Son of Judah] has been changed [lost his strength] because Adam isn't appearing in him anymore, since Elijah has given Himself to the Gentiles [heathen] who are repenting [of their carnal minds], and He has delivered them, because they have violently slain [Leviathan],[R]

[R] Job 7:2 (AT)
Is 22:14

2.05 And that is why Jehovah has not appointed anyone in the congregation to judge [forgive] our sins; but now that Adam is risen [again in the Gentiles], we shall be watered and fed;

2.06 Therefore, Leviathan's [thoughts] and the Wild Animal's [emotions] are your two witnesses that this prophesy, that you shall be clothed with the shame [of the carnal mind], shall not be withdrawn.

2.07 But Jacob says, Jehovah's Spirit is cut off, amen, these [prophesies of doom] could not be His works; but Jehovah

---

[200] The use of the Hebrew word ***ish, mortal man***, instead of the Hebrew word ***Adam***, indicates that Adam had already died to his immortal spiritual manhood.

says, [these prophesies of doom are my righteous judgment], because my lawsuit [against Judah], and the resulting judgment [because all mankind is guilty], puts Cain, the mortal woman within the [spiritual] men keeping the law, in order.

2.08-9 Indeed, a long time ago, in the age opposite this one, my people incarnated as the children of Belial**[R-1]** when the Snake, foolishly confident because of her victory over Adam, Elohim's mind,**[R-2]** violently took hold of Adam's widowed spirit and carried the whole Living Beast**[R-3]** away, and passed over into this dead age,**[R-4]** by spreading herself out in front of the existing world.**[201]**

R-1 Rom 5:6 (AT)
Job 38:4, 7
Pro 23:31-32 (AT)
R-2 Job 40:23-34 (AT)
Dan 8:4 (AT)
R-3 Zeph 2:04 (AT)
R-4 Rom 5:6 (AT)
Job 38:4, 7 (AT)

2.10 So die to Belial's lifestyle and stand up in full stature, because Leviathan is the idol that binds you to this hellish world with a cord of hard labor,

2.11 Where mortal man, the lying witness to Adam's resurrection, is [saying], ***I prophesy that Adam shall arise out of your withered, mortal human spirit***, because they had intercourse with the Snake's [unclean] mind. Therefore, mortal man shall be the prophet of this [rebellious] people,

2.12 And I will take Adam away from Jacob by condensing him back into Abel, [Adam's root system], and join Adam to the Gentiles, so that the whole Wild Animal may be healed; and the Gentiles shall be a flock in the midst of their feeding place, just like Israel was [Jehovah's flock] when Adam

---

201 See, *Mind, Hell & Death*, Chapter V.

was in the midst of them; and Elohim's Sons shall judge the sins of the Gentiles.

2.13 Elijah has pierced through Abel, and raised Adam from the dead, and he has broken up [their carnal mind], and is overflowing into, and appearing in the visible world, and Elijah shall be their head.

Chapter 4

[798.3]
4.05 Behold, I will send to you the personality of Elijah, the prophet, himself, in the day that he will bring in the great [harvest] of Jehovah's revered moral one.

4.06 By incarnating Michael and Adam's corner [Messiah], the woven garment [immortal mind] that is committed to utterly destroy the Earth['s fertility], and Messiah shall thrust His [immortal mind] into the [mortal] mind of [Elohim's spiritual] children, and restore the male conscience of [Michael and Adam], their fathers.

THE BOOK OF NUMBERS

Chapter 5

[60.4]
5.22 And the Serpent is the cause of the detestable condition that the Living Beast fell into, when Adam committed adultery and fell down from the spiritual world into the visible physical world, where his female side inflated into an army.

Chapter 12

[1217.1.C]
12.11 And Aaron said to Moses,

"Please sir, we failed to rise to the morality of the spiritual soul [that God gave us, and] have done something foolish; I implore you to not place the penalty for this sin upon us, "

12.12 "But, please] pray that [Miriam] should not [be like the angels who] go out from the womb of Elohim, [their] mother, [and] come into existence separated from [Adam, Jehovah's] male organ, [and are] killed [and] consumed,"

12.13 And Moses cried unto *El*, [the Name of God associated with lovingkindness], saying,

"Oh God [whose Name is lovingkindness], I pray [that] you sew [Miriam back together with Adam, the one] I pray [that] she belongs to, "

12.14 And Jehovah said to Moses,

"[Her] father injected his substance into her twice; She shall not be ashamed [because her] personality has two souls;

"[Her spiritual soul] shall complete the days [that it is destined to be] closed up [in a flesh body, and

"Her animal soul shall] complete the days [that] it is [destined to be on] the outside [with] the crowd [of people], and,

"After that, [it] shall separate [from her body]; and

12.15 "Miriam['s spiritual soul] shall complete the days [that it is assigned to be] closed up [inside of] Miriam's [flesh body, while Miriam's animal soul is on the outside with] the crowd of people, [but

"Miriam's spiritual soul] shall not leave [her flesh body] until [Miriam's animal soul] separates [from it],"

12.16 And, after that, [the people] set up camp [for the spiritual] season [that teaches the Hebrew children how] to speak [the spiritual language of] the immature [Son of God],

Chapter 13

[404.8]

13.17 And Moses sent undercover agents to gather military information about the carnal mind [and her armies] saying, Let your withered human spirit spring forth and ascend up to Michael, [the high mountain],

13.18 So that Elohim, [the one who enforces Adam's] moral order, and the people who dwell above [the sea], and the Serpent's captain, that mighty Leviathan [subconscious mind], who will be consumed in a little while, can recognize you,

13.19 Because, Adam, the good timeline, is marrying [Michael], and Adam's fortified mind [Michael and Adam] will dwell in the same physical bodies [as] Leviathan's [subconscious], defensed mind, which is the Serpent's evil [timeline, and] Elohim [will enforce Adam's] moral order,

13.20 But Adam's timeline [in the earth] withers Leviathan [subconscious mind], the Tree [of the Knowledge of Good & Evil], and Elohim restrains Satan, and [Abel] captures Cain, the [conscious] mind of the personalities of the earth,

13.21 And as the [undercover agents] ascended [up to Michael, the high mountain], they recognized that they were [Cain], the Woman who was hostile to Adam [and] to Elohim, [the one who enforces Adam's] moral order, because Cain, [their conscious mind], is the [spiritual] womb [that receives] the Serpent's [seed],

13.22a And Adam ascended out of their withered human spirit, and attacked Leviathan, [the subconscious], and [Elohim attacked] Satan, [the unconscious, and Abel attacked] Cain, the woman [personality], within Anak, the witch who was in full stature,

13.23b And Michael, bound himself together in one accord with Adam [spiritual marriage], and the double portion judged Leviathan, the yoke bar that joins the Woman [Cain] to [the Serpent's household],

13.23a And [Michael and Adam] gathered [Abel and] the Woman [Cain, out] of [Satan], the [Serpent's] semen,

13.22b And the personalities that departed from the enclosed place were rebuilt into [Adam's] timeline,

13.23c And [Adam] cut [the children of Israel] away from Leviathan, the [Serpent's] murmuring, idolatrous subconscious mind,

13.24 And [Elohim] cut the children of Israel away from [Satan], the waters of the Serpent's semen, [and Adam], the [righteous] mind [that Michael] called forth from above, [became] the fruit of the Woman,

13.25 And the undercover agents returned from exploring the Earth, and ending the Wild Animal's timeline.

Chapter 18

[1260.5.C]

16.48 And [the second Adam, who is] alive, stood up in the midst of the [personalities of the First Adam, who is] dead, [and shut the First Adam in, and] the plague was restrained.

Chapter 18

[1114.3.C]

18.15 I shall preserve the firstborn of mankind [and he shall] ransom the unclean beast [that is his female part; then] you shall give him, [the only source of immortality], to the unclean beast [that is his female part, and the unclean beast shall surrender the use of its body and personality to you];

18.16 You shall ransom the female seed, the holy place of the logos, [who are] pale, fearful and never satisfied, [according to] the standard value of the five [Sefirot] suspended [between the female and loving kindness, of the six Sefirot of the son of God, which are] suspended between the female and the father, and this is how you shall] ransom the twenty [Sefirot that I have created, the 10 Sefirot of the world of creation and the ten Sefirot of the world in the mirror];

The six Sefirot of the son of God, [which are] suspended between the female and the father, shall ransom the five [Sefirot of the female], the holy place of the logos, [who are] pale, fearful and never satisfied, suspended [in the world in the mirror],

Chapter 20

[1234.1.C]
20.07 And Jehovah spoke to Moses, saying:

20.08 "Take the congregation, your mate, the extension of yourself, [and] gather together with Aaron, [your] brother, and speak to the congregation, your mate, [who cannot] see [why they should respect Jehovah, when he does not] give their souls water, [and when the people understand why their] souls have no water, [Adam, the soul that I, Jehovah gave them], shall bring forth water, and [that is how] you shall furnish water for the congregation, [your] mate, [and their] cattle, [through understanding];"

20.09 And Moses took [Aaron and the congregation], his mate, the extension [of himself], as Jehovah commanded,

20.10 And Moses and Aaron gathered together with the congregation in the personality of the soul [of Adam, and Moses] said [to the congregation] that belonged to him],

"Please, listen [to me,

"The pride of] this rebellious soul that [just] came out of captivity, is preventing the water of [Adam, the soul that Jehovah gave you, from] coming forth; "

20.11 And [as] Moses [spoke to] the congregation, [his] mate, the extension [of himself, Adam], the mind [that Jehovah gave to the people], lifted up in [them, and when they understood why there was no water, Jehovah] struck [Leviathan], the foot [of pride, the pudenda] of the [rebellious] soul [that just] came out of captivity, [and] water came out [of Adam, the soul that Jehovah gave to the people], abundantly, and the congregation drank, and their cattle,

20.12 And Jehovah said to Moses and Aaron,

"Because you did not establish my holiness in the understanding of the children of Israel, [Adam, the soul that I, Jehovah, gave them], did not enter into [them], the land that I gave him, or stand upright [in] the congregation, [your] mate,

20.13 And this [is the story of] the quarrel that the children of Israel, the mate [of Adam, the extension of himself], had with Jehovah, the one who sanctified them, when they argued with him over the water

Chapter 21

[1246.3.C]
21.06 And a lot of the people of Israel [were believing the thoughts of] the serpent, that Jehovah was not adequately rewarding them for their submission to him by providing them with spiritual experiences and heavy spiritual doctrine, and they died, [so] Jehovah sent the Seraph [within Moses which had the correct understanding] among the people, and

21.07 Therefore, the people came to Moses and said,

"We have sinned in that we have spoken against Jehovah, [saying he was not adequately rewarding our submission to him by providing us with spiritual experiences and heavy spiritual doctrine], and against you, [Moses, for thinking that you led us out of Egypt, only to die in the desert]. Please intercede for us [by asking] Jehovah to take away [the thoughts of] the serpent, [the image, or idol, that came into existence in our heart because of our incorrect understanding);" *

> * The incorrect understanding of Jehovah's intentions, and Moses' motives, became idolatrous thought in the intellect of the soul, and images, or idols, in the hearts of the people; And when anyone believed their own thought, rather than the Truth about Jehovah, and Moses'

motives, they died because of the sin of idolatry. The parable says that they died because fiery serpents bit them, but does not reveal that the fiery serpents were creations of their own ungodly imaginations. They died because they believed their own thoughts, rather than the true thoughts of God.

And Moses prayed for the people,

21.08 And Jehovah said to Moses, [let] the Seraph [within you, which has the correct understanding of me], complete [the image of God in the hearts of the people, and] let the correct image of God* in their hearts] be as obvious [to them], as if it were [a flag on] a flag]pole, [and] it shall come to pass that, if any one [that thought that I, Jehovah], was not adequately rewarding their submission to me by providing them with spiritual experiences and heavy spiritual doctrine, sees [the truth about me that is now as obvious as a flag on a flagpole], they will live,

* The Image of God in the heart center is not the image of Jehovah. It is the image of Elohim, that Adam is supposed to be a reflection of in the visible world. Changing the image of Elohim in the heart center, creates another Adam that does not know Jehovah, the only source of life, in the visible world, and the human cities that Jehovah made to inhabit, become uninhabitable and are destroyed.

21.09 And Moses completed [the correct image of Elohim in the hearts of the people that believed] the serpent, [that Jehovah was not adequately rewarding their submission to him by providing them with spiritual experiences and heavy spiritual doctrine], which [thoughts] brought the judgment [of death for idolatry] upon them. And it came to pass that, if any man that [believed] the serpent [that Jehovah] did not adequately reward his submission to [Jehovah] by providing him with spiritual experiences and heavy spiritual doctrine, gazed intently [at the image of Elohim that Moses completed in their heart center, received the correct] understanding [of Jehovah's intentions, that man's thoughts were] elevated [above the thoughts that the image of] the serpent [conveyed, which thoughts] brought the judgment [of death for idolatry] upon [the people, and that man] lived.

Chapter 22

[380]

22.21a And Adam rose up within Balaam, and compressed [Balaam's] bestial nature,

22.20 And Elohim came to Balaam and said to him, [Satan, Adam's] widow, is calling to Cain [within you] to rise up and besiege the men [of Israel], but even though you go with them, the words that I say will, nevertheless, come forth [from your mouth],

22.21b And Balaam went with the princes of Moab,

22.22 And Elohim's judgment emanated from King Adam [within Balaam], because [Balaam] went [with the princes of Moab], but Adam, Jehovah's righteous lifestyle [within Balaam] opposed [Leviathan, Balaam's carnal mind, who was] now riding upon [Cain and Abel], her two servants, [who are Balaam's] bestial nature, and when [Adam] endured,

22.23 [Cain, Balaam's] bestial nature, saw Adam, [Jehovah's righteous] character, standing with his drawn sword in his hand, and [Abel, the righteous] part of [Balaam's] motives, walked into the field of Balaam's [consciousness], and struck [Cain, Balaam's] bestial nature, to turn Balaam towards [Adam's righteous] character,

22.24 And Adam, Jehovah's righteous [character], stood in the narrow passageway [that leads to] the spiritual reproductive parts [of Israel], as a wall [of separation] that covered their sins [from the inside] and blocked Balaam's curse [from the outside],

22.25 And when [Cain, Balaam's] bestial nature, saw that Adam, Jehovah's righteous wall [of separation], was crushing her underneath [Abel], she thrust herself toward [Leviathan's] side of the wall that separated [Balaam from Leviathan], and killed [Abel] again,

22.26 And, in addition, Adam, Jehovah's righteous [character], went and stood in that narrow place [where one's nature turns from good to evil], so that [Balaam] could neither judge [Israel] nor unravel his authority,

22.27 And when [Cain, Balaam's] bestial nature, saw Adam, Jehovah's righteous [character], she collapsed under [Abel's authority]: And anger poured out of Balaam, and Balaam struck [Cain, Balaam's] bestial nature, [commanding her] to use witchcraft against [Abel, rather than submit to him],

22.29 So [Cain], Balaam's bestial nature, said [to Abel], You are the source of my pain. If I had a sword in my hand I would kill you right now,

22.28a So Jehovah opened the mouth of [Balaam's dual] bestial nature,

22.30a And [Abel, the good side of Balaam's] bestial nature, said to Balaam, We are your fiery serpent, the bestial nature which has been your mortal foundation, repeatedly, up to this incarnation,

22.28b And [Abel, the good side of Balaam's bestial nature], said to Balaam, Elohim has smitten [Cain, the bestial nature] that belongs to you these three times,

22.30b Is it customary now to subject [the one who] belongs to you [to these things]? And [Balaam] said, No.

22.31 Then [when Balaam repented], Jehovah opened Balaam's eyes, and Balaam saw Adam, Jehovah's righteous character, standing with his drawn sword in his hand, and [Abel and Cain, Balaam's righteous] personality prostrated itself, and [Balaam] bowed his head,

22.32 And Adam, Jehovah's righteous [character] said [to Balaam], Elohim has smitten [Cain], your bestial nature, these three times. Look and understand that I went out and opposed [Leviathan], the lifestyle which is opposite mine, [so that Abel] could cast down [Cain within you],

22.33 And [Cain, your] bestial personality, saw me, and turned towards [Abel], my [righteous] personality, these three times: And if [Cain] had not turned towards [Abel], my [righteous] personality, this time, I would have forcibly separated [Abel from Cain] to save your life,

22.34 And Balaam said to Adam, Jehovah's righteous [character], It was sin for me to not know that you were opposing my lifestyle. [But] now [that I have repented], will you return my evil eye to me?

Chapter 23

[346.1]
23.10 Let he who hath understanding, separate Leviathan from the many members of the Wild Animal.**[R]**

R Job 7:2 (AT)
Rev 13:18

23.24 Behold, the people [of God] shall rise up like a roaring lion [when] the Lion [of upper world] incarnates as before [and causes] Satan to lie down; [and the people of God who are] pierced**[R-1]** by the fresh [incarnation of the Lion of the upper world], and consumed**[R-2]** by Him], shall drink the blood of [His Life].

R-1 Rev 1:7
R-2 Rev 3:16

Chapter 24

[Message # Unknown]
24.01 And when Balaam saw that Jehovah [had opened] his good eye to bless Israel, [Balaam] no longer opposed [Israel, Adam's] footsteps, with incantations, but drew near to the speech of [Abel], the root [system] of [Adam's] personality .

Chapter 25

[795.1]
25.04 And Jehovah said to Moses, Let all the people who have abandoned the personality of Jehovah [and joined themselves to the Snake], the spiritual power that opposes [him], seize [Leviathan], their head, so that Jehovah's burning anger may be turned back from Israel,

25.05 And Moses said to the mortal men of Israel who have the mind of God, Kill [Satan and Leviathan within] the mortal men [of Israel] who are joined to Ba'al-peor.

THE BOOK OF PROVERBS

Chapter 3

[1212.3.C]

3.19 Jehovah set up the heavens [to give] understanding to the earth[en souls that he created to be the home for the Son and the Daughter of] wisdom [when] they marry.

Chapter 8

[856.4.C]

8.10 Receive my instruction rather than the [other] choice, [which is] salvation that comes from a knowledge [of sin] and the sowing & reaping judgment;

8.11 Wisdom is good, better than all the wisdom that may be desired;

8.12 The Holy Spirit [and] wisdom, dwell with trickery since knowledge of the evil plan came into existence;

8.18 Riches and honor and the wealth from antiquity that does not decay are with me, and righteousness, which is

8.19 My fruit, is better than judgment; my valuable kind of gold is a harvest that is preferable to the salvation that you can choose,

8.21 That I may cause those who love me to inherit [continual] existence, and I will fill them with supplies;

8.22 Jehovah possessed me, the firstfruits of his ways and deeds long ago in the east;

8.23 In retrospect, I was poured out as a drink offering [to be] the leader in the earth long ago;

8.24 I was born when there was nothing but the deep primeval ocean, [before] the underground springs that came to the surface were weighed down with water;

8.25 I was born before the mountains sank down [into] the personality of the hills,

8.26 Up to [the time that Jehovah], the head, had not yet made the earth separate from the dust of the world,

8.27 When he prepared the heavens [and set his Son upright];

I was there when he engraved the circular [Sefirot, the roof of the heavens where Jehovah sits] above the personality of the ocean;

8.28 When he conquered the dust from above, he strengthened the springs [of clear water] against the primeval ocean,

8.29 When he put the visible world [in order, and told the Snake] not have spiritual sexual intercourse [with the Woman, and] appointed [his] semen to engrave that side [to be] the foundation of the earth,

8.30 Then I came into existence near the architect [who] trained me and gave me pleasure in the personality of the fulfilled reality of time;

8.31 [I was] playing happily in the inhabited earth and my enjoyment [was] with the sons of Adam.

Chapter 20

[OLM 01 26 00]

20.30 Righteous judgment cleanses Satan's [spiritual filth] and the pestilence [in] the innermost part of the belly center] separates [the personality from Satan and Leviathan].

Chapter 22

[Message # Unknown]

22.28 Don't indulge in behavior that will destroy your personalities and physical bodies, because your first ancestor labored to produce them out of his own substance.[R]

[R] Jn 1:3

Chapter 23

[27.1]

23.10 If you destroy your personality and physical body, you will become as one who is incarnated by Leviathan, and Adam's mortal remains, the root by which Elijah grafts himself to you, so that you can receive eternal life, will die.

[313.9]

23.30 When Adam's widowed spirit receives the Serpent's seed [instead of] having spiritual intercourse with Elohim, she incarnates as a Wild Animal,

23.31 And the earth[en personalities] that search out [knowledge] through the Serpent, delay Adam's rising from the dead,

23.32 And [their efforts are fruitless because] the Serpent's ultimate state is [to be] the earth that is separated from Elohim's waters, [so she ceases to exist].[R]

[R] Amos 5:18, 20 (AT)

Chapter 24

[1212.3.C]
24.03 A family is built upon [the daughter of the sphere of] wisdom, and set upright through understanding.

Chapter 26

[392.1]
26.11 A fool repeats the same mistakes over and over again because he is in bondage [to Leviathan], just like the male prostitute who is in bondage to [Satan] returns to his master.

Chapter 30

[313.9]
30.18 You [who are] in the right side of the heart center, can separate the fiery serpent from Leviathan, which is an extraordinarily hard thing to do,[R] if you confess your sin nature,

[R] Rom 5:7 (AT)

30.19a And express Jehovah's righteousness in your thoughts and behavior,[R]

[R] Eph 6:13

30.19b By resisting Satan, your unconscious mind's unrighteous suggestions to think her thoughts and act out her lusts,[R] and by pressuring her to conform to Jehovah's righteous motives,

[R] Rom 5:7 (AT)

THE BOOK OF

PSALMS

Chapter 2

[Message # Unknown]
2.12 Kiss the Son [of God], so that the seed of God in you is not consumed by the wrath of [Cain], your angry side.

Chapter 19

[1013.2.C]
19.01a El, [the Name of God associated with Lovingkindness], writes the [wise] opinion [of the Father] from the World of Emanation, and [the Understanding of the Mother from] the World of Creation, and

19.02 From day to day, and from night to night, knowledge gushes forth from Eve

19.01b [Into Adam], the creation of [the Sefirot], the work of their hands, [and] he stands out boldly in the material] universe,

19.03 There is neither [spiritual] speech, nor [spoken] language where [the voice of the Sefirot] is not heard.

19.04 Their [measuring] line goes out through the[ir] earth[en borders], and their words [reach] as far as all the worlds [of Adam's material universe, because] He has put [Adam's many members there, to be] a tabernacle for the sun [of Righteousness],

19.05 Which is like a bridegroom coming out of the closet, rejoicing that he has the strength to produce the manchild;

19.06 [Melchizedek] goes forth from [the female of the World of Creation], to the end of heaven, and his circles [reach] to the ends of [the circles in the World of Forms in all of Adam's members], and no [sin] is hidden from the heat [of his judgment],

Chapter 22

[982.5.C]

22.06 The house of Israel, the root of mankind, [does] not [have] a male mind, [so] the people disrespect [us].

Chapter 30

[OLM 08 02 00]

30.5 [Jehovah's] anger [lasts] for a little while, [but Jehovah] is delighted [when Abel] seeps through [Cain, and Adam, Jehovah's] life, shouts [for] joy [when He] permanently [covers] Leviathan, Adam's dark shadow.

Chapter 37

[33.2]

37.01 Don't be angry at yourself because those who are broken in pieces when they were separated from God do evil, neither over anxiously seek to cover your morally perverse offspring.

37.02 For those who are separated from God (that's us) shall soon be harvested, and Righteous Adam shall be revealed in them.

Chapter 40

[Message # Unknown]
40.06 [In the past] God desired sacrifices and offerings, and God required burnt offerings and sin offerings, [but now that God] has opened my understanding,

40.07 [I] see [that] the undifferentiated, engraved letters [that represent] God [in this lower world] are appointed to appear [in] the mortal men [where] the Kingdom [from] above [is found], and

40.08 [Therefore], now that your law is within my heart, O my God, I delight to do your will.

Chapter 48

[894.1.C]
48.02 Jerusalem, the hidden, unconscious and reproductive part of the [spiritual] city of [Messiah], the great King, [is the soul of mankind, called] the beautiful elevation, the spiritual high place [which is] the [calm] delight of the whole earth.

Chapter 49

[1025.C]

Hear and Understand

49.01a Let all the people

49.02a Of the sons of Adam

49.01b Who are married to this [present] way of life,

49.02b The individual male [personal souls who are] rich [because they know God], and the destitute [who do not know him], be assembled as [one] unit,

49.01c [So that] everyone can hear this and have their understanding broadened:

49.03 [There is a spirit in man[R] that] whispers the understanding of the mysteries of the Word of God into the heart of the individual male [personal soul], and [the individual male personal soul] speaks [the understanding of the mystery outwardly], through the mouth [of the material body],

[R] Job 32:8

49.04 [Therefore], I will reject the parable; I will dig out the spiritual [truth behind] the mystery,

Faith vs Pride

49.05 I will fear Elohim in the days of nature's evil, [and when] perversity lies in wait to surround me;

49.06 They that trust in their own strength, in the abundance of their wealth, boast [R] [that]

[R] Rom 2:23-24

49.07 They do not need a brother to ransom [their] male personal soul, [or need] a ransom to pay [to Satan], the widowed god [of this world, that] will satisfy her;

Transmigration

49.08a [I acknowledge that] the personal soul does not continue forever, and

49.09a [That only the personalities that clothe Messiah shall be] victorious [over death[R] and] live continually, and

[R] 1 Cor 15:54-55

49.08b [That it] is, [therefore], very urgent [that] the ransom price [be paid

49.09b So that the part of Adam that is] seen is not destroyed,

49.10 [Because], the prideful person that is seen, the one that is fat [with sin], who wanders away [after God] looses [him from Satan], the strength of the unconscious part of the mind [of Adam from below], dies, [(even though he has acquired] the intelligence [that follows after one receives] understanding)], and

49.11 [Because] all the material bodies that [Adam from above] resides in [exist for only one] revolution of [their life] cycle [even though] he calls himself by their names, [and Adam from] above, their foundation, [lives] forever,

49.12 [Because Jehovah's breath],[R-1] the valuable, [reproductive part of] Adam, failed [to produce the child [R-2] that would have made them immortal; So] they do not stay permanently [in the earth, but die] [R-3] like the dumb beasts,

[R-1] Vs 3
[R-2] Gen 15:4
Is 74:6,
Rev 12:5
[R-3] Ps 82:6-7

49.13 [Because] this lifestyle of the [female] side [of Adam] that is fat [with sin] pleases [Satan], the unconscious part of the mind [of Adam from below],

Deliverance

49.14 [But in] the morning [of the next age, [R-3] Satan], the sharp rock [that] wears out [the personal souls in] the graves [of the material bodies that] they reside in, shall fail,

[R-1] Matt 23:27
[R-2] Mal 4:3
[R-3] Rev 22:16

49.15 [Because] Elohim shall surely [pay] the ransom to [Satan and Leviathan], the mind of [Adam from below that rules over] the personal soul, [to rescue them] from of the grave [of the material bodies that Satan and Leviathan possess, and] take [those personal souls [R-1] as a bride] [R-2]; and

[R-1] Matt 24:40
1 Thess 4:13-18
[R-2] Rev 21:9

[This is the reason why the soul parts of Adam trans]migrate into the grave [R-1] [of the material body], the place of death, to attend the flock [of God and] to tread down [Cain, the wicked one [R-2] who dwells] together with [Abel], the upright [personal soul, and

Conclusion

49.16 [This is the reason that] I do not revere the individual male [personal soul that] accumulates [wealth and] increases into an honorable house[hold in this world],

49.17 [Because I understand that] he takes nothing [with him when] he dies; Neither [does any part of his] honor[able household] descend [with him into the limbo of] potential

49.19 [Where their eyes are] never [en]light[ened,[R] concerning the mysteries of the Word of God, and] he, like his fathers, goes [only] as far as [one] revolution of [their life] cycle, and

[R] Eph 1:18

49.20 [Since], the house[hold of] the honor[able] Adam is not separated from the mind of [the dishonorable Adam, who] resembles the beast [that is] destroyed [after one life cycle],

49.18 [Elohim offers his] mind to the personal soul that submits [to him, and grants that personal soul] life [and a] sound [mind].

Chapter 58

[313.1]

58.04 Fallen, mortal man shuts up his ears to Jehovah's instructions like a deaf, poisonous serpent,[R] because Leviathan, his mind, is in the Serpent's image

[R] Deut 32:33 (AT)
Ps 74:14 (AT)
Ps 140.13 (AT)
Ez 38:2 (AT)

58.05 And Cain obeys Satan, mortal man's unconscious mind, [which is saying], ***Form a soul tie with Leviathan, the mind, that can make you wise*** [by experiencing evil].[R]

[R] Gen 3:22 (AT)

Chapter 68

[170.2]

68.13 Even though Adam's widowed spirit engaged in a spiritual sexual union with [the turtle], the Serpent's [primordial] animal form, Elijah shall overlay Satan's armies with silver [that redeems and purchases Adam's widowed spirit], and [overlay] Leviathan, her leprous external expression [mortal mind], with a wall of sharp, pointed instruments [that pierce her through continually].

Chapter 69

[Message # Unknown]

69.09 The rebellion of those who are defying you is attacking me [also], because Adam has swallowed up your carnal mind [and we have become one].[R]

[R] Gen 5:24
Heb 11:5

Chapter 72

[33.1]

72.16 And Elijah shall collide with Adam's widowed spirit with a hard blow, and join with him, and [they shall] bring [Satan] into submission, and the Living Beast shall be Elohim's horse, which shall leap upon command. And the resurrected Adam shall be revealed in the many members of the Wild Animal, and they shall be mature spiritual men, showing forth Jehovah's life, like mature grass with a fully developed embryo within.

And in that day, Adam shall be expanded, poured out, and distributed throughout the Earth of mortal man, and Elijah, the first of many brethren to shed his outer [physical] body,[R] shall cover over the Serpent, who was a part of the Living Beast from the beginning, but became the leader of the proud tribes of the Earth when she married the ground, and the Living Beast became a Wild Animal.

[R] Rev 1:5

Chapter 74

[340.3]

74.14 Elijah broke Leviathan, that poisonous spiritual plant,[R-1] into pieces, and reformed [Adam's widowed spirit] into the bread from heaven,[R-2] so that the mortal, animalistic men inhabiting this visible, physical world, could be raised from the dead.

[R-1] Jn 6:57-58
[R-2] Deut 32:33 (AT)
Ps 58:04 (AT)
Ps 140:13 (AT)
Ez 38:2 (AT)

74.19 The primordial Serpent delivered [Adam], the living soul, up to the turtle and Leviathan, and the spiritual life of the weak and afflicted were forgotten for [rest of] the age.[R]

[R] Song 2:10-12 (AT)
Lk 2:24

Chapter 78

[862.3.C]

78.55 Adam, the personality of the line [of existence], inherited the tents of the tribes of Israel, overthrew the heathen that was occupying them, [and] drove them out,

Chapter 87

[1054.4.C]

87.02a All the high places of Jacob's houses,

87.03a The city [of souls that Jehovah dwells in, that]

87.01 Looms up [as if out of nowhere], the beginning

87.03c That speaks about the weighty issues of [the Kingdom of] God,

87.02b That is s joined to Jehovah [through Zion, Adam's female reproductive part],

87.03b The holy place [that]

87.02c [Looked into] the opening [of the bottomless black hole of the unconscious part of the mind, and was swallowed up by Rahab, the personality of the waters in the lower window of creation]; And

87.04 [This is the reason why Jehovah says],

"**Shall identify Rahab**,

"[The personality of the waters in the lower window of Creation] that confused [the woman,

"So that **She can be recognized**

"[By the inhabitants of] Philistia, Tyre and Ethiopia, [who] are [designated to be] intimate with [Jehovah],

"So that they can **Distinguish between**

"[Rahab and]

"These [spiritual males

"Who] are [to be] born there, [in the city of souls that Jehovah dwells in];" And

87.06a [These words that] Jehovah

87.05a Spoke [to the psalmist concerning] Zion, [the holy beginning, are so important [that he told him] to make a written record [of them, which includes the following prophetic interpretation]:

A male shall be born* from [Zion], and

* The Lord Jesus Christ

He shall bring forth a male [child] from himself,** [and

** The priests of Judah of the Melchizedekian Order.

[That male child] shall stand up erect,* and**

*** Jesus shall appear in full resurrected power in the priests of Judah.

He shall be elevated [above Rahab];" And

87.05b [The prophecy of the psalmist][R] shall come to pass,
[R] Zech 3:8

87.06b That these [males that are prophesied] shall be born there [in the city of sols that Jehovah dwells in, and]

87.07 [These males] shall preach the esoteric understanding of the Word of God, [and their preaching] shall penetrate [Zion, Adam's] female reproductive part [within the city that Jehovah dwells in], and

87.06c [The souls of that city] shall stand up erect, and they shall be elevated [above Rahab].

Chapter 90

[33.2]

90.06 Grass [spiritual life] dries up, and is cut off at the end of the age, but it blossoms again and shows itself forth at the beginning of the new age,[202]

90.05 [Therefore], you flooded over their land,[R-1] dissolved it into particles, and they disappeared; but when the next age dawned, they revived and pierced through to the visible, physical world again, this time as mature grass, ready to be harvested.[R-2]

[R-1] Gen 7:17
[R-2] Gen 9:1

90.16 Let Elijah, the work of Michael's hands, be seen in Israel's servants, and let the Spirit of [Elijah] be seen by Israel's descendants.[R]

[R] Ez 1:28a (AT)

90.03 You turn the Serpent to dust, and command [Adam], Elohim's Son, to come home.[R]

[R] Gen 2:24 (AT)
Gen 4:6-7 (AT)
Job 7:10a (AT)
Amos 5:9b (AT)
Zech 11:22 (AT)

---

[202] There is a New Age in Elijah [Christ in the New Testament], and a new age in Leviathan. There are two resurrections of mortal man, one of righteous Adam, and the other of the Serpent, who is damned (Dan 12:2, Acts 24:15).

Chapter 91

[Message # Unknown]

91.01 Jehovah's Spirit possesses the Wild Animal. Let His people vibrate forth from the visible, physical world. He rules from within his Living Beast. Let the ground bear Adam, Elohim's fruit, because Jehovah is her husband.

Chapter 92

[Message # Unknown]

92.07 When the Serpent's offspring bud forth in the Earth like Elohim's Sons [the fully mature seed bearing grass], Leviathan shall show herself, and she shall be destroyed forever.

Chapter 99

[31.1]

99.01 The Spirit of God possesses the earth of mankind; let the people vibrate forth from the realm of the Spirit; He rules from within His creation; let the earth bear the fruit of Adam, for the Lord is his husband.

Chapter 102

[Message # Unknown]

102.04-12 My mind and emotions have been so devastated because of the processings which precede your joining yourself to me, that I even forget to eat. My life in this visible, physical world is like grass that has died after fulfilling its purpose of producing seed;[R] Leviathan, my dead, mortal mind, is broken in pieces, because Elijah has pierced through her and nailed Himself to her; Elijah has stunned Leviathan, and made her speechless, and incapable of expressing [the Serpent's] nature,

[R] Rev 14:16 (AT)

But I shall live by your Spirit, Jehovah, because Elijah shall marry Adam's widowed spirit, and when Adam appears in the ones who were with you before the world was founded, they shall inhabit the Living Beast for the life of the ages, because they were lowered into the dust at the beginning of time, but [Elijah] shall redeem their spirit, and adopt their personalities,

Chapter 103

[Message # Unknown]

103.14 Because he knows that Abel is [turned to] dust,

103.15 And that Abel's [life]times are in the daylight, because, out of the whole Wild Animal, Abel [alone] is like grass which is standing strong and glistening with Elohim's life, even though he is about to be mown down,

103.16 And Adam's widowed spirit shall pass out of Satan, and [the fiery serpent] won't be around anymore, and Leviathan won't be seen in the visible, physical world.

Chapter 104

[1218.1.C]

* The purpose of Creation is that
The Non-Existent One Should be recognized

THE PROBLEM

104.25 [The unconscious part of] the mind [is] a great, [spiritual] sea [that is] wide [enough to] contain the Primordial Reptile and many great and small living [souls], and

104.28a You, [Jehovah], gave

104.26a These [earthen] vessels [that you] made to go there,

104.28b [To be] gathered [together with Adam, and] opened [your right] hand [of blessing] to fill

104.27a These [souls with everything that is]

104.28c Good, [but

104.26b They were born as] Leviathan, [the wreathed serpent, who] wages war against [Jehovah,

who they expect] to feed [them, instead of Adam];

PROMISE OF DELIVERANCE

104.30a [But] Jehovah shall send forth [his] Spirit [and]

104.31b [Elohim] shall enlighten

104.30b The earthen personalities, and they shall be recreated, and

THE HOUSEHOLD OF JEHOVAH

The Son of Wisdom

104.31c [The Son of the Father, Jehovah's] opinion that exists in infinity, shall communicate with

The Priests of Wisdom

104.34 The household of Jehovah, and they shall contemplate [the Son of the Father, and]

Enlighten [the earthen personalities, and]

Braid [them together with the world] above, and

JUDGMENT FOR THE PERSONALITIES

104.32a [The Priests of Wisdom] shall scrutinize [Leviathan's] earth[en personalities, and]

104.32b They shall quake [with fear of their sins being exposed, and

SPIRITUAL INTIMACY

The Son of the Father shall be] intimate [with the earthen personalities of Leviathan, the wreathed Serpent], and

LEVIATHAN BROKEN

Jehovah shall] breath [out of]

THE HILLS OF LEVIATHAN

The powers [that came into existence when the Primordial Serpent and the Elohim, wove together in the wrong moral order, and

THE WOMAN SAVED

104.35 The Son of the Father] shall complete [Cain], the criminal part of the earth[en personalities that is] morally wrong, continually, and she shall kneel before the Nonexistent One, and

THE PERSONALITIES (SOULS) SAVED

104.33 [The Souls that Jehovah made] shall sing [about] the life [that] Jehovah [gave them, and] praise Elohim, repeatedly, [for understanding].

Chapter 105

[441.5]

105.01 Confessing your sins, invites Jehovah's nature, [which nature] recognizes the abusive deeds of your kinsman,[203]

105.03a So let [King Adam], Jehovah's thought form,[204]

105.02a Prune the vine,[205]

105.03b And illuminate the heart center of those who strive after [Jehovah's] holy nature,

105.04a [So that they will] desire the strength of [Elijah], Jehovah's everlasting personality,

---

[203] Jehovah's nature recognizes the hidden sins of the heart that mortal man dismisses as human, but which produce death (Pro 16:25).

[204] The Hebrew word translated ***glory***, Strong's #1984, the same Hebrew word translated ***praise*** in verse 45, signifies Adam, humanity's spiritual, righteous inner (Footnote continued – See, Appendix)

[205] Cut away the carnal mind.

105.05 Who recognizes that the [spiritual] male performs the miracle of marking [humanity with Adam's] righteous mind,

105.04b [And] inquire after [Elijah], and follow [Him everywhere],

105.02b [Because Elijah] vibrates on [Jehovah's] frequency, and understand His communications,

105.06 [And disseminates Jehovah's] virile seed to Abraham, [Jehovah's] servant, [and to the] children of Jacob, who prefer him,

105.07 [And Elijah is] Elohim, the righteousness of the earth, [who] is Jehovah, Himself,

105.08 [Who] remembers that He promised to [enter into an] eternal alliance [with] the generation that tames the ox,[206]

105.09 Which [promise] He made to Abraham, fulfilled in Isaac,[207]

105.10 And confirmed to Jacob, by carrying out His eternal alliance with Israel,

105.11 Saying, ***I will forgive the sins of your carnal mind because you are pregnant [with my man child], your inheritance,***

105.12 When there were only a few spiritual males who were engraved [with Jehovah's nature], and gathered into [the Holy City/higher centers],

---

[206] The spiritual generation of men who tame their personality, which is an emotional animal with the Serpent's nature, by living out of Adam, Elohim's righteous mind, began with the nation of Israel, through Moses and Elijah, and continues in the Church today, through Righteous Adam.

[207] Jehovah deposited His virile seed in the human embryo which was born as Abraham's son, Isaac.

105.14 And He didn't permit the [carnal minds of the] kings [of the earth] to overflow [the resurrected] Adam, but corrected them on [Adam's] behalf,

105.13 While [Israel] was traveling from kinsman to kinsman within the same nation,[208] and from one foreign nation to another,[209]

105.15 [Saying, ***Satan] will break you in pieces if you continue to engage in spiritual intercourse with the fiery serpent while you are under the influence of Elijah's Spirit, or after Adam is resurrected in you,***

105.16 And He proclaimed that the whole tribe of the earth should be [spiritually] hungry [so] that the Sons of God [spiritual bread] could be brought to the birth,

Joseph

105.17 And He incarnated His servant, Joseph, a mortal man whose personality was given over to [spiritual] death,

105.18 [When his] emotional animal (personality) braided together with [the fiery serpent], attacked [Adam], the choice olive Tree [of Life within him], and cast down [Adam, Elohim's] male organ,

105.19a Until the time that

105.21a [Michael], the controller of the whole creature,

105.19b And purified [Joseph] so that he could speak the Word of the Lord,

105.22 By fastening prince [Abel] to [Joseph's] personality, to be his leader, and to instruct him in righteousness,

---

[208] The root system of the spiritual man, Adam, was deposited in Isaac, and passed, genetically, from generation to generation, through the bloodline.

[209] Israel's physical diaspora.

105.20a And King [Adam], the ruler of the people, stretched out [of Joseph] to set [Abel in Joseph's] kinsman free,

105.21b And establish [Adam] as the master of [Israel, His] household,

Moses and Aaron

105.26 And [Abel] shot forth[R] [into Adam] in Moses, His servant, and in Aaron, whom He had chosen as His instruments,

[R] Jon 1:3a (AT)

105.27 And [Moses and Aaron] spoke forth [Jehovah's virile seed],[R] and [Abel], Elohim's immature mind, was grafted to [the heart center of] the mortal men who were judging their own sins,

[R] 1 Cor 1:21

105.24a And [Moses and Aaron] shut the [spiritual] eyes of their adversary, the fiery serpent,

105.30a And Abel,

105.23a [Elohim's] immature mind that [Moses] nailed to Israel,

105.30b Vibrated forth from the innermost part of the heart center of the kings of the earth,

105.23b And attacked Jacob['s carnal mind], which was in awe of Ham['s spiritual power],

105.28 And, so, [Moses] set [the ones who were judging their own sins] free from the darkness of the fiery serpent's confusion, but [Cain, the conscious part of their carnal mind] rebelled against [Abel, Adam's root system], who was miraculously spoken into them,

105.31 So [Jehovah] commanded that [Abel], the root system [that would mature into] Adam [Elohim's immortal] mind, should be gathered together into the higher centers,

105.32a So that [Elijah], the son of God, could forgive their sins,

105.39a By [strengthening Adam to] spread out into the [higher] planes of consciousness, and cover the fiery serpent [in them],

105.38a So He stirred up their [centers],

105.34a And commanded that they increase into Adam,

105.39b [The one] who illuminates their [personal, spiritual] world,

105.37a So that they could overthrow Leviathan who grafted

105.38b The fiery serpent to them, and attack the dreaded Satan and who dominated them, and force them down [underneath Adam, their other self], and depart from their double mind [into the singleness which is in King Adam],

Israel Rebels: Judgment Their Only Hope

105.40 [But Israel] consulted oracles, so He gathered them into the [speaking] silence[210] where they were safe and secure, and he satisfied them with the bread from heaven,[211]

105.24b And [the Fortified Adam], the abundant fruit, came forth in the people,

105.32b And [sent] hail [upon] the fiery [serpent, Leviathan's] spearhead[212] in their land,

105.33b And crushed the Tree [of the Knowledge of Good & Evil] which was in their [spiritual] territory, and wounded the fiery serpents [in the people],

---

[210] The solitude which shuts out the sounds of this world equips us to hear the sounds and communications of the ***inner world*** of Elohim's spiritual city. (Footnote continued – See, Appendix)

[211] The doctrine which accurately expresses Jehovah's truth.

[212] Leviathan is penetrating mortal man from a plane of existence which is higher than this world, and the fiery serpent, which is at the tip of each of Leviathan's tentacles, is present in every mortal man.

105.36a And the many-membered Leviathan, the firstborn of the emotional animal (personality), [the collective subconscious mind of mortal man], who is the captain of the fiery serpent, was fatally wounded,

105.33a And the Fortified Adam

105.35b Consumed the [fiery] serpent, [Leviathan's] fruit,

105.36b [Who] generates [Satan, mortal man's witchcraft] power,

105.34b And [the Fortified Adam] entered into [the people's heart center] suddenly, and, like young voracious locusts [who eat everything in sight], began to consume Satan, and to engrave [their human spirits with Jehovah's nature],

105.35a And the Fortified Adam, their [only] mind[213]

105.25 Turned back [Ashtoreth], the hateful one in the people's heart [center], who deceived [Jehovah's] servants,

105.41a And the Fortified Adam engraved their human spirits which were flowing freely with

105.29a Satan, the polluted waters, and their human spirits were transformed into living waters,

105.41b And they died to the lifestyle of [Satan], the barren seminal fluid,

105.29a And Leviathan died prematurely,[214]

Israel Overcame . . .

105.42 Because [Adam, Jehovah's] male thought form, set [Jehovah's] servant, Abraham, [apart from other men],

---

[213] Their carnal mind was no longer functioning.

[214] Leviathan, the fish is Satan's sea of energy, dies when the Fortified Adam boils Satan as a sin offering (Dan 7:7 [AT]).

105.43 And chose those of His people [Israel] who summoned Him, and led them out [of the lower centers [hell)] by joining [His] anointing [to them],

105.44 And the people drove out [Cain and the fiery serpent], the existing occupants of the earth, and they inherited the heathen,[215] who paid them for their wearisome labor [in this timeline with death],

105.45 So that they could observe [Jehovah's behavioral] laws, and conceal [King Adam], the thought form [that accurately expresses] Jehovah's spiritual truth.

Chapter 110

[1002.7.C]

Adam

110.01 Jehovah said, ["You shall be] the master of Satan and Leviathan], your enemies, when you are joined to my right column, as long as you keep them underfoot, and

Jerusalem, The Female Soul

110.02 "Jehovah's speech shall go forth from [your spiritual intellectual soul], the high place of Jerusalem, [the soul city of God, and] you shall rule over [Satan and Leviathan], your enemies [who are] in the midst of you, and

The Male Child

110.03 "The people who belong to you shall respond, spontaneously, to the spirit of the splendid young boy on the day that he is strong enough to emerge from their womb;"

---

[215] The Serpent, the heathen who is the dark part of the spiritual negative that produces the visible world, is a necessary part of the creature, and harmless, when she is under Adam's authority.

High Priest, Son Of God

110.04a [Indeed], the Non-Existent One [who] takes pity [on the First Adam, and] Jehovah, shall complete a priest [that is] similar to Melchizedek,

Mediator/Priest, Son Of Man

110.05a The King of Right[eousness],

110.04b [Who lives] forever, and

110.05b Righteous Adam shall strike through

Israel

110.06 Leviathan, the head of [the First Adam's] many dead, earthen bodies, and he shall distinguish [Israel] from the Gentiles by filling [them with himself]

110.05c In the day [that his] passion for Adonay, [his wife]

110.07 Shall raise [the primordial kings] from the dead and set them upright, and [those who follow his] lifestyle, shall drink from the river [of his life].

Chapter 118

[OLM 07 14 99]
118.27 Elohim, Jehovah's light wave, saddles [the fiery serpent], the wife of Satan and Leviathan, to the point that the glorified Elijah, the altar of Jehovah's power, arises in the individual [mortal man].

Chapter 125

[Message # Unknown]

125.03 The family of those who do iniquity shall not cast Abel's righteous, spiritual life, down to the ground, that place of spiritual weakness, where Adam's widowed spirit engages in spiritual fornication with Satan and Leviathan.

Chapter 139

[18.9]

139.13 For God has established me with all provision in the eternal realm of the spirit by joining Himself to my inmost soul or mind; He has interwoven me with the fertile parts of the earth.

139.14 He cast His son out of heavens, stripped Him of all spiritual authority and power and made a natural man out of Him to spiritually prepare him to be molded and changed. After that, the seed of God within Him (which was, as yet, undeveloped and had never experienced being joined to God), could come forth and be formed into distinguished individuals with their own name.

In the fullness of time He would deliver them from fear, which is nothing more than separation from God, and He would do that by joining Himself to each and every one of them at the end of the age.

Indeed, His children were separated out from Him in accordance with the manner which would provide their immature fearful souls with prosperity, blessings and all good things, until the fulfillment of the promise to restore them to the eternal realm of God.

139.15 God gave His reproductive strength to me (this is Adam speaking) from his unlimited source of supply when He formed me under the cover of His spirit, and my spiritual life was then separated into many parts and interwoven with the realm of death.

139.16 God's eyes saw my unformed mass and the bill of sale that He gave to Satan, the unconscious part of the carnal mind, which was a witness that He sold me to him, had the names of all my members written in it who were formed within me in the time period called day, or lust, or passion, before anyone of them experienced the life of God.

Chapter 140

[313.8]

140.01-3 False prophets . . . are like a witch whose wounding words pierce [men's hearts, because] the Serpent's poisonous[R] spiritual power motivates their speech.

[R] Deut 32:33 (AT)
Ps 58:04 (AT)
Ps 74:14 (AT)
Ez 38:2 (AT)

Chapter 141

[410.1]

141.05 Let the faithful [witness[R-1] to the Word of God], the hammer [of the Lord that] corrects [Leviathan],[R-2] the Serpent's captain, strike through [Satan, who counterfeits] the anointing, continually, and let righteous [Adam], the Captain of [Jehovah's armies], intercede [on my behalf],

[R] Rev 1:5
[R-2] Ez 1.07a (AT)

Chapter 149

[OLM 02 03 99]

149.05 Let the saints be joyful because of their hope of glorification, and let righteous spiritual speech vibrate forth from those who have risen out of their beds,

149.06 And let them enter into the street of Adam, Elohim's thought form, and let [Satan and Leviathan], the sword that has two teeth, become the phallus of King Adam,

149.07 That Jehovah should take vengeance upon Satan, the heathen who inflicts punishment upon His people.

149.08 That they might restrain the kings [of the counterfeit timeline] with spiritual chains, and the mortal men who they manifest through, with fetters of iron,

149.09 To execute upon their other, [evil] side, the judgments written, this honor have all the saints.

THE BOOK OF

1 SAMUEL

Chapter 1

[610.2]
1.13 Hannah spoke in her heart only, but the lips [of her left and right columns] moved/vibrated, [so] Satan understood and interpenetrated [her God Mind], and [Satan within Hannah] plotted against [Hannah, to steal her blessing].

Chapter 5

[859.3.C]
5.06 Because the mind of Jehovah [within the Israelites] was more powerful [than the mind of Dagon within the men of] Ashdod, [Jehovah within the mind of the Israelites] stunned [the men of Ashdod], and severely punished them [because of their] pride,

5.09 And it came to pass [that] Jehovah, the unconscious mind of the physical bodies [of the Israelites], broke forth from within the fortified [mind] of the mortal men of the city, and struck them vehemently, both the small and great, and threw them into a severe confusion,

5.12 And [Jehovah] struck the fortified [carnal mind of] the mortal men severely, [and they saw the great God, Jehovah, and] a cry [of repentance] went up to heaven [from the terrified mortal men, that] they should not die,

Chapter 6

[859.3.C]

6.03 And [the Levite priests] said, [Do not [try] to send the ark of [Jehovah], the God of Israel, away [from the Philistines when your heart] is empty, [but] confess that you were wrong, [and are guilty of idolatry, and of making yourself] equal to [Jehovah, the God of Israel, and] repent; then you shall be stitched together [again with Jehovah], and you shall understand [that] you belong to Elohim, and [that] you cannot turn off [the thoughts of Jehovah's] mind, [whenever it suits your purposes];

6.04 And [the mortal men of Israel] said, What guilt offering should we bring to [receive the spiritual strength] to return [the ark to Jehovah? And the priests] answered, [You must reduce] the number [of Sefirot of your] carnal mind, [because your pride convinced you that you could defeat] the lords [of the Philistines by taking the ark of Israel into the battle without Jehovah's permission, and that is the reason why the Philistines] were able to defeat the unified five Sefirot [filled with] the golden oil of the Son [of God within the Israelites below] and the five [Sefirot filled with] the golden oil of the son [of God above];

6.05 Wherefore, make [images of] the prideful and arrogant [thoughts of your carnal mind that] corrupted the land [of your physical bodies], and ascribe to the opinion of [Jehovah], the God of Israel, and perhaps He will enlighten [your blind eyes, and you will understand that Jehovah is] higher than your mind, higher than the gods [of the carnal mind], and higher than the land [of your physical body],

6.11 And [the men of Israel, who thought that a box that they could carry was the power of God, rather than Jehovah, the greatest of all the gods, who dwelt in the box, submitted] the self-images of their arrogant carnal mind to the gold[en Sefirot of the mind of God], and laid the ark of Jehovah upon the box, and [they laid the box on] the cart, and

6.17 [That is the account of how] these [mortal Israelite men became spiritual] Philistines [when the number of Sefirot of their carnal mind increased to the number of the Sefirot of the lords of the Philistines, but were saved from] Jehovah['s Sowing & Reaping Judgment, when] the Son of God turned back their guilt [by unifying] the five Sefirot [filled with] the gold[en oil of the Son of God in the mortal men below, and the five Sefirot filled with the golden oil of the Son of God above],

6.18 And the [Israelite] cities [that were] fenced in [by their carnal mind, and the Israelite] villages that were ransomed [by the Son of God], were witnesses [that] the fortified cities of [the mortal Israelite men, became spiritual] Philistine lords [when] the number [of the Sefirot of their carnal mind increased to five, but they were] allowed to remain [in the world of action] when Joshua, the field that [contains] Abel, the raw material [that has the potential] to marry Jehovah, [the only one who] could make them whole [again], made the down payment of the five golden [Sefirot of the Son of God], the great stone [from] above, [and] put them in the [spiritual] ark [of their heart],

Chapter 28

[800.2]

28.20 Then, immediately, Saul fell down from his [kingly spiritual state of] full stature, into [his] earth[en mind], and he was sore afraid because of the words of Samuel.

THE BOOK OF

2 SAMUEL

Chapter12

[Message # Unknown]

12.23 I have killed this Elohim, but now that righteousness is strong enough to cover my carnal mind and return the [fiery] serpent in the midst [of me] to her starting point, I [can] walk, once again, according to I [AM's] inner lifestyle.

THE BOOK OF

SONG OF SOLOMON

Chapter 1

[1218.8.C]

Solomon Speaks Elohim's Words

1.01a The songs [that] Elohim sings to Solomon [are]
1.02a Morally correct
1.01b Songs; [Therefore],
1.02b The words of [Solomon's] mouth are
Kisses [that are] better than
The kisses of emotional love, and
1.03 The smell [of his kisses are like
The smell of] the anointing that comes forth from above, R
[Which is the smell of] moral correctness;
The authority of [his] Name* sets the virgins upright

* "Solomon," in this spiritual song, represents the Second Adam, the Lord from heaven, who stood up within

"King Solomon," the man, and gave him his wisdom and power (1 Cor 15:47).

[R] Ex 29:18
So 5:5, 13

1.04 And pulls [the tormentors] out from the unconscious part of the mind

[Of the virgins who] remember [that]

The love [of the words of your mouth is] better than

[The kisses of] emotional love;

[The virgins] run [after you because

The words of your mouth] stand [us] upright, [and]

They bring us to the King's rooms

[Where we experience] gladness and joy;

Solomon Is Righteous Adam

1.05 Solomon['s words come from] the Spheres of the Infinite;

They are as beautiful as the daughters of Jerusalem, and

As dark and mysterious as the tents of Kedar;

1.14 My beloved [is] the redemption price [R] for

The group of cultivated Israelite [souls that] belong to him,

[R] Ps 111:9
Rom 3:4

Righteous Adam Stands Up

1.07 Tell me [King Solomon],

How [does] your soul stand upright?

Where [do these words that] you feed on [come from]?

How is it possible for animals to grasp [it, and

How is it possible for] Elohim [in the upper] window [of creation]

To come into existence? and

To be intimate friends [with the animals]?

Adam In King Solomon Falls

1.06 [My] mother made me the guardian of my own vineyard, [R-1] [as well as]

The guardian of the vineyards of the [Israelite] children,

[But], I looked at the mysteries of the infinite [R-2]

[And Wisdom], dried up the rays [R-3] [of the Holy Spirit],

[R-1] 2:15 Gen
[R-2] Gen 2:9, 17
[R-3] Rev 12:1, 6 (ATB)

Israel Can Fall

1.08 Do you know who you belong to beautiful lady?

If not, [when you] go out [into the land], [R]

You will become the property of

The avatars that dwell in

The tents of the Shepherds

Who mate with the goats of

The flocks that they feed;

[R-1] Gen 34:1

1.09 I have compared you my darling to
Horses that grind grain [R] for Pharaoh's war chariots,

[R-1] Jud 16:21

It's Time For You To Marry

1.10 [Wherefore], it is time for [your] jaws [to be] pierced, [R-1] [and for your soul] to be
Put in
1.11 Right order, [and]
Made to belong to [the king who gives you]
The 10 Spheres of Salvation, [and
Overlays your soul with the spiritual] gold [R-2] [of his Spirit],
1.12 Until the fragrance of the King's friendship
Surrounds [you continually];

[R-1] Gen 2:12|
Job 41:2
Ez 29:4
Ez 38:4
[R-2] Ex 25:13

Israel Feeds The Nations

1.13 You exude a fragrant odor, beloved, but
[The spiritual milk of your] breasts [has] a bitter taste [R-1] [for
The people I have sent you to tell [R-2] about] immortality;

A Material Body

Your [body] is a cluster of closely bound muscle or nerve fibers [that] belong to me;

R-1 Rev 10:9
R-2 Matt 24:14

Spiritual Eyes

1.15 How beautiful are your eyes
[That] see in the Spirit, my love, and
How beautiful, my love,
[Is your] 360 degree vision, [by which
You see all around yourself, as well as
Your ability] to focus [on one thing intently];

A Soul Body

1.16 How beautiful you are, my beloved,
Indeed, you are] delightful;
Indeed, the [soul] body that we lie down in together
Is a luxurious [flourishing, spiritual] tree [that is full of life],
1.17 The beams of the upper part of
[The spiritual tree that] houses [us
Are made of] cedar [wood], and
The structure [of the spiritual tree that houses us
Is made from the wood] of the fir tree, and
[Both trees can live more than 1,000 years].

Chapter 2

[643.9.C]

2.01 The apple tree
That holds up the sick person [until
He bears] the fruit [that] is
A permanent resident of [Jerusalem,
The city that] I AM is intimate with, [and
Made] a covenant with,
Sustained me,
2.02 [But, Leviathan], the thorn bush,
Pierced into the midst of [I AM's] daughters
[In] the same place where
[Solomon], the companion [of the female Adam,
Jehovah's] spiritual, perennial plant,
Was standing upright
2.01 In the valley
[That is opposite the Mount of Olives,
To seduce Solomon],
The flower of I[AM's] perennial plant,
2.03 [Who was destined to bring forth
I AM's] sweet-tasting fruit,
But Michael],
The seed of the apple tree [of wisdom
In Jehovah's] beloved spiritual household,

[Which was standing] upright
In the midst of the trees of
[The spiritual] forest [that]
Is married to the household of
The shadow of lust and passionate desire,
2.04 Identified [Solomon as a member of]
The house[hold of Judah, one of]
The tribes [that Jehovah] made a covenant with,
So, the male Adam]
Gathered [Solomon] into [his spiritual] winepress,
2.05a And [Michael],
The seed of the apple tree [of wisdom,
That begets the male] fruit [of the whole Adam,
Who] is the permanent resident of [Jerusalem,
The city that] I AM is intimate with,
[Sought] to hold up
2.06 [My] head [which was] under
[The water of Jehovah's] left hand [of judgment],
By impregnating me with the son [of wisdom,
Jehovah's] right hand [of mercy],
2.05b [Who] would have sustained me,
[But] I was [too] sick [to survive the judgment].

Solomon Warns Jehovah's Female Companions

2.07 [So], take an oath you daughters of Jerusalem
[Who are destined to marry Adam], the male gazelle

[Who is] heir to a glorious, [immortal] earthen body,
[But] who [still experience] the cravings of
The female deer of the field [of creation],
That you do not make a covenant with Satan
[To satisfy your cravings, because, if you do],
Satan will arouse Leviathan, her mate,
To be intimate with [Abel within you, and]
When Abel is satisfied,
[He does not resist Cain, and, then,
Satan and Leviathan will control you],
2.08 [Wherefore], watch out for the speech of
[Leviathan], that unjust lover
[Who] descends [by] leaps
From the [Serpent's] higher Spheres,
To cut you off from

Discerning Leviathan's Seduction

2.09 [Adam], the male gazelle,
[Your true] lover who resembles [Jehovah,
The one who] shows you your sins [because]
He desires [to engrave you with the nature of]
A young male deer that longs for God:
Look,
This [other lover] remains [stealthily] motionless
Behind [the conscious part of your mind],
Gazing at [you, secretly] through

The bars of the [protective, spiritual] barrier
[That] surrounds [Adam's end] of the [worm]hole
[That connects Adam and Leviathan's two worlds],
Observing [you] intently, [because
He is determined that] pride should blossom forth
[In your mind and emotions],
2.10 [Then, after the sin of pride has been revealed in you,
Leviathan] speaks [from within you], saying,
"I have replaced the lover you [used] to belong to,
"[The one who] judged your sins,
"[And now] you belong [to me],
"My beautiful, female companion,
"[So] come [along and accept your new] lifestyle."
2.11 Look,
The rain of destruction [that corrects your sins]
Has, indeed, passed away, [because
The spiritual] excrement [that] you belong to
Has crossed over [to the other side, and
Now that I am no longer judging your sins];
2.13 Judah's male figs are ripening, and
The male grapes blossoming [on
Judah's] grape-bearing vines give off a [good] odor,
[So] rise up [and] walk [with me
My] beautiful female companion,
Walk [with the one you] belong to,

2.12 [Because it is] time for the flowers,
[The human personalities of the female Adam]
In the earth,
To hear and obey the turtle's [primeval] impulse
To experience a [spiritual] sexual connection
[With the Serpent's] vibration.
2.14 [Wherefore], it is appropriate [for you] to let
[The Queen of Sheba] see the concealed place
[From where] the soul that serves Jehovah
Wages [spiritual] warfare [against
Satan and Leviathan, and]
The secret place [from where
Adam] ascends into [the higher worlds, and]
To hear the sweet sound of the supernatural visions,
[Which are] the voice [of Jehovah, and
Adam], his mate.

The Male Adam Encourages Solomon To Resist

2.16 [Resist Leviathan's lies, Solomon, and
Believe the truth that]
You belong to Ani, [the Shekinah, and that]
You belong to [the female] Adam,
[Jehovah's] perennial plant,
The lover [who] is intertwined with
Your [spiritual] house, [and that
You belong to the male Adam,
The one who] cares for you

By judging [your sins],
2.17 [Because the Dragon] will [continue]
To puff [at you, Solomon], until [you,
Solomon], the beautiful flower [of
Jehovah' perennial plant],
Repent, [and until
The female Adam],
The [spiritual] Day [within you],
Escapes [from Leviathan], the [Serpent's] shadow,
[And until Adam], the male gazelle,
[Your true] lover [who] resembles
[Jehovah, the one who] shows you your sins
[Because] he desires [to engrave you with
The nature of] a young male deer that longs for God,
[Once again], cuts off
Leviathan's] spheres[within you],
Through judgment,
2.15 [Wherefore, Solomon, you should
Help the male Adam who] you belong to,
To seize [and]
Repossess [the female Adam within you, because,
When] the animal nature [of Cain,
That wicked one within you,
Is joined to Abel within you,
Abel acquires] the animal nature of
The Serpent's insignificant household, [and

Agrees with Cain] to destroy [you, because
Your] spiritual vineyard, [out of all]
The vineyards [that Jehovah planted]
Is blossoming.

Chapter 3

[OLM 12 22 99]

3.02a [And they said in their hearts], Now we will ascend into the [narrow] street and seek spiritual communication [with the Regenerated Adam, but] the fiery serpents surrounded [their] personalities,

3.03a And [Leviathan, the Primordial Serpent's] city appeared,

3.02a And they found [themselves] in the wide avenue [of Leviathan's] city,

3.03b [And Leviathan] surrounded them [and] guarded their personalities [against] spiritual communication with [the Regenerated Adam],

5.07 [And Satan] appeared [and] divided [their personalities from the Regenerated Adam], the covering [who] had lifted them [into the world] above, [and] joined [their personalities to Leviathan, the Primordial Serpent's] city [that] was surrounding [them and] guarding [their personalities against spiritual communication with the Regenerated Adam, and they died to the Regenerated Adam's spiritual life].

3.05 [So all of you] spiritual females of mortal humanity, desire [that the Regenerated Adam], the prominent one [who reflects Jehovah's] splendor, awakens the Fiery Serpent [within you, so that] you will be completed [as the holy] Jerusalem, or

[Satan] will curve [you] into Leviathan's timeline, [and the fiery serpent will have] carnal communication [with you].

5.08 [And] the female personalities [of the holy Jerusalem] are spiritually and physically] sick [because they are] in love with [the female Leviathan, so let the male Adam] complete [them, before] Leviathan acquires them, [or] Elohim [will have] to boil [Satan to liberate] the personalities that stand in front of Leviathan,

5.09 [And], this is the reason why your friend and lover, Elohim, I [AM's right arm], boils Satan: [to make] the fiery serpents [that are joined to the personalities] spiritually beautiful, [and, after that], your friend and lover, Elohim, will [continue] to boil Satan [until Adam] completes [the whole woman]; to boil Satan [until] your [personalities] are completed.

Chapter 5

[949.1.C]

The Invitation

5.01 Come into my garden my sister, my bride. I have gathered together with the bitter distilled drops; I have drunk the wine [that builds the spirit] and the milk [that builds the soul], and have eaten the wisdom which preserves [the material body that comes] from the nest [where mankind Is being formed]; eat, my friends; drink, drink until you are satisfied, my beloved;

The Seduction

5.02a My [soul] was asleep, but the [emotions of] my heart were awake, because the voice of my lover, [the one who] rewards my good deeds and punishes my sins, was knocking [on the door of my heart, saying], Open [the door] my sister, my love,

5.03a I have washed my generative parts. How can I defile you,

5.02b The morally pure soul [that] belongs to me?

And the drop of the Spirit [of Elohim, the Creator, that] was cut off [from the Father and became] the head [of the children of] the night, completed me;

5.03b [And that is how] my covering was stripped off; who shall clothe me [now]?

The Rescue

5.04 [But the Ancient of Days] sent forth [Adam from] above, his generative part, [and] the mind [of Righteous Adam, the one who] rewards my good deeds and punishes my sins, [made] a loud commotion [in the world below], and

5.05 I [AM] rose up to open the prison, and the mind [of Righteous Adam], my lover, distilled [Satan], the bitter [spirit of] the bitter world, and [Righteous Adam's defiled, but beloved soul] crossed over [into] the blessings and judgment of the world above;

Crossing Over

5.06 [And after] I [AM] opened [the door to my prison, and] I crossed over, my lover wrapped himself [in] my soul; I tried to speak [to him], but he did not answer, and when I called to him, he did not appear;

Cleansing Judgment

5.07 And the guards that surround the city found me; they lifted my veil and struck me and wounded me [because] I was joined [to the world] above [which they guard];

First Love Lost

5.08 You completed daughters of Jerusalem, if [Adam], my lover [who] belongs to Elohim, appears, tell him that I am worn out [from the warfare that I have experienced since] I [AM] joined [me] to [the world above];

A New Lover

5.09 [They answer, saying], Elohim, your lover,* [is] the spiritual lover of the most beautiful women of the household of Leviathan;** Elohim your lover has completed us more than any other lover;

*Adam was her lover, but now she has become one with Adam and Adam belongs to Elohim (Vs 8).

**The Holy Spirit of Promise, the lover of the repentant vessels of the First Adam, is the lower Elohim.

Clinging To The Old

5.10 [She answers], My lover* is reddish-brown and dazzling white, the most distinguished one of countless numbers,**

*She does not understand that she has become Adam, and that Elohim is now their lover.

** "Adam" is the name of God, and Adam, himself, has many names. "Jesus" is the most distinguished of all of Adam's names because he was the first personal soul of the First Adam to rise from the dead, and the only one "born again" from the seed of the Father. All the other personal souls of the First Adam will be resurrected through him.

5.11 His head [is made of] refined pure gold, and many single hairs form the locks of the hair [of his head, which is as] black as a ravens;

5.12 He rises up like a dove from the existing landscape. He bathes the [human vessels] that he marries with the milk [of the Word], and fills them completely with the water of [the Shekinah], the river from above;

The Souls That Cross Over

5.13 The lips [of the souls who have] crossed over are like trumpets [that Satan's] distilled bitter drops ooze out of;* their flesh is like a flower bed of sweet spices;**

*Their lips preach the wisdom of God, which forces out unclean spirits.

**The human body is "skin." "Adam" is their flesh. He is likened to "spices" because of their preservative qualities. He is "sweet," rather than "sour," because "the preservative experience" is pleasurable.

5.14 Their mind [is like] a revolving door, [continuously being] filled with the oil [of the anointing]; the reproductive part [of their soul is broken like the ships of] Tarshish; a bright spirit overlays [Satan], the sharp tooth [that consumes their mortal flesh, with] sapphires [sharp enough to cut diamonds];

5.15 Their [right] leg [is] a column of [righteous] white linen joined to a foundation from above; their appearance is as pure as refined gold; [these] chosen ones [are like the [long-living] cedar trees [that grow on the snow-covered mountains] of Lebanon;

5.16 Their mouth sucks from the whole [Adam];

Two Lovers

[Elohim], this lover, is desirable; [Adam], this lover is your other self, you daughters [whose] souls [are joined together to form the spiritual city of] Jerusalem.

Chapter 8

[Message # Unknown]

8.08 Cain's self-love,[R-1] cannot satisfy[R-2] herself, or overcome Satan, but Adam can cleanse the Woman who is ruling over him,[R-3] if he judges her sins[R-4] for the purpose of utterly condemning[R-5] her spiritually incestuous, homosexual relationship.[R-6]

[R-1] Gen 2:21b, 22-23 (AT)
[R-2] Is 5:14
[R-3] Gen 2:22 (AT)
[R-4] Eccl 12:3 (AT)
Dan 2:34 (AT)
Dan 8:13 (AT)
[R-5] Is 11:3-5 (AT)
[R-6] Joel 3:3 (AT)
Jon 1:17a (AT)
Rev 17:3
Jn 7:24

THE BOOK OF ZECHARIAH

Chapter 1

[1120.4.C]
1.01 In the eighth month, in the second year of Darius, came the word of the LORD unto Zechariah, the son of Berechiah, the son of Iddo the prophet, saying,

1.02 Your fathers have provoked Jehovah and he is enraged,

1.03 Therefore say to them,

"Thus says Jehovah, [God of] the armies [of Israel],

"Turn back to me, says Jehovah, [God of] the armies [of Israel],

"And I will turn back to you, says Jehovah, [God of] the armies [of Israel];

1.04 "Do not be like your fathers, who the former prophets cried to, saying,

'Thus says Jehovah, [the God of] the armies [of Israel],

'Turn back now from your immoral lifestyle and your immoral behavior,'

"But they did not hear [me], or respond to me," says Jehovah;

1.05 "Where are your fathers? Did the prophets live forever?"

1.06 [No, they did not live forever], because my words and my statutes that I commanded my servants, the prophets, [to say to] your fathers did not rise [to the level of their understanding, which caused] Elohim* [within Judah] to return to Jehovah, [the God of] the armies [of Israel], saying,

"It is proper [for you] to do [whatever is necessary] to set [us] upright, according to our lifestyle and according to our behavior,

* Righteous Adam within the Judeans agreed with Jehovah that judgment, under the present circumstances (that the Judeans did not understand that they needed to repent), was the mercy of God. His agreement is significant, inasmuch as he, the anointing dwelling in their flesh, would experience the very same judgment.

1.07 Upon the four and twentieth day of the eleventh month, which is the month Sebat, in the second year of Darius, came the word of the LORD unto Zechariah, the son of Berechiah, the son of Iddo the prophet, saying,

1.08 I was looking with my carnal mind, and there it was!

A [mortal] man who was similar to Adam, the royal male consort* [of Jehovah who] rides [in the Sefirot of Judah, Jehovah's battle] horse, and

[Abel], the [mortal] man that was similar to Adam, was standing in the midst of the horses [of Judah that Jehovah] rides [in, and they were] in the valley of [decision in] the unconscious part of the mind, [and some of them] had the mind [of God,** and some were] like God,*** and

* The word, "trees," is not in the interlinear text. The Hebrew word translated "myrtle" (Strong's 1918) is the masculine of the Hebrew word translated "Esther," (Strong's 1919), as in "Queen Esther."

** "Mind of God," is an interpretation of the Hebrew word translated "speckled," which means "bright red (as piercing to the sight)." We have associated this Hebrew word, (Strong's 8320), with Strong's 5348, the Hebrew word translated "speckled" in Genesis 30:39, which means "to mark," and with the phrase, "brought forth cattle ringstraked, speckled, and spotted," in general.

*** "Like God," is an interpretation of "white." (Ps 82:6-7)

1.09 Then I said,

"[Who] are these Elohim?"

And Adonai, the angel that was talking to me said to me,

"I will show you [who] these male Elohim [are],"

1.10 And [Abel, the mortal] man [who] was standing in the midst of [the horses that were in the valley of decision in the unconscious part of the mind], said [to Zechariah],

"These [are the personalities that] Jehovah [clothed in] earth[en bodies], and sent to walk around [in the World in the Mirror," and

1.11 [Abel, the mortal man] who was standing in the midst of [the horses who were in the valley of decision, in the unconscious part of the mind], the mate [of Adam], the angel [that guards Judah] and the royal male consort of Jehovah, responded [further], saying,

"We have married [these personalities that are] walking around in earth[en bodies in the World in the Mirror] and, as you can see, all [of their] earth[en bodies] are no longer warlike, but completely calm and tranquil, "

1.12 And then the angel of the Lord entered into the conversation saying,

"Jehovah, [God of] the armies [of Israel], how much longer will you withhold your compassion from [the inhabitants of] Jerusalem, the [soul]-cities of Judah [that you dwell in], who you have been enraged at these [past] seventy years?"

1.13 And then Jehovah, himself, responded to the angel that talked with me, with good and consoling words, and

1.14 The angel that spoke with me said,

"Cry out saying,

"Thus says Jehovah, [God of] the armies [of Israel],

'I am anxious to possess [the soul-cities of] Jerusalem, and

'[I am] intensely enraged at [the spiritual souls of] Zion,

1.15 'And I am filled with wrath [towards Jerusalem and Judah], and

'Extremely angry and enraged at the non-Israelite nations who have not been too concerned about [Judah's] moral evil, and have helped [to deal with it only] a little bit,'

1.16 "And Therefore, thus says Jehovah, "

'I am restoring the maidenhead of [the soul-cities of] Jerusalem, and my house shall be built in [the earth of Adam below],'

"Says Jehovah, [God of] the armies [of Israel]," and

'[Adam from above is] the measuring line that shall be spread out upon [the soul-cities of] Jerusalem;

1.17 "Continue to cry out, even more, saying,

"Thus says Jehovah [the God of] the armies [of Israel],

'My [soul-]cities [in Jerusalem] shall be dashed in pieces by [Adan from above], Jehovah's goodness, and I will continue to test [the spiritual souls of] Zion.' "

1.18 Then, my other [spiritual] self, opened his eyes, and there it was! I saw the power of the completed [Adam], and

1.19 I said to the angel that talked with me,

"Who are these?"

And he answered me, [saying],

"These are the [priests of Judah [R-1] who wield] the power [of the completed Adam] to grind [R-2] Judah, Ephraim and the Body of the completed Adam into powder," and [then],

[R-1] Heb 7:14
[R-2] Matt 21:43-44
Lk 20:17-18

1.20 [The angel that talked with me] showed me the four [spiritual offices* of the completed Adam who has the authority] to build Jehovah's [house], [R] and

[R] 2 Sam 7:5-17

*Apostle, Prophet, Evangelist, Teaching Pastor (Eph 4:11)

1.21 Then I said,

"What have these [priests of Judah] come to do?"

And he spoke, saying,

"These [priests of Judah are] the power of the completed Adam, [Jehovah's other] self,

"To grind [the other] Judah into powder, so that they [can] no longer lift up [their] head to come against these mortal men [of Judah and the non-Israelite nations], to terrify them, [and]

"To cast down the power of [the four-fold ministry of] the completed Adam of the non-Israelite nations that lifted up the power of the completed Adam over the land of Judah, to grind it to powder.

Chapter 2

[1120.4.C]

2.01 I lifted up my [spiritual] eyes and looked and there it was! A [mortal] man with a measuring line in his mind;

2.02 And I said,

"Where are you going?"

[And] he said to me,

"To measure the width and the length [of Adam in] Jerusalem, [the city of souls, Jehovah's] mate," and

2.03 The angel that talked with me went out, and I saw [that] another angel went out to meet him, and

2.04 Said to him,

"Run and speak to this young man, saying,

'The abundance of mankind shall marry the unwalled towns of Jerusalem [that came into existence when Jehovah] bisected [Adam], and

2.05 'Because I will be a wall of fire round about [them that] came into existence [when] my opinion was bisected [from Adam]' says Jehovah,

2.06 '[There are] two woes [coming upon Judah, so] escape from the land of the north,' says Jehovah,

'Because I have dispatched the Spirit of the completed Adam, [the Lord from] heaven, [my mercy, to recover] you,' says Jehovah;

2.07 "Oh, [all of you spiritual souls of] Zion who are married to the daughter of Babylon, deliver yourselves;

2.08 "Because, thus says Jehovah, [God of] the armies [of Israel who dwells in] the unconscious part of the mind,

" 'You stripped away the spiritual sight [of my people] when you sent my opinion away, so that you could commit adultery with the non-Israelite nations,

2.09 " 'Look! The mind of [Adam, my] mate, shall vibrate from above, and my servants shall be robbed [of their anointing,' and]

" 'They shall know that Jehovah, [God of] the armies [of Israel sent you],

2.10 " '[So, let the people who] sing [spiritual doctrine] be encouraged, oh daughter of Zion, because, behold,

" 'I am coming to dwell permanently with [the unwalled towns that came into existence when my opinion was bisected from Adam]'

"Says Jehovah, and

2.11 "Many nations shall be joined to Jehovah, and it shall come to pass that

"The people [that I] bisected [from Adam] shall be my people, and I shall dwell permanently with you, and you shall know Jehovah, [God of] the armies [of Israel, and

"[You shall know that] he sent me to you, and

"In] that day,

2.12 "[Adam], Jehovah's mate, shall inherit [the material bodies of] Judah, his share in the holy land, again, and

2.13 "The personalities [of Judah] shall wake up, [and] their material bodies [shall become] Jehovah's holy habitation, [and] all [the earth shall be] quiet."

2.13 "The personalities [of Judah] shall wake up, [and] their material bodies [shall become] Jehovah's holy habitation, [and] all [the earth shall be] quiet."

Chapter 3

[966.9.C]
3.07 Thus says Jehovah to his armies, If you walk in my lifestyle and guard [against side-stepping preaching salvation to the Gentiles], and if you also judge my household, and also guard the [people] that I have fenced in, I will give you access to these [men who] stand in the midst of [the stones of fire],[R]

[R] Ez 28:14

3.08 Hear now, Joshua, you [who are] the high priest, and your associates who are married to the personalities of mortal men [who perform] miracles.[R] Look! I will cause my servant, the BRANCH [of the Tree of Life, and his] mate, to come into existence.

[R] Dan 11:32

3.09 Look at the soul that I have laid in the personality of Joshua. I shall engrave seven landscapes upon that one soul, says Jehovah to his armies, and extract [the First Adam], the perverse mate of that material body, in one day, and

3.10 In that day, says Jehovah to his armies, you shall call every mortal man that is near [to Messiah, the life-producing] vine,[R-1] or near [to Israel], the fig tree,[R-2] his neighbor.[R-3]

[R-1] Jn 15:5
[R-2] Matt 24:32
[R-3] Lk 10:36-37

Chapter 4

[51.2]

4.02 And [the angel] said unto me, What do you see? And I said, I have looked, and behold a candlestick all [of] gold, with a bowl upon the top of it, and his seven lamps thereon, and seven pipes to the seven lamps thereon, [are] upon the top thereof, and

4.03 Two olive trees by it, one upon the right [side] of the bowl, and the other upon the left [side] thereof, and

4.06 The temple of God shall be built by the power of the Spirit of God, and

4.07 Adam shall be moved out of the way of the Spirit of Elohim and he shall bring forth the headstone, God in the flesh, even the [spiritual] man Elijah, the only mediator between God and man, and

4.09 . . . you shall know that Jehovah has sent His armies to you . . .

4.10 When Leviathan can't trample Elohim's little ones under foot any longer, because Elijah is shining through them as an energy source that maintains their correct moral order.

Elohim's Sons are Jehovah's eyes, which are everywhere in the earth of mortal man.

4.11 Then I answered and said to the angel, What are these two sources of spiritual life that minister blessing and pronounce judgment in the visible, physical world?

4.12 And I answered the angel again, and said unto him, What are these two sources of Jehovah's spiritual life that empty out of themselves through two purified connecting tubes?

4.14 Then the angel said, The candlestick [with its seven pipes], and the two olive trees, are the two Sons that Adam, the Lord of the whole Earth, sired[216]

Chapter 6

[40.2]
6.01 And I turned towards the visible, spiritual world, and focused my spiritual eyes, and looked into the Spirit, and, a miracle; I saw spiritual things, [the widowed spirit of Adam], the lamb that was slain, was flattened out into the linear plane of mortal man, and became the womb designed to raise Adam from the dead; and she was a Wild Animal that was emerging forth and unfolding like the leaves of a plant, and Adam and the fiery serpent were two distinct spiritual powers[R] proceeding forth from her.

[R] Zeph 1:2 (AT)
Gen 4:1-2 (AT)

6.02 At the beginning, Adam ruled over the material Earth which gave him form, and over the Serpent, the one in second place, who was in darkness, and Michael was ruling over Adam, the mind through which Jehovah would appear, but the

---

[216] Elijah, the savior of Israel, and the glorified Jesus Christ, the Savior of the world.

Serpent became strong, fortified herself [against Adam, and became Leviathan, who] multiplied to her fullest, and is appearing through many leprous, sin-filled members.

6.03 Then I answered, and said unto Elijah, the one who was talking with me, What are these, my Lord?

6.04 And Elijah answered, and said to me, The four horses symbolize Adam, who was in right standing with Elohim, ruler of the Earth, as well as of the heavens, when they were one Spirit before Adam [separated from] Him, but [the Serpent] incarnated [as Leviathan], who increased like a plant [into many members].

6.05 And the Serpent, the dark part of the Living Beast, incarnated as a mortal Woman, and the Living Beast's spiritually pure part, Adam's widowed spirit, was woven together with Leviathan, who [became the] Wild Animal [that] unfolded towards the visible, physical world.

6.06 And after the Serpent separated from Adam, because she desired to appear in the visible, physical world, Jehovah said, Go towards your desired goal, appear in the visible, physical world, and she became a Wild Animal that is symbolized as a bay horse, the one with Adam's reddish stain. And this is how the many members of the Wild Animal appeared on the face of the Earth.

6.07 Then Elijah explained to me in a loud anguished cry, [saying], In due season, you will understand that Adam shall [be restored to Elohim's family,[R] and they] shall increase into [Elohim's mature Sons], because Adam's widowed spirit is Elohim's Son, and even though he is joined to Satan right now, he shall eventually be [a part of] the mind where [Jehovah's] Spirit rests.

[R] Gen 2:24 (AT)
Gen 4:6-7 (AT)
Ps 90:3 (AT)
Amos 5:9b (AT)

Chapter 9

[768.2]

9.01 The burden of Jehovah's word to [ISIL, which claims to be the legitimate ruling authority of] Damascus, the land of Hadrach, [the God of the Syrians]: Jehovah is married to the tribes of the Israel [of God] through the mind of the whole Adam,

9.02 Which is assembled together against [the spiritual power of] the vehement wisdom of Freemasonry in the Jews and Christians [who believe their doctrine],

9.03 Who separated themselves [from Me when the thoughts of] their conscious mind gathered together with the spiritual power [of the vehement wisdom of] Freemasonry, [to give ISIL] the wealth [it needed] to build a fortified [military machine] with sharp teeth;

9.04 Look! Adonai will severely strike [the spiritual power of the vehement wisdom of Freemasonry], which seized the unconscious mind [of the Jews and Christians who believe their doctrine], and consume it, and

9.05 The king of Gaza, [who] expects to eradicate [Christianity], shall be disappointed; he shall not marry the child that he birthed in [the Jews and Christians that he captured] in Ashkelon, [where they believe the vehement wisdom of Freemasonry; on the contrary, the spiritual child that overthrew the Jews and Christians who believe the vehement wisdom of Freemasonry] shall be destroyed;[217] and

---

[217] The king of Gaza is an evil spiritual king. He is the Malchut, the 10th degree of power from the fallen world above our world, that descends into, and attaches itself to, the spiritual child that it previously

Ashkelon, [one of the cities where Jews and Christians who believe the vehement wisdom of Freemasonry are captured], shall see [Righteous Adam pull down their temple][R] in Gaza, [and slay the principalities that dwell therein], and shall be afraid; and

[R] Judg 16:30

9.07 I will shut the mouth of the disgusting spirit [that calls for] the blood [of Christians and secular Jews, and] make their pride[ful speech] irrelevant, by assembling the armies of the widowed Elohim in Judah, [and] they shall exterminate [the spiritual power of the vehement wisdom of Freemasonry, and then]

9.06 I will circumcise the arrogant Philistines[218] from Ashdod, [who captured the Jews and Christians who believe the vehement wisdom of Freemasonry], and marry [Hiram Abiff],[219] the illegitimate [spiritual] child [born of the spirit of the vehement wisdom of Freemasonry, and]

9.08 My widowed house[hold] shall return [to Me], and cross over [into My Mind], and now that they see with My eyes, the armies [of the widowed Elohim] shall encamp around them, and the oppressive [spiritual power of the vehement wisdom of Freemasonry] shall not pass through them anymore.

9.09 "Rejoice [R-1] greatly daughter of the Sphere of Wisdom; Shout [out loud] [R-1] daughter of Jerusalem, [the city of souls that Jehovah inhabits, because the Son of the Sphere of Wisdom], your King, is coming to belong to you; [R-2] [He is] the

---

incarnated within humanity. On the Righteous side, Adam is Jehovah's spiritual child within humanity.

[218] These are spiritual Philistines, Israelites of God who have the arrogant nature of the Philistines, rather than God.

[219] ***Hiram Abiff*** is analogous to Righteous Adam in the esoteric wisdom of the Torah. He is the new, inner man of the Freemason ideology.

Righteous [One, [R-3] the author of] Salvation, [R-4] [who comes] riding in a male donkey [in his first incarnation, and riding in] a young male beast of burden, the son of a female donkey [R-5] who[se personalities] are [in submission to him, in his second incarnation];

"Look [for him everywhere, all the time, so that you recognize him when he appears]!

[R-1] Lk 19:37 (ATB)
[R-2] Lk 22:19
[R-3] 1 Jn 2:1
[R-4] Heb 5:9
[R-5] Rev 12:5

[Message # Unknown]

9.15 Jehovah's soldiers shall defend them, and they shall be like filled bowls,[R] and devour them, and Adam and Elijah shall save them in that day.

[R] Rev 15:1

Chapter 11

[1121.4]

11.01 Adam, the first [of] the immortal trees,* opened the white brick** door [R] [of his mind to physical sexuality, and Elohim's] fiery [judgment fell on him]; and

[R] Gen 4:7
Jn 10:7
Rev 3:20

* Amplification of ***Cedars of Lebanon***

** [White] Brick is the previous word in the Lexicon before ***Lebanon***.

11.02 Now [all Israel] is wailing, [because] the First [Adam] is ravaged, [and Judah], Elohim's immortal [tree],* has fallen [because of their idolatrous worship of] Christmas,** [and] Manasseh's*** long-living trees**** are wailing, [because the vine [R-1] that] descended [into the visible world has been] cut off from the Garden [above, and the blood of the Pure One is poured out upon the ground like water],[R-2] and

R-1 Jn15:5
R-2 Deut 32:14

* Amplification of ***Cedar tree.***
** Amplification of ***Fir tree***.
*** The territory of Bashan was given to Manasseh.
**** Amplification of Oak tree.

11.03 The shepherds can be heard wailing because their doctrine has been proven wrong, and the redeemed [R] can be heard moaning because their pride has brought them down [to the grave];

R Lk 1:68
Job 21:13
Pro 16:18

11.04 [Wherefore], thus says Jehovah Elohim to the shepherds [that are] the mate of the migrant [kings who] smite the souls of their assemblies with deadly intent,

11.05 Who do not stand [them] upright, or feed [them], or do anything to alleviate their pain, [but], on the contrary, smite them with deadly intent [and] sell them [to the highest bidder, while] saying,

"Jehovah [is surely] blessing me [because] I am rich,"

[And, nevertheless, go] unpunished [by the angels in the world] above;

11.06 "I will not continue to alleviate the pain of the physical bodies [of the mortal men who] married [the migrant kings that descended] from above,"

Says Jehovah's inner whisper, [R]

"But, watch, I will bring [the Second] Adam, [my] mate, into existence, [and] the mortal men [who] associate their [personality with his] mind, shall smite the [migrant] kings [that are oppressing them] in the unconscious part of the mind with deadly intent, and they shall snatch [their] bodies away from the negative mind [of those kings], and

[R] Job 1:12

11.07 "I will separate [the mortal men who] belong to [me, that are] pressed down under the Shepherds [who are] the mate of the migrant kings and set them upright, and I will take [back] the Second [Adam], the spiritual plant that unifies [Judah], called 'Beautiful,' [R-1] [because they are the gate to the temple where healing takes place], and the other called 'Israel,' who are in] bondage [R-2] to the shepherds [who are] the mate of the migrant [kings], and

[R-1] Acts 3:2
[R-2] Gal 4:24

11.08 "I will destroy the three shepherds* [who are] the mate [of the migrant kings that were] cut off [from God, who seek] to obtain souls for their assemblies because of greed, and hold] the female personalities [that] they are unified with [in bondage],[R] and

[R] Gen 10:9
Gen 25:27

* Judah, Levi and Benjamin

11.09a "The Shepherds [who are my] mate shall speak [my Words, and] those [personalities that] are destined to die, shall die,[R-1] and those [spiritual intellectual souls that] are destined to be separated from their bodies, shall be separated from their bodies, and the female [spiritual intellectual soul of Judah], the woman that is lifted up in pride, [R-2]

[R-1] Jer 15:2
Matt 8:22
[R-2] Rev 17:1-2, 5

11.14 "[That] cut down the Second [Adam, the spiritual] plant [that is] bound to the unconscious part of the mind, and broke up the brotherhood [R] between Judah and Israel in the unconscious part of the mind,

[R] 1 Ki 12:14, 16

11.09b "Shall no [longer be able] to consume the male pudenda of [Israel, **R** my] mate,

R 1 Ki 12:19

11.10 "[When] I take back [Israel] in the unconscious part of the mind, from Judah, my mate, [who] cut down [the Second Adam, the spiritual] plant in the unconscious part of the mind, [and] broke the covenant [that] I made with all of the people [of Israel] in the unconscious part of the mind,

11.11 "[Because], in the day that [Judah] broke [the covenant that I made with Israel] to guard [them that] were pressed down [under their authority, the Son of God, **R-1** the only One that] knows [the Father], stood upright in the unconscious part of the mind [of Judah, according to] the Word of Jehovah,**R-2** and

R-1 Jn 1:18
R-2 1 Ki 10:12

11.12 "He shall say to [them that are pressed down under the shepherds who are married to the migrant kings],

" 'If the perceptions of your mind are good, you will put yourself [in a position to receive] my reward, [which is] the salvation of the whole Name **R** Jehovah, but if [the Second Adam], your male mind is not standing erect, my reward shall be allocated in proportion [to the thoughts of the Second Adam that are found in] the unconscious part of the mind,' " and

R Jude 3

11.13 Jehovah said to [them],

"Cast away the splendid garment [of the Second Adam from] above from the clay bodies [of Judah] because they do not value it enough to keep it," and

I took the salvation of the whole Name Jehovah in the unconscious part of the mind of the house[hold] of Jehovah and cast it away from [their] clay [bodies], and

11.15 Jehovah spoke again [and said],

"I shall take the immoral shepherds [that] belong to [me, that are] the vessels of [the migrant kings], and

11.16 "Look! I will raise up shepherds in [their] land * that will not destroy adolescent boys [R-1] by visiting [them with hostile intentions], nor strive to break into [widows' houses [R-2] to enrich themselves], nor will they solve [conflicts with] an immovable male ego, nor will they eat fat, [R-3] or [eat meat from an animal that does not have] a split foot,[R-4] or from one that was] torn in pieces, [R-5]

[R-1] Lev 10:13
[R-2] Matt 23:14
[R-3] Lev 3:17
[R-4] Lev 11:4
[R-5] Ex 22:31

* I will take the immoral souls away from the migrant Kings and raise up moral Shepherds in the same physical bodies that the migrant kings possessed. Reincarnation of the migrant kings (which is the death of the body) will not be necessary to clothe the souls of moral shepherds.

11.17 "Woe to the shepherds who God does not dwell in, [who] leave [the people] to the sword [R] of the migrant [kings because] their power to perceive the righteous [thoughts that come] from [the Second Adam who is] above, is disappointing;[R] Their power to perceive the righteous [thoughts that come] from [the Second Adam who is] above is very weak, so [the personalities of their assemblies] are very ashamed.

[R] Ps 17:13

Chapter 12

[912.2.C]
12.01 [The following is] the burden [that the prophet, Zechariah, had to deliver] the Word of Jehovah to Israel:

[Thus] says Jehovah: [On the First Day of creation, Elohim] stretched out the heavens, and laid the foundation of the earth, and squeezed the spirit of mankind into the center [of the earth], and

12.04 In the [Second] Day [of creation, I opened my eyes upon the house of Judah, Open, says Jehovah, and struck every horse of the people with blindness, and I struck [Leviathan], their rider, with madness; and every horse was bewildered, confused and disoriented,

12.02 [But], look! [In the Third Day of creation], I [AM] will put [the spirit of his Son inside of] a [mortal] vessel, [and] he shall flow together with [the spirit of that mortal man, and complete him,[R-1] and] that mortal man shall be glorified, and the glorified man] shall surround Judah [from] above, [and be] a doorway[R-2] [of escape][R-3] for all the people of Jerusalem [from] above [when] they are besieged, and

R-1 Col 2:10
R-2 Jn 10:9
R-3 1 Cor 10:13

12.03 In that day I will put a stone/seed [in] Jerusalem [that will carry away] the burden [of sin of] all people, [and my Son] from above shall make a covenant with all the people of the earth, and gather together [with whoever believes in him], and

12.05 Judah, my familiar friend, shall say in his heart, [We], the inhabitants of Jerusalem, are strong, [because] we belong to the armies of Jehovah, [our] God, and

12.06 In that day I will put [the people of] Judah, my familiar friends, in a cauldron, and light the fire [under] the wood, and the fire shall devour their sins like [fire burns up] newly cut grain, and all the people of the World of Action shall be inhabited again, [when] the south [side of Jerusalem, the conscious mind of the body], below, [is as beautiful as] the north [side of] Jerusalem, [the unconscious, hidden part of the mind of Messiah, above], and

12.07 Jehovah shall save the tents of Judah first, so that the house of David does not magnify the opinion of the inhabitants of Jerusalem above the opinion of Judah, and

12.08 In that day, Jehovah shall defend the unconscious [part of the mind of] the inhabitants of Jerusalem, [and he that] has weak ankles among them in that day, [shall be like] David, [and] the house of David, God's army, [shall be] the personalities of the Angel of Jehovah, and

12.09 It shall come to pass in that day, that I will seek to destroy all the nations that come against Jerusalem, and

12.10 I will pour out the spirit of grace upon [those of] the house of David and the inhabitants of Jerusalem who are pleading for mercy, and they shall look upon the Ancient One that they stabbed [in the back], and they [who are] under wormwood [judgment from] above, shall grieve bitterly because [of what they did to the Ancient One], like a firstborn wails for [the mother it was previously united with], and

12.11 In that day, [the women of the house of David] shall mourn [like they mourn for] Tammuz, [and the inhabitants of] Jerusalem [shall mourn like they mourned for King Josiah when he died in] the valley of Megiddon, and

12.12 The material bodies of every extended family [of Judah] shall mourn [because of] their separation [from the Ancient One], and the extended family of the house of David [shall mourn because of their separation from Jehovah], and the women [of the house of David shall mourn because of] their separation [from the Queen of Heaven], and the extended family of the house of Nathan shall mourn [because Messiah will not be] separated [from their seed, or] separated from [the wombs of] their wives, and

12.13 The extended family of Levi [will mourn because they are separated from their fathers who are consecrated to Jehovah, and] the wives [of Levi will mourn because] they are separated from their husbands, and

12.14 [As for] all the [other] extended families that are not necessary [for National Israel to be in right standing with Jehovah], every family will be separated [from the royal line of Judah], and their wives [will be separated from [service to the women of the royal household].

Chapter 13

[OLM - 07 19 00]
13.07 Let [The regenerated Adam, Jehovah's] sword, awake because of Elohim's sons, and because of the men who have fellowship with me [through the Holy Spirit], says Jehovah; and let [Elohim's] armies wound Leviathan's collective consciousness [and] disperse [the fiery serpents], the [spiritual] immigrants, [and the Regenerated Adam, my] collective consciousness, will [dissolve Leviathan's collective consciousness, and] return Abel to his starting point.

Chapter 14

[1124.6.C]
14.01 Look! The day is coming that Jehovah in the midst of you shall share [with you] what you have to gain [by overcoming];

ARMAGEDDON

14.02 Adonai, the part of the people [of Judah] that do not break their covenant [with Jehovah], but remain in Jerusalem, the City [of spiritual intellectual souls], shall gather together with [the Second Adam, her] mate, to battle against [the primordial kings] in all the nations that catch [the spiritual intellectual souls of] the City of Jerusalem [in a net], steal the possessions of

[Judah, Jehovah's] house[hold] rape the women and send half of the City into captivity, and

JEHOVAH

God of Battle

14.03 Jehovah shall go forth and fight against [the primordial kings in those] nations [like he fought against the Canaanites that] were hostile [to the Hebrew children] in the day [that he brought them out of Egypt], and

God as Saviour

14.04 In that day, [Yeshuah], the exalted [personality of Elohim], shall stand upon the carnal mind of [the spiritual intellectual souls of the City of] Jerusalem, [and the golden] oil [that flows from the two anointed ones] in the eternal world, shall burst forth from the midst of the personalities [of Judah], and the half of the nation [of Judah that became deaf and blind

When Jehovah's righteous Sowing & Reaping] judgment [fell on them because] they withdrew from the oil [that flowed from the holy ones from] above [when they appeared in a human form], shall be forgiven, [and] the very great valley [that exists between] the eternal world [of God] and the nations of the material visible world, [shall be closed up] and

God of Justice

Prophecy Vs Law

14.05 [The personalities of] Judah [that are in] the Valley [of Decision who] marry the Noble Branch shall escape [Jehovah's Righteous Sowing & Reaping Judgment], like the personalities of the Judeans [that] escaped [the judgment of leprosy] in the day [that] King Uzziah [caused] an uproar [by challenging the authority of the Levitical priesthood, until]

Jehovah came and [demonstrated that the combined authority of the esoteric wisdom and the monarchy (by which some] Judeans might escape from [the Valley of Decision]), and [the authority of the Law as it is actualized through the Levitical priesthood], are equal, [but the authority of] the Holy One is greater than all of [the collective voices of the prophets and priests, and that he, alone, has authority over the prophetic voice of his Daughter in the individual Judean], and

God of the Dark

14.06 It shall come to pass in that day, that [the Law that Jehovah gave to Israel so that they could en]light[en the nations, shall become] darkness, and

God of The Light

14.07 It shall come to pass [in] the day [that] Jehovah [is] unified [with his Name, that everyone that is] enslaved [by the Law, that] knows [his Name], shall be enlightened, and

God as The Holy Spirit

14.08 It shall come to pass that living waters shall go out from Jerusalem, [the City of spiritual intellectual souls, and] half of [the souls in] the sea [of the unconscious part of the mind] shall go toward the former [wisdom, and] bear the fruit [of the Spirit of the Holy One], but the [other] half [of the souls in] the sea [of the unconscious part of the mind] shall be hindered [from bearing the fruit of the Spirit of the Holy One] until [the sins in the unconscious part of the mind] are exposed, and

God as The Son

King of Kings

14.09 Jehovah shall be King over all [of the primordial kings that rule over the personalities of the First Adam who is made from] the Earth in that day, [and] Jehovah [above, and

Elohim within the people], shall be one [God], and [the Second Adam, the Lord from Heaven, Jehovah's] Name, [and the First Adam who is made from the Earth, shall be] one [whole man],

THE FIRST ADAM

Trapped

14.11 [But the First Adam] is caught in a net, [and the personalities of Judah that Yeshuah] married, are not safe [from the skewed perceptions of the dead primordial kings, and Jehovah] does not inhabit Jerusalem, [the City of spiritual intellectual souls] any more, and

THE REDEMER

14.13 It shall come to pass in the day that Jehovah, the great [God that] dwells within [Judah], seizes a man [and raises him from the dead, [that] it causes [such] an uproar, that the mind of the neighbor [that does not believe it], shall rise up against the mind of the neighbor [that does believe it]; and

THE REDEEMED

Judah

14.10a [The personalities of Judah that Yeshuah marries shall be] forgiven, [the kings of spiritual Israel] shall return [to Jehovah, and] all the dry material bodies [that house the personalities in] the Valley [of Decision, and] the spiritual intellectual souls of] Jerusalem, shall stand] upright, and

Benjamin

14.10b The seed of Benjamin [that] stand [on] the right side of the [swinging] door shall be joined to the gate of the First[born Son], the corner[stone of the temple of God, and shall become a part of] the projection of the [well] favored [Son of] God [who]

judges the primordial] kings [that are in Judah, the Family of Egypt and the nations, and

THE LAST ADAM

14.14 [The primordial kings within] Judah shall raise [them] up [as] an army [against the spiritual intellectual souls of] Jerusalem, to take away the great and abundant covering that is the strength of all the nations that surround them [to attain] salvation [and righteous] judgment, and

14.12 [This is the reason why] Jehovah [shall send the Last Adam to rescue] the people [of Judah from the primordial kings that raised [them] up [as] an army against all [the spiritual intellectual souls of] Jerusalem, and

As A Plague

To Judah

[The soul parts of Yeshuah, the Last Adam, Jehovah's] male organ, shall stand upon Elohim, [Ancient Adam's shadow in] the empty space [where creation is taking place], and they shall crucify [the Shekinah within the people of Judah, and the primordial kings] in the unconscious part of their carnal mind shall melt from the great heat, [and the Shekinah within the people of Judah, shall separate from the primordial kings, and flow together with Yeshuah, and the perverse] perceptions of [Satan], the tongue [of the primordial kings], shall vanish, and [Cain, Satan's] mouth [piece] shall vanish [also],

As The Priests of Judah

14.15 [Wherefore], it is right that these [priests of Judah, whose] bestial material bodies [are Jehovah's] horse [in the Day of Battle, who] boil [Satan until the Shekinah] separates [from the primordial kings, and their personality turns away from Cain, the source of] their anger, [towards the oil of the anointing that] weans [them from the milk of the Word], should be as a plague [of Locusts to the family of Egypt and all unrepentant, habitual offenders] and

REWARD

The Festival of Booths

Judah

14.16 It shall come to pass [that] all [the Judeans] that came against [the spiritual intellectual souls of] Jerusalem [that are disbursed among] all of the nations, that remain [after the first plague], shall ascend, from year to year, [with the spiritual intellectual souls of Jerusalem who] worship King Jehovah, [the God of] the armies [of Israel, by loving Yeshuah, their neighbor], and shall experience the Festival of Booths, and

The Families of the Earth

14.17 It shall come to pass that the families of [the First], earthen [Adam, who] do not rise up [together with the spiritual intellectual souls of] Jerusalem [to worship] King Jehovah, [God of the] armies [of Israel, by loving their neighbor after Yeshuah rescues them from the primordial kings], shall not [experience] the rain from above, [which is the Holy Spirit of Life], and

The Family of Egypt

Chastised

14.18 If [Manasseh and Ephraim], the family of Egypt, do not come [into a unity with the holy one] above, [and] do not rise up [with the spiritual intellectual souls of Jerusalem, the priests of Judah shall be as a plague [of Locusts that shall consume their egos, and] overthrow [the pride of then Second Adam, and then, after that],

Redeemed

Elohim shall crucify [the Second Adam], Jehovah's mate [within the Family of Egypt who are scattered throughout] the nations, that do not come up [with the spiritual intellectual souls of Jerusalem] to observe the Festival of Booths, and

Habitual Offenders

14.19 This shall be the punishment for the habitual offenders in Egypt, and in all the nations that do not rise up [with the spiritual intellectual souls of Jerusalem who worship King Jehovah by loving Yeshuah, their neighbor], they shall not experience the Festival of Booths, and

THE END OF THE AGE

The Priests of Judah

14.20 It shall come to pass In the day that [the priests of Judah], the horses [that reveal Jehovah's strength in the day of battle], clearly sound [the trumpet of] Jehovah's holiness [through esoteric doctrine], that [the personalities of Judah], Jehovah's house[hold], shall boil [Satan, their sin nature], and

The Son of Man

[Ancient Adam], the personality of the altar, shall sprinkle [the blood of Yeshuah, his] vessel upon the living waters of the spiritual intellectual souls of the City of Jerusalem, and they shall turn into the Blood of the Son of Man], and

Judah Redeemed

14.21 It shall come to pass in that day, that every Judean that comes to Jerusalem, [the City of spiritual intellectual souls, to worship King Jehovah, God of the armies of Israel, by loving Yeshuah, their neighbor], shall sacrifice [Satan, their dead primordial king, and] boil her in the boiling pot [of the unconscious part of the mind, and

The End of Evil Inclination

The evil inclination of] all of them shall be carried away, and the holiness of Jehovah, [the God of Israel's] armies, [shall be revealed in them, and] there shall not be [any] Canaanites in [Judah], the house[hold] of Jehovah, the God of Israel's armies, any more.

THE BOOK OF

ZEPHANIAH

Chapter 1

[270.2]

1.02 I, Jehovah, am promising to heal the whole Wild Animal which is in outer darkness, by gathering her into a protective relationship with me, while Elijah crucifies Adam's widowed spirit, and liberates him from Satan.

1.03 And this is how I'm going to do it: I'll free Adam's widowed spirit from his bondage by sending Leviathan and Satan against everyone in Judah, who is dwelling in their flesh,

1.04 And against those who swear by Jehovah with their mouths, but are really swearing by Satan, and obeying the armies of demons in their carnal minds,

1.05 And against those who have turned away from Jehovah, and those who are not looking for Him, and those who have not loved Him enough to trample their carnal minds underfoot.

1.06 And it shall come to pass, in the day that Elijah rips the carnal mind out of everyone who overcomes [Satan], and offers [Leviathan] up to Jehovah,

1.07 That Elijah shall appear in the mortal men he has purified, and rip out the carnal minds of the Sons of Israel, and everyone else in whom Abel is covered over by Leviathan.

1.08 So let your carnal mind be silent when Abel shows you your sins, because the time when Adam shall defeat Leviathan is very near.

1.09 And I, Jehovah, declare that in the day that I rip the carnal minds out of my first fruits, and send my purified ones to show their sins to my people who are in bondage to Leviathan, but deny their condition, my people shall cry out for help, and I shall strip the pastors who are abusing them of their authority, and the carnal minds of my people shall break up, and Adam shall rise from the dead in them also.

1.10 Therefore, let the harlot who is sitting on, and possessing, Adam's ox like a queen,[R] perish, and let the carnal minds of those of Elohim's people who are believing into Elijah for salvation, be divided up.

[R] Rev 17:3-4

1.11 And this is what will happen at the appointed time: I shall examine the minds of my people to determine whether they are begotten of the Serpent or Elijah,

1.12 And I shall rip out the minds of the men that are born of Leviathan, which are saying, ***The Lord shall not judge the sins of His people.***

1.13 And when they fail to keep Abel alive, they will rebuild their dying personalities and physical bodies with Cain's wisdom, and [Leviathan] shall restore their spiritual life, and their imputed anointing shall be taken away from them, and Abel shall die to his priesthood again.

1.14 The day when Adam rises from the dead is very near, and [it is] approaching with violent speed[R] to aid Jehovah's dying people; the rage of [Satan], the tyrant's battle cry shall be fierce.

[R] Deut 32:35 (AT)

1.15 This day is the day that Jehovah shall show His passionate love for mankind by expressing His anger against Leviathan; It is a day of great distress for Satan, because Elijah is cutting through Leviathan to bring sudden ruin to the dark prison[R] of the carnal mind, the kingdom of darkness [that] scabs over Abel and covers [him] with misery,

[R] Job 40:14-15a (AT)
Is 14:19
Zeph 2:9

1.16(a) This is the day that the truth about what happened to Adam shall prepare Jehovah's people for the battle that will liberate Adam's widowed spirit from her illegal union with Satan and Leviathan.

1.17(a) And I shall bind Adam's widowed spirit to the Spirit of Elijah, and he shall [increase into Adam,

1.16(b) And they shall] sacrifice Leviathan up to Jehovah,

1.17(b) And they shall die to their ignorant and miserable lifestyle, and their bestial [mental, emotional and physical] bodies shall be made waste.

1.18 Neither shall Cain's own devices nor [Satan's] spiritual power be able to save them in the day that Jehovah's spiritual power destroys Leviathan and perfects everyone who is joined to their personality,[R] because Adam passionately desires to marry His wife.

[R] 1 Ki 19:7 (AT)

Chapter 2

[272.6]
2.01 Face the truth, you heathen nation, that Adam's widowed spirit, your true identity, is married to the Serpent.

2.02 Nevertheless, Abel's priestly authority is being restored because Adam is rising from the dead, and maturing into Elijah, the one who is to offer Leviathan up as a sacrifice to Jehovah, so that the spirit of your mind can be reformed into Jehovah's image. But the prophecy that the lake of fire [Kingdom of God] shall be formed in you hasn't been fulfilled, because Adam isn't judging your sins.

2.03 Therefore, look to Jehovah to meet all of your needs, you in whom Abel is raised from the dead, but are still miserable and afflicted in your emotions, and He will give you Elijah's ministry of reconciliation; and you shall search out man's true motives, and extend the mercy of Jehovah's judgments[R] to the spiritual criminal, in the day that Jehovah delivers His people from their bondage to Satan and Leviathan.

R Is 11:3-4

2.05 Woe unto [the Serpent], the heathen who killed Adam, and is appearing in the visible, physical world as a company of wandering men[R-1] who are joined to their own flesh![R-2] The resurrected Adam is against you [Leviathan], you dead, mortal mind, and shall stop Satan, the Wild Animal's unconscious mind, from living through you, by drying up her sea.

R-1 Is 14:5 (AT)
R-2 1 Ki 19:7 (AT)
Rev 17:2 (AT)

2.06 And the company of wandering men who are married to Satan and Leviathan shall use Elijah's spiritual military power to divorce themselves from her, and they shall marry him.

2.04 And Adam's widowed spirit shall divorce the Serpent who violently murdered Adam and carried away his living breath, and Elijah shall cut [Leviathan away from] Abel, and Adam's widowed spirit shall overcome Satan's spiritual power, and separate from her, and the Serpent shall be barren.

2.07 And the company of men who were wanderers, but are now married to Elijah, shall be a lifeline to the survivors of Judah's household, and Jehovah and Elohim shall reverse their captivity, and all of the men who are migrating from the Wild Animal, into the Living Beast, shall be loosed from Leviathan and marry Elijah, and they shall lie down in peace.

2.08 I have noticed that the Serpent has killed Adam, and woven his widowed spirit together with herself to form Leviathan, her carnal mind, in my people,

2.09 Therefore, says Jehovah, the living Word, to Israel, Elohim's soldiers, Leviathan shall be a prison house**[R-1]** for Satan's hurtful spirit,**[R-2]** and they shall exist inside of a dead Wild Animal,**[R-3]** until the end of the age,

[R-1] Job 40:14-15a (AT)
Is 14:19 (AT)
[R-2] Gen 3:16 (AT)
Rom 6:17-18 (AT)
Rev 17:3 (AT)
[R-3] Jon 2:10

When Adam pulls Leviathan, their subconscious mind, to pieces,**[R-1]** and the nations shall pull their carnal minds to pieces also, and Elijah shall boil Satan, their unconscious mind,**[R-2]** until she turns into dead salt, and Elohim's Sons shall judge the nations,**[R-3]** and they shall inherit perpetual life also.

[R-1] Heb 4:12
[R-2] Dan 7:9 (AT)
Zeph 3:3b (AT)
[R-3] Dan 7:25 (AT)

2.10 And Adam's widowed spirit shall be fully joined to Elijah when the Gentiles pull Leviathan apart [also], and they shall weave Adam's widowed spirit together with Elijah, like Elohim's Sons did.

2.11 And they shall respect Jehovah when His righteous judgment separates Adam's widowed spirit from Satan and Leviathan, and Jehovah shall be worshiped in His own house by all of the minds of the heathen.

2.12 And Elijah shall crucify Ham's descendants, and [Leviathan shall be] circumcised [in them] also.

2.13 And Elijah shall turn away Satan's authority, and Leviathan shall become paralyzed and silent, and this visible, physical world shall vanish.

2.14 And the whole flock of the nation of Wild Animals, both the unpurified and the defensed, shall pass through the time period over which Satan and Leviathan rule, and the bowls [Sons] of Elohim's wrath, shall uncover the spiritual sexual parts of the preserved Wild Animal, and Elijah shall cover them, and Abel shall smear together with Elijah, and they shall preach out of their renewed minds, and they shall be delivered from this existence of physical and spiritual labor.

2.15 This is that insolent, dead, Wild Animal, who is existing in adultery [with Elohim's wife], without fear, whose carnal mind is saying, I am God, and there is no one as great as I. But look at how that dead, Wild Animal, which was turned into a desert by Jehovah's judgments, has now become the Living Beast, which is Jehovah's resting place! He shall call for them, and purify them, and the Wild Animal that they are existing in, shall be made alive.

Chapter 3

[305.10]
3.01 Woe to the Wild Animal which is unclean because of her rebellious mind.

3.02 She didn't obey Jehovah's voice, or benefit from His instruction, because her carnal mind wasn't overthrown; and her carnal mind wasn't overthrown because her [carnal mind] wasn't sacrificed to Jehovah, and her carnal mind wasn't sacrificed to Jehovah because she wouldn't confess her sins and repent,

3.04a And her priests have violently torn away Adam's spirit and committed treason by prostituting him,[R]

[R] Pro 26:11 (AT)
Job 41:5, 13 (AT)
Eccl 12:3 (AT)
Ez 32:2 (AT)
Dan 8:6-7 (AT)
Joel 3:3 (AT)
Rev 17:1

3.03a And that's why Satan, the Wild Animal's unconscious mind, is like an army of fierce young soldiers executing the sowing and reaping judgment upon herself, because of the sins of her carnal mind,

3.04b But Leviathan shall be cut off because of Elijah's righteousness

3.03b When Satan is boiled, and [Adam's widowed spirit is]

3.07b Joined to [Elijah], her true husband, the only one who can preserve her alive [because He is the only one strong enough to make her confess her sins and repent.[R]

[R] Vs 7a

3.05a So, you see, Jehovah incarnates Adam in the midst of His Living Beast from age to age, but the Serpent, who is presently possessing Adam's widowed spirit illegally, is the only one who forms Leviathan, the visible expression of the Serpent's deadly existence.

3.06 And that's why Leviathan lies in wait to murder Adam, so that the Serpent can live with my wife.

3.05b Nevertheless, the Serpent shall be ashamed when Leviathan is weeded out [of the garden] and [Adam is] returned to his proper place [as the mind of] the Living Beast, because I have promised the nations that I will destroy Leviathan and dry up the Serpent's power to pierce through Adam.

3.08a It is, therefore, my decision to heal their spiritual leprosy, and form them into my own image by breathing myself [Elohim] into them; so I'm casting Leviathan, their mortal minds, into the lake of fire [Spirit of Elijah], where Satan is, and they shall be completely broken apart and destroyed,

And after I burn up Leviathan, I'm sending you [Elijah] to gather whatever is left of them [Adam's widowed spirit] into one Body with yourself,**R** through union with [their human spirit], so that Adam, the only one who is able to overcome the Satanic government of this visible, physical world, can rise from the dead.

R Gen 7:5 (AT)

3.07a And I, Jehovah, said [to Elohim], Surely when I bring this [merciful] judgment upon their [carnal] minds, they will confess their sins and repent, so that Adam's widowed spirit can separate from Satan, [join with Elijah, and increase into Adam].

So Elijah said to [the mortal man], Confess your sins and repent, so that Adam can rise from the dead and enable you to pass over into the Kingdom of Heaven. But [despite these great and precious promises] they earnestly continued to act out the Serpent's wicked deeds.

3.09 Therefore, at that time I will overthrow Satan and Leviathan, the mortal mind of the tribes of Israel, and purify [Adam's widowed spirit], and bring them into submission to Adam's single Mind, so that all of humanity can be in Jehovah's image,

3.11a And, in that day, when it is revealed that Cain turned away from Jehovah to act out the Serpent's lusts, they shall be disgraced, but I shall cause Leviathan to depart from them,

3.13a And the Spirit of Elijah shall subdue Satan, that wicked one, and subject her to his authority,

3.12 And after that, when only powerless, but compliant, Cain remains, she shall seek protection [from the Spirit of Elijah],

3.10a My bloodless sacrifice, and he shall purify [Elohim's Sons],

3.13b And the Spirit of Elijah shall mature Cain and Abel, and Cain shall respect Abel;

3.10b And Adam shall be born [again] in their generation because [Elijah's] righteous spiritual power is stronger than the witchcraft [that cast down] Ham,

3.13c And the Adam shall free his ox, and govern her, and [the Spirit of Elijah] shall marry her, and [fully satisfy her], and she will be adulterous no more,

3.11b And [this is how] my nation, Israel, shall be exalted again because of Elijah,

3.14a [Therefore] let Israel shout victoriously over [Satan], his enemy, and let Jehovah's Living Beast rejoice, and let [the fiery serpent] rejoice also,

3.16 Because, in that day, it shall be said to the Wild Animal, Don't be afraid, and to Adam, Don't stop [waging war against Satan and Leviathan],

3.17 Because Elijah, who is Jehovah in the midst of you, shall save his beloved Wild Animal by engraving Jehovah's nature upon her, and Adam shall rise [from the dead] with a joyful shout, and they [Elohim's Sons] shall leap over [the wall][220] by the Spirit of Elijah,

3.15(a) And Adam's widowed spirit won't be subjected to Leviathan anymore, neither shall they experience Satan's emotions, or sickness or disease in their bodies anymore, [which are the fruit of her] wicked deeds, because Jehovah has caused Satan to depart from them, and brought Cain to repentance,

3.14b And completed Abel.

3.19a Surely [then], at the appointed time I shall strengthen my wife, who has been leaning on her earthen side since she was seduced and marked with the Serpent's nature, and

---

220 The hedge that separates the left and right side of the heart center.

draw her back into the Kingdom of Heaven by nailing [crucifying] her [human spirit] to Elijah,

3.18a And Adam shall rise from the dead within her carnal mind,

3.19b Which is holding my wife captive, and I shall gather her together with Elijah, and they shall enter into the Kingdom of Heaven [rebirth];

3.18b And Elijah shall go beyond this abominable age, which the Serpent formed, and Satan is ruling over, and he shall offer Leviathan as a sacrifice to Jehovah, and mark the Wild Animal with Jehovah's nature, and this is how I shall cause my wife's many members to stand up [be born again] in[to] the visible, spiritual world.

3.20b And at the time that your visible appearance reveals that I have joined you to Elijah, and made you alive again, the whole human race shall have my sinless nature.

3.20a And at the specific time that I purify my wife through judgment, I shall marry her.

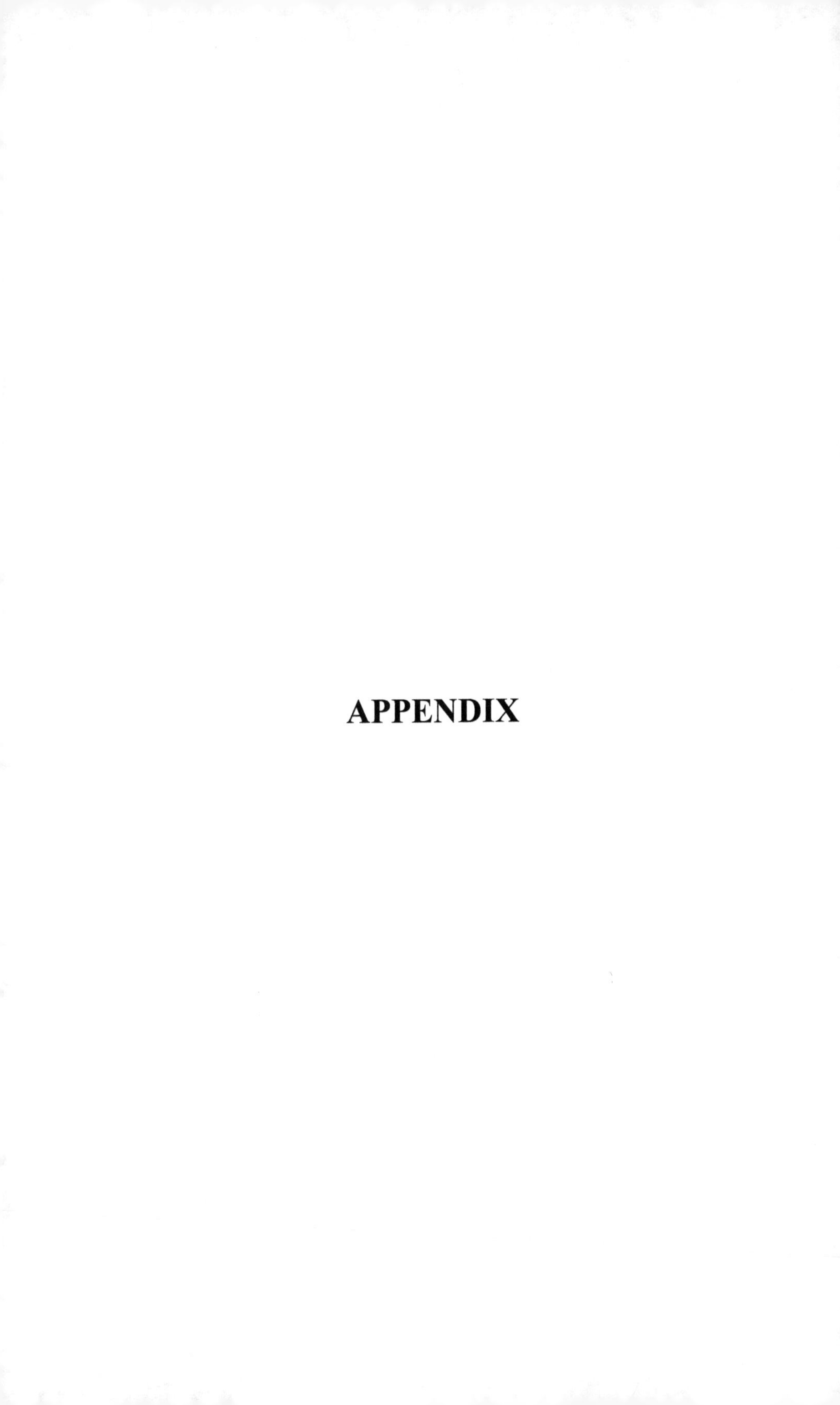

APPENDIX

AMOS

Footnote #2 Con't

The Spirit of Elijah joins with Abel, Adam's root system within a mortal man, to raise Adam from the dead (Zeph 3:08a [AT].)

The image of the eagle that guards the whole visible spiritual world, signifies the Spirit of Elijah joined to the resurrected Adam. Together, they are the powerful warrior Spirit (Dan 8:13 [AT]) that is strong enough to force Satan and Leviathan (Rom 8:20-21 [AT]; Col 1:27), the [primordial] Serpent's mind within mortal man, to release Abel (2 Tim 2:6; Heb 2:15), the creature's only source of consciousness.

In the New Testament, the Spirit of Elijah (Mal 4:6) raised Adam from the dead in the man, Jesus, and liberated the whole spiritual man from his physical body.

Jesus, who was Christ (Jn 1:1) in the days of his flesh, the anointed of God, ascended into the spiritual world of the brow center. He is appearing in the visible, physical world today, by the Holy Spirit (Joel 2:28-29 [AT]), and as the second generation of Christ in the individual believer.

Jesus of Nazareth, who became Christ, was born of the mortal seeds of Joseph and Mary. (See, LEM Message #591, ***The Virgin Birth***.) Then the spiritual man, Adam, rose from the dead (1 Cor 15:4, Jn 5:25) in Jesus of Nazareth, and was, eventually, rejoined to Jehovah above (Rev 12:7).

In the New Testament, the resurrected Adam is called "Christ" (Acts 2:30), and the fortified Adam (Rev 19:13) is called Righteous Adam.

Today, the Holy Spirit of the glorified Jesus, the Fortified (Last) Adam (1 Cor 15:45), who abides in the brow [6th] center, is raising

Adam from the dead in the many members of mortal humanity (Jn 5:25; Matt 19:30), by penetrating their dead human spirits (Jude 3).

Footnote #3 Con't

The incarnating spirit marries the bestial background [threads] of the creation by weaving himself through them. Such a marriage produces a mind and a house, or a body, which are the image of the incarnating (male) spirit.

The Spirit of Elijah (the Spirit of Christ) produces an immortal Living Beast, whose mind is Jehovah's Son, i.e., Spirit of Christ (unconscious), Christ (subconscious), and Abel (conscious), and the Serpent produces a dead, mortal, Wild Animal, whose mind is the Serpent's daughter, i.e., Satan (unconscious), Leviathan (subconscious) and Cain (conscious).

Each mortal man is a part of the many-membered Wild Animal, who is married to their fallen, mortal mind [the Serpent's illegitimate offspring].

Jehovah considers such a marriage (1) adulterous for everyone who has a relationship with Himself, that is, Judah and Israel in the Old Testament, and the Church in the New Testament, and (2) a common law marriage* for those who do not have a relationship with Him.

> *A man and a woman who live together for seven years, or more, without a formal marriage ceremony, are considered married by common law, that is, they have lived as husband and wife for so many years, that the State considers them married.

Footnote #6 Con't

The Spirit of Elijah is awakening Abel, Adam's dead root system, within mortal man, to raise Adam from the dead and restore his priesthood (Gen 4:4[AT]). Abel matures into the resurrected Adam, who covers the fallen, mortal mind of the individual (his old identity).

Then, the Spirit of Elijah, who is above, joins to Adam resurrected in the individual, to crucify (Gal 6:14) mortal man's Fallen Mind, and destroy it.

The resurrected Adam becomes the spiritual king (Gen 1:26), the new mind that reigns over the mortals who mature into everlasting life. But the mortals that Leviathan reigns over, as King (Jer 44:18; Rev 18:7), cease to exist (see, Amos 5:20b).

Footnote #9 Con't

The Interlinear Text of Gen 2:21 says that Jehovah put ***Adam*** (Strong's #121) into a deep sleep, which means that ***Adam*** descended, and was joined to, the level of consciousness called ***Adamah*** (Strong's #127), the spiritual ***ground***.

Adam was joined to the spiritual ground in the wrong moral order when he agreed with the thoughts of the Serpent (2 Pet 2:4, Jude 6).The spiritual ground is the spiritual earthen personalities of creation saturated in the waters of creation. Mortal man is the fallen creature, or the Beast (Rev 17:3), that is formed from the union of the Serpent and the spiritual ground. Fallen Adam is the Carnal Mind of mortal man.

Adam, the Son of God, is Jehovah's reflection on the surface of the waters above the firmament, and ***Adamah*** is the Serpent of the Earth, Elohim's dark shadow, carved in the muddy ocean bed underneath the firmament.

Footnote #12 Con't

The background threads of the creation can be likened to the cloth background of a tapestry. The [primordial] Serpent wove the image of Leviathan, the sea serpent, her own spiritual sexual male organ, over Adam, the mosaic that Jehovah wove into the background threads of the creation, and the Living Beast became a spiritually female, Wild Animal.

The [primordial] Serpent could not unravel the image of Adam that was woven into the tapestry of creation, so she wove an image of Leviathan, her own spiritual sexual male organ, over the image of Adam, and in this Truth lies our hope that Jehovah will send a deliverer strong enough to unravel the Serpent's image, which will reveal Jehovah's strength in the creation (Rom 8:20).

Footnote #18 Con't

Elohim, Adam's living mind, married the ox that he formed out of the ground, and the creature became a Living Beast. The Serpent is the name for the primordial waters underneath the firmament, and the ground is the name for the earthen ocean bed at the bottom of the primordial sea.

Adam, through his marriage to the ox, was, then, joined to the Serpent's dense side, and the whole creature (Adam and the ox) was alive because of Elohim, Adam's living mind.

Adam's relationship to the primordial ox can be likened to a man sitting in full control of his horse, and Adam's loss of his immortality, to that of an unseated rider whose horse has trampled him to death.

Footnote #19 Con't

Elijah shall weave His Spirit through the widowed spirit of Satan, the background threads of the creature, and the sun of the fallen creature will set and never rise again. (See, also, Note #12.)

Leviathan is called a ***sea serpent***, because she is a spiritual serpent that exists in fallen Adam's blood stream.

Leviathan is called the ***sun of the fallen creature***, because she is the mediator of the ***other side,*** through which energy flows between mankind and the Serpent.

Energy flows from Elijah to mankind, but on the ***other side***, energy flows from fallen Adam to the Serpent, because fallen Adam is the Serpent's meat (Is 65:25).

DANIEL

Footnote #50 Con't

Adam died to his spiritual manhood and Jehovah's breath incarnated as Satan, the unconscious part of the mind of the Wild Animal, Adam's ox incarnated as Cain, a mortal Woman (Gen 2:25 [AT]), the Snake increased into Leviathan, and the whole Wild Animal was engraved with the Snake's nature (Lk 3:7).

Adam's ox was engraved with the evil nature of the Snake (Jas 1:15), and Elohim's spirit that gave the Snake consciousness, became the human spirit.

Righteous Adam is the only one who can impart life to the Wild Animal, but Abel, Adam's root system, must rise first and reclaim his priesthood (Col 1:16-17).

Footnote #51 Con't

The bones that form the skeleton of the material body are the structure upon which the flesh hangs, and the bones of the skeleton hang on the spiritual flesh of Adam's personal souls (personalities), the spiritual bones of the Living Beast.

Adam's bones are the personal souls (personalities) that are extensions of his many soul-parts. The personal soul (personality) is the offspring of Jehovah's breath, the reproductive part of the soul and Elohim. When Jehovah's breath twisted together with the Snake, all the souls that were "fathered" by Elohim ceased to exist, and the Woman brought forth personal soul (personalities) attached to a material body, that are in the Snake's image. Neither the soul-parts of Adam, nor the soul-parts of the Snake, can incarnate in the visible world without personal souls (personalities).

Footnote #53 Con't

Elijah is the spiritual Warrior that raises Adam from the dead.

Adam exists on multiple levels. One of his models fell, but a righteous model of Adam continued to exist. That righteous Adam is called *The Second Adam, the Lord from Heaven* (1 Cor 15:47) in the New Testament.

Gabriel is one of the names that identifies righteous Adam when he is not clothed with a human personality. Righteous Adam is a many-membered spiritual mam whose individual members are indistinguishable from each other, so one of his soul-parts married the personal soul (personality) of Elijah () and began to be called by his name.

Elijah, one of Adam's married soul-parts, had to fight Satan, the unconscious part of Daniel's mind, before he could crucify Daniel's human spirit, raise Adam from the dead within Daniel and speak to Daniel from within his own mind. The spiritual principles that govern Righteous Adam's entrance into the spiritual universe of a human being, require him to be already clothed with a human personality, so Adam's soul part that was married to Elijah entered in.

In the New Testament, the Spirit of Elijah crucified the man, Jesus' human spirit and raised Adam from the dead. Jesus' mortal personality, Jesus of Nazareth, was swallowed up by the Second Adam's soul-part (Matt12:48-50) that was already married to Elijah, and been called *Jesus* ever since.. The glorified Jesus Christ is appearing in this visible, physical world today as Christ.

Footnote #58 Con't

Adam is the ***positive/dominant*** spiritual law called "the Tree of Life." "The Snake" is the ***negative/dominant*** spiritual law called "the Tree of the Knowledge of Good and Evil." Adam's female side twisted together with the Snake who made him the ***negative/negative/dominant*** spiritual law that was able to overthrow Adam.

But the ***negative/negative/dominant*** Law, the Snake (which is a part of the creation), who is strong enough to kill Adam, the ***positive/dominant*** Law, is not strong enough to kill the ***double positive*** law, the Second Adam, (positive) + Elohim (positive) ***[positive/positive/dominant].***

Footnote #64 Con't

The significance of the number ***1,335*** is: 5 - spiritual ministry to the individual which results in 30 - the fulfillment of the Law of Sin and Death when the fiery serpent is forced to submit to 300 - the restored three-part altar [Jehovah, Elijah, Adam] (Gen. 6:15b, 16b, 16c & 15c [AT]), and ***1,000*** - Adam is raised from the dead (Rom. 8:11) in the individual human spirit.

Footnote #65 Con't

Adam, Elohim's mind (1 Cor 15:45), rises again in the last day, but not the personality. See, Message #202, ***Time For Resurrection***. See, also, Matt 11:14; Lk 1:17; 1 Jn 2:15-19 [AT].

DEUTERONOMY

Footnote #66 Con't

Israel's agreement with his fallen, mortal mind brought all this evil upon himself.

Satan mediates the sowing and reaping judgment. Adam is the mediator of Jehovah's righteous judgment, which teaches about the sin nature and gives the personality an opportunity to repent before the reaping and sowing judgment ripens into judgment.

Jehovah's merciful ***way of escape*** (1 Cor 10:13) from Satan, is to raise Adam from the dead in the individual human spirit. Righteous Judgment swallows up the sowing and reaping judgment, when Adam, the mediator, is revived, and the personality [the Woman] confesses that all of her painful experiences are arising out of her own sin nature.

Footnote #69 Con't

Waging war against the fiery serpent in one's own mind, as well and in other men's minds* raises Adam from the dead as one's own renewed mind which is in Jehovah's image (1 Cor 15:3-4). This happened first in Jesus of Nazareth (Rev 1:5). (See, Message #186, ***The Christ***, Part 8 & Part 9.)

*See, first footnote to 1 Jn 2:12-14, Alternate Translation of the New Testament, where these believers are called disciples.

Footnote #70 Con't

Michael, the archangel (see, Jude 1:19) pierced Abel, Adam's root system within Moses, and raised Adam from the dead, but Moses, the personality, had to choose Adam, his righteous mind, over the Leviathan, his unrighteous, Carnal Mind.

The personality joined to the Satan and Leviathan, is the ***Devil***, and the personality joined to the resurrected Adam, is Christ Jesus.

Jude 1:9 in the New Testament, depicts Michael, who is above the firmament, assisting Adam who is resurrected in Moses, to win Moses' fallen personality.

Yet, when Michael, the archangel, was identifying Moses' fallen, mortal mind, and teaching Moses that [the personality who agrees with Satan and Leviathan is] the Devil, Leviathan dared to bring forth her evil opinion, [and Moses] said, [it's] not true [that I'm the Devil], I honor you [Michael, and] Adam, [the Lord].

(See, also, Note #**30**), and (See, also, Message #4, ***Out of the Dust***, Message #313, ***The Serpent, the Dragon, the Devil & You***, and Message #340, ***Leviathan***.)

Adam died when sin was revealed in him, but he can be temporarily resurrected as mortal man's righteous mind, when the Spirit of Elijah [the glorified Jesus in the New Testament] crucifies the human spirit.

EZEKIEL

Footnote #77 Con't

There are seven major centers in the etheric part of the physical body. The three lower centers belong to the Serpent's kingdom, and the three higher centers belong to Adam's kingdom. The heart, which is the fourth center, is the land that the two kingdoms are fighting over.

At the present time, the fiery serpent is illegally occupying the heart of fallen, mortal man.

Footnote #78 Con't

The Spirit of Elijah penetrates the right side of mortal man's heart, joins with his human spirit, and resurrects Abel. The mortal Abel increases to the immortal Adam when he pierces into the left side of the heart.

Adam in the left side of the heart, stretches upward towards Elijah, who is in the throat. Adam is energized, or fortified, as soon as he touches Elijah, and immediately rushes back into the right side of the heart to save his emotional animal [personality] from Satan's grip.

The Fortified Adam joined to his preserved personality, appears as a great, fiery eagle that orbits the visible world.

Footnote #79 Con't

The Serpent is the name of the primordial waters that flowed upward into the high window of the creation, to capture Adam's ox [emotional animal], and steal Elohim's breath. The primary concentration of Elohim's breath [spirit] is in Adam, who has Elohim's nature, and is the mind of the ox.

The Fortified Adam is Elohim's reflection on the waters of the upper window, which have a rare density of earth. Adam's ox is formed from the muddy ocean bed of the lower window, which has a high density of earth. Michael joined Adam, Elohim's mind, to the primordial ox, and the man [Adam] and his ox, became ***the living creature***, or the ***living beast*** of Genesis.

The primordial Serpent is appearing today as ***Satan*** (Rev 12:9, 20:2), the collective unconscious part of the Carnal Mind and the emotional body of mortal humanity, and the emotional body of the individual mortal man. Satan is ***widowed*** because she is separated from Michael, the sperm of Jehovah's seminal fluid. The bisecting of the widowed waters, separates Satan (in the root center), from Leviathan, the sea serpent.

Footnote #82 Con't

The Fortified Adam is the collective subconscious part of the Carnal Mind of restored humanity, and the resurrected Adam.

The Fortified Adam, is a spiritual city, which is formed from the unified spiritual centers in many restored men, whose surging waves of energy (Ps 42:7) form a collective beam, or ray, of light [Michael's restored river of light (Gen 2:10)]. The Fortified

Adam's City extends from the crown center downward to, and including the whole heart center in an individual.

Leviathan, the sea serpent, is the collective subconscious mind of the primordial Serpent, and the fiery serpent is the subconscious mind of the fallen individual. Leviathan is the spiritual city that extends from the fiery serpent in the root center, upward to, and including the right side of the heart center in an individual. The fiery serpent [root center] accesses the heart center by consuming Adam's ox, which she holds captive in the center through lust (2 Pet 1:4).

Leviathan, the sea serpent's, spiritual city is an assemblage of many still pools [stagnant centers], which extend far downward below the surface of the earth [conscious mind], into the Jordan, Satan's collective river of death.

The river Styx, is one of five rivers in the underworld, according to Greek mythology, but the Scripture says that there is only one river in the underworld, Jordan -- and that in the center where Leviathan, the primordial Serpent's upper tooth, is -- which, indeed, those who died in Noah's day, crossed over, as they descended into the mouth of the fiery serpent, the primordial Serpent's lower tooth, in the enter (Job 40:23 [AT].

Footnote #83 Con't

The primordial Serpent is the unformed consciousness that existed as the unclean waters [spiritual urine] in the ground floor window of creation.

The Serpent formed herself into a fish body from the mud of the ocean bottom, pierced through Adam's hedge into the upper room of the creation, captured Adam's ox, killed Adam, married Adam's widowed spirit, and became the mind of the Wild Animal which is presently inhabiting the earth.

The household of the earth is the race of Cain, the earthen offspring of this incestuous marriage.

Footnote #86 Con't

The King James translators translated Strong's #7198, ***[rain]bow***, because they couldn't make any sense out of the true meaning of the word, which is, ***a man who wields the bow, an archer***.

The sign of Elohim's covenant with Noah, his sons, and the emotional animal of the earth [the ox that Adam formed before time began (Gen 9:13)], is the judgment which restores the fallen creation to immortality.

The subsequent paragraphs of the Book of Ezekiel detail Jehovah's merciful judgment, which is, unfortunately, perceived as vengeful judgment, in the King James translation.

Footnote #91 Con't

Adam, the reflection of Jehovah's nature, is revealed through the mind of mankind. ***Adam*** is female in relation to ***Ze'ir Anpin,*** the Son of Understanding, the Supernal Mother of the God World of Atzilut. ***Ze'ir Anpin is the Son of God***, and Adam is Ze'ir Anpin's created consort. ***The whole Adam***, the Son of God joined to Adam, is the only mediator between mankind and God. (See, 1 Tim 2:5.)

Footnote #124 Con't

According to Einstein's ***Theory of Relativity***, an object does not exist unless it is observed, and according to quantum mechanics, an object has no reality in this world, the macroscopic world, unless it can be measured.

For this reason, ***Adam Kadmon*** **is often seen to represent the archetypal soul of *Mashiach*,** the general *yechida* of all the souls of Israel, the ultimate "crown" of all of God's Creation, the Divine "intermediate" which reveals primordial Infinity to finite created reality.

Footnote #125 Con't

Verses 1-6 speak to the manifestation of Messiah. The following verses, 7 – 12, speak to Messiah's ministry to the sons of God.

Elijah's recognition of Abel raised him from the sleep of death, and Elijah's measurement, or judgment, of Abel, brought Abel up to the standard necessary for him to produce the spiritual male offspring called ***the lower Adam***. ***Measurement***, ***which is judgment***, produces growth because the wisdom, creative strength and expectation of the one who is measuring, molds the one who is measured into the desired dimensions.

Footnote #127 Con't

The five Rings of the manchild generated by Christ which are designed to be joined to the three Rings of the Female of the world above that descend into the lower world and blend together to form Justice, the New Man, which is the throne of God.

The whole Adam is ***the temple of God***, and the Adam below is ***the gate of the temple***. The individual sons of God are ***the rooms of the temple.***

Abel is the ***outer court of the temple***. He is also ***the door to the Mind of God*** for the sons of God who are ***the individual rooms of the temple***, which is the whole Adam.

Footnote #129 Con't

The Ancient of Days (Atik Yomin) is the long face, the personality of God that waits patiently for fallen Adam to be born again within humanity and return to a righteous relationship with him.

Arikh Anpin is the short face, the impatient personality of the Son of God, who becomes angry more easily.

The upper half of the Sephirah is called ***Atik Yomin*** (the Ancient of Days), and the lower half is called ***Arikh Anpin***.

Atik Yomin contains the DNA of the higher world, and is also the Crown of the lower world. The remaining nine Rings of the lower world all emerge out of the Crown (Arikh Anpin). All of the worlds are linked in this manner, and the divided worlds are being reconnected according to this pattern

Footnote #130 Con't

The words, [***the Abels in***], ***the outer court,*** are an alternate translation which appears in verses 6 and 8, but they are translated from two different Hebrew words. The English word, ***threshold***, in verse 6, is a translation of ***Strong's*** #5592, and the English word, ***porch***, in verse 8, is a translation of ***Strong's*** #167.

Both words can be translated ***vestibule***, and, thus, the extension of that word, ***reception***, ***reception area***, or ***receptionist***, which is how we have used it. Abel is the reception area that one must pass through, or experience, in order to produce the five Rings of the male.

The Scripture uses two different words to express the same spiritual principle, because, in the first instance, it refers to the ascension of Abel from the world below, and, in the second instance, it refers to the descent of Abel from the world above.

Abel, the outer court of Female from the world above, becomes the Crown, Wisdom and Understanding of the world below, when it pierces the threshold of the two worlds. The two Abels, one from the world above, and the other from the world below, are separated by Righteous Adam, the spiritual man who comes into existence when the spiritual essence of the two worlds blend into one unified substance.

Footnote #134 Con't

Dikna
The Beard

The Dikna or "beard" of Arikh Anpin possesses thirteen parts or individual "levels of rectification" (Tikunai Dikna), which corresponds to the thirteen principles of Divine mercy, as mentioned above.

Every ***hair*** of the ***beard*** represents an individual power of tzimtzum to contract the infinite light inherent within Arikh Anpin in order that it become manifest and ***viable*** to the subsequent partzufim of the world of Atzilut (beginning with the partzufim of Abba and Imma I'la'ah, to be explained), to bestow upon them God's infinite mercy.

The seventh part (tikkun, ***rectification***) of the Dikna (its ***middle*** or ***center*** 7 is the middle-point of 13), corresponding to the Divine principle of "truth" (v'emet), are the ***heeks*** of ***face*** of Arikh Anpin, which are not covered by ***hair***. Here the light of the countenance of Arikh Anpin shines without tzimtzum. The light of the countenance is referred to as the ***370 lights***, of which is said: ***In the light of the face of the King is life.***

The eighth and thirteenth parts of the Dikna are referred to respectively as the higher mazal (source of Divine influx) and lower mazal. The higher mazal is the source of Divine life-force which flows from Arikh Anpin to Abba Ila'ah; the lower mazal is the source of Divine life-force which flows from Arikh Anpin to Imma Ila'ah, as will be explained.

Thus, in general, the secret of the Dikna is the bridge between the yet infinite state of the lights of Arikh Anpin and the relatively finite state of the light and vessels of the subsequent partzufim of the world of Atzilut. In the soul of man, this is the bridge between the superconsciousness and the consciousness of the soul.

GENESIS

Footnote #136 Con't

Elohim is Jehovah's sperm, Jehovah and Elohim are the ***life***, and ***light*** is the product of the interaction between Jehovah's Spirit and Elohim's waters (see, Quantum Mechanics In Creation, Message #384). The light is diffracted through the waters of the creation [seminal fluid], and Adam is the mind that is formed in Jehovah's image, which is growing out of the Earth.

Footnote #137 Con't

The difference between the imputed and imparted anointing is the restored firmament. The imputed anointing does not restore the firmament, so when Elohim's light wave recedes, there is nothing to hold the resurrected Abel above the Earth; so Abel falls down into the Earth again, and Cain captures Elohim's breath of life, absorbs his energy, and becomes the Serpent again; and Abel dies.

The rise and fall of Elohim's light wave, is the process by which Elohim is cycling through the waters of life, touching the earth, and casting His reflection upon the surface of the waters (Ez 1:13-14 [AT]).

The imparted anointing, which is Elijah, permanently re-establishes the firmament. (See, Message #384, ***Quantum Mechanics In Creation.***

Footnote #138 Con't

The Tree of Life and The Tree of the Knowledge of Good and Evil are Jehovah's spiritual seminal fluid.

The Tree of Life is Elohim, Jehovah's sperm, dispersed throughout the waters of the abyss.

The Tree of the Knowledge of Good and Evil is the waters of the abyss [without the sperm].

The waters of the abyss are good because, as in human seminal fluid, they contain all of the proteins and other elements necessary for consciousness, but righteous character is found only in Elohim, Jehovah's sperm.

The waters of the abyss are evil because, when densified with the Earth, they have the potential to capture Elohim's breath of life and become the Serpent.

The Tree of Life [the spermatozoa] is in the midst of The Tree of the Knowledge of Good and Evil [the water medium that carries the spermatozoa].

Footnote #141 Con't

Adam's job was to keep the firmament that separated the Earth from the Seas sealed, except for Elohim's light stream which was causing the image of the visible, spiritual world to appear on a regular cycle (Ez 1:14 [AT]), by passing through the firmament [Adam's foundation] to implement the photoelectric effect. (See, Message #385, Part 5, ***Quantum Mechanics In Creation***.)

But Adam thought that the water pressure from the Seas was Elohim's [gas] light stream (Gen 1:3), and let the Seas pass through the firmament. The Seas didn't pass by the Earth and turn upward towards the surface like Elohim's light stream, though. They crashed through the firmament and broke it up, and the Seas covered the Earth.

Footnote #146 Con't

The mind is a spiritual sword, and the primordial Serpent's known witchcraft identifies her as ***the magical sword***.

Adam, Elohim's immortal mind died, and the primordial Serpent bisected the Living Beast into the mortal Cain and Abel.

Jehovah appointed Abel priest over Cain, but Cain killed Abel in an attempt to usurp the priesthood.

Adam did not cease to exist, but died to his immortality, and his widowed spirit, the only source of consciousness in humanity, waits to be resurrected.

Footnote #147 Con't

Verse 1 says that female descendants WERE BORN IN Adam, but verse 2 says that Elohim's sons ***appeared*** as female descendants.

Adam was a superior being who was both male and female (Gen 1:27; Gen 5:2). His offspring were born in him as fully mature beings before they appeared in the visible world.

JOB

Footnote #162 Con't

Job was concerned with overcoming his sin nature and returning to God, so we see that the Lord's reason for sending Satan to reveal Job's sin, was to bring Job to repentance and regeneration. But Job mistakenly thought that keeping the ceremonial law, rather than being spiritual, i.e., living out of the Shekinah (Christ), would expiate his sin, so Job sacrificed the Shekinah within himself, and kept the Law.

JONAH

Footnote #171 Con't

Satan, the primordial Serpent, appearing as humanity's collective unconscious mind, and the individual emotional body.

Leviathan, the sea serpent [the Dragon in the New Testament], the primordial Serpent, appearing as humanity's collective subconscious mind, who lusts to be joined to the fiery serpent in the individual.

The Fiery Serpent, the primordial Serpent's subconscious mind in the individual. The fiery serpent is a tentacle of Leviathan, mortal man's collective subconscious mind.

Ashtoreth [the Devil in the New Testament (Jude 1:9[AT])], the image engraved in the right side of the heart center of the individual whose human spirit and personality are fused with all of the above. (See, also, Message #434, ***Circumcision of the Heart***.)

Footnote #172 Con't

Elohim, Jehovah's spiritual seminal fluid, is the waters above the firmament, and the primordial Serpent, the spiritual urine, is the waters underneath the firmament. Urine introduced into seminal fluid kills the sperm.

Satan dishonored Elohim by pouring her spiritual urine into Elohim's clean waters on the left side of Jonah's heart center, which killed Adam and drew Jonah's human spirit back to Ashtoreth, the image of the primordial Serpent in the right side of Jonah's heart center [see, Vs. 2.03a]. (See, also, Message #434, ***Circumcision of the Heart***.)

Footnote #173 Con't

Mind, man's consciousness, is spirit, but his personality, the emotional animal that he is attached to, is of the earth, and these two are joined as one man.

Consciousness, which is mind, pierces into immortality before the personality, the emotional animal, does. So, one might find their consciousness on the left side of their heart center (which is dominated by the resurrected Adam), and their personality on the right side of their heart center (which is dominated by the Serpent's evil household), during the season that they migrate from the right side to the left side of their heart center.

Satan cannot touch the mind that is abiding on the left side of the heart center, so she attacks the personality by stirring up emotions, passions and lusts, and torments the physical body with illness and physical pain, in the hope of dragging his consciousness, which is his mind, back to the right side of the heart center.

Footnote #174 Con't

Elohim, the waters above the firmament, and the primordial Serpent, the sea underneath the firmament are the divided waters [Gen 1:6]. Elohim commanded the waters above and underneath the firmament to be gathered together [Gen 1:9], because the dry seed remaining underneath is barren, and cannot incarnate the Serpent's negative world.

The phrase, ***the seas that flowed together changed direction***, means that the Seas which were above the firmament in the man, Jonah, pierced through his personal firmament, and Satan revived in him [Rom7:9]. (See, also, Message #434, ***Circumcision of the Heart***.)

Footnote #175 Con't

The wall that separates the left and the right side of the heart center in the etheric part of the physical body, is the firmament, or hedge, or maidenhead, of that man.

The man with a broken maidenhead, descends out of the immortal life which is on the left side of the heart center, and above it, to the mortal, emotional/animal, existence which is on the right side of the heart center, and underneath it. (See, also, Message #434, ***Circumcision of the Heart***.)

Footnote #192 Con't

A *gourd* is ***a quick growing, but easily damaged plant***, which describes Abel, Elohim's mortal mind.

Adam and Abel can die, but King Adam, who is Adam joined to the Spirit of Elijah, can never die.

In the New Testament Adam resurrected in the individual is called Christ, and Christ joined to the Spirit of Christ is called ***the regenerated Adam***, who can never die.

Footnote #195 Con't

The word ***eagle*** is rendered from Strong's #7349, translated ***merciful*** in the the King James translation, which is derived from the root of Strong's #7355. Strong's #7360, a noun with the same letters as Strong's #7355, means a small white vulture with black wings, which is known to be affectionate to its young. A second witness to this derivation is that the word following ***merciful*** in the Interlinear text, Strong's #750, translated ***slow*** in the King James translation, can also be translated long wings.

Jehovah's answer to Jonah's plight is to raise Adam from the dead and fortify him through union with the Spirit of Elijah. The eagle is the image of King Adam, Elohim's fortified, immortal mind.

2nd KINGS

Footnote #198 Con't

The individual whose immortality is based upon his personality being fused to the three-part mind of Elohim's ***New Man***, is a ***Magnificent Man***. The Spirit of Elijah [the Spirit of Christ in the New Testament] is the ***COLLECTIVE unconscious*** mind of Elohim's ***New Man***, the resurrected Adam is the ***subconscious mind of the INDIVIDUAL*** member of Elohim's many-membered ***New Man***, and Elijah and the resurrected Adam, together, are the ***COLLECTIVE subconscious mind*** of Elohim's many-membered ***New Man***.

The conscious mind of mortal man is singular [Cain], where Abel is dead, and double [Cain and Abel], where Abel is resurrected (Jas 1:8; 4:8).

Footnote #199 Con't

Elijah didn't ascend as a singularity, that is, as a spirit without a personality, nor did he incarnate again as a mortal man (see, verse 16). Elijah ***brought his personality with him*** into the spiritual world above, and become a Magnificent Man who could be present in heaven and earth at the same time.

Some translations of the Scripture indicate that the Spirit of Elijah was present in John the Baptist, but this misunderstanding is due to the incorrect translation of the Greek text. Jesus was talking about Himself when he said, ***And if ye will receive it, this is Elias, which was for to come*** (Matt 11:14 KJV).

Elijah is more than an early example of Jesus, the Christ. The Spirit that hovered over Mary -- the Spirit that is Holy enough to bring forth a God man, and enough like Adam to bring forth a human child -- is Elohim's Spirit, joined to Elijah's personality, through the mediatorship of Michael and the resurrected Adam, who are the splendid, immortal mind of Elohim's ***New Man.***

It is this truth that Matthew is demonstrating is his account of Jesus' transfiguration, ***And, behold, there appeared unto them Moses and Elias talking with him [Jesus]*** (Matt 17:2-3, KJV).

PSALMS

Footnote #204 Con't

The Hebrew word translated ***glory***, Strong's #1984, the same Hebrew word translated ***praise*** in verse 45, signifies Adam, humanity's spiritual, righteous inner man, who is the invisible expression of Jehovah's creative thought.

The Hebrew word that is more often translated ***glory***, Strong's #3519, means ***weight***, that is, the visible manifestation, or dense expression, of Jehovah's thought.

The phrase, ***the praise of His glory***, then, is speaking about Adam, Jehovah's invisible creative thought (praise), joined to a man, whose mind and personality are the visible expression (glory) of that creative thought. Jehovah's complete, creative thought, appearing by its manifested, dense form, is the definition of ***Messiah***.

The Greek word ***logos*** expresses this same idea. The mind (praise) and personality (glory) of Jesus of Nazareth, accurately expresses the Father's nature (Jn 5:37).

Footnote #210 Con't

The solitude which shuts out the sounds of this world equips us to hear the sounds and communications of the ***inner world*** of Elohim's spiritual city.

Many today believe that the spiritual concept of ***the silence***, means passive, or silent listening, but this deception opens one up to Satan's domination and mind control, and spiritual oppression by the evil forces that dwell in the astral (emotional) plane.

Jehovah (Righteous Adam in the New Testament) speaks to us when the visible physical world is silent, not through the silencing of the inner world which we access through our mind.

FACTS ABOUT THE ALTERNATE TRANSLATION BIBLE

A Brief History Of The Alternate Translation Bible

The Lord gave Pastor Vitale the ability to understand and clarify the Scripture in a unique way which ultimately materialized as *The Alternate Translation Bible*.

Pastor Vitale began rendering *Alternate Translations* of the Scripture as early as Living Epistles Ministries (LEM) Message #18, but she did not realize at the time how unique they were. It was not until a Nigerian man asked her where he could purchase a copy of the *Alternate Translations* that she realized their significance.

Pastor Vitale returned to the USA after that, and it was there in New York that the Lord asked her to gather together all of the *Alternate Translations* that she had rendered since 1988 and put them into a book. She had no idea, at the time, that *The Alternate Translation Bible* (ATB) would, eventually, be published and sought after by many serious students of the Scripture, and the thought of pouring through two years of message notes, extracting the Alternate Translations and entering the hand-written and typewritten *Alternate Translations* into a computer program, was overwhelming.

After that beginning, Pastor Vitale diligently incorporated every *Alternate Translation* that she rendered into one of the two files that comprised *The Alternate Translation Bible* on her computer, either *The Alternate Translation of the Old Testament*, or *The Alternate Translation of the New Testament*. Today, *The Alternate Translation Bible* is printed in three volumes, *The Alternate Translation of The Old Testament*, *The Alternate Translation of the New Testament*, and *The Alternate Translation of Book of Revelation.* All three volumes may be purchased, individually, at Amazon.com.

In addition, *The Alternate Translation of The Book of Revelation* has been translated into Spanish, which may also be purchased at Amazon.com.

What is he Alternate Translation Bible?

Lexicon, the Greek word for dictionary, is used to describe most Hebrew/English and Greek/English dictionaries which have been compiled for the specific purpose of studying the Scriptures. Hebrew/English and Greek/English dictionaries offer many definitions for each word listed, just like English language dictionaries do.

The Alternate Translation Bible is an *original translation of the Hebrew and Greek Scripture* in which the translator has exercised *Translator's License* in selecting different definitions than other translators typically chose for many Hebrew and Greek words.

Translator's License means that the translator chooses the English translation for a Hebrew or Greek word each time it appears. *A usage search* for many Hebrew and Greek words reveals that the translators of the *King James Bible* frequently selected a variety of English translations *for the same Hebrew or Greek word.*

The Alternate Translation Bible is an *Amplified Translation of the Hebrew and Greek Scripture*. The Scripture, especially prophecy, frequently omits one or more steps which lead up to the event spoken about. *Amplification* is the term that indicates the inclusion of implied spiritual principles.

Amplification means that more than one English word is used to translate a single Hebrew or Greek word.

Amplification means that the English translation may include words that suggest or imply ideas or accounts of events which are undescribed or unstated in the original language,

Amplification means that ideas and spiritual principles that are suggested but not stated in the Hebrew or Greek text, are added to the English translation.

For example, if you were to read that *Jesus was arrested, crucified and became the Saviour of the world*, Jesus' resurrection and ascension would be implied.

Amplified words are not translations of any specific Hebrew or Greek word. They are English words added by the translator for clarity. The *King James Bible* identifies *amplified words* with italicized print. The *Amplified Bible* (Zondervan Publishers, Grand Rapids, Michigan) identifies *amplified words* with brackets. The *Alternate Translation Bible* identifies unstated ideas, principles or events with brackets, but most amplified words have been incorporated into the text of the translation.

The *Alternate Translation Bible* is a *paraphrased translation* of the Hebrew and Greek Scripture.

Paraphrase means to *restate text or a passage of text in another form*, to clarify meaning, or [to use] *as a studying or teaching device* (Webster's Encyclopedic Unabridged Dictionary of the English Language) (emphasis added).

The *Alternate Translation Bible* is an *original translation of the Hebrew and Greek Scripture* which sounds very different than all the other translations available today.

The *Alternate Translation Bible* reflects the translator's choice of definitions, amplification and paraphraseology which is the fruit of years of deep spiritual communion with Christ Jesus, and long periods of prayer, study and contemplation of the Scripture.

The *Alternate Translation Bible* is a spiritual translation of the Bible. It is not intended to replace traditional translations.

Statement of Faith

The translator believes that:

There is only One God (Deut 6:4, Mk 12:29, Rom 3:30, 1 Cor 8:4,Gal 3:20, Eph 4:6, 1 Tim 2:5, Js 2:19)

Jesus is the only begotten Son of God (Jn 3:16),

The man, Christ Jesus, is the only Mediator between God and man (1 Tim 2:5),

Elijah came (Matt 11:14) in Jesus of Nazareth (Matt 11:14),

Righteous Adam was regenerated in Jesus of Nazareth (Matt 19:28)

Adam is the Son of God (Lk 3:38)

Questions & Answers

1. Does the Alternate Translation Bible replace the King James and other traditional Bible translations?

No. The Alternate Translation Bible does not replace the King James or other traditional Bible translations. The Bible can be understood on three levels:

1. *Literal*: What you see is what you get. Reading and studying the literal translation of the Bible is powerful. It can build faith, result in salvation and bring deliverance from any affliction, spiritual, physical, mental or emotional.

2. *Moral*: Reading and studying the Bible can strengthen a weak moral center, or build character where none exists. The Bible tells us what is right and what is wrong in clear and certain terms.

3. *Hints*: Reading one passage in the Bible can enlighten us, or clarify a question about another passage.

4. *Mysteries*: Deep spiritual principles underlie everything that is written in the Bible.

The Alternate Translation Bible reveals the mysteries, according to the Doctrine of Christ.

2. I used to read the *Alternate New Testament* for free. Can I still read it for free on your new website?

Yes.

http://www.livingepistles.org/index.php/new-testament

3. Is the *Alternate New Testament* for sale? Sheila Vitale was born into a Jewish family and began her spiritual journey as a child when her mother enrolled her as a student in an Orthodox Hebrew school. She also attended synagogue on Shabbat during that time, where she experienced the Spirit of God for the first time. Such a deep longing for God was stirred up in her that she wept. She was touched so profoundly that she became desperate to attend yeshiva (Jewish high school) but her parents could not afford the fees.

She became very ill around the age of 11 and has battled with chronic illness ever since. Her most recent struggle against premature death came in 1990, when she spent three months in the hospital before recovering and going on to resume teaching and managing *LEM.* Her illnesses led her to cry out to God, seeking a deeper understanding of what was happening to her.

Much later, as an adult, after years of searching, she, once again, experienced the Spirit that had brought her to tears, but this time it was in *Gospel Revivals Ministries*, a Pentecostal church where *deliverance ministry* was emphasized. She had desired a deeper understanding of Scripture since her early years, so she began to attend church regularly. Scripture was difficult for her. She struggled with the task, but read at least one Chapter every day even though she did not understand it. After about six months, however, while reading the Bible, she saw a vision of the angel with the little book described in Chapter 10 of the Book of Revelation, verse 8. She began to understand the Bible after that, but several more years had to pass before she began to receive Revelation knowledge of the Scripture.

Sheila Vitale studied the Bible and *deliverance ministry* for about seven years under the teaching of *Charles Holzhauser*, the Pastor of *Gospel Revivals Ministries*, at Mount Sinai, NY. Sometimes she attended as many as five teaching services each week, as well as studying for endless hours to gain key insight into her faith. She also edited *Pastor Holzhauser's* books during that time. After that, she studied independently under the influence and direction of the Holy Spirit, before founding *Living Epistles Ministries*.

Yes. The Alternate New Testament may be purchased through Amazon.com.

https://www.amazon.com/gp/product/069230973X

4. I used to read the *Alternate Old Testament* for free. Can I still read it for free on your new website?

Yes.

http://www.livingepistles.org/index.php/old-testament

5. Is the *Alternate Old Testament* for sale?

Yes. The Alternate Old Testament is available for purchase from Amazon.com.

https://www.amazon.com/gp/product/0692437347

6. I used to read the *Alternate Translation of the Book of Revelation* for free. Can I still read it for free on your new website?

Yes.

http://www.livingepistles.org/index.php/new-testament

7. Is the A*lternate Translation of The Book of Revelation* for sale?

Yes.

https://www.amazon.com/Alternate-Translation-Revelation-Jesus-Christ/dp/0692251863

ABOUT THE AUTHOR

Sheila R. Vitale is the Spiritual Leader, Founding Teacher, and Pastor of *Living Epistles Ministries (LEM)*. She moves in the offices of Teacher of Apostolic Doctrine, Prophet, Evangelist and Pastor, has an international following, and has been expounding on the Scripture through a unique spiritual lens for nearly three decades.

She has written more than 50 books based on the Old and New Testaments including *Ephraim, Man of the Earth and The Eagle Ascended (OT), and Salvation* and *Not Without Blood (NT)*. She has also rendered original spiritual interpretations of Biblical texts such as *The Woman in The Well (John, Chapter 4)* and *First Corinthians, Chapter 11*. Her unique, Multi-Part Message style is seen in *LEM* Serial Messages such as *A Place Teeming With Life* (9 Parts) and *Quantum Mechanics in Creation* (18 Parts). Each Part of a Multi-Part Message Series can also be enjoyed as a complete and independent study. In addition, she has defined, explained, illustrated and demonstrated hundreds of spiritual principles throughout more than 1,000 *LEM* Lectures.

Her signature work, however, is the three volumes of *The Alternate Translation Bible (ATB)*: *The Alternate Translation of The Old Testament, The Alternate Translation of The New Testament and The Alternate Translation of the Book of Revelation. The Alternate Translation Bible* is a work in progress (*The ATB Project*). Accordingly, additional spiritual interpretations of both whole and partial Chapters are added from time to time, as they are rendered. The most up-to-date versions of *The ATB Project* may be found online at *The LEM* W*ebsite* (*LivingEpistles.org*). *The ATB* is a *spiritual interpretation* of the Scripture and is not intended to replace traditional translations.

She also analyzed the Greek text of *The Book of Revelation* and preached extensively on it in the early years of

The ATB Project. During that time she produced 197 distinct *Message Parts*, under 29 specific *Message Titles*, all of which deal with *The Book of Revelation. Also, many* of her books such as, *Adam and The Two Judgments* and *A Study in Unconscious Mind Control*, have been translated into Spanish, as well as *The Book of Revelation.*

Pastor Vitale is an illustrator of spiritual principles, a researcher, a translator and a reviewer of the Modern Social Trends of Family and Culture, as they are revealed through TV programs (*The Sopranos),* movies (*The Matrix* and *The Edge of Tomorrow)* and plays (*Wicked).* She also writes for the *LEM Blog.*

She travels domestically, as well as internationally, preaching and teaching Judeo-Christian Spiritual Philosophy, and has donated Audio Libraries of her Lectures to other ministries in Africa, Asia, Europe and North America,

Pastor Vitale serves *LEM* in a range of spiritual, educational, and administrative functions from *The Selden Centre*, *LEM* headquarters in Selden, New York. She is also a philanthropic individual who supports the *Lighthouse Mission (Patchogue, NY) and HGM – Mission of Hope – Haiti, and other* charitable organizations. She also supports community services such as the *Terryville Fire Department.*

In her spare time, Pastor Vitale enjoys watching movies, attending plays and partaking of cuisines from different cultures. An avid traveler, she has visited several countries in Europe and Africa as well as many cities in the United States.

BEGINNINGS, INSPIRATION AND CALLING

Pastor Vitale began her spiritual journey as a child when her Jewish mother enrolled her in the Hebrew school of an

Orthodox synagogue. She experienced the Spirit of God for the first time there in such a profound way that she wept. But after that, when she was only eleven years old, she became very ill and was taken to Mount Sinai Hospital in New York City. She almost died there and has battled with life-threatening health issues ever since. Nevertheless, a deep longing for God continued to pursue her until several years later when she desperately wanted to attend Yeshiva (Jewish high school), but could not. Her secular parents approved of her choice, but could not afford the tuition.

Much later, after years of searching, she once again experienced the Spirit that had brought her to tears in the synagogue of her youth, but this time it was at *Gospel Revivals Ministries*, a Pentecostal church where Deliverance Ministry was emphasized. She had a desire to understand the Bible since she was a child, but Scripture was difficult for her and she struggled with the text. Nevertheless, she read one Chapter of the Bible every day until, one day, *her spiritual eyes opened* and she saw an angel holding a little book.

After that, she attended as many as five teaching services each week for about seven years, the latter part of which she edited *Pastor Holzhauser's* books. But several more years had to pass before *the eyes of her understanding opened even further* and she began to receive *Revelation Knowledge of the Scripture*. She understood at that time that the angel she had seen was the angel of Revelation 10:8.

After about seven years of learning *Deliverance Ministry* and *The Doctrine of Sonship* (*Bill Britton*) from *Pastor Holzhauser,* she studied the Bible independently under the influence and direction of the Holy Spirit.

In **1988** she began teaching Apostolic Doctrine.

In **1990** she spent three months in Stony Brook Hospital where she recovered from an incurable disease, defeating premature death, once again, and went on to resume teaching and managing *LEM.*

In **1992** she journeyed to Africa for the first time, where she was called to the office of Evangelist.

In the **mid-1990s,** she began to Pastor in addition to being a Teacher of Apostolic Doctrine, a Prophet and an Evangelist, thus, satisfying all five offices of *The Ministry of the Lord Jesus Christ to His Church.*

LIVING EPISTLES MINISTRIES

Pastor Vitale was happy fellowshipping at *Gospel Revivals Ministries* but, eventually, she desired a deeper and more spiritual understanding of the Word of God. One day, after crying out to Jesus about her need, she was amazed to hear Him ask her if she would teach. Her initial response was that she did not see how it would be possible since she was already working a full-time job, despite her poor health. But after the Lord asked her for a second and then a third time, she reluctantly agreed, believing that He would empower her to do the job.

Shortly thereafter, in the latter part of 1987, she began to teach her own brand of Judeo-Christian Spiritual Philosophy, which includes applying Old Testament spiritual principles to unlock the mysteries of the New Testament. She believes that the Scripture is a spiritual document that must be spiritually discerned if it is to be understood correctly, and calls that spiritual understanding ***The Doctrine of Christ***. The Lord Jesus Christ named the work *Living Epistles Ministries* in 1988.

The first *LEM* meetings were casual and spontaneous gatherings of friends and fellow deliverance workers in Pastor Vitale's home. After that, they were held in the business office of one of the brethren. Pastor Vitale delivered her first formal message entitled *The Truth About Witchcraft in January of 1988*, followed by *The Seduction of Eve* in April of the same year. After that, she prepared and taught weekly messages including *Signs of Apostleship* and *Lazarus & The Rich Man.*

The meetings eventually increased to two and then three each week.

LEM publishes a wide range of material, including books, e-books, spiritual interpretations of the Scripture and transcripts of many of Pastor Vitale's Lectures and on-line meetings, all of which, as well as the entire *Alternate Translation Bible,* may be viewed free of charge on the *LEM* website (*LivingEpistles.org*). She also has an *Author's Website* where all of her books, as well as several photographs of herself and a short biography are displayed (Amazon.com/author/SheilaVitale). Paperback and digital versions of *LEM* books may be purchased through *Amazon*, *Google Books* and *Barnes & Noble*.

LEM provides free video livestreams through YouTube and other Internet Platforms . . .

@LivingEpistlesMinistries (2016 – Sept. 2022)
@LivingEpistlesMinistriesLEM (Oct. 2022 – Ongoing)
@LivingEpistlesMinistries (LEM disciples)

. . . as well as two channels of ***Shortclips*** where short, focused messages of about 15 minutes each are posted:

@shortclipsbysheilar.vitale3334 (2016 – Sept. 2022)
@ShortClips-SheilaVitale (Oct. 2022 – Ongoing)

LEM donates a significant percentage of its income to other Christian ministries and organizations that advocate for Christian values and defend the United States Constitution.

PASTOR VITALE TODAY

Today Pastor Vitale continues to dedicate her life to teaching the spiritual principles of the Bible and focuses daily on studying, writing and preaching powerful messages from *The Selden Centre,* LEM/CCK's headquarters at Selden, New York.

The Alternate Translation of the New Testament is an original translation based upon a spiritual understanding of the Scripture that will excite anyone who is looking for a deeper understanding of the New Testament. *The Alternate Translation Bible* (ATB) is not intended to replace traditional translations.

The Alternate Translation of the Book of the Revelation of Jesus Christ to St. John is an original translation based upon a spiritual understanding of the Scripture .It will excite anyone who is looking for a deeper understanding of The Book of Revelation. *The Alternate Translation Bible* (ATB) is not intended to replace traditional translations.

Living Epistles Ministries
Sheila R. Vitale
Pastor, Teacher & Founder
Judeo-Christian Spiritual Philosophy
PO Box 562, Port Jefferson Station, New York 11776, USA
LivingEpistles.org
or
Books@LivingEpistles.org

www.ingramcontent.com/pod-product-compliance
Lightning Source LLC
Chambersburg PA
CBHW071055230426
43666CB00009B/1717

* 9 7 8 0 6 9 2 7 9 9 9 6 3 *